DANGEROUS COMPANY

DANGEROUS COMPANY

——

Inside the World's Hottest Trouble Spots with a Pulitzer Prize–Winning War Correspondent

William Tuohy

WILLIAM MORROW AND COMPANY, INC.
New York

Copyright © 1987 by William Tuohy

Library of Congress Cataloging-in-Publication Data

Tuohy, William, 1926–
    Dangerous company.

    Includes index.
    1. Tuohy, William, 1926–   .   2. War correspondents—
United States—Biography.   I. Title.
PN4874.T78A3   1987   070.4'33'0924 [B]   87-5689
ISBN 0-688-06794-8

Printed in the United States of America

First Edition

1   2   3   4   5   6   7   8   9   10

BOOK DESIGN BY ELLEN FOOS

Contents

CHAPTER ONE

The Road to Damascus

I WAS DRIVING the rented Dodge Dart as fast as I could along the rutted blacktop across the Golan Heights toward Damascus. I was threading the car in and out of a long column of Israeli tanks, which had launched the counterattack into Syria. I sped past the ceasefire line, marking the end of hostilities between Israel and Syria in 1967, on the ancient way where, two thousand years before, Saint Paul had been converted to Christianity. Now, the road was a ghastly Via Dolorosa of the 1973 war.

There were burnt-out hulks of tanks, both Syrian and Israeli, some so close together they seemed locked in a death frieze. The Syrian tanks, gun barrels askew, still held the charred bodies of their crews. Long lines of Syrian artillery pieces were abandoned on the side of the road, riddled with bullets from Israeli aircraft. An orange-colored truck, an improvised ambulance, siren whining with the red Star of David flying from the hood, rattled by hurrying wounded to the rear.

Soldiers in vehicles returning to the rear took army-style postcards from the troops moving forward. The postcards were mailed in Galilee, and for some soldiers, would be the last words their families would ever hear from them.

I swerved around a bend and came across a group of gaunt-eyed, unshaven soldiers, who had just come off the front line, singing and dancing the hora, the Israeli pioneer folk dance. In the middle was Israel's chief rabbi, Sholomon Goren, who as the army's head chaplain in the 1967 war had his image immortalized in a photograph of him blowing the sacred ram's horn at the Wailing Wall in Jerusalem's Old City. With the Sabbath due, the tall, bearded rabbi wearing army khakis and a black skullcap told the weary but jubilant troops, "Happy holiday, happy holiday." As if to punctuate the scene, two Israeli Skyhawk jets roared over low, heading deeper into Syria.

A fellow journalist, John Harris, was in the front seat and an Israeli escort officer in the back. We passed a few tiny Syrian villages with their slender white minarets, and rough stone houses. I honked my way past a platoon of Centurion tanks and noticed that the leading one bore the inscription DAMASCUS.

The October morning was crisp and clear with a vast, pale-blue sky overhead. I could see the white shoulders of Mount Hermon with trails of snow blowing off the long summit ridge, where Israeli paratroopers were struggling for control of that commanding terrain.

As I pushed ahead, I noticed that the tanks, half-tracks full of dust-encrusted soldiers, self-propelled artillery, and jeeps were fanning out off the road onto the brown, basaltic plain, leaving the way empty up ahead. As we moved along, now unimpeded, I mentioned to Harris that at this rate we might still make a late lunch in Damascus, and I knew a good place for mezze along the Barada River.

I somehow thought that if we ventured too far forward a military policeman would flag us down.

The signpost on the right-hand side of the road read, DAMAS—36 KM. We were less than twenty-five miles from the Syrian capital with no apparent resistance in sight. But there were also no longer any Israeli armored vehicles on the road in front of us. It began to dawn on me that we were out ahead of the Israeli Army's advance into Syria. There were no military policemen to stop us.

Up front, I spotted some debris covering the road and braked to a fast, skidding stop. I asked Harris to see what it was. He jumped out of the car, ran up to the pile of rock and dirt, and yelled, "The road's been blown." The Syrians had dynamited the road, creating a deep trench, to cover their retreat.

Just then, I heard the pop-pop-pop of automatic weapons nearby. Bullets crackled overhead. I leaped out from behind the wheel and dove for a ditch followed by Harris. Our Israeli Army escort officer, a reservist who ran a hotel in Tiberias, was sitting in the rear seat and I called to him to take cover, but he sat there munching a tomato seemingly oblivious to the danger. Lying in the ditch, I realized that if this was Syrian small arms fire, we were the point element in the entire Israeli advance. Further, we were two American correspondents with Israeli Defense department press cards, an Israeli reserve captain as our escort in a khaki-colored Avis that looked very much like an army staff car, bearing Israeli plates. This was not where we wanted to be; this was no-man's-land. It was a harrowing realization.

After a few minutes, the firing stopped. We glanced at each other and wordlessly dashed back to the car. I jumped behind the wheel. I wasn't about to try to turn the car around there, offering ourselves as a target.

Instead, I threw the gear in reverse, tramped down the gas pedal, and backed up the road as fast as the whining engine would take us. Whatever the Israeli Army was doing, I, for one, was in full retreat. After a kilometer or so, I reckoned we were out of small arms range and spun the car around, heading to the rear. We relaxed slightly.

Harris, a short, blond, amusing New Yorker with a fund of show business stories—he doubled as a war and entertainment reporter—whom I first met in Vietnam, said one had to be fatalistic in war.

"If a bullet's got your name on it, there's nothing you can do about it," he said.

"I'll go along with that, John," I said. "But you can take a few precautions about the bullet that's labeled: to whom it may concern."

Down the road, we ran into Don North, the Cairo correspondent of NBC News. He had a Syrian prisoner in his car: The soldier was a straggler who had readily given himself up. A few hundred yards away, I saw a group of Israeli combat correspondents taking pictures of soldiers flushing out some Syrian troops hiding behind a small hut.

"Surrender, surrender," called an Israeli officer in Arabic. He fired off a few shots in the air from his Uzi submachine gun.

As Israeli soldiers covered them, five Syrian troopers dressed in long, World War I–type greatcoats stumbled forward, their hands in the air, their rifles on the ground. As if it had been arranged by a director, the Israeli television cameramen ground away as the prisoners were stripped of their gear and searched. Like any prisoners, they looked helpless and vulnerable.

Harris offered a cigarette to one young tall and skinny prisoner who identified himself in rudimentary English as Ahmed Jashin. He said he was eighteen and came from Halbe near Damascus. An Israeli officer objected, "Don't give these bastards any cigarettes. Do you know what the Syrians did to our prisoners?" Indeed, the word in the Israeli Army was that paratroopers captured by Syrians in the first few days' fighting on Mount Hermon had been summarily executed and their bodies mutilated. It was not known whether the mutilation occurred before or after death.

In my kitchen Arabic, I told the other prisoners, "*Shway, shway.*" Take it easy. I believed the Israelis would not harm them. Jashin partly in English and partly in Arabic told us, "I was terrified during the battles. We don't know why we are fighting. They just told us to fight up here. We don't have any officers. We don't know where they are. We are just plain soldiers." The Syrians were bundled into a truck and taken away to be questioned by intelligence officers.

I decided to call it a day at the front and headed back through the ruined city of Kuneitra, along the main axis of Syrian advance, noting how far they had gone before being stopped by Israeli tanks. We passed the old customs house, and drove down the jagged Golan escarpment into the lovely Huleh Valley, across the Daughters of Jacob Bridge over the upper Jordan River, and on to Safad, a city of stone houses that served as the headquarters of the army's Northern Command. There, we dropped off our escort officer, who invited us to visit his hotel in Tiberias, and we picked up Charles Mohr, the Nairobi-based correspondent of the *New York Times,* whose rented car had broken down.

I wanted to get back to Tel Aviv, to the press room in the Defense Ministry where we could file our stories by telex or telephone. Communications were uncertain from outlying towns like Safad, and the Israeli Army had a strict rule that no foreign correspondent was to spend the night with a military unit in the field. It was a three-hour drive back and Harris took over the wheel. I was able to rough out my story on my note pad; in Tel Aviv we would check on what the official briefers were saying about the course of the war and triangulate this with reports out of Cairo, Beirut, and Damascus. My *Los Angeles Times* colleague in Jerusalem, Harry Trimborn, would write the overall war story while I would concentrate on the sights, sounds, and color from the front.

This was a key day in the war, Friday, October 12, 1973, when the Israeli counteroffensive into Syria secured the northern front. On the previous Saturday, October 6, the Syrian and Egyptian armies had launched a joint massive assault: in the north across the Golan ceasefire line of 1967; in the south, bridging the Suez Canal into the Sinai desert.

In the Golan, the Syrians had attacked with an army of 1,500 tanks and 1,000 artillery pieces against a pitifully small Israeli defending force of some 170 tanks and 60 guns, commanded by General Rafael Eyetan. The shock of the Syrian armor columns drove back the Israelis, and for three days, the fate of Upper Galilee in Israel proper hung in the balance.

General Eyetan and his slender force bent but did not break under the weight of Syrian armor—waging a series of valiant individual tank battles until the reserves could be mobilized and reach the battlefield on the Golan plain. There were incredible stories of individual skill, effort, and heroism. A tank battalion commander, Lieutenant Colonel Yossi, was caught in the Himalaya Mountains on his honeymoon and somehow managed to fly back in time to join his unit in the Golan in what came to be known as the Valley of Tears. He was finally badly wounded and rescued by a young paratroop officer, Jonathan "Yoni" Netanyahu, a Harvard graduate, who three years later would lead the assault force to rescue the hostages at Entebbe, Uganda, and lose his life there.

Those early days of the war were long ones for us. The round-trip to the Sinai was about ten hours; the Golan six hours. That's just driving time, not our time spent reporting. We left the Hilton too early for breakfast. We'd get coffee along the road and eat a box lunch prepared by the hotel staff the night before. I'd stash away a bottle of wine. At night, after writing our stories, we'd return to the hotel, invariably too late for dinner in the restaurant. But the bar was open, and the first several evenings I dined on peanuts, briny olives, and cheese squares washed down with beer.

It was a pleasure running into Charley Mohr. I had first met him while covering Barry Goldwater's presidential campaign in 1964 and a couple of years later we had teamed up on several operations in Vietnam. Mohr was tall, cool, and knowledgeable, and, best of all, he was a marvelous raconteur. So that evening I offered Charley a place in the Dodge Dart with Harris and myself for a trip back to the Golan the next morning. We were up before dawn and picked up an escort officer in Tel Aviv. We were in luck: He turned out to be Captain Amos Sapir, whose father was the Israeli finance minister, Pinas Sapir, and who had been wounded as a paratrooper in the 1967 war where Mohr became friends with him.

The early starts were necessary in order to get past the military checkpoints in Upper Galilee at the Daughters of Jacob Bridge and up to the Golan Heights before Syrian shelling began. When the guns opened up, military policemen would shut down the bridge to unessential traffic, sometimes all day. But once you got onto the Golan and past the checkpoints, you were pretty much on your own. Nobody cared much what you did—except the escort officer.

The ride north was lovely; it was the best time of the day. I'd drive along the coastal highway, the opalescent Mediterranean on the left, the false dawn spreading over the limestone hills of Samaria to the right. I'd pick up the BBC news in English over the car's medium-wave band from Cyprus. Just before the old Roman town of Caesarea, we'd cut inland, pass the crossroads of Megiddo, the modern name of biblical Armageddon where the climactic battle between good and evil will be fought, according to Revelation; and then through the lush plain of Esdraelon with fields of wheat and cotton and wild flowers, known by its earliest settlers as the Garden of God; skirting Nazareth on the west, with Mount Tabor, reputedly the site of the Transfiguration, in the eastern distances; passing Hattin where Saladin defeated the Crusaders at the Mount of Beatitudes; and reaching the Sea of Galilee at Tiberias. I'd refuel here, and then head due north over a series of hairpin turns into Upper Galilee. At Rosh Pinna, we'd take a sharp right turn to cross the Jordan River at the Daughters of Jacob Bridge and climb the steep slopes to the Golan Heights.

I had almost reached the ghost town of Kuneitra, the former capital of the Golan, when Syrian shellfire began. The previous day we had been lucky. We hadn't run into any artillery fire because the Syrians were retreating and were unable to zero in their guns. Now it was altogether different. The artillery was registered on the main road and bracketed it, sending up dirty puffs of smoke and dust. I slammed on the brakes and we scrambled for a ditch. We lay there with our heads covered by our arms. We may have looked ungainly but we didn't care. We weren't about to look up until the shelling stopped. Usually, artillery is fired in "missions," that is, one, five, ten, twenty, or fifty shells at a time, followed by a slack period.

Most military casualties on the battlefield are caused by artillery rather than by machine guns or bombs, so when the shells begin to hit, the safest place to be is flat on your belly, preferably in a ditch, foxhole, trench, or crater. Burrowing into the ground may not look noble, but a generation of brave, young British officers were killed in

World War I because they chose to stand gallantly above their trenches rather than hunkering down during a barrage.

So we lay uneasily and unhappily in the ditch until the firing eased off. I got back behind the wheel and we continued north, but now the road was empty. Israeli armored units had all dispersed onto the rocky plain, but our "soft" car without overland capability was confined to the road, which, unfortunately, was a prominent landmark on Syrian gunners' maps. I drove to a point near where we had seen the Syrian prisoners the previous day when shellfire began straddling the road up ahead. Once more, we jumped out of the car and into a ditch along the side of the road. Again, the artillery, which was some distance away, ceased and we tried to assess our situation.

Suddenly, from the direction of Damascus, two jets emerged from the haze lying over the road.

"Sukois," yelled Captain Sapir. We hit the deck. I crawled away from the car, a clear target. The Soviet-made fighter-bombers were low, heading our way. At what seemed to me just about the last moment, they banked left, and from their graceful wings, white blossoms—about eight in all—appeared. These were parachute bombs aimed at Israeli armored vehicles deployed just off the road. The bombs exploded between the half-tracks and us. Two more Sukois followed the first brace and dropped their bombs, too. Flat on our stomachs, we were showered with fragments of the hard volcanic rock the blasts threw up. While I cowered in fright, the Israeli gunners in the vehicles opened up with .50-caliber machine guns, but too late to catch the supersonic jets. Then, the troops quickly gunned their engines and moved to different locations so not to be sitting targets for a follow-up attack.

We moved back to a crossroads where some sturdily constructed houses appeared to offer additional shelter from the artillery. An Israeli officer told Sapir that the army's advance was being "consolidated and broadened," which meant the movement toward Damascus was halted and the flanks strengthened. The Israeli high command had decided not to attack Damascus: The capital would be difficult to control with all its civilians and an attack could bring in the Soviets on behalf of the Syrians.

The shelling continued through the morning; an Israeli truck was hit. Ammunition was touched off. Then, two other vehicles went up in flames. "Oh, those poor boys," exclaimed Sapir.

Next, an enormous kettle-drum series of explosions shook the earth and huge geysers of brown smoke billowed from a hill behind us. These were the impacts from the Soviet-made Katushas, the multiple rockets that land forty at a time—one of the more fearsome experiences of the war. Experts say the Katusha is an "area" weapon; that is, they are not very accurate. But that thought was not much comfort when the rockets landed near you. I was nearly scared to death as it was.

I remembered I had a bottle of wine in the trunk of the car. I opened it with the corkscrew of my Swiss army knife. The wine was warm from the sun. It was sweet and terrible. But it was alcohol. I passed the bottle to Harris warning him that it was not Château Lafite. He took a swig, agreed, but cracked, "Well, you got to remember we're in Syria now and Israeli wines don't travel well."

Later, driving back toward Kuneitra we saw the contrails in the sky of what appeared to be an aerial dogfight. I stopped the car for a better look. As the four of us stood there, two Syrian MIGs came streaking toward us on a course perpendicular to the road. Harris and Sapir dived for a ditch on their side but Mohr and I had none, so we just went facedown on the asphalt.

The MIGs bore in, firing their rockets from their wings toward us and some Israeli military units off the road. We lay spread-eagled on the rough macadam surface, feeling absolutely helpless. I cursed myself for having a khaki-colored car, which looked so much like a military vehicle. The rockets exploded a hundred yards away but appeared not to have harmed the soldiers. The MIGs banked to head back toward Damascus, running for home. As we watched, two Israeli Phantoms in dappled camouflage swooped in low over a hill following the MIGs. The lead Phanton loosed a Sidewinder air-to-air missile, which streaked across the sky, exploding in the trailing MIG's tailpipe. The jet went up in a fireball, which dropped from the sky trailing a plume of oily black smoke.

Shakily, I glanced at Mohr. "I don't know about you, Bill," he said, "but I'm beginning to feel like the starlet in the lousy movie who asked, 'Who do I have to screw to get *out* of this picture?' "

Charley had a point. He even had a metaphor relevant to the life of a war correspondent: What am I doing here and how do I get out?

Driving back, we traveled a road in the Golan that traversed the Valley of Tears, filled with the carcasses of knocked-out tanks. It was here the British war correspondent, Nicholas Tomalin of the London

Sunday Times, had been killed as he moved his car while a photographer took pictures of the wrecked tanks.

A Syrian gunner lurking a kilometer away had noticed the brightly painted rented car and fired a Sagger wire-guided missile destroying the automobile. Tomalin, who was forty-one, had covered Vietnam, too. I have always made a point in a war zone to avoid photographers when possible: In the nature of things, they have to take more chances to get their pictures—and these are risks I'd just as soon avoid.

Tomalin was highly regarded by his peers, and in discussing his craft, he once wrote a paragraph that could well serve as his own epitaph: "A journalist's required talent is the creation of interest. A good journalist takes a dull or specialized or esoteric situation and makes newspaper readers want to know about it. By doing so he both sells newspapers and interests people. It is a noble, dignified and useful calling."

On the way back to Tel Aviv, Mohr took the wheel and the conversation worked around to the 1971 war between India and Pakistan. Mohr, who had covered the White House, recounted the time that Pakistani President Ayub Khan, an ex-general, was entertained by Lyndon Johnson in Washington.

Johnson, said Mohr, got on well with Ayub. They were both big, strapping men who liked horses, the outdoors, hunting, and rough talk. Johnson, on the other hand, couldn't stand India's Prime Minister Indira Gandhi.

Johnson professed to be totally confused by Indian dietary and Hindu religious practices.

"Tell me, President Ayub," he asked, "why is it that with all that poverty in India, they don't eat all those cows you see wandering around?"

Ayub Khan attempted to explain the Hindu belief that cattle were sacred and not to be butchered for food.

"I still just don't get it," responded the President. "Down where I come from in Texas, we eat cows, we milk 'em—and why some of those old boys down there even fuck 'em."

We drove to the press center in Tel Aviv where Prime Minister Golda Meir was speaking on the closed-circuit television hookup from Jerusalem. Golda, as everyone called her, turned out to be a solid rock during the first dangerous days of the war when the outcome was still in doubt. Defense Minister Moshe Dayan had wavered. Despite his obvious strengths, Dayan was something of a Hamletlike character in

Israeli public life, procrastinating and indecisive at critical times. Watching Golda's self-assured performance seemed to give me a clue why General Dayan had never made it to the top.

I had interviewed Golda for television with columnist Rowland Evans in 1969 and she was quite negative about the prospects of reaching any accord with the Palestinians. After the interview, she asked us if the cameras were switched off. Evans said yes and she asked, "Are you sure?" He reassured her. Only then did she reach in her purse and pull out a cigarette; she didn't like to be seen smoking on camera.

That evening the bar of the Hilton was livelier than usual: All sorts of characters had been pouring into Tel Aviv. El Al, the national airline, was determined to keep to its ordinary schedules. Isaac Stern arrived to play his violin for the troops. Zubin Mehta, conductor of the Los Angeles Philharmonic Orchestra, turned up. Danny Kaye showed too, along with actor Chaim Topol, a reserve officer who put on his uniform and served as a press escort officer. Journalist friends were all on deck: Phil Caputo of the *Chicago Tribune* who was working on his fine *A Rumor of War;* Bill Hampton of the UPI; Nick Proffitt of *Newsweek;* Hugh Mulligan of the Associated Press; Henry Kamm of the *New York Times;* Jordan Bonfante of *Time;* Jack Laurence of CBS; and Barry Dunsmore of ABC. There were plenty of parajournalists, too, freelancers looking for excitement rather than news. Among the writers at the bar that evening was Nora Ephron, on assignment for *New York* magazine, with whom I worked when she was a researcher and I was a writer on *Newsweek.*

"You don't remember me, Bill," she said, though I did, "but you were one of the few people at *Newsweek* to give me a break. I've always remembered it." At the time, I was doing a cover story on McGeorge Bundy, President Kennedy's national security adviser, and Nora did a first-rate job of reporting on his background at Yale and Harvard, which I called to the attention of the senior editors.

I introduced Nora to the gang. In any war, you tend to team up with old mates, and some new ones, sharing rides, dinners, and experiences. In our group was Mohr, Harris, Proffitt, and Terry Smith of the *New York Times.* Since I was writing daily color stories, I had the luxury of picking my own assignments each day, while people from outfits like the *New York Times* had to rotate field trips with writing the war or political story from Tel Aviv or Jerusalem.

At the bar, I got a worried call from the hotel manager. He told me John Harris had been returned to his room by Israeli medics under heavy sedation and wondered whether someone should spend the night sitting up with him. John had come down with a case of combat fatigue—and after our day of being shelled, bombed, and strafed, I could see why. Most correspondents don't want any fuss made about them, and, satisfied that Harris had been looked after, I advised the manager simply to let him sleep it off, and, specifically, not to wake him in the morning.

Actually, I'm surprised more foreign correspondents don't get badly shaken up. I suppose it's because we know we can usually get out of a war zone after a period of danger. But a soldier has to stay there and take it—hour after hour, day after day, week after week.

The next morning, Mohr and I again picked up Captain Sapir at the Defense Ministry and he asked if we could take another passenger. Harris's seat was free so we, of course, agreed. The newcomer turned out to be Meshulam Riklis, a stranger to me, but who we learned was a millionaire industrialist whose companies, among them Cartier, did something like $2.5 billion worth of business a year. He was also one of fifteen Americans who had contributed $1 million annually to Jewish charities and was a former chairman of the New York chapter of the United Jewish Appeal. Hence, he was a VIP in Israel and Amos wanted to bring him along.

On the drive north, Mohr and Riklis talked about big game hunting, at which they were both experts. Charley, in fact, had just returned from a hunting safari in Botswana's Kalahari Desert, about which he had written a long piece for *Playboy*—before being vectored to Israel.

We reached the point on the road where the Syrian prisoners had been taken but were again held up there because of shelling just ahead. A second car pulled up with Hugh Mulligan and Horst Faas, of the Associated Press. Horst, a Berliner by birth, was one of the hardest-charging photographers in the business, winning a Pulitzer Prize in Vietnam and another in Bangladesh. Hugh was quite gentle, a blithe spirit. Hugh said Horst had a card taped to the glove compartment of his car, for the passenger's edification. It read, DO YOU WANT TO LIVE FOREVER?

As we waited for the shelling to subside, two press buses raced past our position without even slowing down. This was infuriating: It's well known that press buses rarely get you anywhere you want to go. How many times during a political campaign had we berated bus drivers for failing to keep up with the candidate's motorcade? It turned out that the press escort officer, as we had previously, expected a military policeman to flag him down at the appropriate point on the road.

Mohr and I decided we could not bear the indignity of allowing the press bus to get farther than we had and we packed back into the Dodge. I headed for the danger zone. Sure enough, the Syrians chose that moment to open up again with long-range artillery: The car was bracketed by 130-mm shells. I slammed on the brakes, cut the engine, and we scuttled for cover.

I thought, at least, I had cut the engine. I was used to driving a plain shift Alfa Romeo in my Rome base, not an automatic transmission with confusing markings. That's my story. But actually I panicked, leaving the engine idling. As we huddled in the ditch, and the first shells began landing, the car inched ahead on its own.

Riklis saw the car moving, jumped up, and tried to shut off the engine. I yelled, "The hell with the car. Get down " He succeeded in steering the car off the road into a shallow depression where it stuck, the engine still running. Later, Riklis said he had an appointment in Tel Aviv and could not afford to lose the wheels. He had also been at the Anzio beachhead in Italy in World War II, so that explained his impressive coolness under fire.

About twenty shells hit near us, the closest about twenty yards away. For me the desperate feeling of trying to claw into the stony ground for shelter from the exploding artillery rounds was terrifying. Whistle, roar, *blam*! Whistle, roar, *blam*! Like a freight train gone mad. Every shell sounds as if it's landing right on top of you. But the battle-savvy Israeli soldiers on the exposed plain took each new round of incoming artillery in stride.

"Our boys know when to take cover," an officer told me. "When they hear the incoming whistle, they get down low, and, really, only a direct hit or a near-miss can kill you," After the shelling stopped, soldiers crawled out of their foxholes to help us get the car back on the road. It was still working.

I had some cuts on my cheek, probably from trying to burrow into the rocky soil rather than from shrapnel. Horst wiped off my face with after-shave lotion as an antiseptic and said he had watched us through his 650-mm lens. "I thought you were casualties for sure," he said. Faas is not given to hyperbole.

Sapir and Riklis talked to the troops in Hebrew. The latter were

elated because they had shot down two Syrian MIGs that morning.
Sergeant Major Ezra (correspondents were only allowed to use first
names of combat troops) told us, "I swung my machine gun around
and hit the first one. He crashed right over there behind the hill. I'd like
to do it again; it's good hunting."

The soldiers said they were manning an indefinite front, making
sure the hills were clear of Syrian infantrymen. "We move by night,"
commented a slender private named Yoav. "We keep shifting our
positions and we clean them out. But I don't know what's going on
with the tanks. We simply fight at night and rest during the day,
waiting for orders. That's the face of the war for us."

Yoav's wife was an American who lived in Tiberias. "Please give
my wife a call," he said to Amos. "She and my American mother-
in-law have been worried about me."

"You have an American mother-in-law?" said Sapir, a short,
jovial man who had spent four years at Columbia University. Slapping
the private on the back, he laughed. "That's the worst kind."

There were a lot of Israeli soldiers with American connections. At
the tiny Syrian crossroads town of Jaba, for instance, we met a six-
foot, blond-haired private named Dan Kohn, who had gone to Hamilton
High School in Los Angeles, but was now dressed in black combat
boots, the dark-green standard uniform, and a steel helmet with big
goggles. "I just got a letter from my mother in L.A.," he said. "She
wants to get the war over with. I agree. I've got to get back to the
kibbutz. We grow apples, peaches, and pears—and roses for export.
Hey, would you believe I used to work at McDonald's."

At the same crossroads, we found a Syrian farmer of the Druze
sect, whose experience was light-years from Kohn's. Mohammed
Khatib was illiterate, with a worn wife and ten children. Through an
Arabic-speaking Israeli, he told us, "The Syrians came and then left
and the Israelis are here. Everybody has left except for a few old
people like me. My five daughters and four of my sons have gone, too.
My other son was drafted into the army two months ago and I haven't
heard from him since. I did not run away from here because where
would I go? This is my house. This place is my home."

Heading back, we met some soldiers resting and spotted Topol, of
Fiddler on the Roof fame. He and Amos exchanged greetings. "Israel
is a small country," explained Amos. "Topol took the first plane back
to Israel to get into uniform."

As for the relaxing soldiers, Amos pointed out, "In real warfare everyone does not fight at the same time. Battle is not like a John Wayne movie. The war is not won in two hours and ten minutes film-running time. There is a lot of waiting around in war—as you can see right now.''

At military headquarters in Safad, Riklis was ushered in to see his old friend, Major General Itzhak Hofi, chief of the Northern Command. Given our shared experiences, Riklis arranged for Mohr and me to get a top-level briefing from Hofi's chief of operations, a rugged-looking colonel, who had a black tanker's beret slipped through his epaulet. He spelled out Israeli strategy on the northern front: stabilizing the front line within artillery range of the Damascus suburbs, retaking Mount Hermon with its key positions, and rebutting any attempt by the Iraqi and Jordanian armored brigades to assist the Syrians against the Israelis in the area.

As for the newly arrived Iraqis, the colonel told us, "Syria's guests have left their visiting cards here: two brigades of Iraqi armor came to call on us. Yesterday, we destroyed eighty-eight Iraqi tanks.''

And as for the Jordanians, the colonel added, "I hope that Syria's Jordanian guests will change their minds—though we think they are coming our way—before it is too late for them. But apparently King Hussein hadn't got our message. They may be forced to leave their visiting cards on the Syrian desert, too. So, too bad for them.'' He was right. The crack 40th Armored Brigade of the Royal Jordanian Army entered the conflict a few days later and lost fifty tanks in the fight.

We returned to Tel Aviv, where I wanted to mention both Riklis and Captain Amos Sapir in my daily story. I argued that using a proper name would give the story verisimilitude and punch. First names, I said, sometimes sounded artificial. The Israelis were sensitive about using a soldier's last name, particularly an officer, in case he was later captured and his exploits held against him. In this case, I won the argument.

As a correspondent I can understand the reasons for some censorship: current military operations whose exposure might endanger lives is surely a valid reason for censorship by responsible authorities. The question is more difficult when it involves perceptions of what is damaging to national security. Any criticism of the government, however unrelated to operational military matters, has been construed by some censors as damaging to the state—and such material has been spiked or excised.

Most Arab countries then practiced "closed" censorship; that is, you handed in your copy and had no idea of what was done to it until you eventually read your paper. Normally, in covering the Arab world, you tried to wait until you left a country before writing anything of significance. Obviously, you couldn't do that during a big running story like a war. Israel, on the other hand, practiced "open" censorship: The censors would tell you what they were taking out—and why. You could then argue with them; sometimes you won and sometimes you lost.

The next day, I headed for the Golan Heights again, with Amos Sapir as escort officer and Craig Whitney of the *New York Times,* taking Charley's place in the car. We reached the broad, rocky plain that stretched from the Golan escarpment to Damascus, with a handful of tactically important hills between. We were ordered to stop because of a major tank battle that was raging up ahead. Israeli armor was engaging Syrian and Jordanian tanks and the remnants of the Iraqi force.

We halted next to an armored reconnaissance unit, scout cars that usually ranged ahead of the tanks but had scurried to the rear once the battle between the armored behemoths was joined. We tried to glean snippets of information over the scout car radios with Amos translating. The whole plain before us was laced with artillery bursts, sending out continuous thunder. A barrage hit a hilltop and for a moment, as it was covered with explosions, the crest appeared to be blown completely away.

Over the battlefield, the Israeli Phantoms, Skyhawks, and Mirages streaked low, going in after enemy tank and artillery positions. No Syrian aircraft appeared. A great pall of dust arose from the plain, kicked up by hundreds of incoming shells and the powder from Israeli guns. The classic phrase "fog of war" could be taken literally here.

The tank and artillery battle was a fearsome and tantalizing thing to watch—fearsome because of the hundreds of artillery and tank shells that sent up great showers of smoke, followed by explosions that came seconds later; tantalizing because everyone was straining to discern what was actually happening and how the battle was progressing.

An Israeli tank officer in a black beret raised his arm and pointed in the distance. "See that black smoke coming up," he said. "I'm afraid that it is one of our tanks burning. It is too close for one of theirs, unless they are closer than I think—in which case we are in trouble."

As we watched, the firing died down and there was a lull in the battle. Gunners near us rushed to ammo trucks to resupply, commanders remaneuvered their companies and brigades, and canteen trucks magically seemed to appear on the main road. Soldiers popped up from hidden positions and ran over for soft drinks and sandwiches. Some looked lively, others drawn and haggard.

I found a young Israeli tank captain, wearing grimy, armor-force coveralls and a yarmulke, straining to repair a mechanical defect that had put his Centurion out of action. The forward tank repair station smelled strongly of fuel and cordite. The captain told me, "We beat them again today. And with the blessing of God, we will beat them again tomorrow."

Word came over the radio that many enemy tanks were knocked out in their counterattack and the Arab force was retreating toward Damascus.

The captain had been in almost constant combat since the war began and he said he felt a certain amount of shame that his tank unit had to retreat during the initial fighting when Syria attacked with an overwhelming force.

"I am a regular army soldier and we were guarding the frontier when the Syrians hit us," the captain, whose name was Nathan, explained, wiping his grease-stained hands. "When they came across the border, we stopped their first ones, but then more followed. Our tank unit shot a lot of them. It was like fireworks. But then, we got hit ourselves, just south of Kuneitra. It didn't feel very good, getting hit, and we couldn't move because our treads had been knocked out. A friend in the next tank got hit and his gun wouldn't fire.

"He yelled, 'Syrian tanks in front!' and we were able to fire our gun at those T-55s. But they kept coming and we were disabled. So we grabbed our Uzi submachine guns and jumped on one of our other tanks. For two days, we had to retreat—though we were firing at them all the way. Then we got hit with a bazooka during the night. We waited for two days and got a new Centurion so we are back in action. Our tank commander was hit in the leg during our counterattack but we have a new tank commander.

"We still feel bad because we had to fall back."

Just then, Captain Sapir, who had his ear to the radio, yelled, "MIG alert!"

"Don't worry," Captain Nathan told me. "Just stay here next to the tank. The MIGs make a lot of noise but they don't shoot much. We will chase them away."

The MIGs did not appear. The Syrians fired a short group of

artillery shells that landed near us, but not so close that we had to take cover. An eerie calm descended on the battlefield, and, as we prepared to return to Tel Aviv, I was reminded of young Winston Churchill's observation that there was nothing quite so exhilarating in life as being shot at without result.

That evening I telexed my story to Los Angeles from the press room as usual, though other reporters who were closer to deadlines sometimes phoned in their articles. The *Washington Post* was laggard about installing dictation machines for incoming calls and I remember hearing Bernard Nossiter, at the next desk, telling a very inexperienced dictationist, "This is Nossiter from Tel Aviv with the war story . . . Tel Aviv . . . Tel Aviv. *T* like in Tom, *E* like in easy, *L* like in love . . . Tel Aviv, goddammit."

Later that night, I heard that an Israeli armored "task force" had crossed the Suez Canal and was shooting up Egyptian missile sites, artillery batteries, and infantry command posts on the west bank. So far as we could gather, it was still being described as small-scale, possibly only a one-shot effort. When we asked the briefing officer, General Uri Narkis, what was a "task force," he replied cryptically, "It is a force with a task." I also got a tip that we ought to get down to the Sinai the next day.

So Mohr, Nick Proffitt, Sapir, and myself were up and rolling at 4:00 A.M. We drove out two hours before daylight. In Tel Aviv, women wardens would dab your headlights with blue paint as a kind of blackout precaution. But on the road, such restricted vision could be fatal, and once clear of Tel Aviv, I'd wipe off the paint. I'd drive south along the coast, through the old Philistine city of Ashkelon, Herod's birthplace, then into Gaza where Samson wreaked vengeance on his tormentors. In the Gaza Strip, Amos kept a tight grip on his Uzi submachine gun. This was the home of four hundred thousand Palestinians and incidents with the Israeli army were frequent.

We'd enter Egypt with the fading stars very close, the dawn touching the desert with russets and gold. We'd follow the coast with the Mediterranean on our right. At El 'Arīsh, the palm-shaded capital of the Sinai, we'd make a pit stop near an area where the bedouins camped with their camels. We'd have scalding Arabian coffee laced with cardamom. And then, we'd head south into the heart of the Sinai, with undulating sand dunes, immense distances, and often a mirage shimmering on the sands up ahead.

With Amos dozing, Proffitt and I would encourage Mohr to tell us what we called Lyndon Johnson stories.

Covering the White House, Mohr had been flimflammed by President Johnson during the Dominican Republic crisis in the spring of 1965. The President, Mohr remembered, kept changing his public rationale for sending in American troops to the Caribbean island. Johnson would privately give Mohr one explanation—to protect American lives—which the *New York Times* would print, only to find Johnson offering another reason a few days later—to stave off communism. Mohr protested to the President that he ought not to treat the *New York Times,* a serious paper, in quite such cavalier fashion.

As Mohr recalled, the President responded, "Charley, any time you want to know anything, anything at all, my door is always open to the *New York Times.* You don't have to go through my press secretary or anybody else; you just come straight to me."

Mohr took the President at his word. A few weeks later, a report surfaced that Johnson had quietly and retroactively raised the salaries of his White House personal staff. During the President's walking news conference around the Ellipse, Mohr asked him if the report was true.

Johnson stopped cold and turned on Mohr glowering: "Here you are alone with the President of the United States and the leader of the Free World, and you ask a chickenshit question like that!"

I recalled the time that the President took a couple of reporters on an impromptu tour of the private quarters in the White House. He opened the door to the master bedroom, and found Ladybird at her dressing table. She shooed him out. Johnson liked to needle John Kennedy's press friends for the late President's penchant for playing around, even though he was married to one of the world's leading beauties.

"I don't have to tomcat around Georgetown," he said to the reporters, who recognized the allusion. "I got all I want right in there. Rolled over on the Bird last night and again this morning. Not bad for a man of fifty-seven, is it?"

That morning, guided by our escort officer, I pulled into a secret Israeli army base near the Gidi Pass in the western Sinai. On the first day of the war, the Egyptian Army, backed by a force of twenty-two hundred tanks and twenty-three hundred artillery pieces, crossed the Suez Canal on pontoon bridges, overwhelmed the series of Israeli outposts known as the Bar-Lev Line, and occupied the entire east bank

THE ROAD TO DAMASCUS

of the canal up to a depth of a couple of miles. But the Egyptians did not press their assault on the critical Gidi and Mitla passes. I had spent the first three days of the war covering the Sinai battles, until I shifted north to the Syrian front. The Israeli strategy, I was told, was to fight a holding action in the Sinai until the much more immediate threat of the Syrian assault was repulsed—their tanks were at one point only ten minutes traveling time from the Jordan River. Then, the major Israeli attention could be turned to fighting the Egyptians in the Sinai.

Now, a helicopter painted a sand-camouflage hue landed in a whirl of dust and out jumped a familiar figure in dark-green fatigues, a peaked cap, enormous goggles, and a black patch over his left eye. General Moshe Dayan, the defense minister, was here to get a firsthand view of the Sinai fighting. I liked Dayan. I thought that as a Sabra— that is, a Jew born in the Holy Land—he had a better feeling for dealing with the Arabs than many Israeli leaders who had been raised in Europe. But the country's senior politicians viewed him as something of an opportunist, and outside of military affairs, he never made a broader impact in Israel.

A massive, running tank battle was in progress near the canal and the sound of gunfire boomed in from the west beyond the Gidi Pass.

Was this the crucial battle on the Sinai front? I asked.

"Not yet, not yet," said Dayan.

What about the task force on the west side of the canal?

"It is very closely related to the battle of the central sector of the canal."

How long would the task force operate in Egypt proper?

"That is the sixty-four-thousand-dollar question," he said, his ironic smile breaking into a grin.

In a typically graceful gesture, Dayan complimented the fighting qualities of the Egyptian soldiers who had crossed the Suez Canal and successfully withstood the initial Israeli counterattacks.

"It is the Egyptian politicians who should be blamed," he said.

He told us that the northern front was definitely stabilized and that reserves of air and artillery could now be concentrated on the Sinai against the Egyptians.

He sped off to meet his generals and we drove through the Gidi Pass, which with the Mitla Pass, serves as the key defense position guarding the western Sinai. We came to a crossroads position that had been critical in repulsing the Egyptian advance, and found a tank battalion commander resting in the shade of the big M-60 Patton's hulk, his goggles draped around his neck, binoculars across his chest.

"The Egyptian tanks have improved their tactics since 1967," he said, dragging on a cigarette. "But they don't seem to have mastered coordinated tactics. They just go forward all at once without any apparent plan to support one another. The Russian-made T-55s and T-62s aren't bad tanks but our Centurions and Pattons are better. Our guns are accurate—we get hits at maximum range. And they are more comfortable for the crews. Sit inside and see." I did and they were. The Centurions were made in Britain; the Pattons, American-made.

But the battalion commander credited the Egyptians with one of the big surprises of the war—and a rude shock to the Israelis. "They caused most of our tank casualties not with their tanks but with their wire-guided, Sagger missiles manned by infantrymen. Our tanks moved forward in the first days of the war without adequate infantry support, which was a big and bloody mistake. They were able to knock out our tanks before we got close. Now we have learned to deploy our infantry without tanks to neutralize their missile-carrying soldiers. It was a costly lesson."

Indeed, the Israelis were taken by surprise in October 1973, having placed too much reliance on the effectiveness of their armor force alone. I was one of those, who on previous visits, thought the Suez Canal served as a perfectly effective antitank ditch. But, of course, the Egyptians quickly bridged the canal in several places on the first day of the war and moved their armor into the Sinai. The Israelis, whose armored forces had been so effective in the 1967 war, had seemingly forgotten that in most cases tanks should be used with infantry. For Israeli infantrymen might have winkled out the Egyptian gunners whose lightweight missiles were so devastating during the first crucial days of the war. The Israelis hadn't counted on the effectiveness of the missiles carried by the infantry. I realized that even the shrewd Israeli commanders had been preparing, through armor doctrine and weapons, to fight the previous war.

I noticed that the Israeli Mirages, jet fighters, flying overhead had bright Day-Glo paint on their wings. This was to differentiate them from the Libyan-supplied Mirages the Egyptians were using. Similarly, Israeli armor vehicles would use Day-Glo markings on their topsides so they would not be attacked by their own planes.

I had often flown aboard C-130 Hercules transports in Vietnam but here in the Sinai they flew very low, skimming the tops of the palm trees, in order not to be hit by Egyptian ground-to-air missiles, which were very deadly in the first few days of the war. Occasionally, we'd see a SAM-2 missile fired by the Egyptians across the canal streak skyward leaving spiral contrails as it vainly tried to hit a high-flying Israeli reconnaissance jet.

I also met an artillery officer, Yehuda Drori, who told me he majored in strategic studies at the University of Southern California. "I've got a lot of relatives in southern California," he said. "Tell them I'm fine. The only thing I miss out here is the World Series." I only then remembered October was the month for the American baseball classic.

On leaving the unit, we offered to take back postcards from the soldiers. Though it was perhaps indiscreet, Amos read us snatches in Hebrew from some of them.

"What's new with you," wrote a lieutenant to his girl. "With me, everything is all right. I hope you are not worried. We have a lot of food. We get a lot of underwear and socks. No problems on this subject. The only thing is I do not shower. After the war, I will take plenty of showers. The morale is high here. I hope morale in your place is as high as here. If so then I am happy."

"The morale here is good," wrote another soldier to a friend, more poignantly. "It is only a pity that so many people are missing."

Back in Tel Aviv, the atmosphere had lightened: The Golan seemed secure and the Israelis were turning the tide of battle against the Egyptians. There had been no air or missile attacks against Israeli cities. There was time to relax and get a decent dinner outside the hotel. At one of the briefings, I had met a delightful and vivacious beauty, who was also a serious student of Middle Eastern affairs and whose former boyfriend was a ranking official with Mossad, the Israeli secret intelligence service. A gang of us went to Mandy's and had a superlative time. During a war, there's a certain eat-drink-and-be-merry quality to an evening, since you just might possibly be dead the next day, and there's no point sitting around brooding about it.

Most correspondents sometimes speak in a kind of code designed to disguise true feelings: Wisecracking and cynicism are often used as a device to let off steam and to cover up sensibilities, particularly in the presence of others who haven't shared their experiences. Often this comes across to outsiders as a kind of Hemingwayesque bravado that at best seems juvenile and at worst totally uncaring.

At dinner, there were some jokes at my expense concerning my Gucci typewriter case. I had a battered old Olivetti, which I liked. The case developed zipper fatigue but I couldn't get a replacement, even in Rome. So I dropped into Gucci on Via Condotti and ordered a custom-made case to the Olivetti's proportions. Once the knowledgeable Peter Jennings, later to become ABC-TV's anchorman, asked me how much it cost.

"It's like a yacht, Peter," I told him. "If you have to ask the price, you can't afford it. Actually, the case cost more than the type-writer."

Peter blanched and dropped the subject. But Loren Jenkins, then with *Newsweek,* insisted I order him a case like mine. I've always taken the view, by the way, that decent luggage is essential for a foreign correspondent, and that one also ought to dress as well as any ambassador one is interviewing. I've never seen the point in looking like a reject out of *The Front Page.* That way you get sent around to the tradesmen's entrance at embassies and wind up having to tug your forelock before the high and mighty.

Nora Ephron was along at dinner, having become friendly with the group, and she asked to interview me for a story she was doing about war correspondents. The next day, I was taking a break from the front to do a long military analysis, and I agreed to see her. Nora is a dark, slender woman from Beverly Hills, with an edgy voice, who made her reputation doing biting commentary. She asked me to start from the beginning, when I had first heard about the attack and how I responded.

Actually, I'd been working that Saturday in my Rome office putting together a story on the making of the film on Queen Christina with Liv Ullmann and Peter Finch. The foreign desk called me to confirm that the Egyptian-Syrian attack was serious and continuing. The desk suggested I try to get to Cairo. I said I'd head for somewhere in the Middle East, probably Beirut, since the Cairo and Tel Aviv airports were closed. At Fumicino Airport, I bought a ticket for Beirut but hand-carried my baggage in case of a hasty change in plans. Sure enough, at Fumicino I learned that an El Al airliner was standing by and might take off, the first passenger plane into Israel. I called the Israeli embassy in Rome to ensure that I got a seat on it and swiftly changed flights without losing my baggage. We had a man in Beirut, Cairo was still closed, and our correspondent in Jerusalem could certainly use help in a war.

The El Al flight did take off, getting into Lod Airport after dark. Early the next morning, I ran into Barry Dunsmore of ABC News who

had a car and was heading for the Sinai front. I joined him. I spent the
next three days traveling to and from the Sinai before shifting to the
Golan for the Israeli counteroffensive against the Syrians.

I explained this to Nora and tried to make some points about our
calling. Though there are some, like photographer Tim Page, who talk
about the "glamour of war," most correspondents are horrified by the
carnage of modern conflict. But if you are a professional foreign correspondent, war goes with the territory. I tried to make the point that
some of the best war correspondents were also fine political reporters.
If, as Von Clauswitz pointed out, war is an extension of politics by
other means, then a good correspondent ought to know about the
political factors behind any conflict. I wanted to disabuse her of the
notion that serious war correspondents were simply thrill seekers. Nora
took copious notes.

That evening, a handful of us were invited to a private military
briefing conducted by the chief of military intelligence at the Defense
Ministry. For the first time, we learned the extent and significance of
the cross-canal attack, which was rapidly becoming the decisive ma-
neuver of the war. Our aim now was to get across the canal: I teamed
up with Terry Smith of the *New York Times* and photographer Eddie
Adams of *Time,* who when he was with the Associated Press won the
Pulitzer Prize for his shot of the Saigon police chief executing a
Vietcong prisoner at Tet.

We managed to drive as far as Tassa, the military jumping-off
base for the Suez Canal operation, where we were put up for the night.
I bumped into Genevieve Chauvel, the striking French photographer,
who was wearing an attractive bush jacket and pants. "Very chic," I
complimented her. "Yves Saint Laurent?"

"Better yet." She smiled. "It's a Saint Laurent copy by Minh in
Saigon." Minh had outfitted dozens of correspondents from his shop
in Tu-Do Street.

The Israelis offered us tin helmets, overcoats dating from World
War I, and army cots inside an old tent. I preferred to sleep in the car,
having brought along a pillow and a blanket from the hotel. Parachute
flares cast an eerie orange glow over us all night long. The next
morning, we drove down to the canal past a bewildering litter of
burnt-out tanks, guns, and trucks. We parked the car behind the massive levee that marked the canal. Adams struck off on his own and
came up with a powerful shot of an exhausted Israeli soldier cradling
his head in his arms with the canal in the background. It won second

place, the silver medal, in the annual World Photo Awards at The
Hague, the Netherlands, in 1973. During a lull, Terry and I walked
across the makeshift metal pontoon bridge the Israelis had constructed
across the canal, a blue-and-white Star of David fluttering at the far
end. As we stepped ashore, a young Israeli soldier said, "Welcome to
Africa."

The surface of the Great Bitter Lake just south of the bridgehead
was glassy and you could see the merchant ships that had been ma-
rooned at anchor, caught there during the 1967 war. Our escort officer,
not Amos Sapir this trip, would not allow us to hitchhike to the front
lines, but strolling through the palm and eucalyptus groves I found a
paratroop medical unit, with one of Israel's top scientists, Dr. Cyril
Legum, in charge.

"In civilian life I'm a geneticist at Tel Aviv University," he told
me, sitting on a mound of sand next to a trench. "Here I do battlefield
patchups to keep the wounded alive until they can be evacuated. Ge-
netics is more sophisticated but this job is immensely important right
now."

Dr. Legum, lean, pale, and wearing the distinctive red boots of
the paras, said the shelling could be nerve-racking, particularly the
Katusha multiple rockets that were fired every night. Suddenly, a
grinding whistle echoed through the grove. "Duck!" ordered the doctor and pushed me into the trench. "I think that was just a single
harassing round," he said. Another whistle. The doctor grimaced in
embarrassment as the second shell hit. One more round came in. In
professional tones, the doctor explained, "When we're down here in
the trench these things can't hurt us much. And the shells are coming
in from long range and don't interfere with our advance. But that
doesn't help you personally if that lucky shell finds your foxhole. The
direct hits are a kind of cosmic lottery—there's nothing you can do
about them." I wasn't sure whether I was soothed or rattled by the
message.

A fourth and fifth shell landed much closer, the last about twenty-
five yards away and a lieutenant was hit in the head by a metal fragment. The geneticist scrambled out of the trench toward the wounded
man but came in third to two other doctors. "It's just a scalp wound,"
he reported. "He'll be all right."

Walking back to the bridge, I noticed my pants slit up the leg,
from jumping in and out of the trench. The beachmaster, a Brooklyn-
born lieutenant, offered to stitch up the seam with his needle and thread

and told me, "A terrible thing happened last night. Three reservists, all veterans of the last three wars, were sitting together when the nightly barrage came in. They wanted to stay together to talk so they all jumped in the same big hole. They should have picked individual trenches. A shell came in and killed all three."

Off in the distance, a terrifying salvo of Katushas exploded, causing the earth to tremble and the palms to sway. Back at the makeshift bridge, I noticed a young soldier wearing a St. Christopher medal around his neck. "It's from my girl friend in Skokie, Illinois," he explained. "She's a shiksa [a gentile]."

Crossing the canal back to the Sinai, I watched an Egyptian missile spiraling up into the sky after an Israeli jet. It missed. On the east bank, a brawny, bearded regimental sergeant major offered me a hunk of salami and remarked prophetically, "This is the third time I have been fighting in the Sinai—1956, 1967, and 1973. In ten years, I'll be fighting again and so will my thirteen-year-old son." The sergeant, whose name was Eitan Jrushalmi, for Jerusalem where he was born, in peacetime was the chief game warden for the national park system. He concluded sadly, "My great-grandfather and grandfather fought the Arabs who harassed their farm. My father fought in the War of Independence in 1948. I've fought and my son will be fighting in the future. The nation will have to get used to the idea of periodic wars."

I came away disturbed by this deeply pessimistic and fatalistic outlook. But the war was now going well for the Israelis: Armor units under Major General Ariel "Arik" Sharon had crossed the canal and struck west and north. He was followed by Major General Bren Adan's armored division, which rolled due south effectively surrounding the Egyptian Third Army, still on the east side of the canal. The move jeopardized all the gains President Anwar el-Sadat had achieved in the early days of the war.

Back in Tel Aviv, we got the word that a tentative ceasefire had been arranged through the urging of the United States and the Soviet Union.

With the ceasefire, the pace slowed: I went aboard a missile boat in Haifa to do a story on the Israeli Navy, which had fought missile-to-missile sea encounters, with the Syrians and Egyptians, the first such engagements in naval history.

In my writing, I tried to convey the idea that war really *is* hell, wherever it takes place, and that conflict produces suffering and grief for everyone involved. I was introduced to a member of a family that had been singled out for sorrow in the Yom Kippur War. I drove out to a modest house in a Tel Aviv suburb to visit Zvi and Ruth Swet, whose twenty-two-year-old son, Yair, a smiling, handsome, six-footer, was killed leading his tank company in the Golan Heights on the second day of the war. Yair was one of almost three thousand Israeli soldiers killed in the eighteen-day war, which would be the equivalent of two hundred thousand battle deaths for the United States.

The Swets' two other sons, Mickey, twenty-three, and Rami, twenty, also regular army officers in the armored corps, were wounded in the first fierce days. Rami had heard reports of Yair's death over the radio intercom, for Yair was widely known among the troops for his good cheer and the wisecracks he made to keep up morale. The radio message from Yair's tank unit said, "The jokes have stopped. Our commanding officer is gone."

Mrs. Swet, then fifty, was a refugee from Hitler's Austria; her husband, Zvi, fifty-one, a native of Poland, fought in the 1948–49 War of Independence until his legs were blown off at the hip by a land mine. If there was anything to single out the decor of the Swet household from others on the block, it was the framed original drawings by the French political cartoonist, TIM. This was the pen name of Louis Mitelberg, who, on a trip to Israel ten years before, was taken around the country by Zvi Swet. They formed an enduring friendship.

When word of Yair's death reached TIM in Paris, he wrote the family in English and the letter was still on the coffee table:

> Yair, my big Yair, the warm fraternal smile on his face, fallen in the battle of Israel. I will never forget him. He will be living in my memory forever. His face, his stature, his voice are for me the concrete image of what a young Israel means. My brother Zvi and my sister Ruth gave birth to the eternal and biblical state of Israel after 2,000 years.
>
> Twenty-five years later, their son Yair fights again and falls in the battle. Thanks to him the country lives. Allow me to join my tears with yours because Yair is the son and the pride of every Jew.

There was one last story Charley Mohr and I had our hearts set on: getting to General Sharon across the Suez Canal for his account of the crossing. So one morning, we drove down to the canal with a reserve major as our escort officer. After several false starts, we managed to get a line on Sharon's secret location and finally found his command trailer late in the afternoon. Sharon greeted us enthusiastically: Arik, as his troops called him, remembered Charley from the 1967 war.

"Welcome," he said, running a hand through a shock of iron-gray hair. "I just had the chief army rabbi here and I was afraid to offer him these. Have some." He handed us a tin of nonkosher smoked oysters and broke out a bottle of Johnnie Walker Red. It's not generally known outside Israel that most of the generals in the Israeli army are atheists, agnostics, or at least nonobservant.

"I've been fighting for twenty-six years," said Sharon, a great, gruff barrel of a man, taking a long swallow of scotch. "All the rest were only battles. This is a real war. I've got to check the troops dispositions but I want you to have dinner here and stay the night."

Our escort officer interrupted, "General, I've got strict instructions from the Defense Ministry that no foreign correspondents are to remain in the field with Israeli units overnight."

Sharon cut him off. "What kind of an army is this if a major can tell a major general what to do?" he asked, only half in jest.

So that was that. Sharon's reconnaissance officer, a handsome blond colonel out of central casting, showed us the canal, its ramparts, and the salient features that figured in the crossing—and the breakout into Egypt. We returned to the command trailer and over dinner, Arik unlimbered the acetate maps with the blue and red arrows marking the movements of his forces. He gave us a graphic account of the decisive battle of the war, blow by blow.

From Tassa, where we had once spent the night, Sharon showed us how he launched his attack at 5:00 P.M. on Monday, October 15. Using the four brigades assigned to his division, he sent one armor unit west toward the canal to serve as a feint and block off Egyptian tanks. At 6:00 P.M., a second armor brigade—the key unit—pushed off on an end around, driving first for the Great Bitter Lake south of the bridge-head and wheeling north. This second brigade split into three prongs: The left or western element raced for the canal to reach the bank; the center slashed northward to repulse the expected main Egyptian counterattack; and the right or eastern prong moved back toward Tassa to clear the road for the reinforcing two brigades.

Sharon had chosen his bridgehead with care: Its axis of advance drove along the line separating the Egyptian Second and Third armies, always a weak link because boundary-line responsibilities are often hazy. The first reinforcing unit was the paratroop brigade in half-tracks, carrying rubber boats, which moved to the canal. Bulldozers cleared the high sand dikes to open up a passage. Sharon during his years as Southern Commander had prepared for just such an emer-

gency by scooping out and thinning an area along the dike where
equipment could be marshaled and bulldozers punch through the wall
and eventually lay down a bridge across the waterway.

That night, army engineers bulldozed a bridgehead, embarking
tanks on specially built self-propelled rafts, which ferried an armor
brigade tank-by-tank across during darkness. "We achieved complete
surprise," explained Sharon in his booming voice. "We suffered heavy
losses on the east bank in our brigade that was holding off the Egyptian
Second Army to the north. But on the west bank, we found little
opposition. We knocked out twenty of their tanks and we were fifteen
miles west of the canal, our guns pointing toward Cairo."

Sharon paused to light a cigar and his mood seemed to change, a
hard edge to his voice. "At this point, I was ordered to hold back. This
was a bad mistake by the high command. They said we had to lay a
bridge over the canal before moving any more armor across. I preferred to move the tanks on rafts. If they hit the bridge, you've got no
bridge. But if you've got fifteen rafts, and they knock out five, you've
still got ten rafts for the tanks."

Sharon said the high command in Tel Aviv had lost precious time
in not moving a second armored division across the canal immediately
in his wake. Ultimately, Bren Adan's division crossed, and headed
south, but Sharon said the delay had cost the Israeli Army the unparalleled opportunity to encircle the Egyptian Third Army before the
superpowers put the pressure on Israel for a ceasefire with Egypt.

"I could have surrounded the Second Army in the north, too, if we
had been given the resources. I told the high command that we were losing time. They thought we didn't have a pressing problem with time. But
they didn't realize there was going to be pressure for a ceasefire—with
forces in place—so time was the most important factor for us."

At that point, Sharon criticized fellow senior officers by name, in
what, after our stories were published, came to be known in Israel as
the War of the Generals. Sharon never had any love for his successor
as chief of the Southern Command, Major General Shmuel Gonen, and
he accused him of in effect being unprepared for the surprise Egyptian
attack, which captured the string of forts on the Bar-Lev Line. He also
berated the heretofore respected armed forces commander, Lieutenant
General David Elazar, for failing to assess intelligence reports and not
mobilizing soon enough. General Moshe Dayan, too, was needled for
vacillating in the first grim days of the war when it looked as if the
Syrians might overrun the Golan Heights.

As we furiously took notes, our escort major looked increasingly shocked and pained at Sharon's revelations. But the general pressed on. "The trouble was that except for Dayan none of the high command or the Southern Commander bothered to come here to see the situation firsthand. I believe a senior general should come forward to talk to his division commanders, not send the commanders back to headquarters. Though some people are trying to destroy Dayan now, he was the only senior general who knew what was going on at the front here. In this war, there seemed to be much less presence of high officers up forward, and, consequently, they didn't get the best picture of the situation.

"Already, they are explaining they didn't move up an additional division to assist me because the bridgehead was not secure. Well, they just didn't understand the situation. I'm a great believer in good planning—for a general officer mastering the details of the situation. You can do your thinking at home and still plan a good operation. But if you want to exploit a developing military situation, if you want to read the battle correctly, and if you want your people to fight the very best for you, then you must be up with your first tanks."

Sharon paused, as if to let the import of what he had just said sink in. He had criticized the key generals in the army and he added former chief of staff Chaim Bar-Lev to his list of officers who either hadn't been sufficiently prepared for an attack or who had failed to seize the tactical opportunities as they developed. "I suppose it will be up to the historians to decide whose decisions were the right ones in this war," he said. "The trouble is that it is the politicians who appoint the historians to write about the war."

Mohr and I spent the night in a tent and the next morning Sharon personally conducted us on a tour of the battlefield: American-made Pattons and Soviet-built T-62s, lay blackened and twisted in the sand, evidence of the ferocity of the tank battle, the one Sharon had called "a real war."

We piled back into the Dodge and decided not to speak of the story in front of the escort officer. We knew it was dynamite: an exclusive account of the decisive battle of the war and a withering indictment of the Israeli high command by the nation's most popular and successful general. In Tel Aviv, we decided that though our material did not violate strict operational security—after all, the ceasefire was on—the material was so politically sensitive that the censors might find some way to eviscerate it. So Charley opted to fly to Rome, using a code over the phone to New York to indicate his plans, where he could file without fear of official tampering. I spent the whole night writing a four-thousand-word story in my room so that he could take it with him first thing the next morning. The stories sent from Rome did indeed cause a sensation in Israel for some time to come. But I wasn't around to get the reaction.

I received a call in Tel Aviv from my foreign editor asking whether I could get to Cairo to cover the ceasefire talks from the Egyptian side. Though I don't like to change sides in a war, I agreed, and reached Cairo via Cyprus. Next, I was asked to report the postwar Arab summit conference in Algiers. All told, it was a couple of months before I got back to Rome. There, I found a copy of *New York* magazine with the Nora Ephron piece.

I'd thought Nora was doing a piece on correspondents and the nature of war reporting. But her article was entitled "The War Followers" and the opening passages focused on the various oddballs and hangers-on who turned up in Israel during the war. As for the correspondents, she went heavy on the "war is fun" theme and said that most of us romanticized war.

I was appalled by some of the quotes she stuck in my mouth. She garbled a compliment I had paid to Charley Mohr and she had me talking about my "Gucci" luggage. She missed the point that the typewriter case business was an inside joke, a send-up, but how do you explain to a girl from Beverly Hills that the whole thing was a way of thumbing one's nose at fate?

I'm sure it's good medicine for a reporter himself to be on the receiving end of a half-cocked journalistic barrel. But the story did get me thinking. Was I really a war follower, in the sense of being a camp follower? Was I insensitive toward human misery? Or romantic about wars? And what, after all, kept me covering conflicts for twenty years?

God knows, I never intended to be a war follower, or, for that matter, even a foreign correspondent.

———

CHAPTER TWO

Sea Duty

COWERING IN THE sands of the Sinai or the paddy fields of Vietnam, it occasionally struck me that I'd come a long way from Chicago, where I was born and grew up. I had a reasonably comfortable upbringing, the eldest of six children of a lawyer-turned-judge. My father never made much money but he managed to shield the family from the rigors of the Great Depression. I attended Catholic grammar schools on the Far North Side and Loyola Academy, a Jesuit high school. As a freshman, I went out for the boxing team, the Illinois state champions. I made the team, won my first fight, but in my second, got my nose badly broken. That effectively ended my formal athletic career.

Loyola was strong on the classics, but during the early 1940s, I found it hard to get absorbed in Xenophon's retreat and Caesar's wars when the morning papers carried accounts of the U.S. Marines at Guadalcanal and the U.S. Army slogging through Italy. A few days after graduation in June 1944, I enlisted at seventeen in the U.S. Navy, or more accurately in an officer training program, headed for college rather than sea duty. I began my naval career at the unlikely venue of De Pauw University in Greencastle, Indiana. I was impressed by the "fleet men" who had come not from high school but from sea, and who were mildly scornful of us sailors fresh out of high school.

"How many semesters have you been in the Navy?" was a com-

37

mon put-down, and rightly so, I thought. After some infraction at De Pauw, I was exiled to another small officer-trainee contingent at the Montana School of Mines in Butte, where the residents apologized for the tameness of the town because the miners and lumberjacks were off to war.

But Butte was still colorful, "the richest hill on earth," so-called because of the copper mines. There was a row of "cribs" along Mercury Street where the whores would rap silver dollars against windowpanes to attract customers. I was still a virgin, but much too skittish to sample their wares. Besides, they didn't accept sailor students.

One Saturday night in the dead of a Rocky Mountain winter, I was restricted to quarters because I had slept in earlier in the week but, bored, I decided to go out on the town anyway. I headed for the Aero Bar downtown, a place that didn't ask underage servicemen like myself for identification cards. I was sampling a beer when a fellow sailor, a "fleet man," from the school sailed in with a blowsy blonde in tow. They began quarreling. She threw her drink in his face, and he slapped her.

The bartender reached over and tossed a punch at the sailor. In an attempt to defend my mate and the honor of the U.S. Navy, I took a swing at the bartender, which glanced off harmlessly. It was, by the way, the last punch I ever threw in earnest, except for a few defensive parries against ladies. Anyway, a kind of half-assed brawl ensued and somebody pushed me out the back door about the time the shore patrol arrived. I slipped quietly back inside the dormitory, but apparently I was identified, for on Monday morning the commandant called me into his office and queried, "Where were you approximately eleven P.M. Saturday night?"

"The Aero Bar at Fifth and Hennessy," I replied, not so much out of truthfulness as from the awareness that he had me cold.

"What do you want out of the Navy?" he asked.

"Sea duty," I responded.

"Request granted," he said.

The next day, I was on a train to the Great Lakes Training Station back in Illinois, still hundreds of miles from the sea. There, I went through boot camp and signal school in the spring of 1945. But by the time I got out to the western Pacific, the war was over. I spent a couple of months on a signal tower on the island of Manicani in Leyte Gulf, tossing coffee cups at huge dragon lizards that came out to sun themselves. I still hankered for sea duty and wangled what I thought was a transfer to a destroyer in Shanghai. Instead, I was transferred to a submarine rescue vessel, the U.S.S. *Florikan* at the sub base in Subic Bay in the Philippines. But not long after, our submarine squadron sailed for Tsingtao, China, an old German treaty port on the Shantung Peninsula facing the Yellow Sea.

It was fascinating duty, playing hide-and-seek with the submarines: Our ship acted as the target; the subs would let loose their unarmed fish at us set to pass under the hull, and we would recover the torpedoes at the end of their runs. In port, signs warned that the surrounding area was communist-controlled. Two of my high school classmates, Tom Wolfe and Gerard Vanden Branden, turned up aboard destroyers, and we had some roaring binges in Tsingtao.

Our ship finally got orders to sail for the submarine base back at Pearl Harbor. At one point en route, the helmsman let me steer the ship, but I became confused with the compass heading, and we were halfway turned around toward China before the officer of the deck noticed our veering wakes and screamed to high heaven. In Pearl, the Navy was asked for volunteers for Operation Crossroads, the atomic tests at Bikini Atoll. I seriously considered staying on for a while, but decided that since all my high school chums were getting discharged in the summer of 1946 and entering college, I'd be happier joining them than staying in the Navy.

Colleges were full that fall and my marks in high school were unexceptional, to say the least. My father managed to get me and my younger brother, John (who had completed high school in three years and joined the Navy about the same time I did), into his alma mater, Loras College in Dubuque, Iowa, on the Mississippi River. In 1947, I was returning to Chicago for Easter vacation aboard the streamliner *California Zephyr,* when it hit a tractor that had fallen off a flatcar onto the tracks, roared off the rails, jackknifed, and crumpled into a suburban station, pinning me under the wreckage. I was in some pain, which wasn't helped by the woman across the aisle from me, who was uninjured and untrapped but kept yanking at her fur coat which had gotten stuck under me.

"For Christ's sake, lady, take it easy," I moaned.

"This is no place for language like that," she replied testily, and pulled the coat free.

I was lucky to remain conscious during the couple of hours I was trapped to help instruct the rescue team when they finally got to me. In their eagerness to pull people free, they ripped off the leg of an elderly woman near me, who died from loss of blood. I spent a year in Chicago's Wesley Memorial Hospital, getting my legs repaired, undergoing fifteen operations with extensive skin grafting. It left me with a new heel, a severed Achilles tendon, and a slight limp, which normally only shows when I'm tired. But the period in the hospital turned my thoughts to journalism. My father's three best friends were Chicago newspapermen: Edwin A. Lahey, a labor writer and Washington bureau chief for the *Chicago Daily News;* Luke Hunt, managing editor of the paper; and Clem Lane, the *Daily News* city editor.

I entered Northwestern University and eventually graduated with a liberal arts degree. Northwestern has a fine journalism school: I suppose it's a toss-up whether you major in journalism or English, or something else. A humanities curriculum makes you better-rounded, they say, while journalism better prepares you for the practical conditions you face on a paper.

On school vacations, I'd returned to San Francisco, and decided the city was the ideal place to live and the *San Francisco Chronicle* the ideal employer. On the strength of a letter of introduction to editor Paul Smith, I packed my belongings into my car and drove to San Francisco. Smith was out of town the day I walked into the newsroom, but it was my good fortune that the paper happened to be short a copy boy. I was signed on for something less than forty dollars a week.

In those days, a copy boy was something like an intern: You spent months running copy or errands, and fetching food and coffee for reporters and editors, with the occasional chance to write stories. There was no formal instruction; you were just supposed to pick up the knack somehow. I would examine the carbons of stories after editing by the city desk to see how they were trimmed, tightened, or better focused by the sharp pencils of the editors. As a vacancy occurred on the staff, a copy boy or girl was given a crack at being a cub reporter or subeditor. It was a heady atmosphere and I developed an enthusiasm and romantic attachment to journalism that, however misguided, I have not yet lost.

The copy boys—usually about a dozen in all—were a bright and lively group since the *Chronicle* then was considered one of the best-edited papers in the United States. And, of course, San Francisco was stunningly beautiful. Those were the early days of the Beat Generation, and the gay population, while evident, had not yet become so dominant in the city. We copy boys had Ivy League graduates and wartime paratroop officers in our ranks. There was a good deal of banter as we sat at our table making "books," the copy paper and carbons on which reporters would type their stories, waiting for the cry, "Boy!" Then one of us would leap to respond. It was really rather demeaning for us, at our age, to race around the city room with copy or coffee for the reporters and editors, some of whom treated us like the serfs we were.

Once when the call for a "boy" came, Bob Strebeigh, a Princetonian from an old eastern family and a former Marine officer, announced, "At ease gentlemen, I'll take this one."

"That's very democratic of you, Bob," someone remarked.

"Never confuse democracy with noblesse oblige," replied Strebeigh.

I was an usher at Bob's wedding to a beautiful sculptress, Mary Tilden, from one of the oldest California families. I had rented, for the first time, a white-tie-and-tails outfit, and at the dance afterward, I had my eye on a dazzling young Hungarian countess. I asked her to dance, but wearing rented shoes, I slipped on the dancing wax sprinkled on the floor and fell on my ass. As I struggled to regain my footing, the countess glared at me scathingly. The romance ended then and there, and it remains the only time I've ever worn white tie and tails.

As I progressed up the copy boy ladder, we all ran into tough times when the *Chronicle* went through an economic crisis, laying off many in the city room. This meant waiting nearly twice as long for the eventual shot at a reporting job. But when I finally got my chance after eighteen months, I had served longer as a copy boy than anyone else promoted to reporter—a record that I believe still stands at the old *Chron.*

I started off with two front-page stories: the first, a Polio Foundation announcement of a breakthrough with the Salk vaccine; the second on the survivors of a merchant ship sunk in a collision off the Golden Gate.

I covered the basic assignments: the night police beat, Oakland city hall, the courts, weekend fire-chasing. The idea was to get experience on all the routine beats, without getting stuck on any one permanently. In the mid-1950s, San Francisco was a highly competitive newspaper town, something like Chicago of the twenties. We had the *Chronicle* and the Hearst *Examiner* in the morning and the Scripps-Howard *News* and Hearst *Call-Bulletin* in the afternoon, along with the *Oakland Tribune* across the bay. Each morning paper had six different editions, and we operated as if every reader read and compared all six editions of both papers. It may have been myopic but it kept the journalistic adrenaline flowing. Today, with monopolies controlling most major U.S. cities, such competition no longer exists, and it's probably too bad.

On the city desk, Abe Mellinkoff was a tough taskmaster, always on call, always checking in after hours to see what was cooking. Larry McManus was a sharp and sympathetic editor who could lucidly explain to a cub reporter what was wrong with his story and how to improve it. Dick Hemp, Harvard and U.S. Marines, brought a coolness under fire to the desk that kept the clamor from getting out of control. Pierre Salinger, whom we called the French Kid, bubbled with enthusiasm, treating every story he handled as a night city editor as a candidate for the Pulitzer Prize. "It's a hell of a story," he would shout across the city room to news editor Bill German, alerting the news desk to an upcoming piece.

Pierre, by the way, gave me one of my more unusual assignments: Dick Hemp had been on a junket to Pike's Peak, Colorado, to celebrate the twenty-fifth anniversary of the development of the turbo-supercharger by General Electric, and stopped off in Los Angeles on the way back. It seems he got tangled up with an old girl friend, was partying it up, and in danger of missing his shift. Pierre dispatched me on a midnight plane to Los Angeles to find Dick. I had a terror of flying: This was only my second flight and I had several whiskeys to calm my nerves. I toured Hollywood and finally found Dick relaxing in luxury at the home of an old Harvard classmate in Pacific Palisades. I got him out to the airport later in the day, and I had several more drinks. By that time, Hemp was pressing me to get on the aircraft. So the story went down in the lore that I flew to Los Angeles to get him, but *he* had to escort *me* back to San Francisco.

I covered all sorts of stories for the *Chronicle:* fires, bank robberies, conventions, even an execution in San Quentin's gas chamber. I preferred articles that needed a light touch. But I was well down on the list of the paper's humor writers, since we had masters like Art Hoppe, who would eventually do a column; Kevin Wallace, who went to the *New Yorker* as did Bernard Taper; and Tom Mathews, an imaginative writer who went on to the Peace Corps in Washington.

One of my mentors was Stanton Delaplane, a magnificent writer who won the Pulitzer Prize in 1941 and after the war turned to writing a humorous travel column. He gave me trenchant advice on conveying the flavor of one's five senses. He warned me, too, that it was dangerous to remain a cityside reporter for too long: The paper would ultimately chew you up and spit you out. Better to carve out an independent, journalistic niche, he pointed out. Delaplane was not your newspaper romantic. "The good old days never existed," he once told me. "These are the good old days." I was in the Buena Vista Café the night Delaplane convinced the owner, Jack Keppler, that Irish coffee would be a great drink for the foggy San Francisco climate. They spent hours trying to get the formula right, and I consumed most of their rejects.

Another reporter I considered something of a beau ideal was George Draper, the tall, elegant son of Dorothy Draper, the New York interior decorator. George had five wives, including a Guggenheim heiress. He also volunteered for the International Brigade in the Spanish civil war, though he was no communist. In World War II, he was an artillery spotter pilot and won a Silver Star for mounting a bazooka on his wing and knocking out a couple of German Tiger tanks. He was a great competitive reporter with a breezy prose style; everything he covered he did with great flair. In retirement he took up sculpting and still manages to look twenty years younger than his age.

What the *Chronicle* had then—and many papers lack today—were self-assured editors who knew how to improve stories and had no compuction about honing down articles or suggesting they be rewritten. I welcomed evening and weekend shifts because that meant I'd get a crack at stories that during the week would normally be assigned to a more senior reporter. In time, I was promoted to the night city desk and it was exhilarating to be in charge of all that was being covered in the city.

More than once, as the late rewrite man or the night city editor, I would have adjorned after work—say at 1:00 A.M.—to Hanno's Corner across from the office for a couple of drinks when the lighting fixtures would start to shake. We'd return upstairs to check with the University of California Seismological Laboratory before preparing another earthquake (usually smallish) story for the morning headline.

San Francisco was a great place for kicking around; lots of lively bars and people. I went out with several girls but fell in love with one who had just come to work for the paper. She had a fresh kind of beauty that turned every head in the city room—and elsewhere. She was the daughter of an admiral who ran the Navy's Deep Freeze expedition to the Antarctic, a fine officer who was both an aviator and

submariner. We had a riotous wedding at the Alameda Naval Air
Station. The reception was marked by Pierre Salinger's wife ending up
in the pool, a foretaste of what was to come with Pierre and the
Kennedys. But our marriage seemed doomed. She worked the day shift
and I worked nights and we never were able to get our lives to mesh
properly. After two years, we were quietly divorced, so quietly, in
fact, that few of our friends on the paper, where little was kept hidden,
knew about our troubles until later.

After seven years on the *Chronicle,* I developed a yen to try my
hand in New York on the grounds that if I got married again in San
Francisco I'd probably never make the move—and I did want to see
what journalism in the Big Town was all about. At the time, I had also
fallen for a beauteous Englishwoman named Elizabeth who lived in
Manhattan, which provided an additional incentive to move. By chance,
the New York papers were all on strike, but through Stan Delaplane,
I had an introduction to Gordon Manning, then senior editor at
Newsweek magazine. Gordon, who was an exciting editor, hired me as
a "swing" writer for the "back of the book," that is, as a writer who
did pieces for the special sections like Medicine, Press, Education,
Science, and the Arts.

I worked for a different department almost every week and covered a wide variety of stories: For example, I might go to Boston one
week to do a piece on Samuel Eliot Morison on the occasion of his
completion of his history of U.S. Naval Operations in World War II;
or to Philadelphia to interview George C. Scott who was appearing in
Andersonville, the story to run with the review when the play opened
in New York; or to visit Louis Armstrong at his house in Queens (he
had porno pictures plastered to the ceiling of his den and told me he
didn't have a swimming pool because his friends would get drunk, fall
in, and sue him).

I once did a story about George Draper for the Press section after
he had come back from an especially colorful trip to "darkest Africa."
"That was a nice story, Bill," George told me. "Until that came out
in *Newsweek,* my mother always regarded me as a failure."

I learned how to tighten a story, as if with a wrench, to fit the
allocated space, usually much abbreviated. I concentrated on compres-
sion, transitions, and keeping the story tightly in focus since in a
one-column newsmagazine story (perhaps 350 words) you couldn't
wander far afield. I also learned to handle the longer stories, up to
cover length, through melding anecdote, detail, quotes, and glimpses

of personality, rather than simply through ordinary indirect discourse.

Writing for a newsmagazine was replete with frustrations: I quickly learned how many different ways the same story could be approached. In a standard news story for a daily paper, the most important elements have to come first. But in a weekly newsmagazine you can "back" into the story in a variety of ways, all equally valid. Thus a story is much more subject to an editor's whims. An editor can arbitrarily select one lead over another: Do you start with a quote? A scene setter? A historical reference? Or what? Sometimes the lead of the story would get switched back and forth, shifted to suit individual tastes, as the piece moved up the editorial ladder. Some editors, I believed, would unnecessarily mess with a story merely to get a blue pencil into the act—to show they were earning salaries, rather than to improve the piece. All this could be ruinous to a writer's morals. A writer sometimes felt like a puppet on an editor's string; stories turned around for no valid purpose. I often thought that what was sometimes proudly called group journalism on *Newsweek* ought more properly to be described as mob journalism.

The pressure of having your work subject to such editorial whim made for a lot of tension at *Newsweek*. Further, it wasn't rare for your main story of the week to be edged out of the magazine by a late-breaking news event. Or possibly by a top editor's decision that he no longer was so keen on a story he had raved about only a day or two previously. More than one new writer assigned to a major story before he got the hang of the place walked straight out of 444 Madison Avenue after the third arbitrary rewrite of a story he thought was perfectly acceptable the first time around.

My own morale suffered because I wasn't given permanent status: *Newsweek* was then on a financial hold-down with a ban on hiring permanent staff, though I was getting a regular salary as a temporary writer. During that first summer, a fellow writer, Jack Winocur, who was in the same boat, and I decided to go in to see the managing editor, Malcolm Muir, Jr., to demand that we be made permanent—or else. I overslept the day we were to see Muir and Jack called me at home. "Don't try it," he warned. "Muir turned me down and I've just quit." So I hung on as a temporary writer until I did a major spread on the posh New England ski resort, Sugarbush, which Muir liked, and my name was added well down on the *Newsweek* masthead.

At *Newsweek*, early in the week before the news jelled, there was a period of calm with long lunches and time for dalliance between writers and researchers. In those days, most of the writers were men and the researchers women; fortunately things have changed and news-magazines like other publications have become more enlightened and are placing women in senior positions. As events quickened toward the end of the week, the pressure soared and often the writer-researcher team found themselves two against the world. The pressure of sixteen-hour days, writers spending Friday and Saturday nights in midtown hotels rather than returning to the suburbs, and their shared frustrations created the conditions for love affairs between writer and researcher. I had the impression that some of the writers with middle-class families in Westchester, Connecticut, Long Island, or New Jersey, felt that only their comely researchers knew what they were going through in their shared battle against editors and deadlines—consequently romances flourished.

The pressure cooker affected senior executives as well. Publisher Philip Graham fell in love with a woman reporter in the Paris bureau whom he pursued more openly as he became increasingly more manic-depressive. It ended with his suicide in 1963, and to this day, I think his widow, Katherine Graham, still believes that some *Newsweek* executives encouraged the affair, and were thus indirectly responsible for Phil's death. Later, Ben Bradlee made his peace with Kay, escorting her around the Republican National Convention. Ben was a natural leader, and though he liked favorites and had a very short attention span, he had flair and was exciting. Kay made a wise choice in hiring him away from *Newsweek* to the *Washington Post*.

The top *Newsweek* editors were an authoritarian lot, particularly the erratic John Denson. He once reduced a researcher to tears because he kept changing the word "Berber" to "Negro" in a story about North Africa.

She persisted on labeling them Berbers and, in a rage, Denson literally threw the copy through his office door at her, yelling, "All right, you can call those goddamn nigras anything you want!"

Denson once approved a four-color cover drawing of French president Charles de Gaulle, failing to notice that the artist had drawn a French flag de Gaulle was holding with the tricolor running horizontally rather than vertically.

Denson, a native of Louisiana, had little regard for blacks and constantly refused to put one on the cover. Finally, he gave in and used a black bas-relief head on the cover to represent "Emerging Africa." But the color was bad; red was mixed in the print. "That figures," said one disgusted reporter. "When *Newsweek* finally put a black on its cover, he turns out purple."

Denson also had strong views about everyone in the media; thus it was difficult to do a story about a Press section figure without psyching out Denson's views in advance. Once Gordon Manning had been arguing heatedly with Denson about the treatment accorded some press magnate in a scheduled story. Manning was accompanied by the Press researcher, Jerene Jones, an intellectual graduate of Bennington College. She noticed that Denson had a habit of grinding his teeth when angry, as though munching a snack.

"What kind of nuts was Mr. Denson chewing on?" she asked Manning innocently as they headed out the editor's door.

"Mine," said Manning.

After eighteen months in the "back of the book," I was loaned to the Nation section to help out during the 1960 presidential campaign. I flew to Hyannis Port after the Democratic convention to do a piece on the Kennedys and the reaction of the locals to a presidential candidate in their midst. Pierre Salinger of *Chronicle* days was now Kennedy's press secretary, and introduced me to the senator, his wife, Jackie, and brother Bobby. They were witty and lively and certainly understood how to cultivate the press.

The campaign whetted my appetite for stories about the new Kennedy administration, and Manning asked me to become a writer on national affairs. It was a stimulating time: I remember doing a cover story on George Romney who refused to give us advance notice on whether he would announce for Governor of Michigan. Editor Osborn Elliott, who had replaced John Denson, even took Romney to the Racquet Club hoping to get some inside word so we wouldn't be stuck with a long cover pegged to his announcement—if he decided not to run. But Romney said he wouldn't tell us anything until he prayed and got enlightenment from God. That didn't go down too well at the Racquet Club. We held our breaths on that story. But I also did covers on new members of the administration: Robert S. McNamara at Defense; Orville Freeman at Agriculture; McGeorge Bundy, the national security adviser. I looked forward to tackling complicated subjects and trying to make them understandable to the reader.

During this period, I was forced to overcome my reluctance to fly since I was rushed south to do reporting on civil rights stories like the Freedom Riders, traveling with them from Montgomery, Alabama, to Jackson, Mississippi.

In time, I even came to enjoy flying. In Vietnam, watching those tracers approach a helicopter like fiery oranges being lobbed at you, I wondered whatever made me uneasy in a nice, safe commercial airliner. I once flew from Saigon to Bangkok with John Chancellor of NBC News. John fell off immediately into a deep sleep and I told him on arrival that I envied that quality. He said that several years earlier, he had suddenly developed a phobia about flying. He went to a physician, worried that his career as a traveling correspondent might be in jeopardy. The doctor prescribed a heavy tranquilizer to be taken just before a flight. So Chancellor would get on an airplane in an almost comatose state. After six months or so, the phobia passed and he was taken off the medication. But in a kind of Pavlovian reflex, John said, no sooner does he buckle the safety belt on an airliner than he falls asleep.

Like other young journalists, I had long been an admirer of *The New Yorker* writer A. J. Liebling, who did the Press pieces for that magazine. I once met him at a cocktail party and asked him whether there was much difference in the way *The New Yorker* printed his stories and how they appeared in book form later. I was thinking particularly of his pieces on Colonel John R. Stingo.

"Yes," said Liebling. "*The New Yorker* took out some of the references to sex in the magazine version. You see *The New Yorker* has a very strict view: Fucking can't be fun. People who commit adultery in the magazine, as in the John O'Hara stories, have got to come to a bad ending. You can't have a good time with sex in *The New Yorker*."

On *Newsweek,* I helped edit the Nation section during vacation periods and I generally "fitted" the section, that is, made sure that the stories and pictures got into the alloted space. You learned to make every word count as you trimmed a word here or there, attempting the shoehorn the stories into the page. I came to admire writers like Peter Goldman, whose stories were so well constructed that one couldn't find an extraneous word or phrase to shorten it by a line or two.

I suppose the most dramatic story I handled as a Nation writer, with the exception of the one on the Kennedy assassination, was on the Cuban missile crisis. I was writing the main running story with much of the material being supplied by Ben Bradlee, Washington bureau chief and a Kennedy confidant. It was a week in which the fate of the world genuinely seemed to hang in the balance. It was also a week that Elizabeth, my English girl friend, and I were throwing a big party to announce our engagement, which had been planned for some time. I arrived late Saturday night after finishing our cover story, though it was not yet clear how Nikita Khrushchev would respond to the U.S. naval blockade of Cuba.

Elizabeth bawled me out in front of the guests for being so late. "You're so bloody narcissistic, Elizabeth," I replied, "that you think Khrushchev laid on this crisis just to screw up your party."

Words continued throughout the evening and by 5:00 A.M. when I left we were no longer engaged. A few hours later, I was alerted, at home, that the Soviets had capitulated and Phil Graham wanted the magazine totally redone to encompass the momentous news. I showered, shaved, and raced to the office, and with Oz Elliott and a couple of others, rewrote the story. Despite the fact that I had lost a fiancée, I had a wonderful feeling of accomplishment: The crisis was over, we had redone the magazine under great pressure, and we were on the newsstands with a much better story than *Time*.

For my money, Oz Elliott was the best editor *Newsweek* ever had, and he was a pleasure to work with. Oz hired Dick Dougherty, a delightful fellow who was to become George McGovern's press secretary, as a writer in the Nation section. Dougherty soon decided that newsmagazine writing wasn't for him, and Oz told him his trouble was that he had gotten in with "the Gas House Gang," consisting of me, Peter Webb, and Dwight Martin. Dwight, who had been Time-Life's bureau chief in Tokyo during the Korean War, could do anything on a newsmagazine and make it seem effortless. Oz once complained, "He makes it look too easy. That's not a good influence on the new writers." But the fact was that Dwight had always done his homework on a story; he prepared his material with care; and he had the physical presence to intimidate any editor who attempted to muck about with his copy.

Dwight Martin wrote the obituary for Henry Luce in *Newsweek* that was far superior, in the eyes of all of us, to the one that ran in *Time*. He was also known for his journalistic one-liners.

When a researcher complained that Martin didn't take South American politics seriously, he replied, "How can any grown man take South American politics seriously?"

When Kermit Lansner, who had been an art critic before becoming a senior editor, was named as a top editor, someone questioned his journalistic credentials. "What do you mean no journalistic experience?" needled Dwight. "Kermit was the best night city editor *Art News* ever had."

During this period, Janice Wylie, niece of author Philip Wylie and a *Newsweek* copy girl, was found brutally murdered with a roommate in their East Side Manhattan flat. Detectives swarmed over the *Newsweek* office looking for leads. By chance, I had been dancing with Janice the night before her body was found—at a *Newsweek* farewell party for Dwight Martin, who was becoming editor of the *Reporter*. I might well have departed with her, but instead had a nightcap with Dick Dougherty. Later, I learned that one of the senior editors, a summer bachelor, had made a date for dinner with Janice and then decided to call it off. He telephoned her flat and a man's voice answered. The editor rashly identified himself—at the other end was a homicide detective. For want of any stronger clues, the senior editor became a suspect for several weeks. Ultimately, the murder was traced to a dope addict who was surprised by the girls in the course of a burglary and killed them.

On November 22, 1963, I was struggling at my typewriter with a cover story on Bobby Baker, the friend of Vice-President Lyndon Johnson and a Senate influence peddler. The story was not going well: At that point, there simply wasn't enough evidence to hang much on Bobby Baker, but we were committed on a Friday to a cover. Then came the stunning news from Dallas. I switched to a profile on the new President and Peter Goldman did the running story on the assassination, with Bradlee contributing a moving memoir of his friend, Jack Kennedy.

In the ensuing weeks, I spent a lot of time writing about the new Johnson administration. But I found myself getting stale. A newsmagazine writer, after all, is just a glorified rewrite man, almost always working from someone else's material. And if journalists are observers rather than operators, rewrite men, so to speak, are observers of observers.

But just then, *Newsweek*'s top editors decided to assign one reporter to ride herd on the national political campaign, particularly the Republicans' search for a candidate. I was chosen to be the national political correspondent. The next day, I interviewed Richard Nixon in his New York apartment, since we wanted to get a color picture of him for possible use as a future cover. The following day, I took off for the snowy precincts of New Hampshire. The new assignment reinvigorated me: It was exciting getting out in the field again, away from the hothouse atmosphere of the New York office.

In New York, there was an attitude on the part of some high-placed editors that, as one put it, "everything west of the Hudson is

Bridgeport.'' But coming from Chicago and having worked in San Francisco, I found this attitude to be superficial and shortsighted. Still, our newsmagazine story suggestions from Chicago were invariably about crime or dirty politics, never about architecture, city planning, or government. Stories from California usually emphasized some kooky angle, rather than seeing developments there as the sociological cutting-edge of the whole society. I resolved to get a lot of regional feeling into my political reporting.

Our political coverage was consistently ahead of *Time*'s. We first spotted the groundswell in New Hampshire for Henry Cabot Lodge, then ambassador to South Vietnam. We also reported his weakness on the West Coast, in Oregon and California, as Nelson Rockefeller made his move. Perhaps most important, we found that Senator Barry Goldwater was nailing down delegates—while other publications seemed to think that the Republican establishment would deny him the nomination in favor of Rocky—just as Senator Robert Taft had been dumped for Dwight Eisenhower in 1952.

Though President Johnson appeared unbeatable, the Republicans put up a lively fight until the convention in San Francisco: First Lodge surprisingly moved forward, then Rocky in Oregon, losing narrowly to Goldwater in California. Then, there was the effort to get Governor William Scranton of Pennsylvania to step in to stop the senator, but, as William F. Buckley, Jr., told me, ''Scranton's developed the image of a man who can't fight his way out of Elsinore.''

As the tempo of the campaign increased, so did press coverage, and all sorts of journalists pitched up with the traveling circus for various periods. Theodore H. White would parachute in occasionally and pick our brains shamelessly. But Teddy was fine company; he had set the standard with his 1960 book; and gave credit to his sources. Earlier on, David Halberstam joined up and was a fount of information on Vietnam, which only then was becoming a kind of peripheral campaign issue. He sounded a loud and clear warning that neither the Diem regime nor its successors had won the hearts and minds of their countrymen and that the United States was risking much with its increasing involvement in Southeast Asia.

David had known Charley Mohr in Vietnam when Charley resigned from *Time* magazine out of principle because the managing editor, Otto Fuerbringer, a dedicated hawk, had ordered a story for the Press section highly critical of the young reporters in Vietnam. It was written in New York with no input from Mohr in the field.

I spent most of my time with Goldwater, whom I liked personally, but I thought him totally unsuited for the presidency—and I'm not sure he wouldn't have agreed with me. He had an engaging family: One day the family and the press regulars—Charley Mohr of the *New York Times*, Loye Miller of *Time*, Robin McNeil of NBC News, John Rolfson of ABC News, and Walter Mears of the AP—all flew down in private planes to Nogales, Mexico, to watch a bullfight and drink a lot of cheap wine. A cloudburst blew out of nowhere drenching the bullring. I think the fight ended with the bull being drowned. The Goldwater entourage liked a good time and everyone had a salty sense of humor. But this led to hypocrisies because the senator had decided to attack the President on, among other things, "the moral issue," suggesting that Johnson and his administration were somehow tainted.

Speechwriter Karl Hess was pushing the "morals" theme as a campaign issue, and once when Hess was departing the Biltmore bar in Los Angeles with a local Goldwater volunteer on his arm, Warren Berry of *Newsday* yelled out for all to hear, "Remember the moral issue, Karl!"

Another time, I was invited up to the room of a lady Goldwater official in Dallas when I finished writing my story. It was after midnight when I knocked on her door. It inched open and a senior Goldwater campaign official, later to become a member of the Nixon Cabinet, said, "Not tonight, Tuohy."

The Goldwater people, like old bulls, were protective about the women on their campaign staff. Dick Dougherty, who had become a political writer for the *Herald-Tribune,* and I got along well with the women press aides, partly because we were easygoing and tried to keep them amused. But when one topsider in the campaign learned that one of the girls in the press office was having an affair with a "liberal Eastern press" reporter, she was summarily sent back to Washington.

In one sense, I liked jetting around America in the press plane, but it had its limitations. You never got to see much of the cities on the itinerary: You'd land at the airport, get in the press bus in the motorcade to some stadium, and then speed back to the airport. We landed in Butte one day and I never had a chance to revisit the Aero Bar from my navy days. I once flew from New York to Los Angeles to link up with the Goldwater party barnstorming through southern California. But in the barbershop of the L.A. airport, I learned the senator had to be back in Washington for an important vote and we all piled into his plane for the cross-country trip. It's the only time I've flown across the continent to get a haircut.

Actually, Goldwater hadn't much taste for the handshaking and backslapping that national politics requires: He really hadn't sought the nomination; rather, it was the conservative kingmakers who had sought him. At one point, I switched assignments for a week with White House correspondent Charles Roberts and was struck by the contrast. Lyndon Johnson was larger than life, a natural political animal who reveled in the adulation of the crowds, many of whom were simply turning out to see their President. Just as reporters admired Goldwater's charm and even his reserve, they were awed by Johnson's political appetites and his superhuman ego. "There's going to be an extra stop in California," cracked Doug Kiker of the *Herald-Tribune*. "The President wants to walk over to Catalina Island."

And therein lay a great difference: I got the impression with Goldwater of a man not really interested in campaigning for the presidency or the burdens of the office. Johnson cared for nothing else: He wanted it all. He wanted to be President of all the people, as he was fond of saying, and on the stump his campaign was crammed with movement, color, and pulse, corny as it was.

And Johnson was expressive. During my week with him, Goldwater began suggesting that it was the President rather than the challenger who would be irresponsible with the use of nuclear weapons.

Johnson was furious and told a group of reporters. "That goddamn Goldwater. He says I want to drop the bomb. You know what would happen if I called Bob McNamara and said, 'Bob. I want you to drop the bomb'?

"I'll tell you what would happen. Bob McNamara would tell me, 'Fuck you, Mr. President.' "

Strangely enough, though most reporters did not vote for Goldwater, we went to lengths to protect him in some of his own utterances. This was when he began contradicting himself on such key issues as the United States in the United Nations, tactical use of nuclear weapons, and U.S. policies in Southeast Asia and China. As Walter Mears, who covered the senator for the Associated Press, put it: "I think the reporters have been more than fair. We keep trying to clarify his statements and asking follow-up questions to make sure we understand what he means. This is sometimes hard to figure out. After a while you get to know what he means, although he doesn't exactly say it." Eventually, Goldwater cut down on press conferences and avoided reporters, leading his supporters to believe there was a journalistic cabal against him. In a Los Angeles suburb, someone in the audience warned a press aide, "Please tell the senator there are reporters in the audience taking down everything he says!"

In the end, Goldwater failed to line out a solid, positive conservative position: He remained a nay sayer, allowing Johnson to co-opt the positive, political center. As Johnson said: "That goddamn Goldwater is running against the office of president instead of for president." Goldwater counted on the great, silent conservative vote that didn't turn up—until Ronald Reagan mined it properly—and he went down to a stunning defeat. In November, I decided not to vote against the senator. I'd been trying to report his campaign objectively all year, and I thought that might have been marred in the end by casting a ballot against him. I don't hold this up as a model for others; but I felt better in not exercising my franchise. We all wound up at the Camelback Inn outside Phoenix on election night but the party ended early as the size of the Johnson landslide became quickly apparent. I flew back to the East Coast next to Jimmy Breslin, a very raucous companion.

The question for me was, what to do next? What do you do for an encore after an exciting national political campaign? I was delighted to be back reporting from the field and didn't want to sit behind a desk in New York again. Nor did Washington appeal to me, promising only reporting on an already-entrenched administration.

During the campaign, the government of South Vietnam had begun to unravel and the Tonkin Gulf resolution presaged an increasing U.S. military commitment to Southeast Asia. I heard *Newsweek* was planning to beef up the Saigon bureau and the first choice of the chief of correspondents was Larry Collins, then our bureau chief in Paris. Larry and I had joined *Newsweek* about the same time, but he had served as a foreign correspondent in Beirut and Paris while I remained in New York. He had just published *Is Paris Burning?* in French and was wondering how it would do in the English-language version. Larry, by the way, wasn't our only author: Bob Massie (*Nicholas and Alexandra; Peter the Great*) was a writer in the Foreign section; Bob Elegant (*Dynasty; Machu, Mandarin*) was a correspondent in Hong Kong and Bonn; Roger Kahn (*The Boys of Summer*) was a sports editor; and David Slavitt, a swing writer, subsequently produced novels under the name of Henry Sutton.

I volunteered for the Saigon assignment and when Larry decided to resign to devote all his time to writing books, I was named Saigon bureau chief. During 1964, I was trying to court a fascinating Swiss woman I had met at a wedding in New York. It wasn't easy because I was spending so much time on the road. But when the Saigon assignment was confirmed, I asked her if she'd like to get married and come to Vietnam with me. She accepted and on Christmas Eve, 1964, we departed Manhattan for Geneva, en route to Saigon.

Just before I left, Bob Vermillion, one of our deskmen who had been a correspondent in the Korean War, said, "Bill, for Christ's sake, keep your head down. And remember this: No matter how good the story, you're no good to *Newsweek* dead. Don't take any chances you don't have to." It was good advice.

CHAPTER THREE

Fighting by the Book

My wife, Johanna, and I spent much of Christmas Eve, 1964, inside a TWA airliner at the end of a runway at Kennedy airport waiting for the fog to lift before the pilot decided to scrub the flight. I'd been looking forward to an overdue vacation, hoping to approach Saigon slowly via Geneva, Rome, Athens, Beirut, Delhi, Bangkok, and so on. In Geneva, *Newsweek*'s managing editor Kermit Lansner phoned to say the magazine was planning a crash cover the first week of January and wouldn't it be great if I could get out there in time to contribute to the package. What do you say when the managing editor leans on you? So we headed east, I trying to read myself into Vietnamese affairs as best I could. We spent New Year's Eve in Hong Kong and the next day boarded the Air Vietnam flight for Saigon.

The plane descended over olive-drab hills, meandering, tawny rivers, and emerald-green rice fields. Just off our wing, I could see a flight of combat helicopters looking like dragonflies on some unknown mission. We were met at the airport by Bob McCabe, our Hong Kong bureau chief, and François Sully, *Newsweek*'s longtime stringer, who packed us in the back of his car.

On the ride into town, I was struck by the crush of traffic: blue-and-yellow Renault taxis, low-slung, black Citroën sedans, jeeps, overstuffed American cars, motorbikes, motorscooters, and the ubiquitous *cyclo-pousse*, the pedicab. The streets were wide and pleasantly arced over by tall, graceful tamarind trees. The architecture was handsomely French-Colonial. The sidewalks were thronged with men in sport shirts and slacks, women in ao dais, the high-collared dress with pantaloons and skirt in colors like peach and pistachio. In January 1965, the handful of tall U.S. soldiers in the street looked like Gullivers among the Lilliputians.

François drove us around: The noise and bustle of the city was scented with the pungent, exotic smells of the Orient; joss sticks burned at the ancestor shrines of the pagodas, and smells and colors combined in a sensuous riot at the wholesale market, chockablock with endives, strawberries, parsley, lettuce, tomatoes, pineapples, limes, and the sweet-sour fruit of the tamarind.

On the streets, the children smiled and asked for coins. If you complied, you were hailed as "Number one" (a good guy), if not, "Number ten" (bad guy). Though most of the kids seemed friendly, one youth stared at me contemptuously and spat on the ground.

To me, Saigon at first glance seemed reminiscent of Albert Camus's novel *The Plague,* with the city mostly cut off from the countryside. You were taking a risk, I was told, to drive to Cap St.-Jacques for sunning or swimming in the sea. The day we arrived, three U.S. Army officers were shot at while waterskiing on the Saigon River. It was safer to stick to the Cercle Sportif, the French-built club in the center of town that boasted a dozen tennis courts and an Olympic-size swimming pool. I saw a bevy of French and Vietnamese girls in bikinis, and François pointed out the CIA station chief in bathing trunks reading the newspapers.

We pitched up at the Caravelle Hotel and repaired to the rooftop bar in time to see a gorgeous sunset settling behind the twin spires of the Roman Catholic cathedral. I was introduced to the wife of an American official, a pretty brunette, who explained, "I've been here a year and a half. Sometimes it's bad and sometimes it's good. You read about things that happen in the countryside but still you try to live normally. At times, though, you get discouraged. Last night we heard artillery fire—what the servants call boom-boom. But I really like Saigon. True, it's called a city but for us it's more like a small town. After a trip to Bangkok I was really glad to get back—even though our local movie theater had just been bombed."

The next morning Johanna began house hunting. I, in turn, was introduced to what was then a routine part of Saigon life—a political demonstration. A mob of tough-looking youths surged through the central Lam-Son Square, protesting the arrest of several students in a previous demonstration. Most appeared to be only ten to fifteen years old but the fanatical look on their faces was disconcerting. A couple of them started threatening and berating me, and I didn't know what the form was in responding. Luckily, John Shaw of *Time* magazine appeared, grabbed one of the youths, and unceremoniously pushed him away. The mob moved on, shouting, "Down with Tran Van Huong." He was the prime minister and this was my first direct introduction to Vietnamese politics.

That afternoon I called on Barry Zorthian, the short, dumpy, affable U.S. minister for information in what was called by the jaw-breaking title JUSPAO, for Joint U.S. Public Affairs Office. The office was next to the Rex Hotel Officers Billet where a Filipino dance band played on the roof nightly while American advisers barbecued steaks. Zorthian admitted the country was in a mess politically and militarily: The government was built on quicksand and the army had suffered catastrophic defeats over the year's end. Yet the number of U.S. military advisers in the country had risen to nearly twenty-four thousand. And the Vietnamese had the staunch support of U.S. ambassador Maxwell Taylor, a former general; and the head of the Military Assistance Command, Vietnam, known as MAC-V, General William C. Westmoreland.

I spent the first month in Vietnam traveling around the country by car, helicopter, and U.S. Air Force transport. Vietnam was divided into four military regions: I Corps, comprising the rugged five northernmost provinces; II Corps, the Central Highlands and coastal region; III Corps, the area around Saigon with rubber plantations and jungle near Cambodia; and IV Corps, the huge, table-flat Mekong River Delta.

I began in the south and worked my way north, eventually arriving in Da Nang where at the Special Forces base I met A. J. "Jack" Langguth, the young *New York Times* man who was among the brightest of all the correspondents to serve in Vietnam. Langguth, a husky, cerebral Minnesotan, had been kicking around the boondocks with the Green Berets near the Laotian border. "It does not look good, Tuohy," he told me prophetically.

However, I *was* struck by the quality of the U.S. officers and noncoms assigned to Vietnamese army units as advisers. At the time, they were all volunteers and highly motivated. They had a much more realistic view and a more candid appraisal of the military situation than I found among their senior officers back in Saigon.

I had barely finished my first orientation trip around the country when I had to play host to Oz Elliott, *Newsweek*'s editor, and Kay Graham, our publisher, who were on a Far Eastern fact-finding trip.

I introduced them to General Westmoreland, a nice man with something of the Eagle Scout about him. To break the ice, I mentioned I had been impressed by the political astuteness of his advisers in the field: They seemed to have a feel for what was going on.

"No, no," he said, shocked. "My advisers don't get involved in politics. They are instructed not to."

I tried to explain that I meant politics in a somewhat broader context, but without much luck. It dawned on me that General Westmoreland, whatever his fine military credentials, was out of his depth in a war that was essentially political. Poor Westy. He really thought that he could fight this war by the West Point book.

The Elliott-Graham arrival coincided with that of a high-level mission from Washington, headed by National Security Adviser McGeorge Bundy. During their stay, the Vietcong attacked a U.S. helicopter base near Pleiku in the Central Highlands and a barracks at Qui Nhon on the coast, killing nearly thirty American servicemen. Bundy recommended a retaliatory air strike, and U.S. and Vietnamese planes bombed North Vietnamese targets. This was one of the key decisions by Lyndon Johnson to escalate in order to force Hanoi to cease and desist in the south. Another was the use of U.S. warplanes to attack Vietcong positions in South Vietnam which greatly accelerated the level of violence there.

This, in turn, led to the buildup of air bases in South Vietnam, which were the targets of Vietcong attack. Eventually, in March, the U.S. Marines were sent in to protect the airstrips, the first combat troops to debark.

By this time, Johanna had found a lovely little villa, in the residential section of Saigon—I still remember the address, 9A Tu-Xuong Street—and hired a husband-and-wife team to serve as cook and maid. One morning while shaving, I heard an enormous explosion. The old U.S. embassy in the commercial section had been bombed. I rushed out the door and into my rented Volkswagen Beetle and sped to the scene. A car loaded with explosives had driven up outside the main door of the ill-protected building. The driver exchanged shots with embassy guards which drew some of the personnel to the windows. On the ground floor, Vice-Consul Edith Smith had the presence of mind to warn, "It might be a bomb," causing many around her to dive for the floor.

A couple of hundred pounds of plastic erupted in a ball of fire that shot up the building's six stories, tearing gaping holes in the lower three floors. The blast killed twenty-two people, including three Americans, and wounded nearly two hundred. Flying glass inflicted facial wounds on many, and blinded the CIA station chief. I was shocked to see all those pretty girls in bright print dresses streaming out of the embassy, suddenly all torn and bloody. As of that morning in March, some of Saigon's insouciance seemed to vanish, at least for me.

In those days, finding military action was very much hit-or-miss. You'd get word of an interesting action launched by the Vietnamese Army—called ARVN, or "Arvin,"—and link up with the unit's American adviser. You'd leave early in the morning and, depending on what happened, would usually be home for dinner. Often it was no more than a long hot walk in the sun.

I'd pick up a few leeches around my boots and gingerly pluck them off and I was sometimes gasping for breath trying to keep up with fast-moving young troops climbing hills, but it wasn't the stuff of great derring-do. And even when a unit was engaged in heavy action, unless you were with it at the time, it would be over by the time you could get there. Back in Saigon, at home or the Caravelle, you'd change your fatigues for shirt and slacks and clean your combat boots.

Once, Hugh Mulligan of the Associated Press was on a flight to Da Nang with George Esper, a young fellow AP correspondent. George was fresh out of West Virginia: His only experience outside his native state was a two-week stay in New York City. On the plane, he was writing his fiancée back in Wheeling about the strange sanitary impediments of the exotic East. He had shared a room at the Caravelle with Mulligan and asked him what was the unfamiliar piece of equipment in the bathroom.

"A bidet," said Hugh.

"What's it used for?" asked George.

Hugh explained.

"Quit kidding me, Hugh, what's it really used for?"

Mulligan thought for a moment and said, "George, you know when you come back from the field with muddy boots. Well, you put them in the bidet, turn on the spray, and wash them off."

"Why didn't you say so in the first place," said George, dutifully scribbling the information in his letter.

For a *Newsweek* cover story, I joined Captain Charles B. Huggins, who was the adviser to the South Vietnamese reconnaissance company that operated in the area northwest of Saigon. Charlie, thirty-two, a rangy, bespectacled regular from South Carolina, was a dedicated soldier who had volunteered for Vietnam. I questioned him about his leave-taking from his wife and two children.

"I asked her if she understood why I was going," said the captain. "She said she did but she doubted that the neighbors would."

Huggins in a sense represented the cream of the officer corps and in Vietnam walked a delicate line. He could not give a direct order to a Vietnamese soldier and his suggestions to his Vietnamese counterpart officers could be ignored. Yet, U.S. advisers participated in the shooting and held vast implicit power by virtue of their being able to call in U.S. helicopter and air support—or withhold it.

Our lift of two dozen helicopters landed in a dusty rice field deep in the heart of Vietcong territory near the Cambodian border. Pouring out of the helicopters in the blistering 100-degree heat, the steel-helmeted South Vietnamese troops, who wore yellow kerchiefs for identification, dashed across the sun-baked paddy toward the tree line at the end of the field. There, they went about searching a honeycomb of deep trenches and foxholes, first "sanitizing" each hole with a burst of carbine fire or a hand grenade. Close behind the troops came their commander, First Lieutenant Slen Cam Vo, thirty-two, behind him was Huggins with an M-16 slung over his shoulder and a .38-caliber pistol strapped to his waist. After twenty minutes of intermittent fire, Vo's men captured thirty-three Vietcong suspects.

Lieutenant Vo asked for additional time to search for arms caches. After another thirty minutes, they turned up a large rice supply, then called for the helicopters, setting off a smoke grenade to mark their location.

Huggins told me he spent a lot of time in the field, eating rice mixed with fish and the strong-smelling Vietnamese fish sauce called nuoc-mam. He liked his job with the recon company, which specialized in quick, intelligence-gathering forays.

In early 1965, Huggins was a member of an elite U.S. group. As Major General Charles J. Timmes pointed out: "Our military advisers in Vietnam represent the highest concentration of our best officers and sergeants.''

During the previous operation, the 5th Recon was caught in a withering Vietcong crossfire. Huggins and Vo instantly counterattacked while the tall, rangy Huggins, standing upright in the midst of the battle, called in air strikes.

I spoke to Huggins's superior, Major Sidney Chavers, who said, ''Charlie's outfit is the finest in Third Corps. The key to success is the Vietnamese commander. If he accepts the presence of the adviser, his staff will do likewise. But an adviser needs to know that a Vietnamese officer has other pressures besides the military involved in an operation—political, religious, economic.''

Indeed, those pressures often outweighed the military contributions of Vietnamese officers. As one captain told me: ''The things Americans are taught to believe in—democracy, freedom, love thy neighbor, help the poor—just don't exist over here. I haven't been able to justify in my own mind what we are dying for.''

Many U.S. advisers deplored the lackadaisical attitude of some Vietnamese commanders, the absence of careful planning, and the nagging political influence from Saigon.

From Saigon, I flew several missions with a ''Dustoff,'' the code name for a medical evacuation helicopter, with Captain Douglas Moore at the controls. A tall, broad-shouldered graduate of Arkansas State College who had been in Vietnam seven months, Moore had flown 350 missions in three hundred air hours, ferrying some four hundred casualties. His was one of the toughest jobs: flying into dicey areas in an unarmed chopper, and standing by while his crewmen rounded by the wounded and carried them back to the Huey.

We flew northwest from Saigon over the rugged, triple-canopied jungle country, and the bomb-scarred Iron Triangle and War Zone D, two Vietcong strongholds, to pick up two Americans wounded in an action at Song Be, sixty-five miles from Saigon. The accommodating crew let me put on a radio headset.

''This is Six Six Hickory Smoke,'' said the voice on the radio. ''Armed helicopters are reporting fifty-caliber fire.''

''This sounds like a real number ten area,'' said Captain Moore.

That didn't help my peace of mind, nor did the low-level ''contour flying,'' skimming along the deck at treetop level and sometimes dipping below the trees following a river. It was scarier than any roller coaster I'd ever been on, hair-raising.

Moore said he was feeling the nervousness he always does just before going into a hot landing zone. His first mission was the worst, with armed Hueys firing their .30-caliber machine guns and rockets, the ground fire coming back with flares and the tracers streaming by. It was all new and strange to him then, and, scared, he remembered thinking, "What have I gotten into?"

"Viper Three to Dustoff Seven One," came a voice from an Army spotter plane hovering over the Song Be area, "your pickup coordinates are one-six-nine-zero-three-nine. It's a churchyard along the road south of the mountain."

"This is Dustoff Seven One," Moore replied. "I can see you, Viper, but I don't see the churchyard."

"You're directly over it."

"Okay, I've got it here, Mike," Moore said to copilot Lieutenant Mike Trader. "Open the doors. We've got bad guys around here, but don't shoot unless you get shot at."

We thrashed in over the thatched huts, all in flames, and into the churchyard past the crude, wooden belfry with the white cross. I could see the U.S. and Vietnamese personnel in dappled camouflage crouching in a ditch along the road waving us in. Then we set down, and crew chief Ronald Lewis and medic Donald Chambers jumped out with a litter.

They came back with a wounded Ranger adviser, hit in the hip, who didn't want to lie down in the litter rack.

"Tell him he's got to lie down," Moore shouted over the roar of the rotor. "We've got another WIA pickup, so he's got to go on the top tier."

The helicopter was skidding over a bombed-out church—this was a Catholic village—to set down again. Lewis and Chambers were out of the chopper helping a U.S. soldier who was hit in the shoulder onto the second litter.

"Dustoff, this is Wishing Well. Did you get the U.S. wounded out?"

"This is Dustoff and that's a big fat affirmative," said Moore, taking the copter up. On the intercom: "How are those men?"

"They look okay, sir," said Chambers.

Chambers made sure both wounded were comfortable, told them they looked okay, and lit up cigarettes for them. Chambers said to me, "That second guy has a hell of a lot of fragments from a rifle grenade. But we always tell the patient, 'No sweat,' because we don't want them to panic and go into shock."

Captain Moore said he thought of getting out of the chopper to make sure the first wounded soldier was lying down properly in the litter—but a pilot doesn't leave his seat, except in a real emergency. If there are a lot of wounded around, everyone will try to get on at once, overloading the Huey.

"That happened a couple weeks before in a bad ambush near Da Lat," the pilot said. "Then, we were rushed, and the Vietcong opened up from a tree line. One bullet went under my seat, hit the fire extinguisher, bounced off, and wounded my crew chief."

After transferring the wounded Americans to an ambulance at Saigon, we headed for Hau Nghia Province, twenty miles to the northwest. We flew into an area with paddy fields and tree lines, behind which the VC took cover. I could see tracers flying around, but Moore slipped the chopper neatly into a field, and two Vietnamese soldiers ran toward us carrying a wounded comrade on a stretcher. He had a bad back wound, which Chambers and Lewis began dressing. We lifted off in a hurry and flew back to Saigon, coming in over the Vietnamese military cemetery, a sprawling plot of new graves. Sometimes when the choppers brought back Vietnamese dead after a bad battle, the graves were opened, and the soldiers buried immediately.

Moore's strangest mission came the day a pregnant woman was picked up. "We were bringing the woman back from a little village in the mangrove swamps south of Saigon," the captain recalled, "because there was no medical assistance there. Halfway back, our medical aid man noticed the time had come. He quickly undressed her and delivered a five-pound boy—at twenty-five hundred feet."

"I like what I'm doing here," said Moore when we were back in the operations rooms of the 57th Air Medical Evacuation Detachment. "We're like a doctor or fire department in the States. We sit around until somebody wants us and at night we usually keep our uniforms on because that's when the Vietcong like to hit. We've got a hot line right into our rooms and a jeep with a red light and siren on it, and we can move in a hurry. I like what I'm doing here because I think we are saving lives, and it is satisfying to be doing exactly what you are trained to do. It's a big boost for Americans to know that if they get hit, we'll go in after and get them out. We're not killing anyone: We're helping others—the wounded, the hurt, and the sick."

One of the more glamorous outfits in Vietnam was the U.S. Special Forces. They had been given a big boost, operationally, by

President Kennedy, who decided that their skills—demolition, communications, medics, ordnance, intelligence, patrolling—could be used in Vietnam in counterinsurgency work. Yet there always seemed to be some confusion about their role, both in and out of the Special Forces. For their original missions of unconventional warfare was basically designed to destroy. But counterinsurgency was designed to build. Many Green Beret types had developed the attitudes and mystique of the loner, operating way behind the lines to harass the enemy. But counterinsurgency operations in Southeast Asia called for teamwork for training and for setting up civic action projects.

"There was an intellectual mixup as to the nature of our role in Vietnam," one senior officer confided. "Both here and at Fort Bragg headquarters. The fact is our people were originally trained to be guerrillas not counterguerrillas. There is a big difference."

When the Green Berets arrived in Vietnam, they were given the job of training the montagnards, the aboriginal hill tribesmen, mainly because the Vietnamese had little real control in the highlands. The tribes were organized into companies of CIDG—civil irregular defense groups—paid as mercenaries to defend their home areas. The Special Forces established training camps and patrol bases throughout the highlands, sometimes aided by CIA money and personnel. But the Special Forces montagnard program received a bad jolt in November 1964, when several CIDG companies from two tribes tried to revolt against the central government authority. The Green Berets were in the awkward position of having to put down an insurrection.

"We were partly responsible," according to one senior officer. "We had gained their loyalty but they were loyal to us and not Saigon."

This led to the 5th Special Forces Group in Vietnam reevaluating the whole nature of their mission. A new directive was issued: It still called for border surveillance, but also for supporting Vietnamese government programs wherever Special Forces were stationed. As a result, the Green Berets shifted their skills to the more constructive tasks of "civic action" and "nation building."

As a recently arrived colonel, preaching the new message, put it to me, "There are still a few Bolsheviks around who don't understand or don't want to understand the big change in our mission. But we're changing from separatist loners to counterinsurgency specialists who operate as part of a team."

This didn't set too well with some of the more colorful characters who wore the green beret like "Charging Charlie" Beckwith, who operated his "Delta Project" out of Nha Trang in central Vietnam as a hard-hitting, quick-reaction force. One grizzled top sergeant in Nha Trang bitched to me, "Why don't they turn us loose at what we were trained for? Killing Cong. Not all this civic action crap."

But the Army, which was always suspicious of the elite Special Forces, was adamant. The standard A-Team—two officers and ten enlisted men—was modified to include fewer demolition experts and more intelligence and psychological-warfare specialists. When possible, the dangerously exposed camps along the Cambodia-Laos border were relocated where they could be of more assistance to local population centers.

As a city boy and a failed boy scout, I was fascinated by the rugged Special Forces troopers who were trained to survive in the jungle. They were self-sufficient in a way I could never dream of being. On my way to check out one of the new-style Special Forces camps, I spent a night at the headquarters of a C-Detachment at Can Tho in the Delta. I don't remember much except drinking beer and listening to war stories in the bar. But I do recall that the camp pet was a huge python they had captured in the jungle and kept in a large pen, feeding it live chickens and other tidbits. They were as comfortable with it as a favorite hound.

I rode in a jeep with a couple of Green Berets as shotgun on the way to the camp at An Phu, hard by the Cambodia border. The last twenty minutes was by a motorboat up the Bassac River, the south branch of the Mekong. There, I spent a couple of nights observing the A-Team with Lieutenant Robert Anderson, a tall, blond, twenty-five-year-old professional infantryman who came from Newport News, Virginia. Striding around the camp, Anderson mentioned there were some sixty-four thousand people in his district, which produced a lot of rice and fish. He was the executive officer of the twelve-man team and had been in An Phu for ten months. It was a thriving, important district.

"Our problem is that the VC operate from across the border," said the lean lieutenant, pointing at the frontier a couple of hundred yards away. "We have good intelligence. We pick up their units and follow them as they move around the Cambodian side. We've asked for permission for hot pursuit—but have been turned down. I suppose international border incidents would be disturbing, back in Saigon."

Anderson and his CIDG company organized several ambushes each night and he assigned a member of the U.S. A-Team to make sure they were properly positioned by the irregulars. Much of the Green

Berets' work was training—and retraining—the CIDGs and local militiamen. I accompanied Anderson in a plastic speedboat down the
river to a hamlet called Da Phuoc—with four armed bodyguards from
the Hoa Hao sect. The lieutenant supervised the training of the popular
force in basic infantry tactics. He also inspected the construction of a
two-room addition to the school. Anderson said he was in favor of the
civic action concept.

"We've spent eight thousand dollars on civic action projects," he
said. "Bridges, schools, dispensaries, flagpoles, wells, repair work.
Schools are the big problem. They never have enough schools and
teachers. And this kind of thing is important in the long run. This may
be the way to win this war."

I stopped off at Can Tho on my way back to Saigon. A Green
Beret senior officer there, who had done some thinking about the
problem, told me, "The unconventional warfare mystique has sometimes created bad relations with the rest of the Army. Now, we're
trying to overcome the idea that the Special Forces are closemouthed
and mysterious. We're ready to take on any honorable military job."

It was a far cry from the Green Berets of John Wayne.

With the increasing arrival of U.S. combat troops through the
summer of 1965, the nature of the American involvement in Vietnam
changed—and so did the press coverage. We shifted attention away
from the Vietnamese units to the American outfits—the Marines around
Da Nang, the Army to the north and west of Saigon. I had hired Mert
Perry, an experienced Vietnam hand, for the *Newsweek* bureau and we
were on hand to greet the paratroopers of the 173rd Airborne Brigade
who waded ashore from ships at Vung Tau, which the French used to
call Cap. St.-Jacques. Where once the U.S. military advisers had been
thoroughly briefed on Vietnam before arrival, a paratrooper said to
Mert on coming ashore, "Hey, mac, how long you been on this
island?"

As the U.S. military commitment grew, so did the press corps.
Barry Zorthian began holding daily briefings for the expanded media in
the JUSPAO auditorium at 5:00 P.M. They quickly became known as
the Five O'clock Follies, mainly because many military and civilian
briefers often fed the press inaccurate information. For the official
word was optimism: The Vietcong was being repulsed and the government was winning "the hearts and minds" of the people. There was
light at the end of the tunnel.

"I think it is clear that Saigon will win and the Vietcong will lose," a senior U.S. officer told me that summer. "It is gradually becoming clear to both sides that the pendulum has begun its return."

That same optimistic tone reached back to Washington where President Johnson delivered a lengthy report to leading members of Congress. "The incidents initiated by the Vietcong," he said, "have diminished, and the losses they have suffered have substantially increased."

But a couple of weeks later, the South Vietnamese suffered one of their worst weeks of the war with heavy losses in Quang Ngai and Binh Dinh provinces in I and II Corps and the Vietnamese commanders began openly requesting American combat troops for the central provinces. At the same time the civilian government kept quarreling; another regime collapsed; and the military all but stepped in to take over. As one U.S. senior officer put it: "I don't see how we can *not* get involved in the next big battle."

I spent a couple of days flying around the country with General Westmoreland for a *Newsweek* cover story on him. You couldn't help liking Westy, he was so straightforward in his immaculate fatigues and those four white stars on his hat and collars. He was no expert on counterinsurgency, but he did put his finger on the problem that dogged the allies in Vietnam.

"If we can only get the enemy to stand up and fight we will blast him," he said as we climbed into his personal helicopter on the pad at Tan Son Nhut. "But we can't fight him and destroy him until we find and fix him."

The helicopter lifted and began banking and at that moment a bomb went off in the old terminal building, sending a white puff of smoke and debris bursting through the roof. Westmoreland looked at the new hole in the terminal and spoke into his radio. He took the news calmly. "I thought they'd do that one of these days," he said. "They have no concern for human life. I'm always amazed they haven't been more strongly condemned by world opinion."

We didn't bother to investigate the blast any further—there wasn't much point—and Westy, a modern executive general, had a tight schedule to keep.

If Westmoreland had no solutions, he had at least pinpointed the elusive quality of the war. And it was the elusive nature of results that was in part responsible for the continuing friction between media and government.

In the summer of 1965, the question of military censorship came up—with the press corps divided on whether to institute a World War II–Korea type censorship, where reporters handed their copy to military officers who checked it for sensitive material and then approved transmission out of the area. The problem was as Barry Zorthian pointed out: "We don't command in this war. The Vietnamese do. Therefore we can't censor because you can't have an effective censorship unless you control the communications—which are in the hands of the Vietnamese government."

Almost no one wanted to allow the Vietnamese to determine what was censorable or not. Yet some news agency executives said they favored censorship mainly so that it wasn't left to their individual Saigon bureau chiefs to determine what compromised national security. Most of the rest of us thought reasonable guidelines could be worked out between the media and the government—and adhered to. As Jack Langguth put it: "There are no problems that the correspondents and Saigon officials can't solve locally if the leaders in Washington resist the temptation to run the press as well as the war."

In the end, there was no censorship, but reporters risked losing their credentials and Vietnamese visas if they compromised current operations by disclosing material that jeopardized them.

John Paul Vann had become something of a cult figure in Vietnam. As a lieutenant colonel, a couple of years previously, he had been an adviser with the Vietnamese 7th Division in the Delta and critical of their operations. He had influenced reporters like David Halberstam, Neil Sheehan, and Malcolm Browne with his pessimistic views, which differed markedly from the rosy outlook of the U.S. high command in Saigon, then headed by General Paul Harkins. Now, as a civilian, Vann had returned to Vietnam and was the senior adviser in Hau Nghia Province, where the Vietcong were entrenched. He had hesitated to return after Army retirement, but his wife told him, "You're away from home so much giving lectures about Vietnam, you might as well be there."

Mert Perry and I arranged to spend a couple of days with Vann, and we were to drive to Hau Nghia with his assistant, Doug Ramsay. It was a dangerous area and I slept only fitfully the night before the trip from Saigon. Ramsay showed up with a four-wheel-drive Bronco and carrying an M-16. The ride was uneventful and Vann greeted us in Bao Trai with the cheery warning, "This is all bad-news country."

Nightly mortar attacks were common, so Vann, then forty-one, reinforced the bathroom of his two-story stucco villa so that it served as a shelter. In the countryside, the night belonged to the VC, who often mined roads. Each morning a detail of Arvin swept the main routes. The danger of ambush was ever-present. But Vann, the intense, compact, disciplined Virginian, and Ramsay, the lanky, laid-back westerner, made a good team, constantly touring the province, advising, assisting, and stimulating Vietnamese officials on such diverse programs as building schools, training teachers, refugee relief, food distribution, electrification, and hamlet construction.

On our swing, Vann advocated a strong, central government and said that U.S. aid should at least appear to come through the government rather than from American advisers. Vann was against the military policy of large search-and-destroy operations through the countryside.

"We need less reliance on air power and unobserved artillery fire," he said heatedly. "Hell, that only results in the killing of innocent peasants and helps the VC recruit supporters. We need night patrols to regain the countryside after dark. But these are more difficult than shooting off cannons."

Vann's views opposing the indiscriminate use of firepower were not popular with military officialdom.

In mid-August, a Special Forces camp at Duc Co west of Pleiku in the Central Highlands came under siege and the 173rd Airborne Brigade in Bien Hoa was alerted to move on a rescue mission. I drove to Bien Hoa and flew in a C-130 with the brigade north—it was the first time a U.S. combat force had left its home base for action in the interior. In Pleiku, we boarded trucks, and rumbled through high plains reminiscent of Colorado, with mountains in the distance. The road was flanked by tea plantations, their large thick bushes perfect for ambushes. Alongside the highway, sturdy montagnard tribesmen and their bare-breasted women trudged to the fields. Toward late afternoon, the convoy pulled off the road and began digging in for night. The brigade commander, General Ellis Williamson, was angry that he had to halt before making contact with the enemy, but his instructions were to cover the southern flank while a Vietnamese unit made straight for the beleaguered camp at Duc Co.

I was with Karsten Prager of *Time* magazine, Wallie Beane of *Stars and Stripes,* and the redoubtable Horst Faas, the AP's award-winning photographer. A Berliner, Horst would have made a fine company or battalion commander. He, like his brilliant AP sidekick

Peter Arnett, had an instinctive sense for good tactics and could smell trouble immediately. I always felt more comfortable sticking near either of them.

Horst was a great teddy bear of a fellow with a surprisingly soft voice with a pleasant German accent. Always good company, Faas was always well equipped, and not just with photographic gear. He traveled in what passed for style in the boondocks: tins of paté, Tabasco sauce for C rations, and cans of Beaujolais wine purchased at the French grocery in Saigon. He always seemed to have some extra bit of needed accessory in his bottomless pack. For his work in the field in 1964, he won the Pulitzer Prize for photography.

We all bathed in a nearby stream and pitched our tent while it was still light. That night, we underwent the heaviest rainstorm I've ever been in. Rain crashed down all night long; the sky rattled with lightning and thunder. The goddamn water soaked us to the skin. My only consolation, as I lay awake cold and miserable, was that it was too wet for an enemy attack.

The next morning, we moved out to reconnoiter the southern approaches to Duc Co. Our armored column moved up to a country track without any flank security, which worried Horst and me. When we took some sniper fire from off in the distance, a red-faced sergeant barked to no one in particular, "Don't just stand there, dammit, fire back!"

We entered a remote hamlet and the U.S. captain in charge ordered the paratroopers to round up the inhabitants.

"Ask these people where the Vietcong went," he told a nervous Vietnamese interpreter.

An old man who might have been the village elder began speaking rapidly.

"Sit down and shut up, loudmouth," bellowed the captain.

The captain then ordered a soldier, "Take him a hundred yards down the road. Maybe if they think we're going to blow his head off, they'll talk."

The villagers did not talk: Women and children wailed and sobbed. Embarrassed paratroopers began loading two dozen peasants aboard a truck to take them back to the district town. The soldiers were reasonably courteous but the villagers continued to cry. For all they knew, they were being packed off to exile, imprisonment, or worse. I questioned the point of this to a lieutenant, who said plaintively, "Well, if they're not VC sympathizers, what are they doing way out here? Why don't they live in town?"

The captain was suspicious when he saw defensive holes dug in the ground inside huts. He didn't realize most hooches in Vietnamese villages had such shelters for years. He radioed headquarters for permission to "burn this place now so we won't have to do it later," and seemed put out when the reply was negative.

That operation taught me a few lessons: to relieve a relatively small, isolated garrison, the U.S. and Vietnamese forces had tied up thousands of their best fighting men for days, and as far as anyone could tell, the VC or NVA were still lurking around the area, even though they had withdrawn the siege from Duc Co. Further, the aggressive spirit of U.S. fighting troops and the mentality of their combat officers was hardly suited for dealing with villagers in backwoods Vietnam.

I had hardly returned to Saigon, when word came that the U.S. Marines were involved in their biggest battle yet. I flew to Chu-lai in Quang Tin Province and choppered to the scene of the action on the Batangan Peninsula in Quang Ngai Province.

I found five haggard, red-eyed, dust-caked Marines of Hotel Company, 2nd Battalion, 4th Marine Regiment, or "2-4," cleaning their weapons on the perimeter of their command post in the low-lying, scrubby sand dunes. The smell of burnt powder was in the air. The Marine command was claiming a major victory in that first head-on encounter with a main-force Vietcong regiment. But Hotel Company had borne the brunt of the assault, suffered 50 percent casualties, and these "grunts"—infantrymen—were only now coming out of shock.

"We all expected heavy action," one young Marine in a sweat-stained tunic said to me, "but we didn't know it was going to be that heavy."

"I've never seen anything like it before," added an exhausted hospital corpsman named John Peralta who came from Pueblo, Colorado. "I've never seen so much blood."

"To me, it was the worst experience I ever had," said another Marine, Edward Vaughn, who had been singled out for heroism during the action. "I saw a lot of my buddies go down but there was nothing I could do for them but keep fighting."

Just then, a high-velocity U.S. naval shell cracked sharply overhead on its way to a target, and Corporal Vaughn, who came from Beaumont, Texas, perked up and hollered, "Knock 'em out, baby, knock 'em out!"

The terrain looked like a World War II Pacific battlefield: rolling dunes honeycombed with holes and tunnels; an offshore amphibious U.S. fleet. The Marines had learned that 2,000 troops of a Vietcong hard-core regiment had massed in the area, and launched Operation Starlight, a three-pronged assault designed to cut off and crush the enemy forces. The Marines said at least 560 enemy were killed at a loss of 50 U.S. dead and 165 Marines wounded. Senior officers in Chu-lai described the battle as neat and well-executed, but I found that the grunts in the field thought it was disjointed and confused.

Corporal Jim O'Neill was smoking a cigarette and staring into space. He still seemed dazed. I sat down on a paddy dike next to him, and he recalled his surprise when he first sighed a convoy of Marine amphibious tractors, or amtracs, as he and his tank platoon moved around a bend in a trail.

"I saw troops crawling all over our tracs," he said, "and I thought they were our Marines. But then I saw their uniforms and they were a different color green and looked different. I guess they had killed all our Marines, because they opened up on us with the fifty-caliber machine guns on the tracs. They knew what they were doing and were damn good shots. They hit my tank three times. Then I knew we were in real, bad trouble."

After a full day's fierce fighting, O'Neill's platoon managed to beat back the enemy assault.

One of Hotel Company's officers wanted me to realize what his Marines had gone through. "We had to form the wagons in a circle during the night," he said. "We had real bad casualties. I don't know what we would have done if we had any more because there wasn't a Marine who wasn't carrying a dead or wounded buddy to the medevac zone. There were an awful lot of brave kids—I should say, men."

What the battle indicated to me—and the Marines—was that there was no easy way to clean out a determined Vietcong, just as there had been no easy fighting in the Pacific. The assistant commander of the 3rd Marine Division, Brigadier General Frederick J. Karch, was reflective and surprisingly frank when I asked him about the battle. "You know," he said staring at his cigar, "I didn't think the Vietcong would stand up and fight once they ran up against the first team. I made a miscalculation."

The only reporter or camerman to have been with the Marines on Operation Starlight was the tall, gangly, spaced-out British photographer Tim Page whose pictures got a six-page spread in *Life* magazine.

Cameramen—still and TV—took the greater risks than reporters, for they had to get combat shots on film. Just being there was not enough. There were superb photographers who covered the war and whom I sometimes watched in the field—Larry Burrows, David Douglas Duncan, Eddie Adams, Philip Jones Griffiths, Nik Wheeler, John Olson, Kyoichi Sawada, Dirck Halstead, David Burnett, Dick Swanson, Don McCullin, to name some. But the war produced a lot of would-be photographers who lacked true professional skills and whose only hope of selling their stuff was by taking chances in combat to get an extraordinary combat image on film. Without a war, they were lost, lacking the talents of a Larry Burrows, who could and did leave Vietnam to take shots of birds of paradise in Bali and the Taj Mahal by moonlight.

I always carried a camera in Vietnam. For one thing *Newsweek* had a voracious appetite for pictures. But I also found that working a camera gave me something to do with my hands and kept me from being petrified and immobilized in a tight spot.

Toward the end of my first year in Vietnam, I took another long look at the Arvin. By this time, the U.S. forces had swelled to 175,000 with the promise of more to come. The U.S. military seemed determined to take over the burden of the main-force fighting. But there were still a million South Vietnamese under arms. The U.S. command, though it could not say so publicly, was impatient and disappointed with the slow-moving Vietnamese army. Most U.S. officers blamed the failures of the Arvin on the general lack of good leadership, a deficiency that plagued every segment of Vietnamese society. For if well led, the Arvin fought well.

"The number one problem in Vietnam," a senior U.S. staff colonel confided, "is the need for leadership. The quality of the younger officers is good. But, as in all wars, it is the bravest and the best of the young officers who suffer the worst casualties. The big question is whether we can keep these able young fellows alive long enough to benefit from their experience."

Young Arvin officers were exposed to a situation where the senior officers often held their jobs through political or family connections. They generally made money on the side. And constant exposure to corruption and poor leadership among their seniors had a debilitating effect on the junior officers. Then, too, in those days the American officers came to Vietnam all fired up, but served in the field usually for only six months, before shifting to a staff job for the second half of their year's tour. But the Vietnamese soldiers saw the war was a way of life and therefore a sense of military urgency was rare, except when under direct attack. Self-preservation was primary—patriotic aims dim. Once, in my presence, a U.S. airborne officer asked a veteran Vietnamese sergeant why his unit had not closed faster with the enemy.

The sergeant, who had a valorous record, answered simply, "This war is going on and on. I have been fighting for eighteen years. My idea is not to rush to my death. The object is to survive."

At home in Saigon, Johanna managed to turn the villa into a charming oasis with whitewashed walls and green shutters and flowers everywhere. It served as a home away from home for correspondents like Jack Langguth, Charley Mohr, Morley Safer, R. W. "Johnny" Apple, Jr., Dean Brelis, Jack Foisie, Ward Just, Gavin Young, Peter Kann, Garrick Utley, Tom Buckley, Bill McWhirter, Lee Lescaze, Doug Kiker, and even Jimmy Breslin.

Breslin turned up on our doorstep one morning when he found that his expected reservation at the Caravelle had not materialized. I invited him in for lunch. Breslin, a burly columnist with a shape like a fireplug, was his usual profane self. He couldn't quite believe it when he was served an elegant, light soufflé for lunch.

"You got a lot of nerve living like this in Saigon," he grumbled. "I thought I came out here to cover a war, not eat fancy French food."

I did a press piece comparing Breslin to James Reston, of the *New York Times*, who were both in Vietnam at the same time. "This is all so worthless," said Breslin. "All you get is an empty feeling. Win, lose, or draw, the whole country ain't worth one kid."

Actually, Saigon, except for the occasional bombs, was a reasonably pleasant place to live then. The food, French or Vietnamese, was first-rate and in the afternoon you could go to the Cercle Sportif for a swim or game of tennis or a drink. The favored meeting place was the veranda of the old Continental Palace Hotel, dubbed "the Continental Shelf," where in addition to the latest gossip there were wine and women.

One night we had Charley Mohr and Betsy Baker, a writer with *Art News* magazine who was passing through Saigon, for dinner. Halfway through the meal, a tremendous explosion seemed to rock the room. We all scrambled to the floor and into corners of the heavy, stucco walls for protection in case a second blast came. As things settled down, I checked with the MAC-V duty officer and learned that the shock waves had been from a huge U.S. ammunition dump going off at Long Binh, fully ten miles away.

In some ways, it was difficult working for a news magazine in Saigon. The editors were constantly influenced by what they read in the *New York Times*. On Monday, for instance, they'd read a story about a skirmish that had occurred over the weekend. We'd get cables suggesting that we cover the battle. Of course, by then it would be all over. I'd explain that by the end of the week the focus would be on some other action yet to come. I didn't want to react prematurely, sending someone up to I Corps for a story that would long be dated by the time we went to press on Sunday. Back in New York, they couldn't seem to understand that getting around in Vietnam was not quite as simple as taking the Eastern shuttle to Washington. I'm afraid I didn't endear myself to some of the editors when I rudely pointed this out.

The cover editor in New York was particularly difficult. He seemed to think you could assign a photographer to a unit for a couple of days, thereby ensuring a prize-winning combat spread. He couldn't grasp the idea that a unit could go for days without engaging in combat and that even if they did find action, it was no guarantee that a photographer with them would get good pictures. One platoon in a company could be under fire, but a cameraman with a neighboring platoon in the jungle might see nothing at all.

Then, too, I found supplying material for the *Newsweek* meat grinder rather frustrating. By newsmagazine standards, we had a lot of space—an entire section called "The War in Vietnam"—and I thought we did a much better job than *Time*. But sometimes a week's work would be reduced to a couple of paragraphs or a rewrite man in New York would get something wrong, which was bothersome under any circumstances, but particularly irksome when reporting from a war zone.

I put much of the material that hadn't found a place in *Newsweek* into a long lead piece I wrote for the *New York Times Magazine* called "The Dirty Little War Gets Bigger." In the course of my research, I got to know some American specialists in terror and counterterror operations and the uses of torture. Like other reporters, I had seen VC suspects roughed up by Arvin troops on operations. It was always a problem for me as how to work such incidents into the broader story. I didn't want to give undue prominence to something that was just part of the normal brutality of war. If I did see examples of real torture— troops holding a prisoner's head under water—I mentioned it. Yet, the

Vietnamese troopers in their defense would point out that the prisoner probably had knowledge of the whereabouts of an enemy who had just killed some of Arvin's comrades. I never saw any example of torture for torture's sake; the cases I saw were to gain quick battlefield intelligence.

"The Vietnamese do their questioning out of sight of us," one American adviser on revolutionary warfare techniques pointed out to me one night in Saigon, "because we feel guilty about their methods. They say, 'You people are soft. This is a rough, tough war, and this was the way you get information and the only way.' So the Vietnamese major says to the American adviser, 'I suggest you take a walk down the path and don't come back for a half an hour. We're going to do this anyway so it is better if you aren't here.' I myself don't believe in the effectiveness of torture, but it is very difficult to tell a Vietnamese paratrooper whose buddies have just been wiped out to go easy on prisoners."

"There are better ways of getting information from prisoners than torture," added another U.S. CIA specialist who studied the dark, underside of revolutionary warfare. "Sure you can start cutting off fingers and the guy will talk. But you never know whether the information is accurate. If I were being tortured, I'd whip out so much stuff it would take them six months to check it.

"But you can't walk away from torture. You've got to watch them do it, run through five or six guys, even if it turns your insides. Then you ask them 'Why do you do it that way? Did you get any information you could act on? No? Then why not try it this way?' Most of these prisoners have been warned to expect brutality. They're inured. But if you say, 'I'm your friend,' they don't know how to react. Their orders don't cover this, so being humane can be more effective."

"This is not so much a dirty war as a different war," another man who trained counterterror teams told me. "It is total war involving all the people. The U.S. Army thinks terror is unconventional. But terror is not unconventional to the Vietcong. It is part of the human hardware. Assassination would horrify General Westmoreland. Air and artillery, that's what the military understands. But asassination is what the peasant understands. Vietcong terror is bloodthirsty, but selective. It is a scalpel not a hammer. It is aimed at the leaders—in three years, they drove out fifty percent of the natural leaders from the countryside. They went after the very best and the very worst. As a result, there is a premium on mediocrity among civil servants. The purpose of most VC terror is to teach a lesson. They behead a village chief and kill his wife and kids. It's messy but the next chief won't bring his family to the town and the VC will stress this in their propaganda. Usually, they have a specific reason for every act of terror. They don't kill for the sake of killing. But terror is only effective in the short range. If you use too much, people begin to think, Eventually it's going to be me, so I might as well help get rid of these guys.''

Some of the advisers I was put in touch with were training assassination teams in the Phoenix program run by the CIA. One U.S. officer was quite frank about its aims:

"I'm a greater believer in getting the guys responsible for the war, not the ordinary people who are sucked in," he said. "The least bloody way is to go for the head, get the commander, or the deputy political commissar for the whole battalion.

"I believe in bribing guards to assassinate their officers, buying them off, working through their relatives, putting prices on their heads, sowing suspicion by leaving big piaster notes around, everything possible to get at them. In warfare, you try for the command post. Killing their communications and liaison people is like putting out their eyes and ears. I'd rather kill a political officer of a district than his whole company because as long as he's alive he can recruit five companies. Too many people think our job is only to kill Cong, but ultimately it is to convert them.''

The specialist in black techniques criticized the destruction of the village of Cam Ne by U.S. Marines who used their Zippo lighters to set the thatched huts afire, and was filmed by a CBS team led by Morley Safer.

"In burning that village," he said, "the Marines made their mistake in using mass terror instead of being selective. There is not a single hamlet in Vietnam that is one hundred percent VC. The Marines should have found five or six homes sheltering snipers and burned them—and they should have explained why they were doing it.''

Nothing infuriated these unconventional-warfare specialists more than the random use of air strikes and unadjusted artillery fire in the countryside, known at MAC-V as H and I, for harassment and interdiction.

"It's madness," said my specialist friend. "We're always looking for the easy way, the gimmick. This is a war that will be won on foot. Tactical air strikes are fine when the VC are attacking a position but you don't napalm a whole village because of a couple of sniper shots."

Similarly, these counterinsurgency experts were critical of some of the more gimmicky aspects of the U.S.-directed Vietnamese psychological warfare program. As one told me: "Writing Churchillian messages to toss out of a plane is much less dangerous than getting out to the villages personally. Most peasants have a low literacy rate. Leaflets are fine to warn them of air strikes. But peasants don't follow leaflets, they follow people. You've got to have cadres on the ground to follow up. Otherwise, all you'll get is a bunch of activity reports that can be put on a chart some general can read, but without any real results. There is no substitute for human beings in an underdeveloped society like this."

Finally, a U.S. counterterror expert who spoke Vietnamese and had a Vietnamese wife put it to me this way: "Look, there's no humane way to kill a man. Terror is terror. Murder is murder. Counterterror is a word used by Americans because it sounds clean. The important thing is not the degree of cleanliness of the war but the degree of necessity. Let's not kid ourselves. Yossarian in *Catch-22* was right: Wars are basically insane. We are trying to kill each other. But I also believe in Mao's distinction that there are just wars and unjust wars. If you as an American believe this is an unjust war, then you've got to get out because you will get yourself zapped. I don't think you can become really hardened and brutalized if you share the involvement with the people.

"John Donne was right—no man is an island. And that applies to this war. I feel a strong sense of sympathy when I see a brave Liberation Front man we've had to kill. That day the bell tolled for him. The problem is that U.S. combat troops spend so much time on patrol and in bivouac that they have little contact with the people. They are more likely to become brutalized by the fighting and this is a real danger."

These were grim and prophetic words for a nation like the United States that had gotten used to the idea of large-scale nuclear warfare but not small-scale guerrilla wars. I took a consolation of sorts in the words of Brigadier General Samuel B. Griffith, a student of insurgency, who had written, "Guerrilla warfare is suffused with and reflects man's admirable qualities as well as his less pleasant ones. While it is not always humane, it is human, which is more than can be said for the strategy of extinction."

*   *   *

In Saigon, our bureau had increased to four with the addition of Bill Cook; we were now the largest overseas bureau on the magazine and a crackerjack one. I was quite pleased when Editor Oz Elliott cabled informing us that the bureau had been awarded the Headliner's Prize for the best magazine coverage of 1965.

As 1966 rolled around, official optimism was in the air in Saigon. President Johnson called a conference on Vietnam in Honolulu in February and brought along Vice-President Hubert Humphrey, Secretary of State Dean Rusk, Defense Secretary Robert McNamara, as well as Orville Freeman from Agriculture and John Gardner, of Health, Education, and Welfare. Squads of subcabinet officers accompanied them.

I flew to Honolulu on the U.S. Air Force plane of Ambassador Henry Cabot Lodge with President Nguyen Van Thieu and Premier Nguyen Cao Ky. There they all issued the Declaration of Honolulu affirming that the United States and South Vietnam would keep fighting until an honorable peace could be negotiated. Johnson ordered Humphrey to fly back to Saigon and make a swing around Asia to drum up support for the U.S. intervention. On the flight back to Saigon, we refueled at Guam, and I asked Air Marshal Ky, whom I rather liked, what Johnson had told him.

Ky told me the President had urged him to bolster the Vietnamese government and army so that he would be in a position of dealing through strength with the communists.

"The President said he didn't want me to be like the guy in the poker game who calls 'Aces,' and when asked how many, says, 'One.' "

In Vietnam, Humphrey toured the redevelopment projects and told me, not surprisingly, "I'm really impressed by what they're doing. There's a social revolution taking place here."

But Humphrey like other high officials before him were shown only the model projects, rather like Vietnamese Potemkin Villages. Then we were off on a whirlwind swing to Laos, Thailand, Pakistan, India, the Philippines, Australia, New Zealand, and South Korea, a real barnstorming junket. My strongest memory of that trip was the party in Canberra, arranged by Doug Kiker and some of his Australian newspaper friends. The Yanks supplied the booze and the Diggers the willing girls: It was a smashingly successful blast, and in the words of Colonel Stingo, "many a veteran Cellini who hadn't scaled a garden wall for twenty years made a double score for himself that evening.''

In Honolulu, President Johnson had emphasized ''pacification'' and ''nation building'' and ''winning the hearts and minds.'' He pushed his U.S. television executive friends to emphasize in their coverage what was called ''the other war,'' pacification, instead of ''bang-bang,'' the term used in TV to describe combat footage.

But then a U.S. Marine battalion got into a bad fight on Hill 881 just west of Khe Sanh and was cut off for a couple of days. I remember flying into Khe Sanh with Murray Fromson of CBS to cover the battle. When it was over, I interviewed the battalion commander, a lieutenant colonel, who was genuinely surprised at all the media fuss. Though he had lost thirty-five Marines killed in action (KIA), he said, ''We're just out here kicking a little ass.''

By chance, the petite, French photographer, Catherine Leroy, happened to be with the battalion and took some dramatic combat shots that made the cover of *Paris-Match* and front page of the *New York Times*. The accompanying blurb described her as a nineteen-year-old former secretary. The next day, the CBS bureau in Saigon, whose members were among the best in the country and who had seen plenty of action, received a stinging telexed rebuke from New York headquarters signed by the top three news executives. It read, ''If a 19-year-old girl can come up with this kind of combat coverage, maybe our three teams in Vietnam should stop covering the 'other war' and start covering the real one.''

It was a disgraceful insult by a bunch of deskbound executives but it ended the CBS bureau's concern with covering pacification stories.

I found that many TV correspondents were among the most informed in Vietnam, people like Safer, Fromson, Kiker, Jack Laurence, John Chancellor, Dan Rather, Charles Collingwood, Bernie Kalb, Peter Jennings, Peter Kalisher, Sandy Vanocur, Lou Cioffi, Garrick Utley, Bill Plant, John Hart, even Mike Wallace. Mike, Johnny Apple, and I once flew to Hue, and over several scotches, he told us his problems in trying to get into regular television news after building a reputation as the tough, mean interviewer on his New York evening show. Only CBS offered him a shot at a straight correspondent's job. The rest, as they say, is history. The trouble with television then, as now, was that complicated stories were reduced to ''bang-bang'' with no time available for explanations that would give the action some meaning. Still, TV fashioned America's thinking about Vietnam, and it became America's first ''living-room war.''

One night, Walter Cronkite came to our place for dinner with Morley and Murray and several other correspondents. Toward the end of an evening characterized by heated discussions about the course of the war, Walter remarked in a puzzled way, "No wonder the American people are confused about Vietnam. The reporters themselves disagree about what's happening."

Indeed we did. In World War II, which Cronkite covered so ably, journalistic assessments were much easier. The general would show you the map and indicate that the next day's objective was Hill 357, and after that Hill 429, and after that Tunis, or Cassino, or Paris. You could measure success by mileage.

Though World War II and Korea were no less arduous and dangerous, they were far easier to *report*. Terrain was the key. If a hill, a city, an island, was taken, then success was achieved, progress made, and stories to that effect were written. The informed reporter might question certain tactics, or even grand strategy, but the military milestones were clear—you forged ahead until you reached Rome, Berlin, or Tokyo—or the enemy surrendered.

In Vietnam, there were no such classic benchmarks. A prominent hill was taken at bloody cost, then voluntarily relinquished, only to be taken again. A Special Forces camp was surrounded, relieved, only to come under siege again. Over and over, troops fought on the same terrain: War Zone C, the Ashau Valley, the Street Without Joy. The enemy was being killed but was progress being made?

I felt a deep sense of frustration trying to absorb, sift, assess, and write the kaleidoscopic story of what Ward Just called "the East Asian Theater of the Absurd."

At the Five O'clock Follies, the briefers would announce that 250 enemy soldiers were killed in a battle, but when you later talked to soldiers on the scene, you would learn that they only saw 18 bodies. The rest were estimates cranked into the system. Or an admiral would report that the morale of the Navy pilots on his carrier was never higher and they were enthusiastic about the targets they were assigned in North Vietnam. But later a squadron commander would tell you, "We haven't yet hit a target that was worth one pilot or one plane."

Americans were fond of statistics and they rattled forth from Saigon like machine gun fire: troop strength, kill ratios, defectors, imports, redevelopment cases, refugees resettled, hamlets pacified, you name it. But numbers could be illusory and the most notorious of all was the so-called body count, allegedly the number of enemy dead found on a battlefield. Anyone who had been in the field knew there was no such thing. A platoon commander fighting for his unit's life has no time to count enemy bodies. And the Vietcong were diligent about removing their dead. So enemy casualties were only estimates not actual counts, except in rare instances. But Defense Secretary McNamara wanted statistics—and that's what he got, however misleading or erroneous.

It was instructive to accompany McNamara on one of his field trips in Vietnam. He demanded statistics that showed that whoever was briefing him was indeed making progress in his district, or division. The briefers would wheel out the charts with the arrows all going in the right direction, and the blue areas much bigger than the red areas. It made the briefer and the unit look good, and McNamara didn't seem to care whether the statistics truly reflected conditions in that particular piece of countryside. No, for McNamara everything had to look rosy, and he never heard words like these: "This district is in one hell of a mess; the province chief is crooked; the officials are incompetent; the army won't fight; and the VC is getting stronger."

Columnist Joseph Alsop was one of the most upbeat journalists in his assessment of the U.S. effort in Vietnam. But Joe, as he liked to mention, stayed with the U.S. ambassador and had the use of one of Westy's little executive jets, escorted around the country by two full colonels. Joe's views reflected only those of the very top brass, never the company-level officers or the grunts in the field.

More accurately, NBC's Sandy Vanocur, accompanying McNamara to the huge port being constructed at Cam Ranh Bay, and noting the greeting signs for the defense secretary, remarked presciently, "Those signs should read: 'Welcome to Cam Ranh Bay, Gateway to Disaster.' "

CHAPTER FOUR

You Saved Our Lives

AT THIS POINT, the senior U.S. officials were hopeful, though many of us in the press remained skeptical of the reports of progress. These, too, were the days before the morale of the conscript army began to sag badly, before widespread use of drugs, and the occasional "fragging" of officers, when General Westmoreland could tell me, "The performance of American troops has exceeded my expectations. Their ingenuity, resourcefulness, and initiative have simply been magnificent."

I went on a U.S. Marine amphibious operation, the first of several I would cover. With me was Frank McCollough, the *Time* bureau chief and a Marine in World War II. We boarded an amphibious landing ship and, on the morning of D day off Quang Ngai Province, we got into the amphibious tractors in the well-deck of the ship, and buttoned down tightly.

"What's an old guy like you doing here?" a young Marine asked. I looked around, then realized he was addressing me. But it was a good question.

Our trac trundled forward, clanked down the ramp, and sank into the sea. I had a momentary feeling that we were heading straight for the bottom, and my spirit sank along with the amtrac. But we soon bobbed to the surface and churned on toward the beach. Our company landed and moved inland, firing as we went, just like a John Wayne movie. It was heavy VC country. The only trouble was the Vietcong were not hanging around to take on the Marines. We spent the day without contact and it seemed to me that these huge amphibious exercises were only that—exercises with little hope of surprising enemy forces of any size.

By now, my wife was several months pregnant. At first, she decided to have the baby in Saigon, but her French obstetrician was expelled from the country, so she thought she'd better have the delivery in New York. Meanwhile, I had decided to leave *Newsweek*. It was still a congenial place to work; Oz Elliott was the best newsmagazine editor around. But it was simply too frustrating being a correspondent in a war zone. Though we had a lot of space by newsmagazine standards, *Newsweek* was still an editor's vehicle rather than a reporter's. There were just too many aspects of the war I wished to write about that couldn't find the space in *Newsweek*. I had spoken to Sydney Gruson, foreign editor of the *New York Times,* when he came through Saigon. He was interested in my coming to work for him, but it would have meant going back to New York for a breaking-in period. I wanted to stay in Vietnam; I felt I had only begun to learn the ropes and wanted to capitalize on my own experience.

I had noted that one of the problems in Vietnam was the constant turnover in U.S. personnel. "We don't have five years' experience in Vietnam," a senior officer told me. "We have one year's experience five times."

Beyond that, Vietnam was the obvious major story of our time and I wanted to continue to be involved.

Jack Foisie, the *Los Angeles Times* Saigon man and one of the most highly regarded people in the business, introduced me to Bob Gibson, the foreign editor, in Saigon. Gibson was enthusiastic about taking me aboard in Saigon but there was some awkwardness. At the time, the *Los Angeles Times* and the *Washington Post* had launched a joint news service and the *Times* publisher, Otis Chandler, and Kay Graham were friends. She had objected to the *Times* hiring away from *Newsweek* two veteran foreign correspondents, Bob Elegant in Hong Kong and Joe Alex Morris in Beirut. So for the moment, there seemed to be a hold on Gibson's raiding *Newsweek*.

But in New York with Johanna a few weeks later, I lunched with Gibson, who said the offer to switch to the *Times* was open again. I dined with Dick Dougherty, who was now New York bureau chief of the *Los Angeles Times,* and who told me sagely, "The *L.A. Times* is a lot less neurotic than the *New York Times.* You'll be more appreciated with us, you'll be able to do better work, and you'll be a lot happier." That convinced me. I called Gibson to accept. Gruson took me to lunch at Sardi's and said, "I hope you win them a Pulitzer Prize."

All the decision making left me worn out, and Johanna suggested I take a few days' holiday in Bermuda. Because of her pregnancy, she was not allowed, now, to fly. I flew to Bermuda the next morning; she saw her New York obstetrician that afternoon. He said she had been misdiagnosed in Saigon: She was full term and the baby was due almost immediately. She went into New York Hospital that night, and the next morning in Bermuda, I got a call informing me that I was the father of a baby boy. I flew back to New York immediately, and had a hard time getting onto the hospital floor. Charlotte Ford Niarchos had a child in the next room and bodyguards were stopping everyone. We named the boy Cyril, a family name on my mother's side.

My friends in Saigon used to kid me that Cyril's first word was "incoming." That's an exaggeration, but I seem to recall that among his very first expressions, with all the choppers flying overhead was, in the French-style of pronunciation, " 'Elicopter, Papa."

One morning in Saigon, I teamed up with Rowland Evans, Phil Geyelin, then with the *Wall Street Journal,* and my old comrade, Ward Just of the *Washington Post.* We managed to see Major General William De Puy, commander of the U.S. 1st Infantry Division, "the Big Red One." De Puy was the best U.S. general officer I had seen in Vietnam. Wiry, bright, and well-read, he had served a tour with the CIA, had been Westmoreland's operations officer, and had very high standards.

With De Puy, we choppered to Suoi Da, a Special Forces camp in War Zone C that served as the headquarters of the 3rd Brigade, known as the Iron Brigade.

There, the artillery was in full blast. I was always startled by outgoing artillery fire. I am sensitive to sharp noises of any kind and instinctively cringe. It was highly embarrassing to me, when talking to soldiers or marines at a fire base, to hunker down when the occasional 105-mm or 155-mm artillery tube would pop a round off. I rationalized this by reflecting that I'd rather look foolish cringing at "outgoing" than be too slow to duck when faced with "incoming."

The operation was called Attleboro, and was designed, De Puy told us, to search the Zone C redoubt in Tay Ninh Province near the Cambodian border. He wanted to get to grips with enemy forces or destroy the vast supply depots believed to be there.

From Suoi Da, we boarded an assault helicopter for a lift of infantrymen into the heart of Zone C. The landing zone, called an LZ, turned out to be "cold," so the lift went off without a hitch. Hueys in groups of five swooped down to the clearing, hovered briefly as the troops scrambled off, then strained to gather speed and clear the area. Soon after the battalion secured a perimeter around the LZ— one of those clearings that occasionally dot the vast green carpet of jungle in Zone C—General De Puy flew in. He watched the huge Chinook helicopters carry in artillery pieces slung under their broad bellies. As he stood in a muddy road that the Vietcong used for transporting supplies through the jungle, helicopters fired at suspected enemy positions, the machine guns chattering and the rockets making a whooshing sound. The 1st Battalion slowly began to move out, sending small patrols into the nearly impenetrable underbush.

As they moved, the 2nd Battalion began its assault on a second landing zone. I rode in the command helicopter of the brigade's executive officer, Lieutenant Colonel Thomas Maertens, and watched the pilots and artillerymen put on a fearsome display of air strikes and shellfire to soften up, or "prep," the landing sight. Diving F-100 Supersabers, dropped bombs, napalm, and canisters that broke open, letting loose hundreds of grenadelike bomblets, which sprinkled the jungle with cherry-red explosive flashes.

From Suoi Da and other artillery positions, the 105s' and 155s' rounds were barreling into the landing zone with loud *blams* sending up red-brown puffs along the tree line at the edge of the LZ. At 2:30 P.M., after a half hour of prepping, the troop lift began its descent into the landing zone.

But this LZ was "hot." Automatic weapons opened up on the disembarking soldiers and helicopters as they landed. Despite the fierce bombardment, the firing was heavy—and accurate. Once the decision to commit troops on the ground was made, the operation had to continue. Within minutes, three helicopters were disabled by enemy fire. One appeared to crash just as it was landing. The other two, it seemed to me, were hit by bullets as they settled into the LZ. Vermilion smoke began to billow up from the southern half of the landing zone, the signal for enemy contact. Soon the red smoke was rising from several areas.

Over the radio, I heard General De Puy from his chopper give the order: "Alert the reserve battalion."

Meanwhile, someone called for a dustoff, the medevac choppers.

"Where are those gunships?" De Puy's voice crackled. "Let's get them in here."

The general called in air strikes that rained fire on the western side of the landing zone while the helicopters continued to land. Though the three choppers were out of action, their rotor blades askew, other troop-carrying Hueys now brought in more men to the northern edge of the LZ—farthest from enemy fire, where the 2nd Battalion was setting up its headquarters.

"Once we commit," Colonel Maertens explained, "we don't leave those troops alone down there. We keep pouring in more."

By 3:15 P.M., the last of the battalion had landed. Mortars were called to hit the hidden enemy—thought to be the Vietcong 9th Division and the NVA 101st Regiment. Once the enemy did their damage and found the battalion was continuing the assault, they slackened off. Colonel Maertens flew quickly back to brigade headquarters at Suoi Da to get a better idea of the situation in case the 3rd Battalion needed to be committed. As the helicopter landed, one crewman—who had been scheduled earlier to ride an assault ship—told Ward Just and myself, "Thank you for riding with us today, gentlemen. You may have saved our lives."

At the battalion command post, a helicopter pilot radioed, "I've got three KIA [killed in action] and two WIA [wounded in action] aboard. Where do you want me to bring them?"

The helicopter landed at the brigade medical aid station, the three KIAs wrapped in green ponchos, the shroud of the dead. One WIA was only slightly wounded, the other not hit. He was in a state of shock and lay on a stretcher, a lit cigarette between his fingers, staring into space, oblivious of what was going on around him. A medic, bare-chested in the broiling sun, found the weathered, bloodstained wallet of one KIA, and the dog tags of the other two to record their names. The wallet contained the pictures of the dead pilot's smiling young children. Inside the aid tent, the soldier with a leg wound was grinning, happy to be alive. He was a towheaded, twenty-year-old private first class named Cecil Webb, Jr., who came from Salisbury, North Carolina, and he told me, "We got hit just as we landed. My platoon lieutenant helped me out of the copter. This was my fifth battle and I was scared—just like the other four. But I'm okay. I'd like to go back, back to the battalion out there."

*   *   *

During the autumn of 1966, Arnaud de Borchgrave, the chief
correspondent of *Newsweek,* and I flew to Da Nang to cover a series of
U.S. Marine actions called Operation Prairie in northernmost Quang
Tri Province. In Da Nang, we hitched a ride aboard an Air Force
DC-3, which had been converted into a strange, new weapon by add-
ing three side-firing Gatling guns whose appearance when shooting
gave the aircraft the name Puff the Magic Dragon, code-named
Dragonship.

Each night, a Dragonship would fly from Da Nang north to Dong
Ha near the DMZ (De-Militarized Zone), orbiting the area, on call for
Marines in trouble. Shortly after takeoff, after dark, Captain Edward
M. McKee, the congenial twenty-eight-year-old pilot who came from
Mount Vernon, Washington, told the crew over the intercom, "We
just got the word. It looks like we're going to be doing some work
tonight, Marines are in trouble near the Rockpile."

The Rockpile was a prominent outcropping that jutted eight hundred feet high and commanded a view of the main valleys through
which North Vietnamese troops were infiltrating.

I had on an extra set of earphones and as we neared the Rockpile,
a plaintive voice came over the radio: "I've got seven dead men on my
hands already and I don't want another. Two men are critical and are
going to die unless that medevac chopper gets here."

A Marine company had been hit by mortar and recoilless rifle fire
at last light on a ridgeline and so urgent was the situation that the
Marine radio operators turned over the handset to the medical corpsman to describe the plight.

"One man's only got about a half hour to live," said the corpsman in a tense, high-pitched voice.

"Jesus, I wish I could land this bird down there to get those
guys," said Captain McKee, at the controls.

As we circled overhead waiting for instructions, Captain McKee
suddenly exclaimed, "Look at that ball of fire down there! Christ, that
was a chopper going down."

"Sonofabitch," said Captain Bennie Merrill, the copilot. "He
really got hit."

I looked out the window and saw the blaze where a Marine H-34
helicopter had slammed into a hill after exploding in air.

"Advise Bravo controller we saw the chopper go down," said
Captain McKee. "It looks like he may have been hit by friendly
artillery. I don't think anybody could get out of there, but there may be

some medevacs trying. Let's make sure we're out of the artillery zone.''

A second helicopter radioed that there appeared to be no survivors but it would stand by the crash site. The Dragonship was ordered to continue to the beleaguered Marines' position near the Rockpile.

"Tell them we're coming in," said our pilot. "Tell them to give us their position. Let's drop down a little. I don't want to get hit by our own artillery.''

The thought of getting shot out of the sky by our own shells left me panicky. I took a swig from my pocket flask.

Over the Marines' position, I could see the red lights of the helicopters as they fluttered about trying to find a landing zone where they could pick up the wounded men. The full moon showed they were positioned on the side of a steep hill, a difficult place for choppers to land or drop a basket lift. Below, I could see intermittent orange winking as Marine and NVA troops fired at each other. I moved up to the cockpit for a better view.

"Stand by with the flares," said McKee. "Ready, ready, drop!"

The green, jungled hills below were illuminated by an eerie yellow glow from the flares. A river glinted in the moonlight.

"We're dropping flares so they can try to find a landing zone to get those medevac choppers in. This country looks bad enough to land in during the daytime.''

Suddenly, off the right wing of the plane, a cluster of bomb bursts glowed yellowish-brown and red as they hit the earth. Angrily, McKee told his copilot, "That looks like bombing by radar. Tell them they almost dropped their bombs directly on us. Things are really uncoordinated out here tonight, I'll tell you.

"Okay, now we're cleared to fire. Make sure the FACs [forward air controllers] are out of the way. Stand by with illumination flares. Guns all loaded? Stand by to fire.''

McKee hauled the aircraft into a steep left bank, then sighted out of his left window at an area from which the Marines reported receiving fire. He pushed a button on the left side of the steering column and a deafening roar filled the plane as the three guns opened at the rate of eighteen thousand rounds per minute. The six-barreled gun muzzles were bathed in a fiery yellow halo and a stream of cherry-red tracers arced out to the ground.

"There's some choppers at eight o'clock," the captain said. "Tell them they're coming into my line of fire. Tell them to put their lights on so I don't shoot them.''

Copilot Merrill warned, "There's ground fire down *there*." And he pointed with his gloved hand.

"Give me a full gun quick," said Captain McKee. "We're getting shot at—right over west of that flare."

Efficiently and nonchalantly, the gunners reloaded the Gatling guns, which because of their high rate of fire are fired in short bursts to conserve ammo and barrels.

"Keep hosing down that area on the rise west of the river. Everything on that side of the river is enemy. "How's the ammo?"

"Five full boxes," said gunner Robert P. Maddox, who told me he came from Marshall, Texas.

"You're doing a real good job, Bob, real good," said McKee. "Ask them if they want the fire on the hill or the river bed. Thank Christ for this full moon. We can see what we're doing. Otherwise we'd be stumbling around in the dark."

I looked at my watch. It was 9:20 P.M. A report from the ground said the one wounded Marine was in bad shape, not much longer to live.

"The choppers are trying to drop a basket hoist but they're not having much luck," McKee explained to the crew. "They've got a helicopter pilot familiar with the area who's volunteered to try to find a landing zone. We'll hold all our ammo and flares till he gets here."

Fifteen minutes later, the rescue chopper had not arrived. The medic on the ground radioed, "I had seven dead men. Now I've got eight."

He said the other badly wounded Marine could survive until morning when a helicopter would have a better chance to evacuate him. The Dragonship dropped one last flare before leaving station over the Rockpile and a voice came from a Marine position below: "Why the hell did you have to drop that last one on me?"

Four and a half hours after takeoff, we came in for a landing at Dong Ha. "Hey," reported copilot Merrill, "there's a bunch of people shooting at us off the starboard side."

"Well," said Captain McKee, "I guess we'll have to tell somebody here there's some bad guys back there."

We shook hands with McKee. "I hope you had an interesting evening," he said.

*   *   *

The next morning, we hopped aboard an old Marine H-34 chopper—the Marines always had the worst equipment—which wheezed up to a high ridge called the Razorback, north of the Rockpile, and dumped us out with a load of ammo, in a makeshift clearing blown out of the side of a steep hill. Even in midmorning, it was hot as hell in the clearing, and the Marines of 3rd Battalion, 4th Marine Regiment, or "3-4" as it was called, were stripped to the waist, with twigs in their helmets for camouflage. There was some fighting along the ridgeline but the terrain was so narrow that only one or two Marines at a time could get in position to fire ahead at NVA positions. So Arnaud and I sat around talking to the battalion commander, Lieutenant Colonel William Masterpool, and a couple of his sergeants. Arnaud even applied sun lotion to his face and bald pate.

Since we had exhausted conversation about the operation and the colonel was busy on his radio, Arnaud and I got to talking about the best place in Europe for a summer home. My wife's cousin had suggested we go in with him on a house someplace in the Aegean.

"No, dear boy," said De Borchgrave, who lived in Geneva, "not Greece. Majorca is the place. You can get to it from any airport in Europe and spend the weekend there. For Greek islands you've got to take ferries."

The huge black giant of a gunnery sergeant couldn't contain himself any longer.

"What the fuck are you guys talking about? What the fuck are you doing here, anyway? You're fucking civilians."

"Well, Sarge," I said, "it's like this. In the winter, we go to Gstaad; in the spring, it's Deauville; in the summer, St.-Tropez; and now, in the autumn, it's the DMZ. It's the place to be!" The sergeant shook his head.

Actually, I was always surprised at how well journalists were received by the troops. We were in their way but they rarely seemed to mind. Invariably, they welcomed our attention and seemed astonished that anyone would voluntarily share their lot. The difference was, I knew, that I could usually bug out on a chopper when the going got rough. The grunts had to stay there and take it—day after day.

As we broiled in the tropic sun, I chatted with some of the troops as they came back and sat down for their C rations. Most of the time, Marines tried to ignore the fact that death was never very far away but sometimes conversation slipped around to the subject. Or to wounds.

In Vietnam, Marines were eligible for immediate rotation after being wounded three times, thus qualifying for three Purple Heart medals.

I asked them about their fears in combat.

"If you're going to die," the black gunny said, "you like to go down fighting and maybe take somebody with you. You don't like to get hit by shells coming from miles away. Then you just got to lie there taking it. The more you get out on patrol, the more you get used to it. Funny. It's when you just go out now and then that you get scared all the time."

"It's getting short," added a young corporal who had the Marine emblem tattooed on his upper arm, "that makes you think of getting killed. When you first come here, you don't give so much of a damn because you've got a job to do. But after about eight months you get worried about getting through your thirteen months alive."

"It's getting a bad wound that gets me," said another Marine whose helmet was festooned with green shoots. "The sights you see back in the Navy hospital are really pitiful. Jesus, I've seen Marines there that would be better off dead."

"I don't know," said the gunny sergeant. "There's nothing worse than being dead. I really hate to see a guy check out. No more having fun, drinking beer, having a girl, anything else. He just ain't going to do nothing. It's when you see a Marine lying there, ready for the junkyard, that you realize how much you want to live. Just one inch makes the difference whether or not you're fini.

"It's funny, you can get nicked by the Charlies on three different days and go home with three Purple Hearts and you're a big hero. But if you get the Big One, you go home with one Heart, in an aluminum box. It kind of makes you wonder just how much life can go out of you from that one little hole."

Late that afternoon, we still hadn't been able to move from the LZ. A resupply chopper came in hoving off the tilted clearing, and impulsively we decided to clamber aboard to return to Dong Ha for the night. There I met a "bird dog" pilot, Air Force Captain Robert Bentley, who flew a tiny, single-engine observation plane over the DMZ within easy sighting range of North Vietnam. He offered to take me along on his mission the next morning. It was something I had wanted to do. De Borchgrave, though, opted to try to get back to the Razorback.

At the airstrip, I buckled myself in the rear seat of the O-1 spotter, put on the headphones, and was treated to a Cook's tour of the DMZ, which in 1966 had never been officially entered by American forces except for a few special patrols. Captain Bentley, who was thirty-two and had grown up in Syracuse, New York, had mastered the art of keeping the tiny, slow-moving aircraft aloft, dodging NVA gunners by twisting, banking, diving, and never flying in the same direction for more than a few seconds. Bouncing around the sky, twelve hundred feet up, made it difficult for enemy gunners to draw a bead on us, but it definitely unsettled the stomach.

From my perch, I could see the little Ben Hai River, which formed the boundary between North and South Vietnam, rising in the high mountains of the Annamite Cordillera and winding northeasterly before flowing through a six-mile-wide coastal plain to the South China Sea. I easily identified the Ben Hai River bridge, where the occasional exchange of prisoners took place and was, for that reason, not bombed. On the north side of the river, I noticed a police station with a tall flagpole, and the dark-red standard of North Vietnam hanging limply in the heat.

Captain Bentley, who had been flying in Quang Tri Province for ten months, seemed to have an old-shoe familiarity with everything in sight and provided me with a running commentary:

"Look over in North Vietnam. See those two roads coming south. They link up with that east-west road and we think it's the feeder into the trails that come south. Take a look at that village below us. See how new some of those huts are. They've all got bunkers and other fortifications inside. See those trenches connecting the huts."

A jagged line of deep trenches was cut into the red earth, and young banana trees had been planted alongside the trenches to provide cover.

"All those huts down there have been built since last May," said the pilot, as he swooped and turned and tilted. "None of the houses have gardens like farmers always have. We think they're the barracks for soldiers when they move south. See all those trails off to the northwest. Nobody lives in this area so there's no reason for all the trails. Now, I'll show you the fifty-caliber positions."

Bentley dropped low over four grayish-brown circles that, at first, looked like small bomb craters, but on closer inspection turned out to be doughnut-shaped holes dug to hold .50-caliber dual-purpose machine guns.

"There are a dozen over there and a bunch more to the south. They mount the tripod in the center of the hole and, using the trench, they have a three-hundred-sixty-degree field of fire. They man these positions when the troops are moving through. We've counted about two hundred eighty machine-gun emplacements.''

Off in the distance, I could see shell bursts near the Razorback and the Rockpile. An echelon of Phantom jets flashed near us on a bombing run to aid the Marines. But there was no observable activity just below.

"This is Bird Dog," radioed Captain Bentley. "All quiet in the DMZ.''

Back in Dong Ha, I learned that De Borchgrave had been through a bitter fight with "3-4" on the Razorback, and suffered a shrapnel gash on his forearm in the battle for Hill 400. The hills and mountains in Vietnam, as elsewhere on military maps, have their heights designated in meters and that's how they get their names. I was envious at Arnaud's getting a great combat story while I larked about over the DMZ. On the other hand, I had to admit to myself, it may have been just as well. I was not cut out to be a real Marine.

Dong Ha was an active forward base, the headquarters of the 3rd Marine Division. I found by chance some members of the elite reconnaissance battalion, who made small-unit, long-range forays into the DMZ and other dicey areas along the border. One team was led by twenty-three-year-old Bob Barham, a cool customer from Malibu. His mission was to capture prisoners or spot North Vietnamese gun positions and call in artillery or naval gunfire from U.S. warships offshore. Since Marine infantry were universally known as grunts, the long-range patrollers—who wore floppy hats and carried as many as eight canteens of water apiece and carried lightweight weapons—called themselves supergrunts.

I did not ask to go along on a patrol—not that they would take anyone. But even if I had had the courage, which I didn't, I wouldn't have wanted to jeopardize a long-range patrol with my game leg.

"It's a little scary out there," Barham told ne, as he honed his K-Bar knife. "That jungle gets kind of crowded. It's risky but we know what we're doing.''

The tall, rangy Barham had been a juvenile officer with the Los Angeles Police Department and he planned to take a history degree at UCLA and then teach high school. He was quite a Marine I was told by others; he had won both the Silver Star and the Bronze Star for leading long-range patrols.

"The DMZ is so close by that we just walk over," he continued, offhand about it all. "There are trails all over the place and a lot of people out there, even if those bird dogs can't see them from the air all the time. Sometimes we try to ambush them, when they're heading back north after a battle. They know we're around but they don't know where. They'll try to draw our fire hoping we'll give our position away. I suppose the scariest thing is at night, surrounded by gooks. The thing to do is just stay quiet."

"There's sure a lot of people milling around out there," cracked a corporal named Cook. "But I've never seen anybody I knew."

The supergrunts were proud of their professionalism and in a sense felt sorry for the average Marine.

"Hell," said Cook, "those poor grunts just don't give a damn. They bunch up and make a lot of noise. They figure that because they've got plenty of people around they can make a lot of noise. Then they don't understand why they get hit."

I asked Barham what sort of personality made a good long-range recon man.

"I think what you need is a man who's an introvert on patrol and an extrovert when he's off patrol."

"What's an extrovert?" asked Cook.

"Someone who's gregarious," said Barham.

"What's gregarious?"

Barham gave Cook a playful punch.

I was fascinated by the long-range patrol men, who usually moved in teams of four and never more than six. It took a special kind of resilience and resourcefulness to operate at long distance in enemy territory. The recon teams were unique to Vietnam, where there were no fixed front lines. They generally tried to avoid contact, lying quietly along jungle or mountain trails, noting enemy movements, and moving away to a predetermined rendezvous where they were extracted by helicopter.

I sought out an Army team in Pleiku in the Central Highlands. There, with the 4th U.S. Infantry Division, they were known as LARPs, for long-range recon patrol. The team leader was a young sergeant from Detroit named John Sanderson and I ran into him just as he came off a successful four-man patrol near the Cambodian border, in one of the most inhospitable areas of Vietnam. Sanderson was dusty and weary as he debriefed the patrol. The soldiers' fatigues were stained a rust color from the laterite soil, and their boots were siena-colored, no longer green.

"This time we were tracking some North Vietnamese coming our way," Sanderson said, turning to me. "They almost ran over us. At one point we were within ten feet of them as they moved down a trail in the jungle. We were so close that we could have spit on them. They looked well fed, healthy, with good weapons. They looked bigger than the South Vietnamese."

For two days, the LARP unit watched the NVA movements, the sergeant said, once quietly calling in artillery fire on enemy troops. In all, the patrol spotted about 25 enemy soldiers, estimating they were part of a 125-man company. Toward the end of the second day, the patrol tried to follow the enemy column.

"We stopped to make a communications check," Sergeant Sanderson recalled. "Another NVA unit was coming up the trail and stumbled onto us. We fired at them and killed two of them. Then we faded away and called in artillery to cover us as we made our way back to the pickup spot. Once they see us, our goose is cooked and we have to get out fast."

The team had been inserted and was extracted by helicopter, said the sergeant, but occasionally they had to rappel in and out of the helicopter by rope when an LZ was not available.

"It can be nerve-racking," said Sanderson. "But I like it. You've got the edge on Charlie out there. We're ready for him and he's not ready for us. You have to remain flexible. You have to stay quiet and you can't get rattled. We make our decisions as we go along. There's no better feeling than to know you are able to live like Charlie and beat him at his own game."

Perhaps the most intensively trained of all the recon teams in Vietnam were the U.S. Navy SEALs, who operated from Nha Be, ten miles south of Saigon in the Rung Sat zone, which for years had been a Vietcong stronghold in the mangrove swamps of the Saigon River Delta. SEAL stands for sea-air-land commando.

I drove from Saigon one morning down to Nha Be, once a ramshackle fishing village where the government had built a vast oil tank farm. I located the makeshift SEAL camp under some palm trees and sought out a patrol leader, Lieutenant Ted Grabowsky, who as luck would have it had just returned from an all-night mission in the mangrove swamps. Grabowsky was still wearing his wet suit, gun belt, and other paraphernalia. His blond hair was wet, and he offered me a cup of coffee and talked about his job and his patrol.

"The secret of this kind of work is being able to control yourself," he said, "going hours or even days without speaking or smoking, not rattling equipment, and remaining cool and calm no matter what comes up. It's not a job for everyone. A jumpy person doesn't last long on these patrols. But it's a great challenge and we wouldn't be here unless we wanted to be. We're all volunteers."

The lieutenant, who looked younger than his twenty-six years, said that on most missions the SEALs wore standard tropical boots with quick-drying canvas uppers and solid rubber lowers. "But if we expect to do more swimming than walking," he explained, "we'll wear our 'coral' shoes." These were Peter Pan-like footwear that protected the soles of the feet yet were light enough not to hamper swimming. And the patrols wore camouflage makeup designed by Elizabeth Arden, non-soluble in water, colored black, green, and yellow.

"It gets spooky out there at night," said Lieutenant Grabowsky, warming to his subject. "There's a lot of noise and wildlife in those swamps: crocodiles, monkeys, deer, fish. The mud snaps and gargles when the tide goes out. The lungfish begin blowing and they sound just like a human taking a deep breath. They make a hell of a lot of noise. Nobody talks, of course. We communicate by hand signals and occasional whispers. There's no smoking. Even when we make our regular radio checks with the base, we do not speak. We just depress the mike button and they can hear the click at the other end.

"We set up an ambush at the bend of a stream. It was quite dark before the moon came up, when I saw a sampan creeping along the stream. I could make out two men in it, and when they entered the killing zone, I opened up with my M-16. The men in the sampan never knew what hit them. We tossed hand grenades in the water to make sure and then swam out to investigate. We found two bodies floating in the water and in the sampan were loaded rifles and Chinese-made rockets. Since the ambush had given our position away, we had to move to our extraction zone, set up our defense perimeter, and wait for our helicopter pickup at first light the next morning."

One of Grabowsky's team, Boatswain's Mate First Class Thomas McDonald, recalled a strange encounter in the swamp. "We were inserted at night," he told me over a beer at Nha Be. "It was a mission where we had to swim in from a rubber boat. At the bank, in about three feet of water, I saw what looked like a stump. The stump started moving closer to me. I stopped. It came closer and closer and when it was about six feet away, I saw that the stump had two eyes and was pointing its snout at me. It was a crocodile all right. I moved back about three or four feet, pointed my M-16 at him and fired. The gun blew up—I guess water got in the barrel—but the explosion didn't hurt me. I don't know whether the bullet hit the croc, but I bounced him on the snout with the rifle barrel a couple of times—and then backed off as fast as I could. I didn't see him anymore, and I think he got the worse of the bargain. But the shooting gave our position away and we had to call for extraction."

"Another time," McDonald recalled, "I was sitting in the water on patrol and felt something crawling around my leg. I reached down to check and grabbed on to a big snake. I just flicked my wrist and tossed it as far away as I could. Before SEALs training, I wouldn't have touched a snake with a ten-foot pole. But they don't seem to bother me now."

"What sort of man joins the SEALs? I think it's a kind of man who is an extrovert and has a basic drive toward getting involved in things where there's plenty of action," Lieutenant Grabowsky said. "The SEALs not only work hard but they play hard. On days off, they go scuba diving, or in the States, maybe parachute jumping. Basically we're a pretty easygoing bunch. We aren't bloodthirsty and we don't like to be sensationalized. We got into the SEALs because it seemed to be the most interesting job in the service."

There were plenty of black soldiers and Marines in Vietnam and in the early stages of the war they served and suffered as casualties in numbers disproportionate to the rest of the U.S. population. However, few blacks had reached the upper echelon of the officer ranks. One who did was the irrepressible Chappie James. Chappie exuded charisma and he spoke his mind.

Formally, he was Air Force Colonel Daniel James, Jr., who stood six feet, four inches tall, weighed 230 pounds, and used to wear a black flying suit with his silver eagles of rank and command pilot's wings on his chest. Chappie was by far the tallest fighter pilot in the U.S. Air Force and was vice-commander of the 8th Tactical Fighter Wing based in Thailand, flying F-4 Phantoms on missions over North Vietnam. James used to wear a black panther on his flight helmet and had calling cards embossed with a Phantom superimposed on a striking black panther. But he discarded his trademark because of his displeasure with the black antiwar movement known as the Black Panthers and black power leaders like Stokely Carmichael, head of the Student Nonviolent Coordinating Committee.

I ran into James one afternoon in Da Nang where he was at the air base on a brief visit from his home fighter wing. He didn't waste any words with me:

"This black power garbage is for the birds. And Stokely Carmichael is a big mouth who is making a profession out of being a Negro and he's got no damn business speaking for me."

Chappie wanted to make sure I knew he was not simply a mouthpiece for the white military establishment. "I'm not going around bareheaded and on bended knee," he said heatedly. "I'm not a nonviolent man. I'm a fighter. But I respect the law of my country. There's no excuse for rioting and stealing. A thief is a thief. In the end, everybody loses. I resent Stokely's setting himself up as a spokesman. This SOB is leading too many kids astray, setting back the civil rights movement. And when he advises Negro servicemen to come back and fight at home, that's sheer stupidity."

James called my attention to his own credentials in the civil rights movement. "Hell," he said, "I was in the original sit-in back in 1943." James was an Army Air Corps cadet who with nearly one hundred others refused to accept the segregated practices in effect at Selfridge Field in Michigan. They were all arrested and threatened with court-martial but they held their ground and the charges were dropped.

After he was commissioned as a pilot, James flew B-25 bombing missions; he later shifted to fighters and logged 101 missions over Korea in P-51s and F-80s. As a deputy wing commander, he had completed 56 missions over North Vietnam when I saw him, and was shooting for 100.

"I want to join the Century Club," he said, chuckling. "That's kind of a status symbol. Otherwise you can't in good faith join the boys at the bar."

I asked him if he wasn't getting a bit old to fly a Phantom in combat.

"Maybe I don't fly quite so fast as I used to," he replied, "but I fly a lot smarter. I'm going to keep flying as long as I can. At forty-seven years old, you find the old eyes running out on you a bit and it's a little tougher bouncing back in the morning."

He told me he wore his black flying suit—rather than the standard Air Force blue—because his jet squadron was originally trained as night fighters.

"It adds to my natural camouflage." He smiled. "And it lets me zap around North Vietnam with impunity."

*   *   *

I spent a good deal of time with the Marines in I Corps. They had an enormously difficult task: to stop infiltration across the border and protect the coastal villages and cities in an area long a Vietcong stronghold. The Marines were created—and their equipment and tactics designed—for assaults: to storm beachheads, overrun the opposition, take casualties quickly, and win the battle. Then return to ships for the next assault. I didn't think most of them were temperamentally suited for digging into fixed position and undergoing artillery and mortar attacks. The Marines had no siege mentality, yet their role in the northernmost Quang Tri Province called for them to hold down a static post like the patch they called Leatherneck Square.

This was a rectangle of rolling scrub and paddyland just south of the DMZ, bounded on four corners by Dong Ha at the southeast; Cam Lo on the southwest; Gio Linh on the northeast; and Con Thien, the most exposed, on the northwest.

Con Thien was just a couple of miles from the DMZ, within easy reach of enemy artillery and mortar fire. There, the Marines faced their predicament with gallows humor. The camouflage canvas cover on one Marine's helmet had the inked inscription JUST YOU AND ME, GOD. RIGHT? Another Marine stuck in his helmet band a rosary, a pocket Bible, and four aces of spades. In Con Thien, the newcomer was warned, "Stay close to a hole. The shit can come flying in at any time."

When I arrived, I heard some sad news. First Lieutenant Gatlin "Jerry" Howell was a thirty-one-year-old San Franciscan, a tall, broad-shouldered Marine who seemed to exemplify what was best about the Corps. I had accompanied Howell's platoon on the first amphibious landing in the Delta not long before. There, I had gotten to know him: He had taught school in a slum district of San Francisco and had spoken with pride of the teenagers in his platoon, some of them high school dropouts, who had been headed for a life of truancy and delinquency, but who instead had found, as he put it, a sense of self-confidence, responsibility, and community in the Marines. Having completed nearly a year with a line company, he was transferred to a staff job in the 1st Battalion, 9th Regiment, "1-9."

"The idea was to put him in the rear where he would be safe," an officer friend told me. But the battalion was shifted to Con Thien. His old platoon was caught in an ambush near Con Thien and Lieutenant Howell hastily assembled a relief force and led it through fierce opposition to rescue the remnants of the devastated unit. He found only two men of the platoon alive. Then, for the next three days, almost without sleep, Howell fought back through to retrieve the bodies of their comrades. Three days later, Lieutenant Howell was in the bunkered battalion command post at Con Thien when a 152-mm shell with a delayed fuse hit the roof, killing nine and wounding twenty-one Marines. Jerry Howell, officer and gentleman, was among the dead.

In Con Thien, happiness was mail from home and a hole to jump into when someone yelled, "Incoming!" Each day, patrols were sent out to find North Vietnamese, their weapon was the vaunted M-16, which most of the grunts scorned as inferior to the enemy's AK-47.

"Why is it," a sergeant asked me rhetorically, "that they always seem to have better weapons than we do? This goddamn thing is no good. The other day the M-16 of my point man jammed after only one round. You could drop the old M-14 in the mud and it would still fire dirty. Same with the AK. But this fucking M-16 has to be spotless or it won't fire right. When you're in the middle of a firefight in a wet paddy you don't have time to be running a goddamn rag through your barrel. Why don't they get us a good weapon?"

It was a question I couldn't answer.

In Con Thien, I wondered what it must be like to be a "point man," even with a trustworthy weapon. Of the hundreds of thousands who served in uniform during the Vietnam War, only a small percentage were troops in contact with the enemy. Of course, still fewer were at the sharp end of the stick. Safest were those who made up the whole stateside apparatus; then there were the Saigon headquarters, then corps, division, regiment or brigade, battalion, company, platoon, squad, and in the squad, the single soldier or Marine leading it, called, appropriately, "the point man." Of the many dangerous jobs in Vietnam, his was among the riskiest. The point men were a special breed, usually young soldiers with finely tuned reflexes on whose skills the safety of all depended.

At Con Thien, I met one of the best: Clarence Meadows, a towheaded, skinny, lance corporal from Houston, Texas, who was attached to the 3rd Recon Battalion, which operated between Leatherneck Square and the DMZ. The prospect of ambush was always present. Just returned from a three-day patrol, a skimpy yellow fuzz covering his face, Meadows opened up when I asked about his job.

"The main thing about being a good point man," he drawled, "is that you have to like the job and have confidence in yourself. Actually, I like it up in front. I like to know where I am, where I'm going, and what's happening around me. I don't like being with a big bunch of people. The main qualities you need are the ability to see good, listen hard, move cautiously, and stay quiet. You've got to be careful and observant and look for places where you might get ambushed. A lot depends on your own instincts—it's a matter of judging those bad guys over there. Sometimes you follow the trails and sometimes you avoid the trails.''

In searching for enemy troops, Meadows said, he used his senses. "First you smell them, then you hear them. The gooks have a sour smell like when you open a can of sardines.'' When Meadows spotted an enemy, his next move depended on the nature of the mission and the composition of his squad. If the mission was to bring back a prisoner or documents from a body, Meadows said, he might risk a firefight to get what was needed. But if the mission was simply to make a sighting and report the enemy's whereabouts, the point man might decide to lie doggo and quietly pull out.

"When I make contact,'' said Corporal Meadows, "I order my lead fire team to one side to lay down a base of fire and the other fire team moves to the other side. Then I decide what to do. And if I am with a squad where I think the Marines are getting short in the country and don't particularly want to take chances, I may throw some white phosphorus grenades for a smoke screen, lay down a fire base, try to get some enemy equipment, and then pull out. I don't believe in losing a Marine's life for a lousy weapon or a piece of gear to bring back to headquarters. But if I'm with a bunch of go-to-hell Marines who don't give a damn, then maybe we'll have a shootout. On patrol, you've got to know who in the squad is strong and who is weak. That usually determines your decision on what you will do if you run into the gooks. When the odds don't look good, I always try to *dee-dee* [Vietnamese for 'scram'] out of the area.''

What motivated a man to volunteer for one of the most demanding assignments in Vietnam? "Well,'' said Meadows. "You just naturally have got to want to be a good point man.''

On one trip to the Central Highlands, Ward Just and I ran across a battlefield psychiatrist attached to the U.S. 4th Infantry Division, which was fighting North Vietnamese forces west of Kontum near the Cambodian border. As Captain Yossarian, the antihero of the war

novel *Catch-22,* classically pointed out, if you try to plead insanity—
in order to opt out of the war to stay alive—you will be judged emi-
nently sane. Captain James Randall, a thirty-three-year-old psychiatrist
to the fifteen-thousand-man division, explained his task this way: "It
is to help a man find peace with himself, but also to make him an
effective soldier."

Dr. Randall had seen from four to six soldiers every day during
the six months he had been in Vietnam. Often a soldier's reaction, said
Randall, was expressed by the sentiment, "You're the only person that
a guy can talk to around here and get some answers."

Randall's job as a professional was to soothe a human being's
anxieties—but his duty as a military officer was to make a man fit for
combat, ready to kill and face the possibility of being killed.

So Dr. Randall's definition of cowardice was less strict than the
official military one: In his view, cowardice was when a soldier voluntarily and "with intent" abandoned his position against orders. If a
soldier did this involuntarily, he would not be a coward in the eyes of
the psychiatrist—though he might be so classified by military authorities.

"When we hit an adverse situation," explained Captain Randall,
"we experience anxiety and fear. It often depends on how you react
whether you are judged a hero or a coward."

Dr. Randall cited the example of a soldier in the division who
told him, "Doctor, something is wrong with me. When I'm out there,
I'm not afraid. I'm careless. I'm taking all kinds of chances." After
exploring the case, Randall found that before the soldier's first
helicopter combat assault, his stomach was knotted up with cramps
from anxiety.

"He was so damn fearful, he had to deny it," said the physician.
"He ended up taking chances. Though he was full of fear, he might
have been the type to win the Medal of Honor."

In another case, a soldier was horrified when his unit destroyed a
village. "He felt people were calling him a coward," said the psychiatrist. "The medics sent him here and I found he thought himself a
coward. But actually it was just his reaction to the situation. He was
not a coward."

If a man had a severe reaction to combat, Dr. Randall, after
counseling him, tried to send him to his outfit as soon as possible. "It
is good for the man to get back to his unit, with which he identifies. If
we keep them here too long, they begin to get the message they're no

good, they can't cut the mustard. This could damage their psyche permanently.''

One common experience of men in combat, said the psychiatrist, was the sense of isolation on the battlefield. The reaction could be expressed, ''I feel I'm out there all alone. There's no one out there to care about me.'' Indeed, soldiers are encouraged to yell if necessary to each other, reminding themselves they are not alone. The Army also adopted the buddy system to dispel the sense of isolation.

''The buddy system works well,'' said the doctor, ''except when a man's buddy is killed. Then he may break down because his buddy is gone.''

Remarkably, at that stage of the war, only about 6 percent of those hospitalized in Vietnam were psychiatric or mental cases.

At the 3rd Marine Division hospital at Phu-Bai, a young Marine arrived, mute, tremulous, and hollow-eyed. His platoon had been ambushed by North Vietnamese regulars near the DMZ and badly cut up. The attack was followed by a vicious mortar and artillery barrage that seemed endless to the Marines under fire. The nineteen-year-old corporal had spent six months fighting in almost daily contact with the enemy. He was bone-tired and the ambush, finally, was more than he could take.

He told his platoon commander that he could no longer go out on patrol. ''I've had the course,'' he said firmly.

In the language of previous wars, the Marine was a classic victim of shell shock, which was now called combat fatigue. If the Marine's condition were allowed to deteriorate, he could easily have become another piece of the flotsam and jetsam of wars: the veteran suffering permanent psychoneurotic damage. Instead of holding him on the line, his platoon commander, who had been alerted to recognize such symptoms, ordered him evacuated.

''The boy was in a semicomatose state when he got here,'' explained Lieutenant Commander King G. Price, division psychiatrist. Price put the Marine under heavy sedation—Thorazine, an antipsychotic drug—and within minutes the patient fell into a deep, uninterrupted sleep that lasted thirty-six hours. ''When he awoke,'' said Dr. Price, ''he had no recollection of the worst phase of the ambush and his symptoms had disappeared. We chatted about the experience and I explained that what happened to him was a normal thing in combat. After more rest, a shower, shave, hot chow, and a movie, he was ready to rejoin his outfit. It was important for him, medically, to get back to his buddies as soon as possible. All this does not sound terribly psychiatric but in most cases it works.''

Dr. Price indicated that soldiers who come under artillery attacks are more prone to combat fatigue than those who are on the move. ''As a result of artillery attacks near the DMZ,'' he said, ''we see a new syndrome. This comes when a combat soldier, particularly one with Marine assault training, finds himself in a situation where he is helpless and can't fight back—when there is no self-determining factor, as in an ordinary skirmish where a man feels he may be able to fight his way out.''

Curiously, among those most prone to combat stress, Dr. R. E. Strange, a Navy psychiatrist aboard the U.S.S. *Repose,* told me, were the battlefield medics. ''The medic has a specifically different mission from an infantryman,'' he said. ''He deals with the injured and dying and the dead. The hospital corpsman develops a fantastic sense of responsibility to his unit and these boys really feel bad when they lose a patient. They say, 'I should have been able to do something about it,' or 'Why couldn't I save his life?' They are very intimate with the squad or platoon they are assigned to. Everybody goes to the 'doc' with their problems. From the psychological standpoint, the ordinary Marine is out there to kill somebody, so he can work out his anger and frustration. The medic, though, bottles up much more of these emotions.''

If, after the initial shock of combat fatigue had worn off, a man showed no psychological damages but made a conscious decision that he would not fight again, his case shifted from a medical to a disciplinary problem. It was then up to the division psychiatrist to determine that fine line and decide whether the case was medical or disciplinary. ''It's the toughest decision I have to make over here,'' confided one military psychiatrist.

In Saigon, I checked with senior Army physicians on how men reacted to stress. Lieutenant Colonel George L. Mitchell, the Army's chief consulting psychiatrist, told me, ''The integrity of the group, the unit, is all-important. The stronger the sense of group identification, the less chance a man will crack up. Each man reacts differently to the same set of stimuli. We all can accept a certain level of stress, but, as this increases, we develop defense mechanisms, including combat fatigue. A lot of healthy, young soldiers come to Vietnam convinced of their own indestructibility. This is a healthy reaction to the threat of death. But sooner or later the realization usually bears down on them that they can really get killed. At this point, stress sometimes begins to tell. Then, too, the group gives a good soldier confidence. If something happens to destroy the integrity of the group—a bad fight where officers or senior noncoms are killed—the soldier loses a very important stabilizing force.''

But as to why one man will perform effectively and another crack up, General Hal B. Jennings, Chief U.S. Surgeon in Vietnam, said simply, ''That's still one of the big questions in military medicine.''

Everything in the bush wasn't quite so grim. I flew to Quang Duc Province up in the highlands where I knew the U.S. provincial adviser. We all drank a lot of rice wine and got initiated into the Rhade tribe, though luckily they didn't cut off the head of a bullock. I was presented with a tribal bracelet. But even then, there were complications. We were having a beer with the province chief, a lieutenant colonel, when a group of Vietnamese Army rangers came into the roadhouse and proceeded to tear up the joint. They were drunk and waving their weapons around and the colonel made no move to speak to them. It taught me something about the tenuous hold of Vietnamese Army commanders over unruly troops in the boondocks.

In Vietnam, the U.S. Navy's main force was the blue-water Seventh Fleet and over the years I boarded aircraft carriers on Yankee station, running daily bombing strikes against North Vietnam, as well as destroyers and in 1967 the battleship U.S.S. *New Jersey* for missions firing against targets in the DMZ and North Vietnam. But the most colorful naval outfit was the in-country riverine forces, the river patrol boats that conducted around-the-clock surveillance of the Mekong, checking one thousand to two thousand junks and sampans each day for illicit arms and supplies. They relied on speed, maneuverability, and firepower to keep from being blasted out of the water by Vietcong gunners. I flew down to the Navy base at Can Tho, the largest city in the Delta, located on the Bassac, the southerly arm of the Mekong as it flowed majestically to the South China Sea. The base had about it the air of an old *Terry and the Pirates* cartoon strip. The tiny boats, though they carried no armor, bristled with .50-caliber machine guns and an odd assortment of makeshift weapons the ingenious crews devised. The crews themselves were a raffish lot: for the most part bearded, moustached, tattooed, well-muscled, foul-tongued and sporting black berets, a custom they adopted from the Vietnamese sailors who manned the country's fighting junks. They wore green combat fatigues and bore colorful nicknames like Cambodia Joe, Monster

Boss, and the Nabisco Kid, the last a chief gunner's mate who gave out cookies to Vietnamese children.

In a Navy increasingly given to sophisticated weapons like long-range missiles, the men who ran the PBRs—Patrol Boat, River—were a throwback to an older style of fighting. As a grizzled boatswain put it after I stepped on board: "I used to be a big-gun man on the high seas, but now the heaviest weapon I have is a fifty-caliber machine gun. We don't stand miles offshore bombarding the enemy. We're shooting at each other from twenty-five yards away. When you're going up one of those narrow channels with Charlies on both sides, man, you've got problems."

In Navy doctrine, riverine warfare was defined rather stiltedly as "operations necessary to achieve and maintain control of a waterway system and its contiguous areas, or to deny their use to the enemy." In Vietnam, that boiled down to the job of patrolling the vast, table-flat area south of Saigon that contained one third of the nation's population, most of its rice, and twenty-five hundred miles of waterways. In the Delta, riverine operations were complicated by shifting currents, shoals and tides, and by high river banks, dense vegetation, and abrupt turns—all of which served as excellent cover for the Vietcong.

In the bar of the Bassac River base, I noticed a weathered plank that had been nailed to a tree at the entrance to a tributary of the Mekong; it warned, in Vietnamese, IF YOU BRING YOUR BOAT UP THIS RIVER WE WILL KILL YOU.

The boats were thirty-one-foot runabouts powered by twin marine diesels of 220 horsepower apiece driving water pumps. The pumps sucked in river water and discharged it in a jet; the boats had a top speed of thirty miles an hour. Steering was done by swinging the nozzles. The deepest draft, at rest, was eighteen inches. The only protection was the fiber glass hull. "You could throw a rock through it," a PBR man observed dryly.

The Navy had mounted twin .50-caliber machine guns forward of the wheelhouse, and a single .50 in the stern, often with a grenade launcher attached. Each boat carried two M-79 hand-held grenade launchers, a shotgun, several M-16 automatic rifles, and the crew's sidearms.

I tagged along on Bravo Patrol, Boats 59 and 60, led by Lieutenant Commander Donald D. Sheppard, who had decided to bring an American flag to the district chief at the village of Mac Bac about five miles up the tiny Ba Tieu River from the main stream. When the nature of the day's patrol was revealed at an early morning briefing, the sailors received the news with something less than glee. "I don't mind so much going up that little river," commented one. "It's the coming back down I don't like. That's when they know you're up there and can lay a nice, fat ambush."

The crew checked me out on the use of the guns in case of an emergency, but I figured if they needed my help, it would be a lost cause. Smoothly, the olive-green boats moved out onto the great caramel-colored river, maintaining an interval of two hundred yards. We sped by a village populated with refugees. "The Vietcong opened up on us a couple weeks ago from this place," said patrol officer Bill Potter. "That's one of Charlie's favorite tricks. They move their automatic weapons into a friendly place to shoot at us and we can't fire back, or we're liable to kill a lot of innocent villagers."

Our pumps in Boat 59 broke down and we floated helplessly for five minutes. But repairs were made and we were again under way. "We had a big firefight here the other night," said Potter. "The Charlies tried to overrun that outpost. We got down here chop-chop with our fifties and grenades and helped drive them off. Those soldiers have been our buddies ever since."

We boarded and searched a few suspicious-looking sampans but found no contraband. We entered a designated "free-fire zone" where the Vietcong were believed to hold several islands.

"That zone is a VC training area," a crewman remarked. "We call it Charlie's Fort Benning."

Bravo Patrol swung into the Ba Tieu River, ready to navigate the treacherous passage up to Mac Bac. With the Stars and Stripes fluttering from the mastheads, the two boats slowly pushed upstream, the gunners prepared for action. There was none and the trip was uneventful. Commander Sheppard jumped onto a pier with the flag under his arm. He presented it to the district chief, Captain Tran Van Bien. The goodwill mission was sealed when we all adjourned to a nearby café for beer.

On the return trip, Bravo Patrol opened up on the free-fire zone, the .50-caliber machine guns making an incredible racket as the yellow flame spurted from their barrels. The other crewmen triggered off grenades with the launchers. A brisk wind came up along the river and the boats began slapping into the waves, sending spray over both the bows and the crews. As the fourteen-hour patrol drew near Can Tho, the sailors kept a sharp eye on the shoreline, ready to spot telltale signs of activity.

Later over a cold can of beer, electronics technician Thomas Schmidt, twenty-six, from Richland, Washington, told me, "There is rarely a dull moment. Out on the river, you never know where or when an attack will come. Our morale here is high because our lives depend on each other."

And a young lieutenant wearing military greens reflected, "The way I see it, this Vietnamese family is off in a sampan to catch a few fish, and here comes this rugged, little boat ripping a shot across the bow. It's carrying tall, round-eyed white men wearing thick armored vests with all sorts of weapons, who board their boat—which is their home—and search through everything. Then, just when they are most terrified, these huge Americans give the kid a bar of candy and the father a pack of cigarettes and smile and wave them on. The next time we pass that sampan on the river, the family waves back. I swear to God that means something to me. You can talk all you want about your firefights, but I think this other kind of thing might add up to more in the end."

A couple of weeks before Thanksgiving in 1967, I flew to Phnom Penh to cover the visit of Jacqueline Kennedy, who had been invited to Cambodia by Prince Norodom Sihanouk. Phnom Penh was a glorious place in those days; I had taken Johanna to see Angkor Wat in the jungles in northern Cambodia; and now, the reporters stayed at the Hotel Royale, ate shrimp soufflé, and hung around the St. Hubert Bar with the girls after our stories were filed.

Jackie was showered with rose petals strewn by little flower girls. She seemed apprehensive, as if she might make some diplomatic gaffe. She asked Sihanouk if he could help seek the release, on behalf of old friends, of Doug Ramsey, the adviser I had met two years before in Hau Nghia Province and who was captured by the Vietcong. I had saved the photos I had taken on that trip, and, when I got back to Saigon, sent them to Nancy Tuckerman, a friend of mine, who doubled as Jackie's social secretary. I figured Ramsey's family might like the snapshots.

Sihanouk denied the Vietnamese were using Cambodia as a sanctuary, and he gave the press carte blanche to investigate suspected communist bases near the Vietnamese border. I set off in a Land-Rover with the AP's Horst Faas and George McArthur and we spent eighteen hours in a fruitless search. On the way back to the capital, George, then a noted roué, and I got to discussing women. He liked the young

Asian girls, he said, but I insisted I preferred a woman with a little mileage on her—who didn't chew gum and who had heard of Ronald Colman. As we bounced along the trail, our kidneys rattling, George replied, "Well, Bill, I'll accept your point. I'll take a woman with some mileage, too, but not all over a road like this!"

Two days later, Faas and McArthur did find indisputable proof of a Vietnamese base camp near the border, but I was not with them. I was ordered back to Saigon, because my number two man, John Randolph, had been kicked out of the Central Highlands during a dramatic battle. Randolph was a tough, gutsy correspondent who had won a Silver Star in Korea saving the life of a wounded American soldier. But he had a quick temper and had gotten into an argument with a military policeman at the U.S. 4th Division headquarters in Pleiku. He was summarily ordered out of the division's area as a penance. This was unfortunate for the paper because the Battle of Dak To was under way.

Dak To was the site of an abandoned Special Forces camp in one of the most inaccessible areas of Vietnam, northwest of Kontum near the Laotian border. It served as one of the entryways from the Ho Chi Minh Trail funneling into the Central Highlands. The 4th Battalion of the 173rd Airborne Brigade had been on a sweep in the area when they stumbled onto a well-entrenched North Vietnamese force. The battle began on a Sunday, and for five days the unit was virtually cut off, a kind of "lost battalion" that captured the world's headlines. A second battalion fought its way to the first, but they remained surrounded and under fire, and the third battalion geared up to go in. Several helicopters were shot down. An American jet had dumped a five-hundred-pound bomb inside the U.S. defense perimeter. More than one hundred paratroopers were killed: It was shaping up as a severe American defeat. The enemy fire was so heavy that resupply and medevac helicopters couldn't land in the jungle-covered hill.

I flew to Pleiku and stayed at the press camp Wednesday night. Among the press corps was Dean Brelis, then with NBC News, who walked out in the dark to take a leak, fell into a trench, and broke his leg. The next morning, I hitched a chopper ride to the forward position of the 173rd Brigade.

At the time, most helicopter pilots had instructions not to bring in reporters or photographers to the battalion. So we more or less scrounged around trying to find a pilot who might take us: a resupply ship, a medevac, or one carrying in fresh troops. I ran into Ray Coffey, then with the *Chicago Daily News;* Ed Behr of *Newsweek,* and Oriana Fallaci, the Italian journalist and interviewer. I had come through Rome not long before and it turned out we had a mutual friend in an old girl friend of mine who, I informed Fallaci, was now living with a well-known Italian screenwriter. "I had to come to this hellhole to find out about my friends," she said.

Coffey and I decided to try our luck with an outlying helicopter unit, one of whose pilots agreed to take us aboard. I steeled myself for the crunch: The helicopters had to hover and drop almost straight down to get into the tiny LZ, easy targets for North Vietnamese gunners. I took off my flak jacket and sat on it. This would give my vital private parts more protection. We kept circling for what seemed hours, which only added to the tension. I told Ray, "I'm not sure what I'm doing here, but you, you've got six kids, what the hell are you doing here?" Ray only smiled and shrugged. It was at times like these that I tried to calm my nerves by rationalizing that, after all, I could be slowly dying of heart disease behind some desk in L.A.

We finally lowered to the landing zone just as the fight was ending. This particular half-acre of hell was a wasteland of torn trees, bomb craters gouged out of red laterite soil, shattered timber bunkers, napalm-blackened foliage, and metallic shards of U.S. bombs. In the final assault, an enemy shell landed next to a sergeant carrying demolition charges to use against North Vietnamese bunkers. The blast set off the charges. "He just disappeared," another sergeant told me. "There was nothing left of his body. The blast killed one other man and wounded at least two others."

We helped the paratroops line up the remains of dead soldiers in their green plastic body bags. I mentioned to some of the troops that it was Thanksgiving. "These have been the worst five days of my life," said Dennis W. Hale, an acting squad leader from Buffalo, New York, who was in the lead unit of the first ambush on Sunday. "I didn't know it was Thanksgiving. But I heard about it this morning. You just can't understand how I feel. This is a holiday for me—just being alive after what we went through."

Another paratrooper who went through the full, five-day ordeal said his name was Larry Blair, a point man from Pittsburgh, Pennsylvania. "I've had enough of it up here," he said sitting on a shattered log. "We've been fighting all day and mortared all night. I really don't need any more of that."

Blair told me he thought the hill could have been taken more easily "except for that damned bomb that hit us and a couple of friendly artillery rounds."

The five-hundred-pounder had landed in the middle of a company position, he said, killing the company commander, the chaplain, most of the medics, and many of the wounded they were attending. I was impressed by the way, as sunset darkened, the noncoms were still very much paratroopers in command: barking out orders, maintaining discipline, and making sure the dead in their body bags came out along with the living.

"We paid a hell of a price for this little piece of ground," said First Sergeant Jerry Babb. "But after paying the price we did, we were determined to get to the top of this hill." And his radioman, Bobby R. Dominquez, his face darkened with sweat and dirt and his eyes hollowed from the ordeal, looked at me and sighed. "I got plenty to be thankful about. Who cares about turkey?" He dug into his C rations. "I am alive and that's the main thing. It will be a long time before anyone forgets this goddamn hill."

Back in Saigon, Johanna was getting increasingly unhappy and I can't say that I blamed her. Conditions were deteriorating; she was worried about the safety and health of our son; and she was not amused by my suggestions that Saigon was a better place to live than, say, Dacca. Our Vietnamese couple was still with us: Hai loved Cyril, but they were having their own marital difficulties.

Still, the whitewashed villa with the green shutters and red tile roof was immaculate and the candlelit dinners with fresh flowers were welcomed by our friends. But Johanna never could be sure how many of her guests would turn up. You could get caught in the field without any means of communicating that you'd be late or absent. And however much Johanna would try to direct the conversation toward the arts and literature, it would invariably turn to the war, and everything connected with it. Ward Just of the *Washington Post* was a frequent guest and captured the flavor of our evenings in a subsequent short story that appeared in the *Atlantic* magazine called "The Short War of Mr. and Mrs. Conner." Johnny Apple, the chunky, energetic bureau chief of the *New York Times,* now married to Edie Smith, who had been wounded in the U.S. embassy blast, would drop by as did Tom Buckley, of the same paper, and his wife, Barbara. They were both fine writers and natural competitors.

One late evening, Johnny was pushing Tom to return to the office to put together the nightly "war" story for the paper. As Buckley protestingly rose from the table to leave, someone cracked, "Tom, I didn't know that Johnny was your boss."

"Apple is my boss," countered Buckley, "only in the sense that Pope Julian the Second was Michelangelo's boss."

Another guest was the irrepressible Dorothy Chandler, mother of our publisher, Otis Chandler, and known to everyone as "Buff." She was appointed by President Johnson to a committee of women sent to Vietnam to observe progress in pacification. The editors worried that Buff might be used by the President. No danger of that. We had lively dinners at the villa where plenty of dissenting voices were heard and Buff was given frank assessments of Vietnam that often did not square with the official version.

In those days, we reporters were friendly with some of the young political officers at the embassy or those assigned to provincial headquarters, men like Frank Wisner, John Negroponte, Dick Holbrooke, Paul Hare, and Bill Stewart. When one of us returned to Saigon from the United States or Europe via Iran, we'd buy a huge tin of caviar at Tehran airport and feast on it that night. At that time, we saw a lot of Dan Ellsberg, who was also working for the Rand Corporation as a defense consultant and went out on infantry operations to observe tactics. We knew him as a dedicated hawk, long before he would turn against the war and give the Pentagon Papers to Neil Sheehan.

Going into the field, I'd usually team up with a fellow journalist. Ward Just and I became regular traveling companions. He was outgoing and ebullient and came from the Chicago area. He couldn't see anything without his glasses and was constantly worried about losing them and becoming a risk to the troops. His problem was that he was utterly fearless and was influenced by Hemingway. Thus, he was prepared to take chances I thought rash. He was badly wounded by an enemy grenade while accompanying a patrol of the 101st Airborne.

We had worked on *Newsweek* together and had a lot of friends in common. He was wonderful company and after a couple of days talking to generals and grunts about whatever operation we were on, it was a relief to break out a flask and gossip with a fellow amateur.

CHAPTER FIVE

Signals for the President

SOME FOREIGN CORRESPONDENTS are concerned about competition with other reporters. I've always considered myself reasonably competitive and have no intention of getting beaten on stories. Yet I am gregarious; I like good company, particularly in sticky places. I thought the war in Vietnam had enough for everyone, and I did not consider the *Los Angeles Times* in direct competition with the *Washington Post*. And for me the anticipation of good companionship while covering a story reduced my own apprehension of the danger or discomfort involved. So in Vietnam I found a good deal of camaraderie among certain journalists just as there was among the soldiers. The sense of shared experiences was one of the positive sides to Vietnam—and to war reporting in general. I formed friendships with reporters in Vietnam that I expect to last for the rest of my life, though I might not see a Ward Just or a Tom Buckley for a couple of years at a time.

Occasionally, Jack Foisie, our Bangkok bureau chief, would fly into Vietnam to help out. Jack was everyone's favorite, a slight, wizened, humorous reporter, who had covered World War II and Korea, and was a kind of latter-day Ernie Pyle in the Vietnam War. He always carried two canteens on his belt. As George McArthur put it: "I don't know what he's got in that second one, but it sure makes him smile a lot."

During one period, Jack came into Saigon, and headed north to cover the Marines from Da Nang. He was feeling bad, but hadn't let on to me. In Da Nang, he began passing blood in his urine and collapsed. He was medevaced to a U.S. Navy hospital ship offshore. The ship's senior doctor diagnosed his ailment as a tumorous kidney and recommended that it be removed. But the ship had gotten under way for Subic Bay in the Philippines and it was due for a brief dry-docking there, during which time the power on the ship would be off and the operating room shut down. Jack developed a liking for the doctor and the ship, and flew back to Saigon from Manila, with the intention of returning for surgery when the ship cleared dry-dock. I was appalled.

"You're not going to go back to Subic, you old bastard," I said. "You're going to Los Angeles for the best medical care the States can provide."

I argued with Jack that I had nothing against Navy medicine, but he needed the best kidney man he could find at a major medical center. Jack remonstrated; he didn't want to make a fuss. I insisted that though he was my senior in most every way, I was in command of the *L.A. Times* Saigon bureau and was ordering him home. Finally, he gave in and returned to California for an operation. Luckily, the kidney they removed, although tumorous, was not malignant.

Toward the end of 1967, arguments over how well the United States and the Vietnamese government were doing continued. There was such a profusion of evidence and statistics available on every side that journalists could and did come to wildly differing conclusions. Bob Shaplen in *The New Yorker* didn't see eye to eye with Mary McCarthy who came to Saigon for the *New York Review of Books* and who, by the way, was delightful company. Joe Alsop with the generals had a different view than Mike Herr with the grunts.

Earlier in 1967, Lyndon Johnson had called another Vietnam conference, this time in Guam. There was much talk about peace feelers from Hanoi and whether Washington was getting any "signals" from the other side. Johnson held a background briefing for the foreign reporters gathered in Manila and he was asked whether he had received any signals from Hanoi.

"Signals?" exploded the President. "I'll tell you about signals. I got my antennae out in Washington. I got my antennae out in London. I got my antennae out in Paris. I got my antennae out in Tokyo. I even got my antennae out in *Rangoon*! You know what signals all my antennae are picking up from Hanoi?"

The world press was hushed.

"I'll tell you what the signals from Hanoi are saying: 'Fuck you, Lyndon Johnson.' "

So we went into 1968 with only glimmerings of light at the end of the tunnel, and even those glints were viewed by some skeptics as merely the reflection of false hopes. In Manila, one knowledgeable American diplomat had told me, "Unfortunately, we backed into Vietnam step by step. At each stage, we tended to do only what was necessary to meet the challenge—but we never caught up with it. Now we are on a plateau with a lot of people developing doubts."

It seemed to me there was no central truth about Vietnam, except that the amount of blood, treasure, and time needed for the United States to gain a satisfactory result was higher than the American public was willing to pay.

I wrote at the time: "There is no pleasant project as the United States enters another year of war in Vietnam. The unhappy outlook, barring some dramatic reversal of fortune, is for slow, continuing progress in pacification, for more bitter fighting, for more U.S. casualties, and for much heated argument during the presidential election year over how well or poorly U.S. policy is working in Vietnam."

That argument was soon in coming—at Tet.

By this time, Johanna was finally fed up. She made up her mind to close down the house and leave with Cyril for Switzerland. I flew them to Bangkok and put them on a Swissair flight to Geneva. Then I took a few days off for R and R in Singapore. I overdid it and found myself on a flight back to Saigon with a terrible hangover. I decided to lay off drinking for a few days. I checked into the Continental Palace, the old colonial hotel with its slowly revolving overhead fans on Saigon's main square. In a way I was relieved: I no longer had to worry about the safety of a family in Vietnam.

A few days later, the annual Tet festival celebrating the Vietnamese new year, began. Half the Vietnamese Army had special leave and the Vietcong struck with a dramatic, nationwide series of attacks on January 30. Early the next morning, the Vietcong hit Saigon. A couple of loud explosions shook downtown Saigon. The Vietcong had blown a gap in the concrete wall surrounding the new U.S. embassy. By the time I arrived, most of the shooting was over: U.S. embassy guards had managed to keep the Vietcong assault force out of the main building, though a platoon of the U.S. 101st Airborne Division was helilifted to the embassy roof. But, more serious, the Vietcong penetrated several parts of the capital—as well as a dozen provincial capitals—by far the widest simultaneous assault of the war. A truckload of U.S. military policemen had been gunned down just outside Tan Son Nhut airport and all hell was breaking loose around town. A group of Vietcong were holding off the national police force in a building only a grenade's throw from Independence Palace, the seat of the presidency. Thus, with more than half a million U.S. soldiers in Vietnam, the enemy was nevertheless able to launch a well-coordinated attack inflicting heavy casualties on allied troops. With the help of a thirteen-hour time difference from Los Angeles—in our favor—John Randolph and I put together a long, comprehensive piece on the first hours and days of the Tet Offensive.

I remained in Saigon during the overall story on the Tet Offensive. After several days, the situation was stabilized: the Vietcong were driven out of all the major cities except for the ancient imperial capital of Hue.

There, the North Vietnamese had flown their flag over the citadel, and bitter street fighting was under way between their forces, and the U.S. Marines and South Vietnamese. I flew to Da Nang, and then helicoptered into Hue, landing under fire near the American military compound on the south side of the Perfume River. The U.S. compound was near the southern approach to the main steel six-span bridge, crossing to the north bank of the Perfume River. That night, enemy sappers attached charges to the bridge and set them off. At first light, I saw that two of six steel spans had collapsed in the river.

I ran into Gene Roberts of the *New York Times* and we joined up with the 2nd Battalion, 5th Marine Regiment, or "2-5," moving along the south bank of the river clearing houses of NVA: It was the kind of street fighting U.S. troops had not been involved in since World War II in Europe and the 1950 battle for Seoul in South Korea. As he directed his troops under fire, Lieutenant Colonel Earnest C. Cheatham, the tall battalion commander and a graduate of Loyola University, Los Angeles, explained, "It's an intimate type of fighting—we have to highball him and drive him out. We have three companies, more than three hundred men fighting house to house, but maybe only thirty-five or forty are engaged at any time. You can't get any more Marines that close to them at one time."

For the first two days of the fighting for Hue, the Marines who were used to war in the paddies and mountains had trouble fighting in the city streets. Some companies suffered 50 percent casualties, so many that some wounded were treated and immediately returned to duty. Colonel Cheatham was using the second-floor veranda of the province chief's mansion as his command post. Outside, ceremonial urns were used as aiming stakes for Marine mortars. A maid, grateful for being liberated, was passing out bottles of liquor from the province chief's private stock to the victorious Marines.

"You can tell these troops are young," said Cheatham, "because they don't bother with cognac. They prefer Pepsi-Cola. The Willies and Joes of World War Two would have been aghast."

Cheatham pointed to a gap in the lawn and said, "You see that Marine helmet and gas mask and the mortar hole? You can pretty well guess what happened to that Marine."

About forty yards away, two enemy rockets slammed into a Marine recoilless vehicle knocking it out and sending up a cloud of dust. "That was close enough," said the thirty-eight-year-old colonel. "Let's take cover."

"There's an awful lot of destruction here," Cheatham said later. "We had to blow our way through every wall of every house. It's a shame we have to damage such a beautiful city. In this kind of fighting, we're like a football team—eight, nine, ten, or eleven men. Four men cover the exits of a building, two men rush the building with grenades, while two men cover them with rifle fire. We hope to kill them inside or flush them out for the four men watching the exits. Then taking the next building, two other men assume the hairy job of rushing the front. It sounds simple but the timing has to be just as good as a football play. Sometimes we will be directing fire into one room while our troops are entering an adjoining room. That's kind of scary."

Cheatham lit up a cigar and remarked, "This is a funny kind of war. A block in front of us Marines are getting shot. Six blocks behind us they are buying cigars and cigarettes at the PX in the Army compound."

In addition to the main bridge, the NVA also knocked out the key crossing on the only highway between the big rear base at Phu-Bai and Hue. Soupy, cold weather prevented helicopters from getting into the landing zone at Hue.

I managed to get out of Hue on a chopper with wounded Marines, whom we left off at Phu-Bai. I got another lift back to the press camp at Da Nang, where I could file my stories. The next day, I was bound for Hue again; but it was difficult to get in, because it was cut off by land, and the lousy weather kept helicopter traffic to a minumum. Some reporters tried to get up the Perfume River with the Navy but

Eddie Adams of the AP and I found a helicopter willing to take us. I was unhappy with the door gunner, because, as we were flying toward the city, we picked up enemy fire. Seeing those tracers coming at you like big oranges is very unsettling, particularly when you realize that for every tracer you see there are four other bullets you can't see. The gunner was furious at the incoming fire and insisted that the pilot circle so he could shoot back. I thought the gunner was crazy. As far as I was concerned, I was prepared to let the Vietcong alone. Anyway, we landed on the precarious north side of the river. There, I found Charley Mohr of the *New York Times,* David Greenway of *Time,* and Al Webb of the UPI. We linked up with D Company of Battalion "1-5," which was trying to fight its way along the wall of the citadel against the well-entrenched NVA soldiers whose flag still fluttered from the tall flagpole.

The first night we spent in a hooch near the headquarters of Delta company commanded by Captain Myron Herrington, who was twenty-nine and came from Charlotte, North Carolina. The area was eerie: The scene looked like something from the western front in World War I— tangled barbed wire, shell holes, crumpled masonry, shattered trees, a riddled flare parachute, tin roofing, and hundreds of shell casings and C ration cans.

"The neighborhood is deteriorating," cracked one Marine. "I'd like to move out."

In the field with troops, you turn in when the sun goes down: They don't like lights serving as targets for the bad guys. I'd been carrying an inflatable air mattress, which I blew up and placed under me in the tiny hut. As I lay there, I could hear the huge shells fired from U.S. Navy ships in the South China Sea passing overhead. Through a hole in the roof, I could see flares being dropped all night long. Then, I heard a dispiriting sound: the air seeping out of my mattress through a gash caused by a piece of shrapnel on the cement floor. I spent the rest of the night trying the impossible—getting comfortable on a rough concrete floor.

The next morning, under a continuing leaden sky, we gathered at Captain Herrington's tiny command post.

"I'd like to make this the final push for the main wall to get this over with and get home," said the captain. "I sure wish we had some nice sunshine so we could get some air support, but it doesn't look like we're going to."

We were crouched in a triangular outcropping from the wall of the

citadel with a group of Marines, who could actually see the North Vietnamese from time to time in the next bulwark along the huge wall, about
two hundred yards away. D Company had received some bad news.

"They found the chaplain," one Marine told another.

"He all right?"

The first Marine shook his head.

"Dead?"

"They found him shot in the head," said the first Marine.

"Goddamn," said the first. "The chaplain was all over the place,
always going in with the squads."

A brick parapet rimmed the outcropping and one of the Marines,
in a kind of wild gesture, decided to raise an American flag. I spotted
Lance Corporal Thomas H. Mitchell, who was twenty-one and came
from Nashville, tying an American flag onto a long branch he had cut
from a tree. I unlimbered my Pentax and tried to focus on the corporal,
a brawny Marine with several days' growth of beard, who at that
moment tore off his helmet and ran across to the parapet shouting,
"Remember the Alamo. Remember the citadel." Mitchell stuck the
branch with the Stars and Stripes in the backrest of a chair which he
then set atop the parapet, just down from the NVA position. As the flag
snapped against the wind, the corporal said, "There it is. It's up. . . .
Now watch their mortar rounds come in." With the evident satisfaction of one who has just thumbed his nose at the enemy, he added,
"The hell with them!"

Below the citadel wall, Captain Herrington said to his radio operator, "Call headquarters. Tell 'em we've got the American flag
flying over the citadel wall." Then to me, he said, "It may have been
crazy of that Marine, but this sure is a shot in the arm for our morale."

Later that day, I pigeoned my film rolls out of Hue for the AP's
Horst Faas in Saigon. They reached him and went out on the Wirephoto
service, under an anonymous AP credit. The sequence of the flag
raising was prominently displayed in many U.S. papers, including my
own.

Wes Gallagher, general manager of the AP, who happened to be
in Vietnam, told Horst, "That was a great picture from Hue. Give the
photographer a bonus."

The captain ordered his company to assault the key southwest
corner of the citadel wall. However, he had only two effective platoons
instead of the normal three—so much had the company suffered during
the seven days of attrition in the battle for Hue's citadel.

Herrington sent the first platoon along the huge wall of the citadel. As we advanced, a Marine shot an enemy sniper out of a shattered tree. We pitched up in an abandoned and gutted house. I felt like an intruder, for there were intimate signs of those who lived there until a couple of weeks before: a double bed, photos of a lovely Vietnamese woman and a man in a business suit, Chinese movie magazines, a tape recorder, paperback books, a photograph album, and, strangely, a Sears, Roebuck catalog.

In a situation like that, I chose to stay with the company commander, partly because I assumed it was safer, and partly because he had the radio which made it easier for a reporter to get a broader idea of what was happening in the inevitable fog of war.

The first platoon advanced along the wall, coming within fifteen yards of the corner position. Suddenly, the platoon was hit—as Lance Corporal Charles Fout, a twenty-one-year-old from Covina, California, told me minutes later: "We were moving up the wall. I think they must have let us come that close, because they suddenly opened up on us. They hit us with a machine gun across the road, flanking us, and then threw grenades at us. That's how close we were. They got the lieutenant, the platoon leader, and then they got me—first with a bullet through my arm and then with a grenade that went off in front of me. It singed my face and nicked me. That's my third Purple Heart."

Back at the CP, I crouched next to Captain Herrington's radio operator, who relayed the bad news. "Let's lay some mortars on them," the captain ordered his gunners in the rear.

The first platoon began to fall back and a Marine was knocked off the wall onto the street. The situation was becoming more confused. Greenway and Webb were in a separate hut. Then I saw Charley Mohr dart out of the door of the house we were in but he didn't say why he was taking off. "My right flank is getting chopped to hell," Captain Herrington said quietly, bent in the doorway of the temporary command post. Explosions sounded all around but I couldn't tell whether they were ours or theirs.

"Corpsman, corpsman," came a cry and a fast-moving medic brought a wounded eighteen-year-old squad leader into our hooch, shot in the left forearm. "They are really hitting us up there," he said as his arm was bandaged.

Then Captain Herrington ordered up a tank, one of two of the original five still operating. It let loose several 90-mm shells. But it was hit by three enemy rockets fired down the road, straight as a midwestern main street, and pulled back.

Off to the left a couple of houses over, a Marine sergeant was shot through the throat. Mohr, Webb, Greenway, and Marine combat correspondent Steve Berndtson began dragging him to safety. Then a mortar round hit close by, wounding Greenway, Webb, and Berndtson, all of whom received fragments in the legs.

At that point, another wounded Marine ran into the makeshift command post and gasped to Herrington, "Skipper, they've got this place zeroed in with mortars and you'd better get out fast."

We all helped drag or carry the wounded through the backyard shambles to the original command post in the main wall, where the vain attack had begun an hour before. The wounded Marines were carried on wood doors or slung in ponchos. They were treated by hospital corpsman Al Kent, a young medic from Hancock, Michigan, who that morning learned that his closest buddy, also a medic, had just been killed.

In a race with death and reduced to basics, Kent put his lips down to the Marine's gaping throat wound and tried to clear a breathing passage for him by sucking out bits of cartilage and clotted blood.

"God," he said, his lips smeared with blood, "I tried to get out all that junk but I think there's some fragments left. Oh, damn these gooks."

Kent inserted a tracheotomy tube into the Marine's throat and then loaded him onto a stretcher. I helped put the stretcher on the flat bed of a Mule, a small, carry-all vehicle, and then rode along with the Marine to keep his body in place as we raced back from the command post to a medical aid station near the helicopter pad. There, I saw other Marines lying mute and suffering, waiting patiently for evacuation. We placed the stretcher with the wounded Marine on the ground. But he died there, before a helicopter got in.

Later, the platoon leader showed up at the aid station, having also been patched up by corpsman Al Kent. The lieutenant was hit in the throat, too, but less seriously, and coolly plugged the gap with his finger.

Though I hadn't had a drink since Singapore, I carried a pigskin flask of cognac and offered a slug to David Greenway, whose leg wound was painful but not crippling. He could hobble with the aid of a makeshift crutch and I helped him aboard a chopper when it finally arrived. Al Webb's wound in the calf was more serious and he spent several weeks in the hospital getting all the ligaments and nerves repaired. That evening, Mohr and I helped load the wounded on helicopters and carried them off in Da Nang.

The day left me angered and puzzled. Why, I wondered, did the Marine high command commit only one understrength battalion against the well-dug-in, crack NVA forces holding the citadel?

"We need help," a platoon sergeant told me, in the way you sometimes talk to children. "And we need it now. But it looks like they're going to make us hack it alone."

A combat-ready, full-strength Marine battalion consists of more then one thousand men. But that day, "1-5" had less than five hundred "effectives," fighting one of the toughest battles in Vietnam.

"For every house on every block," an officer explained to me, "we have taken a Marine casualty. We're getting some replacements but we're losing them as fast as we get them."

It seemed to me the old story: Though there were five hundred thousand U.S. troops in Vietnam, there were only a handful—far too few—at this particular sharp end. Further, the Marine command almost seemed to relish the fact that they had to make do with less men, less equipment, and less firepower than their counterpart U.S. Army divisions.

And for some reason, their helicopter pilots had instructions not to fly in ceilings less than five hundred feet, despite the fact that the whole bloody battle to regain Hue was fought under the low-lying clouds of the monsoon season. I remember one harassed medic at the landing pad, shouting into his radio to Phu-Bai asking for help: "I don't care if you've got a weather hold or not! We've got five emergency cases here and six priorities. We want something done immediately and we want a reply, pronto!"

He turned to me and said, "Christ, I may get court-martialed for talking this way but I can't understand why we can't get helicopters in to get the wounded out."

So depleted were the U.S. Marines that in the final assault on the imperial palace to drive the North Vietnamese out of Hue, they were ordered to provide a covering role only.

The morning of the assault, Charley Mohr and I had been with some Marines, and Charley had tested their weapons. Mohr carried a personal Beretta as a sidearm, and, of course, the Marines were fascinated with something as exotic as James Bond's favorite weapon. The Marines let Charley use their sniper rifle while they triggered off a couple of rounds from the Beretta. The whole thing made me uneasy. I didn't see any reason for us drawing unnecessary fire from the NVA so that Charley and the Marines could play games. Some correspondents in Vietnam carried weapons and, in a few instances, used them. I felt uncomfortable and did not carry anything, on the grounds that if my firepower were ever to be needed, there would be presumably a lot of dead bodies and fresh weapons available. However, if a trooper asked me to ride shotgun and handed me an M-16 during a jeep ride, I would dutifully accept the rifle as if I were a John Wayne Marine.

In the afternoon, Mohr and I joined up with the elite companies of the 1st Vietnamese Infantry Division for the attack on the historic, walled shrine, the climax to the twenty-five-day battle for Hue. I was with Major Tran Van Dinh, a handsome twenty-eight-year-old officer who wore a bit of red cloth flying from his left shoulder for identification. It was a tense moment for me at 2:30 P.M. when Major Dinh gave the word to charge the palace walls. It was like something out of the Middle Ages. The heavily laden Vietnamese troops rushed across one hundred yards of green lawn toward the main gate. The approach was flanked by nine giant cannons cast in bronze and bearing mystical characters, installed as symbolic guardians some 165 years before. Past these silent guns, the Vietnamese soldiers charged, shouting and screaming battle cries. I hobbled behind, feeling very exposed. But there was no opposing fire, so we poured across the moat and through the Emperors' Gate and over another bridge past a lotus pond. The NVA troops holding the palace had apparently decided to slip out the previous evening during a tremendous artillery barrage aimed at rooting them out.

Mohr and I met George McArthur of the AP and we headed for the imperial courtyard, where only four of the twelve "Blue of Hue" porcelain urns were undamaged. The imperial stone lions and the dragons guarding the throne room were intact. We gingerly entered the high-ceilinged throne room, which measured one hundred by sixty feet. It was caked with dust and broken plaster and littered with shattered timbers from the roof. Three unexploded 105-mm shells lay on the colored tile floor along with metal shards of other shells that did explode. The throne itself was a smallish chair of red lacquer and rich gilt. It seemed undamaged. It was perched on a triple-tier dais with a golden canopy overhead. I thought to myself it was not every day you liberated a royal throne room.

Despite the damage from shellfire to the palace, the grounds were in much better shape than the houses in the rest of the citadel, and the palace looked as if it could be restored. "This is the end of resistance here," said Major Dinh.

*   *   *

At that time, however, the U.S. Marines were still under siege at Khe Sanh, the forwardmost base in the northwestern corner of the country. I had been on the waiting list for transport into Khe Sanh since the Marines decided that no more than a half-dozen reporters could be accommodated at any one time. At one point, the media contingent slipped to two men: David Douglas Duncan, the *Life* photographer, and John Wheeler, a tough, determined reporter for the AP. Duncan, an ex-Marine tried to convince Wheeler that Khe Sanh was about to be overrun and that he should get out while he could. Duncan didn't know Wheeler, who told him bluntly that if anyone was staying behind it would be John Wheeler.

My turn came for the flight into Khe Sanh. Murray Fromson of CBS and I went out to the air base to board a transport. But low clouds were delaying any flights that morning. So we sat waiting on the hardstand at Da Nang. I have learned that sometimes my inner tension while waiting for a mission expresses itself through drowsiness. So I was nodding off, lying on the concrete with my pack as a pillow, when I was awakened by a diversion. A young Marine—perhaps deranged, perhaps perfectly sane—attempted to depart Vietnam by hijacking a Pan Am jet charter at gunpoint. While we watched, he was talked out of it and led away by military police.

We boarded an Air Force C-130 and the pilot let us sit up on the flight deck with the intercom earphones over our heads during the ride. I took off my flak jacket and sat on it, as was my custom, to protect my vitals, and soon we were making our descent through the soup.

Then the radio from the Khe Sanh control tower crackled, "We have a Marine C-130 on the runway on fire, burning." Moments later, the C-130 carrying twenty-five hundred gallons of fuel for the Marines exploded on the short airstrip. "The runway is closed indefinitely," ordered Khe Sanh tower.

"My God," said Captain Kenneth Strom, the pilot. "That North Vietnamese bastard at the end of the runway got him with a machine gun. That could have been us! I've got eight Air Medals and two Purple Hearts and I don't need any more."

On the way back to Da Nang, Captain Strom, who came from El Paso, Texas, turned over the controls to the copilot and explained to me, "This run is no picnic. The weather is usually lousy. You have to get down low and avoid the mountains. Then you have to come in through those hills and sometimes they've got enemy gunners shooting up at you—and down at you. It's damned hairy."

The next day, we waited most of the morning, but finally the weather cleared enough over Khe Sanh, and we took off aboard a Hercules. This time we broke through the goo with the four-thousand-foot strip dead ahead. But enemy mortars had opened up trying to knock out our taxiing plane. Everyone leaped off the back ramp as the plane was "speed-off-loaded" and ran for the dubious comfort of some skimpy-looking bunkers at the edge of the parking apron. Murray Fromson darted like an expert broken-field runner but was hit by the powerful prop blasts of the turbojets and was knocked flat, badly banging his knees. For the next ten minutes, until the plane unloaded, and turned around to take off, we huddled in the bunker. Then we ran to a trench line and jumped in, when a Marine warned, "Here comes another mortar magnet. Keep your head down." That was the term Marines used for the transports that invariably attracted a few rounds from the NVA gunners. Sure enough, two mortar shells hit nearby so we stayed down until the second plane unloaded and took off. We half trotted to the headquarters of the 21st Regiment, where the commander, Colonel David Lownds, spelled out the strategic situation for us.

Lownds was a cool officer, I thought. He showed none of the gung-ho bravado that many colonels affected with the press. He was of medium size, wore a uniform as worn and stained as any grunt's. He had thinning ginger hair and a long, pointed moustache he liked to stroke. He talked to us from a sandbagged opening to his command bunker, the nerve center of the Khe Sanh base and the only concrete shelter on it. He had a son-in-law in the Marines, a captain who had been wounded in Hue. Lownds himself was forty-seven and had two Purple Hearts from World War II, won at Saipan and Iwo Jima.

He assumed we knew, he said, that the road to the coast, National Highway 9, was cut by North Vietnamese troops. No convoys were reaching Khe Sanh. Morning fog cut down the C-130 and C-123 flights to about a quarter of those scheduled. The ceiling was usually too low for choppers to operate. The town of Khe Sanh, three miles south, was occupied by NVA, and the U.S. Special Forces camp at Lang Vei, three miles southwest had been overrun by the enemy using tanks for the first time.

Colonel Lownds commanded five thousand men, including a battalion of Vietnamese rangers. But he faced, he thought, as many as twenty thousand NVA regulars in those hills at this remote corner of the country.

I asked him about comparisons being made between Khe Sanh

and Dien Bien Phu, another mountain valley where the French were surrounded and defeated in 1954.

He pulled on his moustache. "No, I don't see any real comparison. The French simply didn't have the resources I have available. I can call on air, and artillery from bases along the DMZ."

"Concerned?" he replied in an understated way to my second question. "Sure. Anybody who wouldn't be concerned is a fool. But worried? I'm not sure. I have the assets. I can do the job."

The siege of Khe Sanh with the stepped-up artillery attacks had begun a couple of weeks before. "The first few nights," Lownds remembered, "the incoming came down in buckets. Now, it only comes in occasionally. No one counts the incoming anymore. We take a few rounds and we take a few casualties. Sure, he's trying to knock out our airstrip. But there's not much you can do about it. Two or three of his people pop out of their holes, pop off a few rounds of mortar when a plane lands, and then they are back in their bunkers by the time we return their fire. It's a cat-and-mouse game. He's trying to knock out the aircraft and we're trying to sneak in the planes between the shells.

"We have our three meals a day. We get ammo. We get our bunker material and steel matting. We get our barbed wire. I don't know that I'm hurting yet. We don't get our mail on time. And we didn't get paid for a while. But all these Marines understand what the situation is. We've got good Marines, some of the best. I'm proud to be their leader."

For a man in the eye of the hurricane—and in the bull's-eye of the American press—Colonel Lownds said he didn't worry about the "whys" some critics were asking about the strategic tenability of his position against a concerted, mass attack.

"Marines for years have done what they are told to do," he said glancing at his GI watch and indicating he had to get back to his post. "My mission is to defend Khe Sanh. I am going to perform that mission."

Once a beautiful mountain valley with tea and coffee plantations, Khe Sanh when I visited the place looked like a ravaged, red-dirt moonscape, a devastated patch of land at the end of the line. Although the Marines controlled the tops of the close-in hills, North Vietnamese gunners were entrenched in the farther hills and had a clear view of the base—when the fog lifted. The gunners were good—the base bore the scars.

Khe Sanh was a creepy place with heavy ground mist sliding in over the valley floor and lying all night like a winding sheet. The Marines believed there were tigers in the mountains and that on some nights they could hear them. There were tigers in the Annamite Cordillera, but the tigers there now were more likely to be wearing NVA uniforms. Walking across the base, a Marine escort told me, "It's really spooky out here at night. It's like seeing *The Hound of the Baskervilles* on the late, late show. It's quiet but you hear strange noises."

We hiked to my digs across the lumpy, ill-defined topography of Khe Sanh. Everything aboveground—tents, heavy equipment, sandbags, tin roofing—was riddled with fragments. Empty C-ration cans, shell casings from outgoing and shell fragments from incoming were all over the place. In Khe Sanh, the area around the airstrip was known as the H Zone, for "hit zone." This contained the bunker for the Marine crash crew that tried to save victims from burning planes, the colonel's CP, and Charlie Med, the regimental aid station. This general area was called Downtown.

"Hey, man, Downtown is an easy place to get blown away," my Marine escort observed. The term referred to those hit by artillery fire, who were sometimes quite literally blown away.

We linked up with Seabee Andy Severin, a cheerful, heavyset fellow, who did nothing to ease my apprehension by saying, "Waiting around Downtown is like Russian roulette. Sometimes nothing hits you, but sometimes a few hundred meters off, a guy is blown away."

"I'll tell you something—some of these bunkers Downtown, you don't even have to go outside to get hit. You can get blown away right where you're at."

Severin and the Seabees—Detachment B of the Navy construction battalion—were to be my hosts and I quickened my pace toward their bunker. It was, I learned, the best-constructed bunker on the base. I liked that. As we reached the Seabees' billet, I noticed we were surprisingly close to what the grunts called "the lines," the perimeter, consisting of coils of barbed wire backed up by waist-high trenches, punctuated with fighting holes and sleeping bunkers. It was cold and windy now that night was approaching, and I saw a couple of Marines shivering. Their bunkers looked pretty flimsy to me.

In Khe Sanh, happiness was a well-constructed bunker. The Seabees' was fashioned of wooden beams, crushed rock, sandbags, and ammo cases filled with dirt. Severin, who was a Steelworker 2nd

Class and came from Palisade, Colorado, proudly showed me to a bunk—a bunk, yet. I was impressed. I had heard that the Seabees had one of the most dangerous jobs in Khe Sanh—repairing the airstrip, the vital lifeline to the outside world. I asked him about it.

"Yeah, it's rough," he said. "I mean you feel pretty naked out there. After a shelling, we run out on the strip and work for five minutes filling up a shell hole. Then we catch another incoming and we have to run for it. You can't get very much sustained work done under those conditions. And, you know? It gets harder and harder to get out of your hole and back to work."

The Seabee in charge, Lieutenant Junior Grade Martin J. Kux, who was twenty-four, slipped in the bunker and added in a matter-of-fact way, as if running a contracting firm back in Canandaigua, New York, "When we get hit, our equipment operator goes out to estimate the job. On a small job—that's a small hole—we send out the minimum number of men needed so we won't endanger too many. On a big job, everyone turns to so we can finish it as soon as possible."

The chief estimator turned out to be a twenty-five-year-old Wilbur Carl, who explained his strange calling to me. "When he pops in his artillery," said Carl, "we've got to go out and fix it. If it hits the steel runway matting, we try to cut the jagged edges smooth with a torch and then fill up the hole and lay new matting. You never know when he's going to shoot at you. We kind of like the morning fog here. We can do our work and he can't see us although he can hear us moving around."

Carl, who learned his trade in Midland, Michigan, said one factor contributing to the danger was that they worked around noisy equipment—bulldozers, cranes, generators—and the clangor of engines drowned out the faint sound of incoming fire.

"The roar of the equipment keeps you from hearing incoming," he said, "so the thing to do is keep an eye on the Marines on the side of the strip. If they start to run, you run. You keep looking for a hole while you're working, and when it comes in you pray you don't get hit and you hope that you can make it to a hole. If the stuff is really coming in, it's better to crawl under your machine."

One Seabee who joined our group almost didn't make it. Jim Post, another equipment operator, took his second wound at Khe Sanh—mortar fragments in his upper right arm—a couple of mornings before. He wore his fresh bandage and, rather sheepishly, said, "I was with a couple of buddies. I heard the incoming and tried to hide but I guess I just wasn't hiding good enough. The rounds came in and the next thing I knew blood was running down my arm. But I was lucky: The other two guys got blown away.''

The stories unsettled me but I was reasonably content. After all, I was in the safest bunker in Khe Sanh. I ducked outside to take a leak in a ''pisstube'' and had a beer and some chow warmed up by a camp cooker. I got into my sleeping bag and was reassured by a huge steelworker named Bill Trottno, an older man of thirty-four who had a wife and four kids back in Oxnard, California. ''No sweat. When that attack comes, we've got light antitank weapons and M-16s. It's real John Wayne stuff and we're going to fight. The grunts on the lines will take care of them and so will we. Sleep tight. Pleasant dreams.''

Early the next morning, I was up in the gray mist to visit the Marines on the lines. Unlike Con Thien, Khe Sanh was a big sprawling place with Marine positions on the nearest hills and the NVA on the farther and higher mountains. Death could come swiftly, borne on the flying steel of quiet mortars or the slight thin whistle of a rocket.

I found a squad with several black Marines who seemed to set the tone for the group with their banter under fire. These were grunts with the 3rd Platoon, B Company, 1st Battalion, of the 26th Marine Regiment, and they took as their motto a variation of the Twenty-third Psalm. As James Puyol, a dark, wiry, chipper squad leader from Brooklyn, put it: ''We say, 'Yea, though we walk through the valley of the shadow of death, we fear no evil—for we are the meanest mothers in the valley.' ''

And on ''the lines,'' the Marines had a simple gesture to reassure and encourage one another after a barrage of incoming. It was the classic thumbs-up signal, originally between airmen, meaning, ''Everything's okay for now—take care.''

Just then, a rocket exploded nearby and sent off a severe shock wave. The five Marines I was with at that moment dropped to the clay floor. A second rocket landed even closer, shaking the sandbagged roof and spraying red laterite around. The noise and concussion were like physical blows.

''Oh, shit!'' exclaimed Lance Corporal Puyol; then he smiled and lapsed into child's talk. ''Oh, golly gee. I thought I heard that rocket take off. I heard that hissing sound and we should have been on our faces before it hit. Sorry, men. Old Vic is really after us today.''

During the war, the nickname for the Vietcong or the NVA went through several transmutations among GIs and grunts. First it was the initials "VC." Then it became the military equivalent of these initials, "Victor Charlie." Then, simply "Charlie." Next, the really sophisticated infantrymen—many of them blacks—began referring to "Charles" or "Mr. Charles." Now the grunts in Puyol's squad were calling him just "Vic."

Puyol's men manning the southern perimeter had amusing phrases inked on their helmet covers. WHY ME? said one. Another: IF YOU SEE THIS HELMET IN THE GROUND, DON'T KICK IT—I'M UNDER IT.

The squad had come to admire the professionalism of the enemy. "We're not fooling around with the girls up here," said Corporal Ken Bragalone, a twenty-year-old from Youngstown, Ohio, with a dark stubble on his chin. "We're fighting the North Vietnam Army. They are good men. It's like fighting Marines, like fighting yourselves."

The men particularly admired an enemy soldier they spotted on Hill 471, two and a half miles away, whom they called Luke the Gook after a similar character the Marines met in Korea.

"Old Luke is one tough hombre," said one Marine. "We watched him through our binoculars. He climbed out of his hole to take his morning constitutional. We called in an air strike. They hit him with napalm. He came out of the hole again to look around. The air hit him again. And afterward he came out again and started to dig some more. I just can't understand why we can't get that gutsy little bastard."

I looked through the binoculars from the fighting port in the bunker, and, sure enough, there was Luke and a couple of friends on a ridgeline moving around in a big bomb crater.

"Vic knows how to pin our asses down," admitted Corporal Richard Hunt. "One of those little bastards was right out there in the fog this morning trying to cut the wire. I couldn't see him to shoot him. That's the second time Vic has done that to me. So far, I've got a couple of NVAs that I know of. But Vic has tried to scarf me up, too. I got two Purple Hearts now. One more Heart and I get rotated home. But you know, I'm not really trying for my third one because it might be my last one. My buddy got blown away with only four days to go."

I crawled in another bunker with more Marines as two explosions sounded.

"That's from those goddamn mortar magnets," said one Marine, referring to a U.S. transport aircraft.

"We try not to sweat it," added one of the more senior noncoms I found that day, a tall, weary-looking staff sergeant from Chicago, who introduced himself as Edward Evans and forced a smile. "I've learned a lot up here," said Evans. "When it's real quiet you can sometimes hear the incoming mortar. It sounds like a snake slithering over straw. Rockets make a hiss and you've got about two seconds to duck if you can hear them. Now, the artillery sounds like a freight train going off the tracks. Outgoing fire makes a thin ring like a bell."

Then a private piped up, "When the incoming first started coming in, I tried to differentiate between the various types. But now I just don't give a damn." I personally got the feeling that I'd never be able to differentiate between the two: It was all "outcoming" or "ingoing" to me.

I asked one Marine why the trenches on the lines were only waist-high. "Our trenches used to be up to our shoulders," answered a lanky corporal from Baltimore named S. L. Boone. "Now, it's down to our waists because of all the stuff coming in. And natural erosion. We got to keep digging to stay ahead of the game. But it's tough with Vic shooting at you. He shoots that fifty caliber around like he's playing games or something."

Another mortar round hit, not far away, and a visiting Marine from another company yelled, "See you guys later. My bunker is safer."

I decided to follow his example and, crouching low, made my way back to the Seabee bunker.

There, I noticed a flower-power buff. Seabee J. D. Eshenaur, a husky, blue-eyed construction man, had written his name and home-town, SIMI, CALIFORNIA, on his helmet cover in flowing psychedelic script. There was also the exhortation, LOVE! And another line read, CHEYRIL IS MY LIFE.

"I'm big on the flower-power movement," he told me, laughing.

Another Seabee sneered, but Eshenaur admonished, "Don't knock flower power."

"Shit," said the other Seabee. "Flower power ain't gonna stop no incoming."

One of the Seabees told me of a gruesome incident that happened a few days previously.

"We were out there with a front-end loader," he said, "trying to move some stuff around in the impact area. We were taking a few rounds on the strip. I looked over and a Marine was running about ten feet away and a mortar round came in. I looked over the sandbags at him and the poor Marine looked like two hundred pounds of pork that somebody kicked off the back of a truck. You couldn't even tell it was him. I was just sick, looking. I dragged away another Seabee who got wounded in the arm. Just before that Marine got killed I said, 'Look at him and his funny helmet.' He had put a cowboy, go-to-hell hat on over his helmet.''

Everyone in Khe Sanh seemed to agree that morale got better the deeper you dug in the ground.

''It's unbelievable how our people can stand up under these conditions,'' said Seabee Bill Trottno. ''Americans are kind of hard to beat. It's going to take more than these bad guys can dish out. The trouble is, though, the longer you stay in a bunker, the harder it is to go out in the open again, where you can get blown away.''

Paying another visit to the lines with the grunts, I asked about morale and was surprised how high it seemed to be, since they might have been pessimistic about their plight. One young corporal even complained about the antiwar protestors in the United States. Sitting in a fighting trench, wolfing down a can of C ration peaches, he grumbled, ''They call us Marines underpaid, underage, oversexed hired killers. Tell 'em to go fuck themselves. They can protest all they want. They walk around with their long hair and all that stuff. But we ain't moving from here. Let Vic come. We're ready. If everyone was a lover and nobody was a fighter who the fuck would defend the United States?''

The main thing that worried the Marines was having to undergo shelling—to be on the defensive. That's not what they were trained for.

''This artillery works on your nerves,'' said Private First Class Lloyd Nagle, as he sighted his M-16 over the parapet of a fighting bunker and tried to find a target. ''You just have to sit back and take it when you can't see them. The worst part is sitting around waiting, knowing they're out there and not being able to do much about it. I just wish they'd come at us over the wire. We're waiting for them.''

Nagle's squad-mate, Joe Sayles, a private from Detroit, added, ''This is supposed to be the turning point of the war. Khe Sanh. Well, that's what we're waiting for. He has overrun every other place around here except Khe Sanh. Let him come.''

Sayles offered me a cigarette, and expressed surprise that any civilian like myself was crazy enough to come to Khe Sanh.

''It ain't much fun being a being out here on the lines,'' he said, lighting up, and instinctively cupping the flame from the lighter. ''But one thing I know. Everybody on the base respects the grunts. If we didn't have good morale up here, our people would be cracking up.

Then it would be easy for Vic to overrun us. But our attitude is, don't sweat it.''

One afternoon, I dropped by the Seabees to collect my pack, say good-bye, and see if I could get a lift out of Khe Sanh.

I gave the thumbs-up signal to Ron Frye, a handsome, clean-shaven Seabee I knew had been based at Khe Sanh for seven months, and asked him how he was holding up.

''Well,'' he said with a wan grin, ''you can say I'm nervous. In fact, I'm scared to death. It wasn't so bad before. But now I've gotten edgy. Still, I want to stay here and see this siege through.''

If getting there wasn't half the fun, getting out of Khe Sanh was worse. I waited with a half-dozen Marines who were wounded or due for rotation in a makeshift bunker by the airstrip. We were hoping a transport could land and then we'd make a run for it.

I heard some explosions from rocket and mortar fire.

''How much incoming will this bunker stop?'' an Air Force man asked a Marine lieutenant.

''Fragments,'' he replied. ''A direct hit would blow it all away.''

Another incoming, this one closer. A Marine popped his head inside the bunker and said to no one in particular, ''That one got a jeep and a forklift truck.''

''Now I know how a clay pigeon must feel,'' said a waiting corporal with a wounded arm. ''This airstrip is the center of the bull's-eye.''

I wondered about moving to a heavier bunker but that would have meant traveling farther from the strip and a longer dash for a plane. I sensed some of the helplessness that was the daily lot of the grunts at Khe Sanh. They say that it's the waiting that gets you. True.

A controller stuck his head into the bunker. ''There's a plane unloading at the end of the strip. He doesn't want to get hit up here on the parking apron. You can try to run for it if you want.''

We decided to go—a headlong dash over the red earth, pitted every dozen feet or so with mortar craters. Out of breath from the dash and the burden of helmet, flak jacket, camera, and pack, I decided that this was hardly the way a man entering his middle years ought to spend an afternoon. We waited for the 105-mm ammunition to be rolled off the cargo plane, a lumbering, ancient C-123. Then we tossed our gear aboard the rear ramp and scrambled aboard, bellies on the aluminum deck hanging on to the combat strapping. For minutes that seemed like hours, the loadmaster fiddled with the rear ramp trying to get it to close. At last the plane began to roll down the runway, all of us tightening up against mortar or machine gun fire. Then wheels up, our bellies still exposed. Finally, the blessed relief of the cloud cocoon that spelled protection from ground fire.

The NVA never did launch a full-scale assault against the Khe Sanh. Eventually, the Marines simply abandoned the position, as they had so many other forward firebases in Vietnam.

I returned to Saigon after a month in I Corps concerned about the quality of the Marines' top leadership in Vietnam. There was no question but that the grunts were as tough and determined as any troops in the country, but I wondered whether their senior officers and strategists did them justice. I came reluctantly to believe that the Marines' top commanders had not sufficiently prepared their troops for the kind of war that evolved along the DMZ, that is, positional warfare with static defense bases. The Marines never seemed to be properly dug in to resist the kind of heavy artillery attacks the NVA threw at them. I heard other criticisms directed against the high command: vast, time-consuming amphibious operations that did not result in contact with the enemy; dangerous forays into the DMZ by understrength units; rash and costly frontal assaults on entrenched enemy positions of limited value; failure to employ their helicopters properly, particularly in the evacuation of wounded. One of the key problems was that the Marine structure, doctrine, and training was designed for hitting the beach, gaining an objective, and then pulling back to shipboard. But in Vietnam, the Corps found itself fighting over the long haul in rugged areas where the more heavily designed Army divisions, with their engineering support, would be better suited. But the Marines wanted a piece of the action and they got it—albeit with ill-designed equipment and having to make do with the worst of everything. Well, as the average grunt would say, "Semper Fi!"

Back in the capital, I found the same old political antagonisms prevailing—even in the wake of the Tet Offensive: northerner versus southerner, Buddhist versus Catholic, one political sect versus another.

As peace talks were due to open in Paris, Vietnam presented the unseemly spectacle of a war-torn nation whose civilian leadership was as fickle and flighty as a bunch of prima donnas. "What this country needs is a man on horseback," said a Vietnamese friend. "The trouble is we don't even have a good horse."

I dined with Keyes Beech of the *Chicago Daily News* and his lady friend, Georgie Anne Geyer, also of the same paper. They didn't see eye to eye on the war, he being much more hawkish than she. There was another problem: As two professional foreign correspondents working for the same paper, which rarely could afford two of its overseas reporters in the same place, they were doomed to lead more or less separate lives most of the time. Later they did split up. GeeGee was bright and resourceful and one of the best correspondents around, as were some of the other women journalists who served in Vietnam: Dickie Chapelle, killed by a land mine while on patrol with the U.S. Marines; Margaret Higgins of Korean fame, who picked up a tropical virus that hastened her early death; Kate Webb, the plucky Aussie with UPI; Martha Gelhorn, who had covered Spain with her husband-to-be Ernest Hemingway; photographer Catherine Leroy; the AP's Jurate Kazickas, a striking beauty who was wounded in the rump at Khe Sanh where everyone at Charlie Med volunteered to assist the medic patching her ass; Frankie FitzGerald, who concentrated on the Vietnamese civilians and wrote *Fire in the Lake;* and, after my time, Edie Lederer of the AP and Gloria Emerson of the *New York Times.*

It was not easy to be a woman correspondent. All too often, some male journalists would suggest, unfairly, that women reporters used their sexuality to get stories. And if being a foreign correspondent was a rather odd and complicated way of making a living for a man, what was it like being a woman? Many of the women correspondents I knew were faced with difficult choices. Foreign correspondents assumed that wives would wait behind for them and tend a home and children. But could women correspondents depend on finding husbands who would hold still for the constant round of traveling? Several women correspondents I knew decided that they would have to cease traveling and remain in one place if they were going to take the time to find a husband and have a child. Often, the men whom women correspondents might meet and fall for were reporters themselves and there was the problem with home offices of reconciling where two professional foreign correspondents would base—should they decide to marry or live together. No, life as a correspondent was difficult for a woman—in or out of a war zone.

I did a piece on Oriana Fallaci whom I hadn't seen since Dak To, and in her heightened Latin style she told me over an espresso in the garden of the Hotel Continental, ''I hate this war blindly. It's not even tragic, just stupid. Any respect I might have had I lost at Dak To. I found all these American kids. One was looking for someone to talk to and saw me. His voice was high and soft like a lamb's. He was scared. A few hours later, I saw some American bodies. He was one of the bodies. When I got back to Saigon, I had an hysterical crisis. I am not a crier but I went into my room and cried until I thought I would die. Don't tell me about the flag. Don't tell me about the country. Don't tell me about honor and glory. I don't accept them. I am a woman. I know how difficult it is to put a human being on earth, and I know what it takes to keep that human being alive. I think about my little soldier, dying in a strange land. He did not want to be here.''

I showed La Fallaci a copy of my story on her and she replaced it in my box at the hotel with the endearing note: ''Tuohy. You are the only man who has never betrayed me.''

In May 1968, the Vietcong struck again in a new offensive, sometimes called the Second Tet. Again, they managed to get inside Saigon and hole up in the Cholon area where Vietnamese Army efforts to clean them out were fruitless at first. Among the victims in the first day of the fighting were four journalists who shared office space with me in the Reuters villa or next door at *Time*. The story of their death was related to me by Frank Palmos, a freelancer from Melbourne, Australia, the only one to escape.

Palmos; John Cantwell, of *Time;* Bruce Piggot, of Reuters; Ron Laramy, also of Reuters; and Michael Birch, of the Australian Associated Press, had been driving around in a Jeeplike, low-slung minimoke looking for action. They followed a helicopter gunship overhead that was making rocket attacks on a suspected Vietcong position in the heart of Cholon. ''I told the others we ought to stay on the big streets where it was safer,'' said Palmos, ''but they said to push ahead so we drove up a small alley that couldn't have been more than twelve feet wide.''

They continued up the alley though they saw the residents fleeing in the opposite direction. That was a sure formula for disaster. At the head of the alley, they saw a roadblock manned by VC. The young men in the open vehicle called out, *''Bao chi. Bao chi,''* the Vietnamese phrase for ''journalist.'' A tough-looking Vietcong officer pointed his .45 pistol at arm's length, snorted sarcastically, *''Bao chi!''* and fired two shots into one correspondent's head. Other VC opened up with automatic fire, leaving four dead in the vehicle. Palmos, sitting at the rear corner, fell out, played dead for a few moments until the firing stopped, and then ran for dear life down the alley, weaving and ducking until he got around a corner. He managed to lose himself in the fleeing crowd.

To me, the pointless deaths seemed a classic case of a group of young men in a war zone, without proper experience but who nevertheless wanted to be thought macho. Probably all of them were apprehensive yet no one could come out and say the obvious: "That's it. We've gone far enough. Let's turn around and get the hell out of here."

The next day, I was with General Nguyen Ngoc Loan, the South Vietnamese police chief, whose photograph shooting the Vietcong suspect was indelibly etched on the world's consciousness by Eddie Adams at the time of the Tet Offensive. Now, Loan was leading his men against a building occupied by Vietcong and took a bad hit in the leg. With me was Pat Burgess, a giant of an Australian reporter, who gathered Loan up in his arms and rushed him to an ambulance that had been summoned. I know that for years General Loan was the symbol everyone against the war loved to hate, but he was loyal to his men and fought alongside them. That was more than you could say about a lot of officers. As Adams has pointed out, the Vietcong lieutenant who was shot by Loan had just murdered a South Vietnamese police major—one of Loan's best friends—and his whole family.

"Everyone condemns Loan for shooting this guy," said Eddie, "but if you were General Loan and there was a war going on and your people were getting killed, how do you know you wouldn't shoot him, too? I just happened to be there."

The government had a difficult time rooting out the Vietcong in May, and every day we'd pick a new location to follow the war, almost on our back doorstep, so to speak. The Vietcong hoisted a flag over the Y-Bridge, so-called because it split into two sections halfway over the canal marking the southern boundary of Cholon. As we approached the bridge, an Arvin soldier warned, "VC—*beaucoup* VC." Gunfire rattled through the area. Rocket-laden helicopters let loose their explosives a few blocks away, and the racket filled the streets. But the soldiers were taking their time in their house-to-house advance. They had been through this before and were in no hurry to mount a massive assault, which they might not survive. So we'd hang around the Y-Bridge for a while, perhaps talking to an English- or French-speaking officer to get some idea of what was going on and then drive back to the Continental, where life went on for what passed as normal in Saigon.

One morning, Horst Faas, Jurate Kazickas, Donald Wise of London's *Daily Mirror,* and I joined the Vietnamese Marines for an operation in the Saigon suburb of Gia Dinh. Don, by the way, while

covering the 1967 Arab-Israeli war, received a cable from his editor
pointing out: "You privileged to report history," which, when you
think of it, is not a bad way to describe what our calling is all about.
Once he received a query from his editor demanding "How you spend
three hundred pounds in less than three days?" Don cabled back: "I
give up, how?"

The operation was to use tear gas to winkle out the Vietcong holed
up in houses. It turned out to be something of a Keystone Kops comedy. First, we boarded three big army trucks at the battered Caltex gas
station that served as a command post. But then we hung around
waiting for a half hour, during which any well-placed enemy mortar
shell could have wiped out the whole marine force. Eventually, the
convoy moved up the street toward barricades behind which were
believed to be enemy troops hiding in houses. As the trucks rumbled
along, the marines ripped open the cardboard canisters to extract the
tear gas grenades. Some impatiently used their bayonets to dig out the
grenades.

"Not that way, you bloody idiots," yelled Don Wise, who had
been a paratroop major and knew a thing or two about military gear.
But the marines kept digging and, sure enough, a grenade exploded
with a loud pop sending a spray of tear-gas powder and fumes through
the open truck.

"Good Lord," gasped Donald, "he's done it."

Unaware, the driver kept speeding along while we and the two
dozen marines coughed and choked, unable to don gas masks because
of the press of bodies. After much yelling and shouting, the driver somehow got the message and halted the truck. We all tumbled out, gasping
for breath, eyes streaming, throats raw, and lungs starved for air. Up
ahead, a couple of marines in the forward trucks had pulled the same stunt
and their trucks were stopped, too. So instead of a crack marine company
going into action with a supposedly effective device, dozens of troops
lined the street crying and coughing. The operation was held up for another half hour while the marines pulled themselves together.

"I suppose we can be thankful that wasn't a fragmentation grenade," said Wise sourly.

Finally, we walked through the backyards of middle-class housing, lined with orchards and foliage. The marines moved cautiously
but quickly, firing short bursts. Alongside the road lay two dead
Vietcong, one a young body who had been placed on a litter with a
previous wound when hit.

"I think the tear gas has driven away the VC," said the company commander, Captain Nguyen Van Pham. "I don't think we have much trouble today."

Up the street, a pretty girl of about twelve was selling lemon juice and coconut milk. As we ordered a round, two dump trucks drove past filled with the lime-dusted bodies of enemy soldiers who had been found in a mass grave by another Marine company. As the stench spread over the soft-drink stand, a little boy wrinkled his nose, and the girl matter-of-factly dabbed her nose with a touch of cheap perfume.

In the evening, having written a story, I'd sometimes go to the roof of the Caravelle Hotel for a drink. From there, you could see the action in the Saigon suburbs from another perspective. Drinks were served by a white-jacketed waiter, miniskirts were adjusted, and binoculars readied as the jets roared in.

"It's showtime," cracked a television man in the burnt-orange dusk ten stories above the city.

"Here they come," said a blond, miniskirted American secretary to her boyfriend.

Two droop-nosed F-4 Phantoms screamed over the city and dived steeply—down, down—then pulled out. A great flash erupted where the bomb hit the target areas, presumably Vietcong concentrations. The television man timed the interval between the flash and the sound.

Ten seconds—or about two miles away. A second jet bored in, skimming the rooftops, and an explosive fragment from a bomb skyrocketed into the sky. They were bombing the hell out of that location, whatever it was. A block away, on the rooftop of the Rex Officers Billet, customers at the nightly cookout enjoyed the brilliant tropical evening colors, as well as the deadly spectacle. The crowd at the Caravelle—journalists, government people, officers—exchanged pleasantries and the latest information on the fighting around the outskirts. The talk was more up-to-date than the 5:00 P.M. military briefing.

"Did you hear that a short artillery round killed four U.S. soldiers and wounded a dozen others?" asked someone.

"Yes, I was there. Spent the afternoon on my stomach with my face in the mud. Hardly had time for a shower."

After the nightly performance, when the jets had whined off in the distance, a pretty French girl exclaimed, "Those bombs, some show. *Pas mal,* not bad. Those Americans are really something. Incredible."

I attended the farewell news conference of General Westmoreland in June 1968. At fifty-four, he still looked the very model of a soldier in crisp green combat fatigues, his iron-gray hair neatly brushed back. I asked him whether he thought the war "at this stage can be won militarily." "Not in a classic sense because of our national policy of not expanding the war," he replied, adding that "our national policy is not to extend the ground war beyond the territory of South Vietnam." Then the general, who rankled under the restraints of fighting an enemy that, in his view, had a free hand in moving troops through Laos and Cambodia, summed up: "The enemy can be attrited. The price can be raised and it is being raised to the point where it could be intolerable to the enemy. It may reach a point where it is a question of destroying his country and jeopardizing the future of his country if he continues to pay the price."

It seemed to me that it was Westy's view—later taken up by the so-called revisionist historians—that if the military had a free hand to bomb Hanoi or invade the north, the United States would have been the victors in Vietnam. I doubted that argument: It would have meant a long occupation of North Vietnam, an unacceptable prospect for the American people and military. Westy, I was told by his close friends, had wanted to leave Saigon for the job of Army Chief of Staff on a successful note but the winter-spring offensive and the worldwide headlines it produced dashed any hopes of the four-star general leaving as a conquering hero.

Saigon had its pleasant interludes. One Saturday morning, I attended a wedding. It was a day that a citywide, emergency alert drill had tied up all traffic, security guards surrounded the chapel, and a monsoon rain cascaded down like a broken water main. Still, at 10:30 A.M. at St. Christopher's Church, a touch of rural England in southeast Asia, Helen Bowen, a pretty British embassy employee was married to David Kenney, a handsome young U.S. foreign service officer. The security guards were around to ensure the safety of the U.S. ambassador, Ellsworth Bunker, and his deputy, Samuel Berger. The ceremony went off without a hitch.

The Anglican prelate who performed the ceremony mentioned that weddings among Westerners were rare in Saigon but he added that any two principals who had experienced the ordeals of Miss Bowen, who hid for five days from the Vietcong in Hue during the attack, and Kenney, who had spent considerable time in the provinces during his two years, ought to be able to handle marriage successfully.

The prelate suggested that when one was shelled by 122-mm rockets, one's thoughts ought to turn toward one's maker—and he said he hoped to see many of the guests at the Saturday wedding at the regular Sunday-morning service for the British community of a couple hundred diplomats and businessmen the next day. He pointedly indicated that many of the Saturday guests were not among his Sunday regulars.

The British ambassador gave the bride away, and afterward at the reception at his residence, the U.S. deputy ambassador, Robert M. Komer, the pacification chief, remarked to me, "My God, what's happened this weekend in the countryside? Half our senior advisers are here."

"It was all very charming, didn't you think?" said a longtime resident as the couple rolled away. "It almost made Saigon seem human again. A jolly good show."

However, like the upbeat stories in Vietnam, this one had its downbeat side. On the flight to Hong Kong, Helen left her new wedding ring, a family heirloom, on the wash basin of the lavatory. Not being used to wearing it, she only remembered it later and by the time she got back to the lavatory, it was gone.

During my time in Vietnam, I'd sometimes run into mysterious types in the field, usually wearing white, short-sleeved shirts with ties. Characteristically, they'd respond to introductions with a tight-lipped "John Smith, embassy." These were the field men of the Central Intelligence Agency, or as they were more familiarly known, spooks. For in Vietnam, the CIA appeared to be almost ubiquitous. The agency was involved in a variety of so-called open activities not generally associated with the classic secret missions of the CIA. As the United States became more deeply involved in fighting the war in Vietnam, the spooks were asked to perform a growing number of overt tasks, such as training the Vietnamese revolutionary development teams, helping establish the Operation Phoenix counterterror assassination teams, advising at the National Interrogation Center, and providing the funds and training for some of the montagnard tribal troops.

"We were given these assignments because there was simply no one else and we had the money," one CIA officer told me.

And a senior government official added, "The CIA performs better than any other civilian agency in Vietnam. They have better guys and a smaller operation with relatively flexible procedures—so they can zero in on a problem without being hampered by a huge bureaucratic framework.''

The CIA was particularly involved in the revolutionary development and pacification programs. Thus, a CIA man might be a regional director or senior province adviser, doing the same job as a foreign service officer, an Army lieutenant colonel, or an Agency for International Development (AID) man—all of whom served as provincial advisers in the pacification program. The CIA at first didn't want to get into revolutionary development—training the teams that then spread out around the country helping the peasants.

"But President Johnson knew that if you wanted to get a job done, you got the agency to do it," an embassy official told me. After that, the CIA's "paras," paramilitary types, began arriving in Vietnam to work in the programs, many on a contract basis, and many ex-military officers.

"I began running into guys I hadn't seen since China, Burma, and the Chinese offshore islands," remarked one old Asian CIA hand.

Eventually, the program was turned over to an "open" agency, namely the U.S. military. The Saigon CIA station chief, whose office was in the embassy, told me privately, "I think this is a good thing for us. If the agency is going to survive, it has to limit itself to collecting intelligence and conducting clandestine operations—small, high-caliber, short-term, high-concentration efforts with a minimum of visibility. The RD program was not this kind of thing."

For a long period, the CIA was involved in SOG, the Special Operations Group, American officers who inserted Vietnamese spy teams in North Vietnam, which was among the more dangerous jobs in the country. I knew an Army major who had been seconded to the CIA for this job, and a brilliant operator he was. He had served in Korea and Vietnam before joining the CIA and was heavily decorated. After one harrowing mission, in which he was dropped into the jungle at the end of a rescue helicopter's cable to pick up a wounded member of one of these patrols, he was recommended for a Silver Star.

"I've already got a couple of those," he said. "I'll take a DFC [the Distinguished Flying Cross, and a slightly lesser medal] instead. It'll look good with the fruit salad on the uniform."

The spooks were highly suspicious of outsiders but they weren't hard to recognize in the field. As one CIA man explained over a beer: "There are forty-four provinces in Vietnam, and there are only a handful of foreign service officers in the political section of the embassy. So the U.S. grass-roots reporting comes from the agency because there isn't anybody else out there in the grass. When you meet a lone American in the boonies, you can usually bet he's one of us.''

And another insider told me, ''The spooks are less naïve and more cynical than the foreign service officers. They tend to assume that nothing is permanent, that people shift sides, that few idealists hang on to their beliefs when the going gets rough. The trouble is that like the rest of the American establishment, they are Europe-oriented and they tend to impose Western solutions on an Eastern society.''

In Saigon, I learned, the agency had its own warehouse filled with sophisticated weapons and other gadgets. It had its own clinic staffed with a doctor and three nurses. It ran its own airline, Air America, which also served as a contract carrier for AID. The spooks tended to live together in new apartment blocks or compounds, keeping to themselves professionally and socially, aloof from outsiders.

''There's no particular mystique about us,'' one CIA officer told me. ''We have the same problems everyone else does. We worry about our families at home, paying the mortgage on the house, getting our kids through school. Our divorce rate is high. One officer on his second tour of duty here, who liked the work and would have extended if possible, was told by his wife that he better get home after this hitch was up, if he still wanted a home—and a wife.''

Over the years, I had tried to maintain cordial personal relations with the U.S. information minister, Barry Zorthian, as well as with the chief military spokesman, Brigadier General Winant Sidle. After more than four years in Saigon handling—or manipulating, as some might say—the media, Zorthian departed. We had a long, friendly farewell chat, and Barry opened up in a way he rarely did in public.

Slouched in a leather armchair in his office, digging into a pack of cigarettes, he reflected: ''The U.S. government has made its share of mistakes in dealing with the press, and the press has made its share of mistakes. And somehow we have not succeeded in communicating the nature of this war to the American people. I suppose this is partly because of the nature of this war. There was no sudden, dramatic enemy crossing of the frontier as in Korea. And it is partly because of the gradual way we became involved here, bit by bit. In past wars, American public opinion was favorably formed before the impact of the war hit home. Here, the ghastliness of the war hit before American public opinion was formed. And the most prominent aspects communicated have been the deaths, the civilian casualties, the impact on the Vietnamese. It is more difficult to communicate the imperatives—aiding an ally, stopping the spread of Communism on a vital area, repulsing aggression—for our being here, the reasons why we are going through this hell."

Barry stared pensively across the room in which he had held hundreds of briefings, and continued, "The press has certainly covered the facts in this war. But the great differences come in making judgments about those facts. We have never agreed on the significance of those facts. I sometimes think we ought to train every senior government official or general in dealing with the media. Too many officials believe the press is something to be avoided at all costs. Well, you just can't do that in the modern world. Nor should you. The media today are so omnipresent, so absorbing, the public gets to know about foreign affairs almost instantly. Thus, people can form opinions which have an impact on the government. The government can no longer tell its people that, in the field of foreign affairs, we know best."

I asked Zorthian about the problem of censorship, and his answer pretty much squared with what I had observed. "I don't think censorship would work, and even if it did, I don't think censorship is a good thing in the modern world."

Barry was philosophical about the press, whom he often saw as his adversaries.

"There are not really any villains in the press here," he said. "By and large, the press has been conscientious and has exercised responsibility. But they are faced with pressures built into the system: deadlines, the needs of editors, and so forth. So the press could do with some self-examination, too. But the government has got to be credible and be realistic. Our system of government is based on mutual trust and good faith, and if the people don't believe what the government tells them, then we as a nation are in real trouble."

I, too, was nearing the end of my tour in Vietnam. But toward the end of 1968, I learned of an appalling story. A squad of U.S. Marines had cold-bloodedly killed five Vietnamese civilians in a hamlet near Hue. This had occurred in May 1968, after the Mylai massacre, but the incident came to light before the U.S. Army episode at Mylai did.

I flew to Da Nang where I found that the seven Marines charged with the murders were undergoing separate courts-martial, for what then was regarded as the worst U.S. atrocity in Vietnam. The crime was being quietly but widely discussed among the Marines and elicited, I found, quite different responses.

"It is the worst thing I have heard about in Vietnam," a Marine captain told me.

But a lance corporal in the same company differed. "I know those guys," he said. "They're okay and I hope they beat this rap."

The seven defendants were members of the 3rd Platoon, A Company, 1st Battalion, 27th Regiment, 1st Marine Division. They were operating near Van Duong bridge in the hamlet of Xuan Hoa in the war-battered rice fields a mile and a half east of Hue. On the May 5, at 4:30 P.M., the patrol leader, Lance Corporal Denzil Allen, a tall, skinny twenty-year-old who came from Lebanon, Indiana, was ordered to take six men and set up an ambush three hundred yards away from the platoon base at the bridge. The area was heavy with Vietcong: The day before a Marine had been killed by a guerrilla sniper.

En route to the ambush site, the patrol picked up two unarmed civilians, fifty-year-old Nguyen Cuu Phu and Nguyen Van Den, fifty-three. Corporal Allen questioned them—though it was not clear how he thought he could communicate—and decided they did not have proper identity papers. Corporal Allen and Private First Class Martin R. Alvarez, Jr., also twenty and a talkative Detroiter, led the two Vietnamese behind a house, stood them in front of a ditch, raised their M-16 rifles, counted to three, and shot them. The two Vietnamese showed signs of life. Allen and Alvarez fired again. They dumped the two bodies in the ditch and covered them with straw. Returning to the patrol, Allen said, "You didn't see nothing."

That night, back at the patrol base, the fifteen Marines were hit hard by a North Vietnamese Army attack. The sergeant in command was notable for his "unexplained absence," the military term for abandoning his post.

Corporal Allen took over command. He was a natural leader, a man other soldiers followed. He deployed the Marines in bunkers and trenches and then called in artillery on the position to blunt the attack. After hard fighting, the enemy was repulsed. No Marine was killed. Allen's cool resourcefulness under fire earned him high praise from his company commander, who said he was going to recommend the lance corporal for the Navy Cross, the next highest decoration to the Congressional Medal of Honor.

At first light the next morning, a nearby platoon sent out a patrol to reinforce the men at the Van Duong bridge and picked up three

Vietnamese civilians: Huynh Van Phuc, thirty-two, Ho Cam, forty-three, and Ho Lau, sixty-five. As the Marines reached the base, someone ominously was heard to remark, "You should not have brought these people here."

Corporal Allen, now the man in actual command, questioned the Vietnamese, and, according to the report, "somehow developed the idea that two of the prisoners should be put to death by firing squad." Allen led the civilians to the bridge, lined up Phuc and Lau along the edge of the canal, arranged the squad in a semicircle, and counted to three. The firing squad shot the Vietnamese, who fell into the canal. One victim appeared to be alive and a Marine tossed in a grenade to sink the bodies.

Then Allen and Lance Corporal John D. Belknap, a blond, strapping twenty-one-year-old who grew up in Forsyth, Georgia, took the remaining Vietnamese, Ho Cam, to a small house. They bound his hands and stood him on a chair. Allen fashioned a noose of white nylon and looped it around Cam's neck. The other end was tossed over a beam.

Belknap kicked the chair out from under Cam, and he dropped gagging, his feet just touching the floor. Allen kicked Cam in the groin. Belknap kicked him in the chest. A thin, twenty-year-old lance corporal named Anthony Licciardo, Jr., from Lowell, Massachusetts, kicked him again. This was done, Belknap said, to cause Cam to die quickly. But Cam remained alive. Licciardo hit him on the head with a sandbag. The rope broke and Cam fell to the floor. Allen pulled out a bowie knife, stabbed Cam in the chest, and slit his throat. Allen and Licciardo carried the body to the canal and threw it in.

When the patrol returned to the base, one member informed the platoon leader of the incident at Van Duong bridge and an official investigation began. Marine examiners later said two of the five victims were on the local blacklist as Vietcong agents, the third was a brother, the fourth a cousin, and the fifth a friend of one of the men on the blacklist.

Since the trials were still going on and the appeals yet to come, the defendants and those already convicted were instructed not to discuss the case. So I sought out Captain Sandy McMath, a twenty-six-year-old Marine lawyer and son of former Arkansas governor Sid McMath, who defended Corporal Allen. He told me that Allen had pleaded guilty but that he had had a growing history of aberrant behavior. McMath believed that under ordinary circumstances he could plead Allen not guilty by reason of insanity but that such a plea did not carry much weight in Vietnam.

"The reaction among Marine courts," he said, "tends to be, we all go through mental stresses and strains here. Sorry about that." So Allen was sentenced to twenty years' hard labor.

In his defense of Lance Corporal Denzil Allen, the man the other Marines looked up to because though he was only twenty he was a second-tour veteran, Captain McMath cited questions raised by Allen's brother back in Lebanon, Indiana.

"Isn't it ironic," asked Joe Allen, "that an immature young man—not old enough to vote, or legally take a drink or get married or buy a car without parental consent—isn't it ironic that we train such a boy as a killer and then hold him strictly accountable and demand exaction for a mistake made when making the gravest decision of all: taking a human life?"

I discussed the case with officers and enlisted men and found a wide range of reaction, as might be expected among men fighting in a puzzling and frustrating war.

A major told me, "You expect unspeakable atrocities from the Vietcong but not from Marines. There are thousands and thousands of Marines who have served thirteen-month combat tours in Vietnam without killing civilians."

But a lieutenant was more ambivalent. "I think they ought to go to jail," he said. "But if I was one of the guys with the unit, I might say, 'What the hell!' "

And at the lower ranks, the attitude toward the defendants was more sympathetic.

"Those guys aren't cold-blooded killers," said a corporal who knew them. "They had been in a hairy fight the night before. The VC don't give us any slack. So why should we give them any? The gooks were on the blacklist so that's not murder. The Marines thought they were justified. Shit, we're in a war, ain't we?"

I spoke to Navy Lieutenant Lawrence Richards, psychiatrist for the 1st Marine Division, who examined some of the men, and he said that Corporal Allen as acting squad leader would appear to be the motivating force. He pointed out that the role of squad leader in Vietnam has been found to be the most stress-prone in combat because of the heavy responsibility for the lives of the men in an eight- or twelve-man squad, a responsibility that was even heavier when shouldered by a relatively young and inexperienced soldier.

"Why they did it is one of the imponderables," said Lieutenant Richards. "My suspicion is that there was some sort of group process that occurred. But we don't know about it at this time."

And so the explanation for the events at Van Duong bridge eluded me as they did the experts, and probably even the men themselves. What *was* clear, though, was the cruel fact demonstrated once again that war brutalizes. And as for Lance Corporal Denzil Allen—leader, hero, murderer—an officer who studied the case said simply, "The Marine Corps created a killer. There came a time when the stress was such that they couldn't control him. And now they have to lock him up."

Afterward in Saigon, I thought about the case and came to the conclusion that one of the defendants had been badly treated, that a serious miscarriage of justice occurred at his court-martial in Da Nang. Private First Class Robert J. Vickers, a tall, black, angular, pleasant-mannered Marine who was born in Dothan, Alabama, and had been a truck driver in civilian life, was the only one of the accused to plead not guilty. Most of the other Marines who admitted their guilt received sentences as light as two years' imprisonment. They plea-bargained with the government and charges were reduced from premeditated to unpremeditated murder.

But Vickers was forced to stand trial on a charge of premeditated murder, and though the evidence against him was circumstantial, he was found guilty by a six-member court-martial and given a mandatory life sentence. I thought that the severe sentence given Vickers, compared to those of the other Marines involved, cast a harsh and unfavorable glare on the quality of Marine justice in Vietnam. So I flew back to Da Nang to see Vickers at the Marine brig there.

Vickers told me he was part of the patrol that picked up the three Vietnamese on the morning of May 6.

"We entered the patrol base with three suspects," he said in a small interview room. "The VC tried to overrun the base the night before, setting off satchel charges, and I wanted to see what they had done to a bunker. I was talking to another Marine about explosives and all of a sudden I heard somebody say, 'Let's shoot 'em,' or something like that. I turned around and saw two Vietnamese men at the end of the bridge with a group of Marines. I started walking toward them and when I got four or five feet from them, one Marine said, 'One, two, three; ready, aim fire,' and the rounds went off. I walked off to the edge of the bridge and saw them lying in the water."

Vickers told me, as he had the court, that he did not fire his M-16, which he carried slung through his ammunition bandolier in a "ready" position. "I was actually behind most of the others. If I had fired, I would have hit some of the Marines standing in front of me."

"I didn't believe it would be done. It just happened so fast. I didn't know exactly what was happening. I just wanted to know what it was all about. I had no idea I would be charged with anything because I hadn't done anything. If I had done something, I would have admitted it like my fellow Marines did."

The main weakness in Vickers's case appeared to be that when initially questioned by investigators, he denied taking part in the incident or knowing who did.

"I didn't want to testify against my fellow Marines," he told me. "The investigator wouldn't say what the charges were. I said I hadn't seen anything. The investigator told me he would get us—and he did."

Vickers's lawyer, Navy lieutenant William J. Cosgriff, who had practiced in St. Paul, Minnesota, said bluntly, "Vickers's only crime was curiosity."

In the brig, Vickers was a model prisoner and during a riot in August he had helped calm down rampaging prisoners and was promoted to trusty—even though he might be expected to show nothing but bitterness over his fate at the hands of Marine justice.

"I was old enough to know what I was getting into when I joined the Marine Corps," he told me. "I always tried to do what I was told the best way I could. I came into the Corps to try to do a good job. But I just don't think the treatment I got was right. If all courts-martial here were like mine, something is wrong. Now, I wouldn't want to go back to duty. I liked the Marine Corps and in a sense I still do."

I wrote a long story about the Vickers case, which appeared on the front page of the *Los Angeles Times* and was widely used by the L.A. Times-Washington Post News Service. I learned later that readers in several cities contacted congressmen to protest Vickers's conviction. The Marine Corps subsequently freed Vickers of all charges.

But now my time was getting short. I was about to shift to Beirut to cover the Arab world and be reunited with my wife and child. I was eager to go but found myself unexpectedly sad about leaving that torn and lovely country. And so there'd be no more hanging around dusty airfields waiting for rides to dicey places with strange names. No more cold C rations or hot landing zones. No more wondering in gyrating helicopters, what am I doing here?

I would leave behind, rapidly fading, what had once been household names to me: DMZ, Hueys, AKs, Dong Ha, the Delta, dustoff, LZs, Rolling Thunder, My Tho, Tiger Switch, the Parrot's Beak, napalm, KIAs, WIAs, MIAs, Agent Orange, the Rockpile, Marble Mountain, Khe Sanh, Yankee Station, the Y-Bridge, Arclight, Tan Son Nhut.

After four years, I had found no certainties, no conclusive answers about the war. There were plenty of advocacy reporters among the press corps but I wasn't one of them.

I had come to Vietnam admiring the Kennedy generation of public servants, the McNamaras, Rusks, Bundys, and the new breed of geopolitical generals and admirals. I left Vietnam believing most Cabinet wizards I met shortsighted and misguided. I found admirals who hadn't done their homework; generals determined to fight World War II. I would not automatically trust their kind again.

I had tried to be accurate and fair; I may well have failed. Morally, I did not condemn the American involvement. Indeed, if President Johnson had somehow been able to win the conflict in 1966 or 1967, I thought, there would have been little concern with the "morality" of the war. I did not subscribe to the view that the media somehow "lost" the war by negative reporting. It was lost, I became convinced, because Americans are an impatient people and are incapable of waging large protracted wars without a clear and clarion sense of national prupose.

I was once chatting with a Vietnamese girl in a bar on Tu-Do Street, and she asked me if I'd be returning after dinner. I said maybe.

"I don't like maybe," she said. "I like sure."

Ah, yes, don't we all? But I found no surety in Vietnam. It was full of maybes.

On my last day in Saigon, I lunched with Peter Arnett and Horst Faas. We did not talk of fallen comrades but rather how best to invest whatever money we had saved from our salaries. On my last night, I went to dinner at Keyes Beech's house with GeeGee Geyer and Charley Mohr. Later, I had planned to drop by the bar next to the Continental to say good-bye to my friend Linh. She was the cashier. She was comely, a widow. Her husband had been a lieutenant colonel who was killed in a battle in Tay Ninh Province a couple of years before. Occasionally, she'd come to my room in the hotel after work. She was cool and undemanding and knew that one day I would leave.

At Keyes's, we got into the usual argument about the morality and conduct of the war. We drank a lot of whiskey. By the time I got back to Linh's bar, it was closed and she was gone. I rose early the next morning with a headache and took a taxi to Tan Son Nhut airport. From the car, I thought I saw Linh standing on the side of the main road waiting for a pedicab but I wasn't sure. I didn't stop—and the car was soon caught up in the crush of traffic and it was too late. On the plane, I thought I should have stopped.

A few weeks later, I was passing through New York on home leave when I got a call from Dick Dougherty, our New York bureau chief.

"I've got good news for you, Bill," he said, "but keep it quiet until Monday when the announcement is made. You're getting the Pulitzer Prize for International Reporting. For Vietnam."

CHAPTER SIX

Across the River Jordan

I HAD THOUGHT the Vietnam story was all-absorbing—and it was. Many of my colleagues never got the experience out of their systems. They were obsessed with Vietnam and it darkly colored their futures. But if Vietnam was central to the American consciousness in 1968, I soon found that the Middle East appeared to be more central to the fate of the world. As a story, it had everything: oil, politics, religion, the Arab-Israeli conflict, the superpower involvement and the rise of Palestinian nationalism. Further, the backdrop was the birthplace of Western civilization: the Holy Land, Mesopotamia, the Nile Valley. The Arab world, which I was assigned to cover from Beirut, stretched four thousand miles from Marrakesh to Muscat with 120 million people and fourteen separate countries. The world of Islam was even broader. And Israel, Cyprus, and Turkey were all less than an hour's flight from Beirut.

Two days after I arrived in Beirut to live, Israeli commandos raided the airport south of town, leaving fourteen jet airliners smoking ruins. The attack was in retaliation for a Palestinian assault on an El Al jetliner at Athens airport a few days before. The world was beginning to ask the questions: Who are the Palestinians? What do they want? I tried to find out.

Beirut was then the center for Palestinian political activity, though when I got there, it was still known as the Paris of the Middle East with a strong Gallic influence stemming from the French mandate period between world wars. It was a lively, raffish town, part Western, part Oriental, full of diplomats, spies, political exiles, journalists, and maneuverers of every sort. Even then, Beirut seemed ripe for revolution. The rich lived in luxury apartments or mountain villas, and believed in a conspicuous display of wealth. The poor sheltered in hovels as depressing as any Calcutta slum. The economic class barrier was reinforced by religion and politics: The Christians tended to be richer and more conservative; the Muslims, poorer and more radical. Despite the growing internal tensions, Beirut danced until dawn at discos like the Caves du Roi and the city was a stimulating place from which to cover the Arab world. But the life could be difficult for the wives of correspondents; the men would often dash off at the last minute to catch planes for Amman, Cairo, or the Gulf, leaving the women behind to grapple with the mundane chores of running a household or serving a dinner without the host. Beirut, as I was to learn personally, was something of a graveyard for marriages among the foreign community.

In coming to the Middle East, I had little background in the intricacies of the political situation. I had grown up in a Chicago neighborhood of Catholics, mostly Irish Americans, and Jews. One way or another I had probably acquired the Israeli or Zionist view of the Middle East: that Israel was a plucky little David, a nation of settlers returning to their rightful land, who had fought a war for independence against avenging Arab nations. They made the desert bloom and solidified that birthright with the stunning victory in the 1967 Six-Day War. I had heard of the Palestinians but was only vaguely aware of their role in Middle Eastern affairs. I don't think I had any anti-Semitic leanings; in fact, I rather admired the Israelis for their energy and military prowess; and was mildly scornful of the Arabs for their inability to run anything properly. So I accepted what was pretty much the U.S. stereotype of the Arab-Israeli conflict.

To learn something about the Palestinians, I first sought out intellectuals in Beirut who, of course, had been living with the problem for a generation. I found Professor Walid Khalidi, the distinguished historian, in his small office on the cypress-lined campus of the American University in Beirut. Khalidi was a small, compact man in his fifties with graying hair who had taught at the university for twenty years. He had studied in England and spoke with an impeccable

Oxbridge accent that seemed to match his well-tailored tweed jacket. He quickly sketched a thumbnail history of the Palestinians.

Palestine, the original Holy Land, had been part of the Turkish Ottoman Empire after the Muslim conquest until after World War I, when it was placed under British mandate. Following the war, the Zionist influx swelled, shifting the demographic balance in Palestine, and in 1948, the United Nations partitioned the country into Jewish and Arab sectors. The Arabs went to war, but lost and Israel conquered 40 percent more territory. Meanwhile, the Hashemite Kingdom annexed the West Bank of the Jordan and Egypt took the Gaza Strip. The first Palestinian exodus began, which was intensified by the 1967 war.

Khalidi blamed the West, particularly the British and the American governments, for the condition of the Palestinians. "The capacity of the Western mind to see the Arab-Israeli situation in purely Zionist terms is unlimited," he said in a voice that seemed to alternate between anger and despair. "Americans appear dazzled by Zionist propaganda. Our own rhetoric at times has been moronic, for home consumption, giving the Israelis the chance to say, 'See what they mean to do to us!' We are where the Zionists claimed to be at the start of their movement."

Then, the professor, in a voice ringing with emotion, said to me, "What an irony! We Palestinians have become the Jews of the Arab world."

He pointed to a spot on a detailed map of Jerusalem on the wall behind his desk and, looking first at me and then the map, said, "That is my house. Right there. I was born there. I want to live there, where my people lived for hundreds of years. But I am not allowed to go there, though Jews from Europe, or anyplace else, can. My people are accused of being aggressors. Who are the aggressors? How do I prove to the Israelis that my home is my home? It is a fantastic dilemma— a Kafkaesque nightmare!"

He got up from behind his desk and walked around behind my own chair, as if to give drama to his next point. "We are all on a tightrope. We thought we had a safety net in the West Bank with access to Jerusalem—which means so much to us. Now there is no safety net—there is nowhere in the world we can go and call home. But if the Zionists concede us the same premises of their own cause, returning to a homeland, they should expect us to continue to fight to regain our country."

A few blocks away in Beirut, I called on an editor at a Palestinian research institution in an old arabesque building filled with musty files. His desk was piled high with papers. He pushed his spectacles high on his forehead and offered me mazbout, sweet Turkish coffee in a tiny cup.

"We have switched positions with the Jews," he explained. "We are members of a Palestinian diaspora. But if the Jews never forgot Palestine after two thousand years, why should we forget our homeland after only twenty years."

The editor like other educated Palestinians I met pointed to the similarities between Palestinian Arabs and Jews. "We both sprang from the same soil," he said. "We both tend to be energetic and educated and we both have a deep sense of living in exile—often unwelcome guests in foreign countries.

"But since the 1967 war, Palestinians have taken matters into their own hands and developed a prestige and dignity among Arab nations they never had before. The word 'Palestinian' is being brought home to the world."

I then set out for the ramshackle Palestinian refugee camps in Lebanon, Syria, and Jordan, the fertile breeding grounds for young Palestinian terrorists who believe violence will win them back their ancestral homes in Haifa, Jaffa, and Jerusalem. They dreamed of olive trees and orange groves as they sat in grim huts on muddy lanes, encouraged in this mind-set by their elders.

In Jaramana, Syria, I found an eleven-year-old girl with soft brown eyes, dark curls, and a ragged dress who explained, "I'm from Haifa. I hope I will go back. My mother tells me that Palestine is my land, and we have a very beautiful home if Haifa."

Like many of the thousands of refugees, the girl's parents viewed their depressing surroundings as a temporary inconvenience, referring to themselves as *al-aidunn,* meaning "those who are going back." And they still have in their memories the imprint of ancestral villages, though their families may not actually have lived there for three generations.

At the time, many of the Palestinian leaders preferred to live in tents rather than UN-supplied prefab huts, because, as one put it, "We don't like to live in huts. They make you feel at home. Tents make you feel you are going back to your country." A Palestinian who was interpreting for me told me privately, "I, too, come from Haifa. I have been a refugee since 1949. Realistically, I don't think I am going back to Haifa. But I want my children to think so. Therefore, we always behave as if we were leaving for Haifa tomorrow."

In Amman, the hilly capital of Jordan, I made contact with leaders of Al-Fatah, the major Palestinian resistance organization. It was done through intermediaries: I'd send word through a contact that I was in town and wished to see one of the top people. Then, that evening or the following night, a bearded Palestinian wearing a kaffiyeh would come by the Hotel Intercontinental to take me to a stone house for a chat with one of the Fatah hierarchy. One night about midnight after many cups of tea, a senior Fatah chieftain told me bluntly, "Our strategy is to liberate the whole land of Palestine by means of an armed struggle. Our aim is to get rid of a state called Israel and reconstruct a Palestinian state with self-determination among those who live there—with equal rights for Arabs, Jews, and Christians. Our revolution will carry on this fight. The Israelis are good fighters but they are as hammers against mosquitoes, our guerrillas. We are stateless, homeless, landless. We have not got anything to lose. This is a generational war—and history is with us."

This was an overriding theme I would encounter over the years: a refusal to recognize that Israel was there to stay. The Palestinians I met were also loath to admit how riven their movement was by internal dissension.

For almost from the first, the Palestinian liberation movement became badly fragmented. Al-Fatah, under Yasir Arafat, was the largest and most active. In the context of militant Palestinian politics, Al-Fatah was the most moderate. The Popular Front for the Liberation of Palestine was led by a Christian physician, George Habash, and was much more militant and Marxist. There were even more radical offshoots like the Popular Democratic Front for the Liberation of Palestine, and a branch of this called the General Command. Further, Syria and Iraq had set up Palestinian organizations in their countries, whose leaders were fiercely anti-Israeli and pledged to oppose any peace settlement in the Middle East that would recognize the state of Israel. Often it seemed that the leaders of the various factions detested rival Palestinian leaders more than the Israelis they were nominally fighting. Thus, the meetings of the Palestine Liberation Organization, the PLO, were rent by quarrels and differences over tactics, strategy, and political goals.

Ranging outside of Amman, I rode up the stony hills west of the capital toward the Jordan River Valley to visit Palestinian guerrilla training camps. The first was a children's base, called an *ashbaal,* Arabic for "lion cub." There on a barren plain, two twelve-year-old boys stood at attention at the entrance, one carrying a Chinese-made submachine gun he seemed to have difficulty holding; the other wearing a bayonet strapped to his waist. Inside, about seventy-five youngsters in khaki jackets and pants were taught to march in ranks of four in close-order drill. They came from a nearby Palestinian refugee camp; they were between ten and fourteen, and were taught calisthenics, drill, tactics, political theory, and the handling of weapons. If they passed their courses, I was told, they were eligible to go to a "youth training center," after which at the age of eighteen they could become full-fledged commandos. The camp was operated by Al-Fatah, and an instructor told me, "We don't accept all the children who want to become Lion Cubs because we simply don't have the facilities to train them. Sons and relatives of other guerrillas have first priority."

Significantly, I thought, the boys were told they were members of a "Palestinian revolution" whose goal was to overthrow the state of Israel to enable the Palestinian refugees to return to their ancestral homes.

"We tell them that they are the new generation whose duty is to regain their homeland," said the instructor.

One young fellow who took the code name "Guevara" told me when I questioned him, "Our training is very difficult. We have to train in winter and summer no matter how hot or cold. We must win our Palestinian revolution."

Young Guevara, who looked short for his twelve years, said he was born in a refugee camp near Jerusalem and expected to return to where his parents lived in Jaffa. "Every person gets homesick for his country," he said. "Only in his own country can one live happily. We should not have to live in misery but with dignity in our country."

Later, Tom Ross, of the *Chicago Sun-Times,* and I were taken in the back of a covered vehicle to a secret Palestinian operational camp in the limestone cliffs and caves overlooking the Jordan Valley. The camp was named for Abdel Hamod, a graduate in petroleum engineering from Cairo University who, they said, was killed during a raid on the Israeli-occupied West Bank in 1968. The Al-Fatah invariably used the term *fedayeen*—"men who sacrifice"—to describe their front-line members. The Israelis called the fedayeen terrorists and we journalists, for want of a better term, mainly called them guerrillas or commandos. At the camp, Tom and I spoke to a solidly built physician who said he was thirty-five and identified himself simply as Dr. Mohammed. Most of the guerrillas used code names, including the Al-Fatah leader, Yasir Arafat, who took the nom de guerre, Abu Ammar. Similarly, most

Israeli leaders who fought the British during the mandate period in Palestine took coded nicknames—and are still so known to old friends.

"I am a doctor to Fatah," said Mohammed in excellent English, pulling aside the red-and-white checked kaffiyeh, the bedouin headdress popular with most guerrillas. "And this is my only practice."

I asked Dr. Mohammed about casualties and he said the losses were not 80 percent as sometimes claimed. "Our losses are light," he said, but he refused to estimate the number. But he added, "What is a revolution without sacrifice?"

He said the guerrillas were taught that "Zionism is an imperialistic movement supported by the United States and other Western powers."

I inquired whether the Fatah knew that 70 percent of the food provided at Palestinian refugee camps was funded by the United States.

"Everyone knows that seventy percent of the food at the camps comes from the people of the United States," he replied testily. "But at the same time the United States gives us food, it gives jets and weapons to Israel to kill us. That is a contradiction. A loaf of bread doesn't kill anybody but a bullet does."

The doctor said he joined a guerrilla raid across the Jordan in the Beitshan Valley, which feeds into the river from the Israeli side just south of the Sea of Galilee.

"You have no idea what it feels like to cross the Jordan River," the doctor continued, eating from a can of bully beef. "When you cross the river, you are going home, home, home. You feel that some day it is going to be yours. History flashes across your mind and then you concentrate again on the job."

Mohammed said his group's mission was to find a guerrilla captured by the Israelis and supposedly still held in an army outpost near the border. "We didn't find him," said the physician. "But we gave them something to remember. We blew their post sky-high. We didn't count how many Israeli soldiers were inside, but there must have been at least ten. We crossed the Jordan River again the same night. We suffered no casualties."

Fact or fiction? Who could know? Like Vietnam, a major problem in the Middle East was trying to assess any statements having to do with statistics, particularly those that were politically loaded. It served the guerrillas' interests to inflate any figure in order to show they had inflicted heavy casualties on the Israelis. I gained the impression that the guerrillas were not consciously or calculatingly lying. Rather, they deeply believed their own propaganda and statistics. There's a major strain of fantasy and wish-fulfillment in Arab thinking, I learned, and they saw the world as they thought it should be rather than as it was. The Israelis were not above lying to correspondents but it was done in a hardheaded, pragmatic way, seeking a specific end, rather than merely indulging in fantasy.

In 1969, the Palestinians moved armed troops into eastern and southern Lebanon from Jordan via Syria. I made several trips to the beautiful Bekáa Valley in eastern Lebanon to check the extent of this process and found sharp differences over their presence.

Late one night, Mike Kubic of *Newsweek* and I found a Palestinian unit that had penetrated into Lebanon despite disclaimers from the Fatah leadership. "We moved here to show the Lebanese government that they cannot force us out of Lebanon," the commander of a two-hundred-man unit told us. "The fight against Israel must be the fight of all Arabs, including the Lebanese. They can't stay neutral, as they would like. We don't want to harm the Lebanese civilians but we insist on our right to have free passage into South Lebanon to attack Israel and liberate our land."

That was a frank statement of Palestinian military intent; we got a much more candid view of what the guerrillas were really planning from their people in the field rather than the statements made by their leaders at high-level conferences.

But the Palestinian presence was resented by the Lebanese population because it drew fire from Israeli aircraft and army patrols. I drove to Rachaya, an old fortress town on the eastern side of the Bekáa guarding the routes from Syria into southern Lebanon. I found a senior Lebanese Army officer who, reflecting a widespread view, complained, "I don't like these Palestinian commandos. I don't understand why they are shooting at us, why they force us to shoot at them, why Arabs are killing Arabs. This is Lebanon. We are Lebanese. We would like to see our government in control."

A Lebanese official in Rachaya echoed the officer. "Why don't they fight the Israelis instead of us?" he asked. "Let them fight in Palestine, not in Lebanon where they are responsible for our villages being destroyed."

One afternoon in 1969, I heard the news flashed over the BBC that the Iraqis had just executed fourteen persons for treason, including nine Jews, and displayed their bodies in Baghdad's main square. I was with Tom Ross and we taxied to the Iraqi embassy to seek a hard-to-come-by visa. To our surprise, we were given entry documents on the spot. We each raced home to pack and managed to get the late flight from Beirut to Baghdad. We were the first American reporters to get into Baghdad since the 1967 war, when Iraq broke off diplomatic relations with the United States.

Baghdad was clenched by fear and suspicion. As one diplomat told me: "People are depressed and terrorized." The regime-generated spy phobia had turned neighbor against neighbor. "You don't have to be a Jew to be scared stiff in this town," the diplomat said.

Phones were tapped, hotel rooms bugged and searched, all cables censored. There were no external phone lines available. Iraqi Army troops were everywhere. Secret-police plainclothesmen loitered in the lobby of the Baghdad Hotel, where I remembered uneasily that during one coup d'etat foreigners were pulled from their rooms by the mob and dragged to their deaths behind automobiles. The regime had encouraged the populace to turn out to view the bodies hanging in the square. "It was a barbarous sight," said one eyewitness. Tom and I managed to find the local synagogue, whose chief rabbi was a member of the Sassoon family. He told us that a couple of nights before in the Baghdad prison, a rabbi had begun to pray in Hebrew, administering the last rites for the nine Jews condemned to die on charges of spying for Israel. But the Iraqi authorities interrupted the rabbi, demanding that he recite the prayers in Arabic. The rabbi replied that the traditional prayer for the dying, the hashkabah, existed only in the Hebrew language. The Iraqis refused to allow the prayers to continue and the men were hanged the next morning without benefit of the last rites.

The experience led me to investigate the plight of the Jews in the Arab world across a three-thousand-mile sweep.

During 1969, I sought out ghettos from Damascus to Casablanca, peered into synagogues in Cairo and Algiers, and talked to Jews in Tunis and Tripoli. I found the condition of the Jews improved in inverse relation to the country's involvement in the Arab-Israeli conflict. Thus, Sephardic Jews received the best treatment in Lebanon, Tunisia, and Morocco. Conversely, they were dealt with most harshly in Iraq, Syria, and Egypt. All the Jews in Yemen had emigrated to Israel, and there were none to speak of in Saudi Arabia, Jordan, or Kuwait. I found that the fears of the Jews remaining in their native homelands were heightened by Israel's successes against the Arabs on the battlefield. As the Arab leaders suffered reverses, they viewed the

Jews as potential fifth columnists and therefore suspect. And as the Arab-Israeli conflict dragged on, even Arab countries reasonably sympathetic toward their Jewish communities worried that they had to placate their Muslim population, who needed a convenient scapegoat for the failure of the Arab countries to eradicate Israel. The more enlightened Arab leaders I spoke to privately deplored the emigration of the Jews because the countries were losing some of their most valuable citizens—doctors, lawyers, technicians, merchants.

"We have the same civil rights as all Egyptians," a Jewish leader in Cairo told me.

"But do you get them?" I asked.

He answered with a mocking laugh.

What rankled Egyptian Jews, and those in other countries, was that they were not permitted to leave. "We feel alone and isolated," said one. "We would like to get out but we can't."

In Beirut, a Jewish lawyer confided, "The major discrimination we find is not from the Lebanese but from some American, British, and French firms which are afraid to hire Jews."

The figures on emigration I was given in Israel were startling: The original Iraqi Jewish community of 130,000—Iraqi Jews traced their history back twenty-five hundred years—was now only about 2,500 left; the Syrian community was reduced from 30,000 to 3,000; in Egypt, the colony of 80,000 had dwindled to 1,200; in Tunisia, there remained 13,000 from a 1948 population of 100,000; in Algeria, a community of 140,000 had gone down to 2,900. The only relatively bright spot was Morocco, with 45,000 of the former 225,000 Jews still remaining and entitled under the constitution to hold public office. A Jewish member of the Casablanca community told me, "Two years ago, after the 1967 war, I had my bags packed. But the luggage is back on the shelf and I plan to stay indefinitely."

In the late 1960s, most major U.S. publications maintained a correspondent in Beirut, with responsibility for the Arab world, and another in Jerusalem. I found that those in Beirut often sympathized with the Arab position, and particularly the Palestinians. Many in Jerusalem, conversely, seemed to reflect the Israeli line on political matters. Aware of this, the *New York Times,* for instance, for many years would not assign a Jewish reporter to Israel. I planned to remain as emotionally neutral as I could and I resolved to visit Israel. Having spent four years in Vietnam without getting north of the 17th Parallel, I wanted to see both sides firsthand in the Middle East. But it was thought that if the Arabs discovered you'd been to Israel, you'd be declared persona non grata and of no further use to your publication. In fact, reporters at the bar of the St. George Hotel in Beirut used to speak of "Dixie" when referring to Israel, for fear of being overheard by security agents. But I decided to cross the line.

I talked the Jordanian authorities into letting me cross the Jordan River—and return—over the Allenby Bridge, on the grounds that the West Bank was occupied territory and should be reported upon. Coming from the guerrilla caves of Jordan and driving into West Jerusalem was like flashing forward several centuries. The guerrillas seemed fixed on the notion that the Israelis were temporary Middle East residents who would soon wilt in the face of Palestinian pressure and return to their lands of origin. But it didn't take long for me to sense the deep, abiding commitment to the land in most areas of Israeli society. I rode in patrols with the Israeli border soldiers along the Lebanese frontier and the Jordan River. I traveled to outposts on the Golan Heights in occupied Syria. And I drove across the Sinai desert to talk to soldiers stationed in the forts along the Bar-Lev Line on the east bank of the Suez Canal, who were undergoing almost daily bombardments from the Egyptians in what was becoming known as the war of attrition.

Kefar Ruppin was one of my destinations: the kibbutz nearest the Jordanian border, which had been attacked by the Palestinians from across the river. The kibbutzniks were determined that the guerrilla operations would not be allowed to disrupt their daily lives in any significant way. "The guerrillas have made this a very busy place," said Czech Noy, who invited me into the cafeteria for coffee and told me he took his name from his native Czechoslovakia. "We have received maybe two hundred fifty shells in all, rockets and mortars. The Fatah tried to cross the river at night and plant mines on our side. But we are able to find the mines. Now they come across the river, shoot their rockets, and run away."

In nearby Degania, the first kibbutz founded in Israel, I arrived just after a rocket attack and a pretty nurse named Tamar Bondy told me, "It didn't do much damage but you couldn't believe the noise they make. It's terrible. The last time the explosions came, a man here died from a heart attack." That previous evening, the residents were instructed to take shelter during a night rocket attack but a twenty-one-year-old girl, the wife of a soldier who had returned on leave, said she and her husband had been sitting on the kibbutz green when the rockets screamed in. "We were supposed to go to the shelter," she reported. "But we stayed out on the grass. When your husband comes home, who needs public shelters?"

And at a northernmost forward outpost on Mount Hermon, on an outcropping six thousand feet high, overlooking a guerrilla infiltration route, a young, blond, bareheaded Israeli sergeant, said with a touch of disdain, "The commandos are a bunch of cowards—terrorists. They come a great distance—only to shoot our women and children and run away without fighting us soldiers. Some heroes!" The sergeant, who came to Israel as a child aboard the illegal transport *Exodus,* added by way of finality, "We know what we are living for and we know what we are fighting for. And we aren't giving up these Golan Heights."

I continued to visit Israel whenever feasible, though my prime responsibility was covering the Arab world. I interviewed Prime Minister Golda Meir on television with Rowland Evans, the U.S. political columnist. Golda was as tough and shrewd as they come and she never once agreed that the Palestinians had any right to a homeland, or even that there was a legitimate entity with the name Palestinian. She parried every question on the subject with remarks like, "You seem to be more interested in the welfare of the terrorists rather than their victims." And she, naturally, brought up the subject of the impossibility of dealing with anyone sworn to destroy or dismantle her country. Of course, she had a point. The television interview showed me, by the way, that it is a lot easier for a politician to get off the hook in front of a camera—with its insistence on the effective use of the time. If you press too much to get an answer, you, as the interviewer, come across to the viewer as a bully.

Back on the Arab side, I would quietly point out to Palestinian and other Arabs that it appeared to me that the Israelis were determined to remain in the Middle East indefinitely, and it might not hurt for them to get used to the idea. Invariably, I was looked upon as a naïve American reporter who had swallowed too much Zionist propaganda and failed therefore to perceive the historical rightness of the Palestinian cause. It concerned me that this mentality led to the continuing refusal to recognize the state of Israel and thus freed the government in Jerusalem from entering into any kind of serious discussion on the establishment of a Palestinian political entity.

In 1970, Israeli operations against the Palestinians were heating up again. By this time, the long periods away from my wife had led to a separation that became permanent. It is not easy being the wife of a foreign correspondent, with all the sudden, extended departures from home, and I suspect the marriage attrition in our field is higher than most any other. Divorce is an occupational hazard for us. As Jim Hoagland of the *Washington Post* put it, "The profession makes what many people see as unreasonable demands and you need a mate who can accept that."

I was seeing a striking Lebanese beauty whom a friend christened "Justine" after Lawrence Durrell's heroine of the *Alexandria Quartet,* a truly Byzantine lady. Justine owned a speedy little BMW and she was fearless as a chauffeur plying the boondocks of Lebanon. Once, we drove into the Bekáa Valley to report on an attack by Israeli jets on guerrilla positions in the Arkoub region on the western slopes of Mount Hermon. Charles Murphy of ABC News had narrowly missed serious injury by leaping into a ditch to avoid the rockets from the jets. Justine and I picked up a couple of wounded guerrillas who flagged us down on our way out of the danger zone. En route to the rear, one guerrilla decided that riding in a BMW with tape cassettes playing wasn't a bad way to evacuate, and he and his gun-toting buddy suggested we take them all the way back to Beirut. Justine, speaking in Arabic, convinced them we were only dropping them off at a first aid station and returning to the fray ourselves.

I had taken Justine with me on a trip to Egypt and had experienced no trouble with hotel authorities over sharing a hotel room. Only belatedly, I realized we had no problems because we had occupied a suite. I wanted to take Justine to see Petra, the Nabataean "rose-red city half as old as time" in Jordan, and we flew to Amman, which the Romans called Philadelphia. There, the guerrillas were threatening the army again, so I had to cover that story for a couple of days. The first night the Intercontinental Hotel in Amman was full, except for the Royal Suite. The desk clerk knew me and gave me the suite for the price of a single. It actually had three bedrooms and a large sitting room at the penthouse level. The next day, the hotel jam eased and we were transferred to a standard double room. But that evening a really nasty-looking character inquired about me at the desk. At first, I brushed it off. But I detected a note of apprehension among the reception staff. The next day, the fellow repeated his inquiries, identifying himself as a secret policeman. He said Justine and I were wanted down at police headquarters.

There, we were accused of cohabiting in a single bedroom while our passports—collected by the hotel—were registered under different names. This, suggested the police lieutenant-colonel conducting the questioning, could lead to our being arrested on a very serious charge in a traditional Islamic state. I had learned that in the Arab world, where the Ottoman legal code prevails, you don't plead guilty to anything.

So I swore that we had been married in Cyprus and had come to Jordan on our honeymoon. "We mislaid our wedding papers," I said indignantly. "I thought this was a civilized country where married couples were not subjected to such harassment." Et cetera, et cetera.

I'm sure the colonel didn't believe me for a minute. But it was my story and I was sticking to it. I was worried that Justine, whose family was prominent in Lebanon, could get into real trouble. But she maintained her cool while I spoke, then interrupted.

To the colonel, she declared in Arabic that surely he couldn't conceive of a proper Arab girl living in the same hotel room with a man to whom she wasn't married. I'm convinced the colonel knew she was lying, too, but she gave a beautiful and gutsy performance and the police chief found it difficult to challenge her. So he said, in effect, "Okay for now, but she'd better be on the next plane out of Amman." She was. I drove to see the hidden city of Petra alone.

Back in Amman, I called on the U.S. ambassador, L. Dean Brown. I wanted to do a piece on him because he carried a sidearm and was determined not to be captured by any of the various militant groups that might decide to hold a U.S. diplomat hostage. Whenever Brown left his desk to go home, he slipped a .38-caliber Smith and Wesson police special in a tan leather holster and clipped it onto his belt underneath his jacket. He was known as "the pistol-packing ambassador."

I sympathized with the point of view of the trim, fit, graying fifty-year-old diplomat, whose bodyguard was a tall, tough Jordanian, a retired captain in King Hussein's Royal Guards who carried a submachine gun. Brown, an infantry officer in World War II, told me, "I may not be able to hit anything, with my eyesight being what it is these days. But if necessary, I *do* expect to shoot and make some noise. I *don't* intend to be taken hostage. If they really want to kill me, there is not a lot I can do about it. They could set up a machine gun along the road and get me. But taking me prisoner is another matter."

Like other envoys, Brown was appalled at the kidnapping of

diplomats by various insurgent groups as a means of achieving their demands. "I would hope that I would not be an embarrassment to the U.S. government by being held a hostage," Brown said quietly. "There are many demands one can conceive of that could be made upon the Jordanian or American government by taking diplomatic hostages."

During 1970, almost daily clashes would break out in Jordan between the bedouin army, loyal to King Hussein, and the Palestinian guerrillas who had set up what amounted to a state within a state. The Palestinians established their own roadblocks and often controlled entry or exit from Jordanian cities. In May 1970, I heard a report in Beirut one evening that Morris Draper, the political counselor of the U.S. embassy in Amman, had been kidnapped. So the next morning I was on the 7:00 A.M. Middle East Airlines flight to Amman along with Jesse Lewis, of the *Washington Post*.

We hailed the first taxi we saw and told the driver to take us by the Intercontinental Hotel to drop off our bags and then to the U.S. embassy, located on one of Amman's several stone hills, known as a *jebel*. It could only happen with an Amman taxi driver: snaking down a wadi, or valley, the cab ran out of gas—right in the middle of a firefight between some Palestinians and the army. We scrambled out of the Mercedes and crawled behind a nearby wall for cover. In Amman, with those stone hills and twisting wadis, it was always difficult to tell just where firing was coming from. We found ourselves near an old stone house rented by Ken Wilcox, a British television cameraman, who offered us refuge. In his garden, I found an eighteen-year-old Palestinian clad in a uniform, with a long, old-fashioned rifle. He said his name was Ussamah. "They told us to guard this street and not let the army come past," he said. "I don't want to shoot Arabs but if they shoot at me, I shoot back."

He was joined by a sixteen-year-old companion named Abu Abed, who said he was a newcomer to the ranks of Al-Fatah. As I stood there, Abu Abed accidentally discharged his rifle, which went off with a loud bang and nearly blew his foot off. He was not hurt but the shock caused him to drop the weapon, which he then sheepishly picked up. To save face, the eighteen-year-old Ussamah said, "That was a sniper bullet. See. They're shooting at us." He added out of Abu Abed's earshot, "He is young and hasn't had much training yet."

Ussamah, who learned his excellent English in Jordanian schools, said fervently, "I hope all this shooting will stop soon. We should be down in the Jordan Valley fighting the Israelis not shooting at each other in Amman. I really don't understand what is going on.'' That made at least two of us.

When we finally reached the U.S. embassy after the firing had subsided, we learned that diplomat Draper—later to become, with Phil Habib, a roving ambassador in the Middle East—had been released. He had been picked up in some kind of mix-up; it was not a proper kidnapping. So sometime in midafternoon, we taxied back to the hotel, which, we found once inside, had been occupied by Palestinian guerrillas, bearing Soviet-designed Kalashnikov automatic rifles. The leader told me that they were from the Popular Front for the Liberation of Palestine (PFLP) and that they had presented King Hussein with a series of demands that would guarantee Palestinian forces complete freedom of movement in Jordan.

At the hotel, we also learned that Jordanian communications had been shut down to the outside world, so there was no possibility of getting stories out by telex or phone. I tried to get our taxi driver to take us to the Syrian border, hoping to transit through Damascus and back to Lebanon by road. But he said the guerrillas had told him not to leave Amman. At first, the PFLP members told us to stay in the hotel for our own safety, since there was still plenty of firing going on around the capital. But as the darkening sky lit up with tracer fire, the moustached commando leader wearing a black-and-white kaffiyeh called the hotel guests together in the coffee shop and said to us in halting English, ''I do not like to use the word. But there is no other. You are hostages! The Americans, British, and Germans will be kept in the hotel as hostages until the king meets our demands. If the soldiers continue to shell the Palestinian refugee camps, we will not be responsible for your safety.''

Well, I thought, that was it. At least, we were not being strung along anymore, and we knew where we stood. There were eighteen American civilians, fifteen Britons, and three West Germans. The other fifty guests—French, Russian, Japanese, and Arabs, mainly tourists seeing Petra, the Roman ruins at Jerash, or the monumental Wadi Rum canyons—were allowed to leave if they chose. But the hotel for them was as safe as anywhere else in Amman. I showed them the unfinished nightclub in the hotel basement, which was a natural shelter, and most of the guests bedded down in the would-be disco for the night. I spent time with them taking notes for my story but decided to sleep in my room. In the lobby, I was confused by the varying explanations offered by the guerrillas as to why we were being held hostage.

At first, they said it was to assure the protection of those in the camps—which doubled, as they did in Lebanon, as homes for the Palestinians and as bases for their guerrillas. Then they said the king must order a ceasefire and give the commandos special status. I went to bed and slept for a couple of hours, rising about 5:00 A.M. to get a line on what was going on. A hotel employee told me that Jordan radio early in the morning said that the king had ordered a ceasefire, complying with the Palestinians' original demands.

But in the lobby, I found that our captors had changed signals once again. Now, they said, we would be kept hostage until Hussein fired some of his top military officers—otherwise the guerrillas would blow up the hotel with the hostages included. It was a hell of a prospect.

The guerrillas were surly. One kept jabbing his rifle in my stomach when I demanded to know why they were still holding us. My temper was getting short; I had banged my bad leg in Cairo and noticed I had an infection on my heel. I didn't want to hang around Amman but it looked as if we might be held for days. Communications were still down and there was no way to get the story out. Based on past experience, I knew that once power was restored, the news agency reporters—there were three with us—would have direct lines to Beirut. I'd probably get beat on my own story. So I decided to escape.

By this time, the guerrillas had put armed guards on all doors leading outside. I had to find an alternate way out. I walked up to my room and hid my traveling bag and typewriter on the closet shelf so that the guerrillas wouldn't know the room was occupied. I headed back downstairs and probed the interior hotel grounds, trying to see what lay beyond the back wall of the garden behind the swimming pool. But a couple of guerrillas on the roof screamed at me and pointed their automatic rifles in my direction, ordering me back. I then slipped into the unused cabana wing of the hotel and found an unlocked room. The window overlooked the rear side of the hotel. I figured I could rip up the sheets on the bed and tie them together, then let myself down outside the window. But I had only seen this done in movies. The drop was about twenty feet. I might be spotted by passing guerrillas—or fall if the sheets tore. Still, it was an ace in the hole.

First, I wanted to explore a long passageway I had noticed on the basement level the night before while trying to find the kitchen to get some water for a girl who had broken her leg falling off a pony at Petra. I sneaked down the corridor and hid behind a boiler trying to figure out where I was. I peeked around the machinery and saw that I was near the rear service entrance. However, there was an armed guard standing by the ramp to the road. I ducked and walked back into the hotel proper. A few minutes later, I saw the same guard strolling through the basement, so I assumed the rear entrance was watched only intermittently. I figured that the rear door was my best shot. It was now about 11:00 A.M. and we were getting steak for lunch from the wood-burning stove in the kitchen. I decided I'd make my escape try on a full stomach. Jesse Lewis turned up, and since we had been together the previous day, I told him of the plan and how I was going about it. I suggested that it would be better if I tried it alone, and, if he heard no firing, after a suitable period he might follow me, if he chose.

I walked down the corridor again, this time taking an empty glass to use as a prop in case I was stopped. "Just looking for water," was my story. Sure enough, I passed a guerrilla guard who stopped me and directed me to the kitchen for water. I got a glass of water, then returned to the corridor. I hid behind the boiler and peered around toward the entrance. An employee came out of a door at the entrance but walked away. Seeing no guards, I strode out from behind the boiler, and walked past the entrance with even strides, my head straight ahead as if I had some business somewhere. I walked out of the hotel, past an open space where I could be watched from the rear entrance, and waited for a moment behind the cabana building. Then, I walked across an area about one hundred yards wide where I could be seen by the guerrillas on the roof. I felt like running but I didn't. No shouts or shots came, and in a few minutes I had reached the city street pattern. I quickly turned a corner and walked to the British embassy about three blocks away. There, I gave all the information I had about the British hostages to the ambassador, Sir Philip Adams, and he called the U.S. embassy, which sent a car over. Jesse Lewis, whom I had known in Vietnam, was already at the chancery by the time I arrived. He had followed me out and walked directly to the U.S. building. We gave Morris Draper a fill-in and learned that the U.S. military attaché had been murdered by a guerrilla gunman at his villa door. We sat down to write our stories, unsure whether we could get communications to the outside world.

The Amman airport was still closed, but late in the afternoon, we heard that an Alia, Royal Jordanian Airline, plane was flying in from Saudi Arabia. It would be at the airport long enough to refuel before heading for Beirut to overnight to avoid possible damage to the plane in riotous Amman. There were no taxis operating and the embassy's cars were tied up on special missions. It looked as if we wouldn't make that last plane out of Amman. Then by sheer good luck, a Red Cross sedan rolled up at the embassy. We asked the driver whether he could take us to the airport, mentioning we were journalists, identifying our newspapers.

"You're with the *Los Angeles Times*," he said. "Do you know Bill Tuohy?"

"Be my guest," I said. He turned out to be Robert Jenny, a professional Red Cross specialist from Geneva. He was a friend of my wife's and had had lunch at our Saigon villa while I was stuck up in Hue during the Tet Offensive in 1968. He was nervy and savvy and raced us to the airport via back roads where the commandos had not set up roadblocks. At the airport, the Alia Caravelle was about to take off. We were hurried through customs and immigration and rushed aboard. The crew was unshaven and had nothing to offer but Pepsi-Cola but that was fine with us. We landed at Beirut to be greeted by a mob of media people all clamoring for information about the hostages in Amman. I took a taxi to my office, and filed my long detailed story by telex, most of which I had written in Amman, and had time to enjoy a pleasant dinner.

The next day, I filed a second story, this one based on the guerrillas I had talked to, and I thought about going back to Amman. I figured the guerrillas might have it in for me for escaping, but there was talk of a settlement in the air that evening in Beirut. MEA announced it would be flying at 7:00 the next morning. I was on the flight, got to the Intercontinental, found that the hostages had been released during another makeshift truce between the Palestinians and the bedouin, picked up my baggage, and paid my bill. The U.S. embassy ordered all dependents evacuated. It made a good windup story and I was happy to see my fellow hostages at the airport all hale and hearty and none too worse for the ordeal. I was satisfied, too, that the hotel people would not get the idea that a foreign correspondent would run out on his bill.

If there's a lesson to be learned, it is that it is best to break away from your captors as soon as possible—before they get a good line on you. Most times this might be impossible, but I think in a hostage situation, it is best to make a break for it—if indeed you plan to get away—as soon as you can.

From Beirut I flew to Cairo, to interview President Gamal Abdel Nasser in his private office in the Kubbah Palace. He seemed relaxed during the conversation. "There's one thing I would like to ask of you," he said. I thought Nasser, a tall, strapping man in a dark business suit, would rule out discussion of some major topic like his recent visit to Moscow. Instead, he asked, "Please speak slowly. My English is not so good."

Nasser insisted he had to go to Moscow for new armaments because the United States continued to supply sophisticated military hardware to the Israelis. He called the Israeli deep-penetration air raids into Egypt—which were a weekly occurrence during the "war of attrition"—a reflection of the "arrogance of power."

I asked him whether he foresaw another general war in the Middle East, and, as if anticipating 1973, he replied, "As we have been here seven thousand years, we have faced many problems like this. We are very patient people. We will be patient until we are ready to deal with our enemy. As long as Israel continues to occupy Arab territory, it is our duty to liberate the territory."

I found Nasser to be charming, soft-spoken, and effective in putting across the Egyptian point of view, however controversial. I wondered why his chief media adviser, editor Mohammed Heikal of the newspaper *Al Ahram,* did not take the opportunity to get him together on a regular basis with U.S. journalists, particularly those from television. I assumed Heikal wanted to keep Nasser to himself, so to speak, so that he, as the information adviser, was the only conduit for the Egyptian leader's thinking on major matters of state.

I asked about his personal future and Nasser replied, "You can see my good health. I said to my people that I will stay in my job until there is complete withdrawal of the Israeli forces from our occupied territory." That withdrawal would come—but not in Nasser's lifetime.

On trips to Egypt, I took a certain amount of perverse pleasure in responding to the frequent Arab charge that the U.S. media was "controlled by Zionists." Once, learning that Israeli warplanes were accused by the Egyptians of hitting a school during one of the "war of attrition" raids, I insisted that the authorities take us to the location and we would report on the damage and casualties. Though the Egyptians finally permitted us to visit a hospital and see the bodies of some of the thirty children reported dead, they refused to let us inspect the actual location of the alleged bombing. Thus the facts concerning the incident remained shrouded in mystery and did nothing to counter Israeli defense minister Moshe Dayan's claim that the children's school was in the middle of a military installation.

For their part, the Israelis were masters at the art of winning friends and influencing visiting politicians and journalists. They knew how to put their best foot forward. But the Arabs were their own worst informational enemies. Time after time, prominent journalists or politicians from the United States would arrive in Arab capitals with promised appointments—after having had the red carpet laid on by the Israelis—and cool their heels for days in hotel rooms before departing in disgust, empty-handed. It was an anomaly to me that despite the importance Arab governments attached to domestic propaganda—control of state radio, television, and press—they seemed to be at a total loss in dealing with visiting journalists who were at least willing to hear their point of view. If reporting from the Middle East, particularly from those U.S. journalists taking a swing through the area, seemed one-sided in favor of Israel, I used to tell Arab information officers they had only themselves to blame—not the "Zionist-controlled media."

The Egyptians were, I found, personally warm toward Americans. And if they found you sympathetic, they were kind to you, despite the fact that the United States was, in their view, overly supportive of their enemy, Israel, which then held all of the Sinai desert. I always had a good time in Cairo: It has pulse and power, and is the largest city in Africa, center of the Arab world, and the intellectual capital of Islam. Though dusty and decrepit, it throbbed with life and maintained something of timelessness about it.

The bureaucracy and government was a nightmare, though. You rarely could get to see senior officials, but there were a handful of available junior officials to get a fairly good sense of what was going on. And after a hard day's work, some of us would repair to the Arizona, a nightclub on the road to the pyramids, and chat up the local girls garlanded with jasmine blossoms, who would practice their English on us. I met one knockout who was a failed belly dancer. She prompted me to do a story on new twists in belly dancing in the Middle East. The food in Cairo wasn't bad, and the city, at this period, was still suffering the effects of the 1967 war. So tourism had not yet got back into high gear, which meant the empty hotels welcomed you. The Nile Hilton was our headquarters, as it was for several international airlines, and more than once I danced under the stars with a stewardess from Lufthansa or Air France.

Cairo, like Amman, was a frequent commute for us from Beirut. During one visit, I took a train to Alexandria to investigate the extent of the deployment of Soviet Sam 2 surface-to-air missiles and found them being installed in and around that ancient port. It was a major story. But it gave me pause. Had I been picked up by security police while nosing around Alex, I might well have been jailed as a spy. For what I was doing—confirming and locating the existence of new antiaircraft weapons—could well be said to jeopardize Egyptian national security. My only response was that I wasn't relaying the information secretly to any foreign power or the CIA but publishing it on the front page of the *Los Angeles Times*. But there was no assurance whatsoever that the Egyptians would accept such an explanation as an excuse for gathering sensitive information.

While in Alex, I spent time looking around the city that Lawrence Durrell's *Alexandria Quartet* had made look like a glittering, sophisticated, dazzlingly beautiful, and intriguingly evil place. But it seemed to me that old Alex had come upon hard times; the snap was gone from her garter. As a United Nations friend put it: "Alexandria is like a dress ball with only old ladies in attendance." But the museum was superb with sculptures of Leda and the Swan living it up. And the girls on the spacious, sun-splashed boulevards had a wonderfully pharaonic look as if they had just stepped off pedestals in the Egyptian Museum.

Alexandria, to me, seemed like so many cities I visited in the Middle East, whether Algiers, Casablanca, Damascus, Port Said, or Baghdad: They had lost much of their glamour and it came as quite a disappointment to one who was raised on Hollywood movies to find how tawdry the present-day reality was. Where were the snows of yesteryear? Where were the boys of the old brigade?

Egypt was a delight in which to roam: I explored the Upper Nile Valley as well as the Delta, the temples at Luxor and the Valley of the Kings, and the lovely Ptolemaic temple of Isis on the island of Philae, which was spared from the rising waters of Aswan by archaeological reconstruction. Outside the temple of Karnak, a hawker showed me a piece of what he said was an original bas-relief from a column inside.

"It's real," he said revealing the piece covertly.

"It looks like an imitation," I said.

"Yes," he replied, "a real imitation."

However, some guides, being literate, would engage me on the subject of the U.S. role in the Middle East. My boatman paddling out to the temple of Philae, who doubled as a high school teacher, told me, "Educated people in Egypt deplore the Nazi Holocaust. But why do the Jews have to have a state in the Middle East. Why not in Germany?

The war with Israel has brought the Russians, whom we don't like, into the Middle East. Here, we think the real problem is the Palestinian refugees. If America can solve that, you will solve the problem of war in the Middle East.'' Always the solution seemed to turn on the Palestinians.

During the summer of 1970, relations in Amman between the fedayeen and the Jordanian Army went from bad to worse. The bedouin officers were increasingly restive with the compromises Hussein, their sovereign, was making with the Palestinian leaders, particularly the Marxist PFLP, to keep peace in the kingdom. So the stage was set for the deadly Black September.

On the evening of September 7, 1970, some of us were having dinner with *Time* magazine's chief of correspondents in the roof restaurant of Beirut's Phoenicia Hotel when we were alerted that a Pan Am 747 jetliner had been hijacked and had landed at Beirut airport. We drove out to the terminal but the plane was kept well away and then it took off for Cairo. We returned downtown and reports came in that a TWA Boeing 707 and a Swissair Douglas DC-8 had also been hijacked by Palestinian commandos and landed somewhere in Jordan. Around midnight, the flash came from Egypt that the Pan Am had been destroyed by the hijackers on the ground at Cairo, luckily with no loss of life. But the whereabouts of the other two aircraft remained a mystery.

So the next morning, a handful of us boarded the daily 7:00 MEA flight to Amman to search for the missing jetliners. At Amman airport, Loren Jenkins of *Newsweek,* who shared office space with me in Beirut, and John Bulloch of the London *Daily Telegraph* and I found a taxi whose driver seemed to have some vague idea where the planes were— an abandoned World War II airstrip known as Dawson's Field, twenty miles northeast of the capital. Our driver turned off the main road, and took us on a crazy ride across the desert, with plumes of dust enveloping the Mercedes. After a half hour or so, wondering whether we were on a wild-goose chase, we crested a rocky rise and there in the distance was an incredible sight: two huge airliners, side by side, in the middle of what appeared to be a vast salt flat, like Bonneville, Utah. The tall, red-and-white tail markings of the TWA and Swissair jets shimmered in the burning sun, while from a tent pitched in front of the airliners flew the red, white, green, and black flag of the Palestinian captor groups. The planes, taken over in midair, had been instructed to land on the hard desert floor the previous night. A makeshift runway had been arranged placing oil drums, with burning gasoline, in twin rows, and the skillful pilots had landed safely on the flat desert surface.

Inside the two planes were 288 passengers and 17 crew members. Except for children, the passengers and crew were not allowed out of the cabins: The youngsters, about 20 in all, gamboled under the aircraft wings in the precious shade. Around the planes, the guerrillas had dug defensive trenches and positioned a dozen or so vehicles. Farther away, in another larger circle, the Jordanian Army tanks, half-tracks, and armored cars were deployed with their gun barrels pointing at the two lonely airliners.

For the time being, it was a standoff between the bedouin troops and the Palestinian fedayeen, or "the beds and the feds" as one American journalist tagged them. A Jordanian tank major asked us, "What can we do? We have to obey their orders to stand clear because there are three hundred people aboard. They've threatened to blow up the aircraft if we come any closer." So as the dust devils whirled across the desert, the Jordanian Army chief, General Mashour Haditha, conferred with the leaders of the radical Popular Front for the Liberation of Palestine under the wing of the TWA 707. The PFLP were the boys from the June hostage-taking at the Intercontinental Hotel, but now they were demanding as the price for freeing the passengers that Palestinian prisoners held by West Germany, Britain, and Switzerland be released.

Late the first afternoon, the guerrillas did allow most of the passengers to go but they kept all those with Jewish names "for interrogation." There were about forty, since the TWA plane had been en route from Tel Aviv to New York when it was hijacked after a stopover in Frankfurt.

The next day, the Palestinians commandeered still another jet, this one a British Airways VC-10 flying from Bahrain to London. After two more days of negotiating in the desert through Red Cross officials, the guerrillas unexpectedly removed all of the remaining passengers and crew and blew up the three jets with dynamite. They hung on to about forty men and women whom they said they would consider "prisoners of war," pending the release of their own convicted terrorists from European jails. The situation was further confused when the overall guerrilla organization, the PLO, declared that the Popular Front had been suspended because the action of the radical group was endangering the Palestinian cause by taking civilian hostages.

The two-score hostages were taken to the Wahdat refugee camp in

Amman, an entrenched base of the PFLP, which had been, in effect, off limits to the Jordanian constabulary. The situation was extremely tense: The guerrillas had humiliated King Hussein before the world. The officer corps was highly restive. The guerrillas had moved into Irbid in north Jordan and effectively occupied the second city in the kingdom. The king appointed a military government, which was totally unacceptable to the Palestinian guerrilla leadership, and shooting erupted throughout the capital.

We veterans of past troubles filled the bathtubs in our rooms: Water would be precious if the power went off. The scattered shooting soon escalated into a full-scale civil war. On the morning of Thursday, September 17, at first light, the army opened up on the guerrillas full-blast, with artillery shells landing on the Wahdat camp.

All power in the city was shut down: That meant no light, no heat, no running water in the hotel, and no communications to the outside world. The fighting continued all day, with the streets raked with gunfire. As before, the hills, meandering wadis, and stone buildings in Amman made it difficult to detect which way the shooting was coming from. An army officer warned us all—there were close to 120 reporters, cameramen, and broadcasters in the hotel—not to go out on the street, or risk getting shot. The army also ordered that no pictures should be taken from the hotel of their troops. We seemed to be in the center of a Jordanian army stronghold and the Defense Ministry was not far away. The officers said anyone using a camera might be shot on sight. On the first morning, some cameramen had filmed soldiers breaking into shops in the hotel arcade, which did not add any luster to the Royal Jordanian Army. The army was conscious of its image.

On our second floor Ole Olson, a Swedish cameraman, was shot in the right thigh while taking pictures: He had not gotten the word from the army that picture taking was verboten. We bandaged him up and I gave him a shot of cognac from the trusty flask I carried for such emergencies. We found a Jordanian doctor in the hotel lobby who managed to summon an ambulance, somehow, and get him to the hospital.

Via radio, we learned that the guerrillas claimed to have taken over a "liberated zone" in north Jordan and had appointed people's councils to administer the cities. The PFLP was throwing down the gauntlet to the king, and it appeared to us that this time the fight would be to the finish. The army moved in with 106-mm recoilless rifles into the hotel parking lot and opened fire in the direction of the Palestinian

positions. The back blast was thunderous and it shattered all the huge
plate-glass windows in the lobby as well as floor-to-ceiling mirrors,
leaving shards and splinters everywhere. Within hours, the lobby was
a real mess with light fixtures, sprung from concussion, hanging cra-
zily from the ceiling, and glass and plaster dust covering everything.
Bullets began bouncing off the hotel's facade, and it wasn't long before
we began talking about "new holes" in our rooms to differentiate from
previous bullet hits. In all, the hotel was hit by bullets or shrapnel at
least three hundred times.

On our floor, the hotel's youngest guest, despite the problems,
was holding up fine. She was the eighteen-month-old daughter of the
Indian chargé d'affaires who had moved into the hotel when his embassy came in the line of fire.

The infant, named Reihaneh, became a mascot on our floor and
since we had bathtubs full of water we were able to make sure her
mother, Kahlelli, had an ample supply for the daughter whose name,
her father said, meant "fragrant flower." I advised the reporters who
hadn't been through this kind of go-around in Jordan before to conserve their water: We didn't know how long we would be without the
stuff or how much we might need. It is instructive how little water you
actually need if you take a proper sponge bath daily and use warm beer
to brush your teeth.

At night, many headed for the basement's unfinished disco to
sleep because it was by far the safest place in the hotel. But I found it
stuffy. My friend Arnaud de Borchgrave, the chief correspondent of
Newsweek who had the room across the hall, and I tossed our mat-
tresses down on the floor of the corridor. If you carefully placed the
mattress next to your room's bathroom, you had the maximum number
of walls between you in the corridor and incoming fireworks. We all
had transistor radios and tuned in the BBC or Voice of America. We
heard reports that some U.S. authorities were suggesting an American
military effort be mounted to save the hostages presumed to be in the
Palestinian refugee camps. It was a ridiculous suggestion: Shooting
one's way into a guerrilla base to rescue hostages would only ensure a
grim fate.

On Saturday morning, the journalists in the hotel held a mass
meeting to discuss sanitary discipline and other matters of mutual
interest. The litter in rooms and corridors was accumulating. The
toilets were stopped up in many rooms. Some people had been raiding
the larder—we got our meals directly from the wood-burning stoves in

the hotel kitchen. In short, pestilence became something more than just a term from the Four Horsemen of the Apocalypse. We thought that we ought to act jointly—not every man for himself. Michael Adams, a Briton who had been negotiating on behalf of the hostages with the Palestinians and who had been an RAF prisoner of the Germans in World War II, pointed out that when he was captured, he and his mates thought they would be soon released. But they were held for six years. So, he said, we ought to prepare for a long siege. We agreed to set up a committee, headed by Adams joined by Arnaud de Borchgrave, Eric Rouleau of *Le Monde,* Murray Sayle of London's *Sunday Times,* Bert Quint of CBS News, Herman Lundquist of a Swedish newspaper chain, and myself. We appointed floor leaders to organize a general cleanup; another group under a British sound-man, who had been with the Royal Engineers in the war, was assigned to dig outside latrines; and a French reporter checked into the commissary to make sure the food was conserved and fairly rationed.

I doubled as floor leader for our second deck. Doug Kiker of NBC News, an old and trusted pal from the 1964 campaign trail and later Vietnam, was my number two. We knocked on every door and suggested all trash be moved to a spot near the elevator (not working) where I arranged sheets to bundle it up and out. We would burn it in the empty swimming pool. Everyone was helpful except for a couple of French photographers, who had been living in squalor at the end of the corridor. They had even sneaked into other rooms to take a crap. I suggested a cleanup was in the best interest of all. They told me to piss off. Then, Kiker rapped on their door and said somewhat more forcefully, "The request is no longer voluntary. We want you to clean up this pigpen—or else." They grumbled, "Dirty Americans," and so on. Finally, Joe Faletta, the tough little cameraman with Doug's crew, banged into the room. We called him the Enforcer.

"Listen, you Frog bastards," Joe said. "If you don't get this room cleaned up in thirty minutes, I'm going to throw your asses off the floor—and if it has to be out the window, so much the better." The Frenchmen cleaned their rooms and remained docile.

We made a clean sweepdown of the floor in proper military style and aired out all bedding. Morale went up accordingly. We obtained water from an outside source, to flush all toilets, so that they were clean, and in the future, outside latrines could be used.

The firing continued all day and most of the night, and restricted as we were to the hotel, we knew precious little about what was going on in Amman and the countryside. The soldiers were getting jumpier and we laid down a rule that no cameras were even to appear at windows. The soldiers, I suspect, thought we were a bunch of spies anyway. Middle East troops don't immediately comprehend what a bunch of journalists would be doing in the middle of a civil war. In our rooms, we would lie on our bellies near the balcony doors to watch the progress of the fighting. Guerrillas would fire off a few rounds at the army from a stone domicile. The soldiers in turn would wheel up a tank and blow apart the offending house. At night, the military would fire a mortar flare, which would descend slowly, casting an eerie glow over the city. A commando would then try to knock out the flare with a burst from an automatic rifle. But this would only serve to reveal his position, and the army would open up.

One morning a soldier ran into the hotel looking for Arnaud. He noticed the *Newsweek* correspondent using his binoculars from his room, and the trooper thought it was a camera lens. He was going to arrest the American spy, he said. Doug Kiker and I stalled the soldier until we could find an Arabic-speaking reporter who calmed him down and persuaded him to leave. That afternoon, Arnaud suggested we take a sunbath since there was not much else to do, and he always favored the out-of-season tan. We crawled across the floor of my room, on the sunny side of the building, and lay on our backs with our heads sticking out on the small balcony to get the rays—without being spotted by the "beds" or the "feds." The door of the room was open and a couple of French reporters walked by, noticed two sets of upturned shoes, assumed we were corpses, and exclaimed, *"Mon Dieu, ils sont morts!"* My God, they're dead! Another time, we decided to leave the hotel and try to walk to the British embassy about three blocks away. We came under heavy fire about halfway there: Arnaud swore the bullets came close enough to raise one of the few strands on his head. We scuttled back to the hotel. I found I was missing my silver felt-tip pen, a gift from a woman friend in Gstaad, and I said I was going back to try to find it. Arnaud said I was crazy. But I found the pen there in the gutter where we had scrambled for cover.

One morning early, a couple of minibuses rolled up. An enterprising French diplomat had arranged to evacuate those French nationals who wished to go to 'Aqaba, the twin city of Eilat on the Gulf of 'Aqaba. It was all done stealthily by the French and left a bad taste in my mouth. But I thought they were damn fools to go to 'Aqaba. The port was not functioning because of the civil war. There were no paved roads overland into Saudi Arabia, and the Saudis anyway weren't letting in anyone without visas. The Israeli border was closed. The only sensible way to get out a story would have been to rent or borrow a small boat in 'Aqaba, row out past gunshot range, and then head for Eilat, where the Israelis would let you in. It might be worth it for a worldwide exclusive, if you didn't have to base in the Arab world. But the French evacuees didn't even do this. Several days later, when the shooting died down, they sheepishly returned to the hotel. That whole period gave a fascinating insight into how we reacted under pressure: who pitched in to help and who ducked any work; who were upbeat and who simply complained or sneered. It was a test of character as much as anything else.

During the week, the civil war had risen to the scale of a major international crisis. The Syrians sent a brigade into southern Jordan, which was blocked by a bedouin armored force. The Israelis threatened to intervene. The U.S. Sixth Fleet moved into the eastern Med and the U.S. 82nd Airborne Division was alerted. The Soviets promised countermeasures. But we were apprised of this only through our transistor radios and remained hunkered down and immobile.

After a week or so, two Red Cross representatives showed up at the hotel, having flown into Amman on a special plane to negotiate for the release of the hostages, believed still to be in the Palestinian camps. They told us a Russian television cameraman, in town to do a tourism story, was killed in his hotel on the first day of the conflict. One Red Cross official said they were taking some critically wounded people out of the country, but he declined to take any news copy with him. However, the visit raised the possibility of additional Red Cross flights—with space for outgoing journalists on board.

Our hotel committee decided that we should set up a system of priority for any seats on a Red Cross flight that might be made available to us. Ordinarily, most of us would have been competing tooth and claw for a seat, but having worked together on hotel arrangements reasonably well for the past several days, we thought perhaps we could act with civility on an emergency exit flight. Most of us gathered in the hotel patio and the meeting was interrupted by only one mortar round. "Incoming," yelled ABC's Charlie Murphy. Then, the meeting continued. The problem was, we had correspondents representing every facet of the media, and therefore differing personal and professional priorities. As well, there were several nationalities involved. Journalists tend to be independent and anarchic and not given to sorting out matters involving mutual cooperation. For instance, the news agency men were interested in getting out a high-speed bulletin because no word had yet reached the outside world from inside the civil war. Television correspondents thought they needed personally to get out in order to go before the camera for their stories. Some journalists were just fed up and wanted out and insisted that we all equally draw lots: Forget about professional considerations.

I suggested that the first person or persons on our list if there was room for only one or two must agree to take all other copy and film out. And since the news agencies had a big backup staff in Beirut—or anywhere else a Red Cross plane might head for—I had no objection to having the first three numbers assigned to the Associated Press, UPI, and Reuters, chosen among them by lot. I also pumped for the television people to be next in line since it was important for them to get their faces on camera, and their photographers had been observing the rule not to shoot film from the hotel for the sake of all of us.

I ended my pitch by declaring that I was planning to stay behind in any case, and had confidence that Eli Antar of the Associated Press, Bill Hampton of the UPI, Doug Kiker of NBC, or others like them would get our copy to the appropriate recipients in Beirut for transmission to our home offices. My argument seemed to work. We gave priority to certain media, then all drew lots so that the 120 of us each had a number, which determined the order in which we would board any plane with a limited number of seats available, whether ten, fifty, or ninety. Each person had his or her number on a card and could line up at the airport accordingly. The Pied-Piper French mission to 'Aqaba returned, rather with their tails between their legs, and begged for priority consideration in our sequence. We eventually allowed the Agence France-Presse man a place high on the list.

That evening, King Hussein spoke over Amman radio and announced that the army would stop fighting. This could lead to a proper ceasefire. The hotel staff broke into cheers. They had not seen their families for the past week, staying in the hotel and trying to keep the kitchen going. That night, however, a conversation I was having with De Borchgrave and John de St. Jorre about the future of Jordan was interrupted by half a dozen "new" bullets slamming into the side of the hotel. "A great little ceasefire," remarked St. Jorre.

Firing continued during the night but seemed to slack off at dawn. Arnaud went down for the morning meal of rice and bully beef and I stayed in my room, bringing the "reporter's notebook" I was keeping up-to-date in case the Red Cross should suddenly appear on an evacuation mission. I heard a couple of heavy-caliber bullets slam into De

Borchgrave's room across the hall and looked in. Two .50-caliber rounds had come through the window, entered his closet, and holed his suits hanging neatly there. I walked down to the basement kitchen and told him, "Arnaud, I have bad news for you. You're no longer the best-dressed correspondent in Jordan."

At 11:00 A.M. the long-awaited news came that the Red Cross was hoping to evacuate those who wished to leave—at 12:30 P.M. Three big buses escorted by Jordanian Army vehicles rolled up to the hotel and a hundred colleagues boarded them. The military buses were de-layed in getting under way and by the time the departing journalists reached the airport, the Red Cross plane had already left because of the danger from stray fire. But the next morning, it returned and all the outgoing media people were able to board it for home.

Less than a score of us remained behind. The Dirty Dozen, as we tagged ourselves, included Arnaud, Roland Flamini of *Time,* John de St. Jorre of *The Observer,* Murray Sayle of London's *Sunday Times,* and Eric Pace of the *New York Times.* That evening, we learned firsthand through U.S. diplomats of the abortive Syrian invasion, re-sisted by Jordanian armored forces, that seemed to threaten interven-tion by the United States or Israel on the side of Jordan while the Soviets prepared to back up the Syrians.

I had sent out with Doug Kiker my long diary which the paper splashed above the masthead and ran for five thousand words. The great thing about the *Los Angeles Times* is that they give you plenty of space when necessary. Journalistically, it has been an extremely re-warding place to work under editors Nick Williams and Bill Thomas and publishers Otis Chandler and Tom Johnson.

For the next six days, the Red Cross flights would fly in empty— journalists were forbidden to board—and evacuate anyone who wished to leave. Some of the Dirty Dozen began peeling off, taking copy to Beirut for those of us still behind. This meant that during that time we had a lock on the story. A U.S. diplomat friend had given me the keys to a turquoise-colored Ford Mustang belonging to a Marine guard, who had been evacuated. Each morning Pace, St. Jorre, Sayle, and I would bum a tankful of gas from the army motor pool and drive to various locations to see what was going on during the ceasefire. We had the story to ourselves and each day filed a piece on some aspect of the aftermath of the conflict. The copy was pigeoned out with friends or the sympathetic Red Cross stewardess.

*   *   *

During this time, the hotel lobby looked like something out of an Eric Ambler thriller: the hostages emerging from the ruins of the Wahdat camp, residents who had been stuck in the smaller hotels around town, diplomats, military attachés, army officers, even various guerrillas in civilian clothes coming in to see what was going on. The hotel staff had performed admirably under difficult conditions, and, when you realized that most of them were Palestinians, then looking after us all without rancor was little short of amazing. As the manager told me: "We gave instructions to all our staff to treat everyone equally. We stressed that passengers of Jewish faith be given special service, particularly their children."

We visited what was left of Wahdat camp. We saw the bulldozers digging a trench to bury the bodies and I told Eric Pace that we ought to watch closely, however grisly. For the number of those who were killed and being buried would always be a contentious figure—the Palestinians inflating the number of their "martyrs," the government deflating the figure. The area had been pulverized by government shellfire during the fighting, and as we watched the inhabitants come out of their shelters, one said, "Hitler didn't do as bad as King Hussein did." That bitterness remained. But the king had won a signal victory. He had broken the structure of the Palestinian militants that let them to operate independently inside the Hashemite Kingdom. And it allowed him to put the Palestinian guerrillas on the defensive and eventually to drive their armed bands out of the country less than a year later. They were not again to be a power inside Jordan.

During our Amman siege, President Nasser died of a heart attack in Cairo, and the focus of the Middle East story shifted to the Egyptian capital. The first day that Amman airport finally reopened to civilian traffic, I drove with the *Washington Post*'s Jon Randal through Syria and then back to Beirut.

Justine was giving a cocktail party at the home of her parents on a hill overlooking the Mediterranean. She was an accomplished hostess and one of the guests was Abe Rosenthal, the executive editor of the *New York Times*, who was on his first trip to the Arab world. Abe had also been in Cairo and told Justine that he was struck by the hospitality shown to him in Egypt and Lebanon and found a certain similarity between Jews and Arabs. "After all, Abe," she said, "we're all Semites, aren't we?"

Toward the end of 1970, in the remote land of Oman at the eastern tip of the Arabian Peninsula, the young Sultan Qaboos Bin Said, with the help of the British Secret Intelligence Service, overthrew his aging, despotic father, Sultain Said, and took over the throne. Arnaud de Borchgrave in Geneva and I managed to get visas—the first U.S. reporters to do so since the coup—and we rendezvoused in Dubai, the gold-smuggling capital of the world. Dubai is one of the emirates on the eastern fringe of the Arabian Peninsula that were once known collectively as the Pirate Coast, because of their raids on shipping in the Persian Gulf. In the 1970s, the British in their role of gendarmes east of Suez banded the quarrelsome sheiks ruling Dubai, Abu Dhabi, Sharjah, Ajman, Um Al-Qyaiwain, Ras Al-Khaimah and Fujairah into, first, the Trucial States, which, with independence, became the United Arab Emirates.

From Dubai, I drove over to neighboring Sharjah to visit the headquarters of the Trucial Oman Scouts, that romantic and dashing desert force that served as the peacekeeper among the fractious bedouin tribes. I arrived not long after dawn to hear the strains of bagpipe music wafting across the sands and found uniformed Arabs in red-and-white headdresses and spanking gray uniforms marching with precision on the parade ground, under an empty pale-blue sky. An officer in starched tropical kit explained, "The bedouin tribes often robbed the coastal fishing villages with impunity. They might kidnap a girl or steal a camel. But the creation of the Scouts put an end to all that."

When word came in of trouble—a quarrel over a well, an accusation of theft, a boundary dispute—the Scouts saddled up in Land-Rovers and sallied forth. The sight of the soldiers—garbed in the bedouin headdresses, slate-gray tunics with scarlet piping, and tan corduroy trousers, and carrying kunjah daggers and automatic rifles—signaled the presence of law and order in the desert. "The sheiks aren't impartial in matters affecting their individual emirates," said an officer. "But the Trucial Scouts are known to be fair and that's what makes them so valuable here."

From Dubai, Arnaud and his lustrous wife, Sandra, and I flew to Muscat, the capital of Oman. At that time, Muscat was still a medieval village, where, under the deposed sultan, there was no dancing, no music, no movies, no radios, no moving about after dark, no traveling without permission—and more important, no public health service, no schools, and no hospitals. They locked the gates of Muscat at sundown. There were no hotels but we were offered rooms by the lone physician in the sultanate, an American missionary named Donald Bosch who performed two thousand operations a year at his tiny clinic operated by the Dutch Reformed Church in America. We arrived in the middle of celebrations marking the thirtieth birthday of the young sultan—who had been trained at the British military academy Sandhurst—and the winding streets were filled with Baluchi women, unveiled and darkly lovely, dressed in robes of emerald, vermilion and sapphire, and Omani tribesmen in turbans, bandoliers of cartridges, old muzzle-loading muskets and the classic silver daggers, kunjahs, at their waist.

Arnaud and I had an audience with the sultan in the palace: He was a handsome, bearded man with deep brown eyes who usually wore a turban and a long robe, but who was now dressed in the British-style uniform of a field marshal. He told us about the background of the bloodless coup and how the British helped him oust his father, who refused to consider any reforms. The old man was packed off to Britain in a Royal Air Force transport and pensioned off at the Dorchester Hotel in London. He lived well, for oil was discovered in Oman.

"I want my people to feel free to do anything they want as long as they don't go outside of the law," the sultan explained. "Basically our people have simple customs but they need education, medical services, roads, communications, and more modern methods of improving agriculture. This is what we have to provide." He pointed out that the estimated population was around seven hundred thousand though there had never been a census. In the old sultan's day, throughout the country only about five hundred boys were enrolled in school— and no girls. Now, he said, there were four thousand boys and one thousand girls studying in school. The sultan told us he would welcome contact with the United States and since then there has developed an alliance between the two countries, which guards the Gulf today.

But in 1970, the new sultan's greatest problem—aside from modernization—was the Marxist-fed rebellion in southernmost Dhofar Province, bordering South Yemen.

The Dhofar rebellion began as a tribal dispute between the old sultan and dissident tribal chiefs, but it changed character as the ruler became more intransigent and unyielding to popular aspirations. The rebellion then became fueled by Russian-inspired agitators in northern Oman and Chinese-trained revolutionaries from South Yemen, who operated from safe bases across the desert frontier in southern Dhofar. The Omani Army was bolstered by British troops seconded to the sultanate, including the crack Special Air Service (SAS). Arnaud and I flew to Salalah, the capital of Dhofar, some six hundred miles south

of Muscat in a vintage RAF Caribou transport used by the SAS. We
found the situation tense, with the army in command of the lowland
plain but the insurgents operating in the mountains above Salalah. The
town itself was ringed with barbed wire and it looked like some kind
of small Vietnamese garrison town transposed to the desert. An SAS
intelligence officer told us, "Oman is the only nation threatened by
Chinese and Russian communists at either end of the country at the
same time."

In late 1970, the British were planning to beef up the forces in
Dhofar and call on a detachment of Iranian troops from across the Gulf
in order to shut down the Marxist insurgency. "Everybody knows we
can't let this go on like this next year, and still expect to win," a senior
British officer told me. "So we plan to fight through the monsoon
season and not come down from the mountains. We need to maintain
our presence in the highlands all year round because there is now a split
between the hard-core Chinese-trained revolutionaries and the simple
Muslim rebels. The mountain people resent the doctrinaire ways of the
dedicated Maoists. That split is bound to help us."

The stakes in Oman were enormously high: The country controlled one side of the entrance to the Gulf at the Strait of Hormuz, the
oil tanker lifeline to Japan and Western Europe. The British augmented
their force with helicopters and Strikemaster counterinsurgency jets—
and the strategy finally worked. After small but pitched battles in the
mountains, the Omanis with the help of the British SAS, in a kind of
Anglo-Saxon Beau Geste setting, succeeded in getting the upper hand
over the insurgents, driving them back into South Yemen. And with
the reforms introduced by Sultan Qaboos, the rebellion was quelled.
Relative peace and quiet returned to Dhofar and it has remained qui-
escent.

Back in Muscat, Arnaud and I wanted to give Dr. Bosch a bread-
and-butter present for his unrivaled hospitality. We searched the flavorsome suq for some worthy gift. But the doctor asked us to donate
blood. He said, "A pint of blood here will literally mean the difference
between life and death for someone." For Arabs—particularly in backwoods countries like Oman—had a fear of giving blood because they
thought it would affect their virility. Thus, there was nothing much
available for emergencies. Arnaud and I presented ourselves to the
Danish nurse at the tiny clinic and rolled up our sleeves. Arnaud is
fearless in a combat situation. But he is squeamish when faced with a
needle or the sight of his own blood. He presented his arm looking

rather peckish. He looked even greener as the nurse sunk the needle into his vein. He had his head turned away from the needle as he lay on the cot. I couldn't resist.

"Arnaud," I said in mock horror. "My God, what's happening to your blood?"

"What is it? What's wrong?" said the former Belgian Count de Borchgrave, Count du Saint Empire, and Baron d'Elderen, his voice rising.

"Your blood," I repeated. "It's coming out blue."

In 1974, I flew from Beirut to Cairo and drove to the Suez Canal. There, I found myself in a U.S. Navy helicopter flying on a minesweeping operation over the canal and peering down at the battleground I had observed on foot during the 1973 war. I realized that so topsy-turvy was the world of the Middle East that the Americans, who were reviled during the war, in the space of a mere six months could have arranged a ceasefire between Egypt and Israel and be actively engaged in clearing the Suez for shipping.

In Alexandria, I managed to get permission to visit the El Alamein battlefield where the British Eighth Army stemmed the advance of German General Erwin Rommel in 1942 and turned the tide of the war in the Middle East.

If there's anything to give a foreign correspondent a chance to reflect on the futility of war, it's a visit to a military cemetery, particularly one that's far from native soil. El Alamein had three: British, Italian, and German.

A still-handsome woman in Alexandria remembered the young Allied soldiers rolling through the city on the way to battle. "I will never forget their sad faces as they waved from trucks," she told me. "They looked so young. It all seemed so worthwhile then."

And a United Nations official, who fought in the war and visited the cemeteries, recalled, "You wonder now what they were all doing here. These boys, some only seventeen, had come from thousands of miles away—from South Africa, New Zealand, India, Germany, and Italy to die in this barren place. The landscape is so accusing, not at all like the military cemeteries in France, where at least the lovely, green land seems as if it might be worth dying for. What were they all doing here? What strikes me about this strange place is not the great battle, not the turning point of a war, but the essential absurdity of war. It is really a terrible denunciation of war. Look at those tombstones—all heroes when they fell. Does anyone remember them, or know what they did here—or even care?''

In the spring, with desert wild flowers in bloom, El Alamein was strangely beautiful, but infused with a sense of silence, loneliness, and emptiness. At Arlington National Cemetery, there's a feeling that the sacrifice of the men who lie under the crosses and Stars of David may have been worth it. In the desert, it seemed more problematical.

The three cemeteries at El Alamein appeared to reflect, architecturally, the respective national traits of the countries they represented. The Italian monument was a tall, white marble plinth inscribed *Ai Caduti Italiani,* "To the Italian Fallen,'' with the list of names inside the mausoleum: Balzone, Mario; Batista, Carlo; Bellini, Marco; Ignoto, Unknown. A mile down the road is the German memorial, a kind of buff-colored Teutonic fortress, with names in black and gold: E. Heim, 1910–1942; A. Heinlein, 1918–1942; W. Henrich, 1920–1942; Unbekannter, Unknown. An inscription reads: "The price of pride is high, and paid for by the young.''

To the east, the British cemetery garden is simple and austere with the servicemen in graves, the epitaphs provided later by next of kin: C. A. Watkins, Royal Artillery, 18: "He was so young to give so much. A boy but brave as any man. God bless you, son, Mum.'' P. S. Cramer, Royal Infantry, 23: "To the mosaic of victory, we contribute this priceless jewel.'' Captain C. G. Lubson, 22: "The precious dust of our lovely lad from England is hidden here.''

And headstones reading: "A soldier of the 1939–1945 war known but to God.''

I noted the headstone of A. McLearie, Royal Navy, killed aboard H.M.S. *Fiji.* "At rest. Your grave I may not see but some kind hand may place a flower for me.''

I found a scarlet wild flower and laid it on the grave.

Osborne Elliott of *Newsweek* and Kay Graham of the
Washington Post at a Special Forces outpost in Vietnam, 1965

(Left to right) Ward Just of *Newsweek,* now a highly acclaimed
author, Phil Geyelin of the *Washington Post,* and columnist
Rowland Evans with the 1st Infantry Division in Vietnam, 1967

Arnaud de Borchgrave
Hill 400 in Vietnam,
1966. Arnaud was with
Newsweek at the time.
is now editor-in-chief o
the Washington *Star* an
a best-selling author.

My wife,
Johanna, in our v
in Saigon in 1965

Bill Tuohy among the ruins at Palmyra in Syria, 1969

When the bullets are flying, the only safe place is on the ground. Tuohy takes shelter beside his bullet-riddled car in the parking lot of the Intercontinental Hotel during the Jordanian civil war, 1970.

Charles Mohr of the *New York Times,* John Harris of the
Hearst newspapers, Amos Sapir, the son of the Israeli finance
minister, and Bill Tuohy take a break during the Yom Kippur
war, 1973.

The forbidden city in Peking was chilly after the Middle East, 1973.

On the set with John Huston in the Atlas Mountains for the filming of *The Man Who Would Be King*

Tuohy rides the highline between ships during Operation Sea Dragon off the coast of North Vietnam.

On a break during the
battle for Hue, 1968

Johnny Apple (left) of the *New York Times* and Bernard Kalb
(right), then with CBS and later with NBC and the State
Department, comment on my graceful trip via the highline.

An unidentified Marine
medic, his mouth
bloodied after being
unable to resuscitate a
wounded buddy in Hue,
1968

After a jubilant Marine
flag raising in Hue, 1968

Tuohy with General Vo
Nguyen Giap in Hanoi,
1984

In the Imperial Throne Room after the battle for Hue, 1968.
(Left to right) Ann Bryant of the *Overseas Weekly*, Tuohy,
Charles Mohr of the *New York Times*. (Rear) George
MacArthur of the Associated Press, later with the *Los Angeles Times*.

CHAPTER SEVEN

La Dolce Vita

I HAD BEEN covering the Middle East for three years when foreign editor Bob Gibson cabled me in Beirut that our man in Rome, Lou Fleming, was returning to Los Angeles.

"Do you like fettucini?" he asked.

I liked Beirut, though I had split with Justine, and Johanna was moving to Geneva. But when an opportunity like Rome comes up you either take it pronto, or wait several years for a possible second shot. So my answer was, *"Sì."*

At the time, Rome was relatively quiet: The Red Brigades had not yet committed their worst outrages and Pope Paul VI was not making much news from the Vatican. I had an apartment on Via Margutta, just like Gregory Peck in *Roman Holiday,* and my office was a ten-minute walk, in Piazza di Spagna. In my *Newsweek* days, I had done a lot of back-of-the-book stories, including entertainment pieces. Saigon and Beirut had been threadbare in such features so I thought I might take a look at *la dolce vita.* After all, Rome was a European film-making center, "Hollywood-on-the-Tiber," and the *Los Angeles Times* was a natural vehicle for pieces about film-making and film-makers.

I looked up Hank Werba, the veteran Rome correspondent for *Variety,* the show-biz bible, but he quickly pointed out to me that Via Veneto wasn't what it used to be in the days of King Farouk and the glittering cast of characters etched on film by director Federico Fellini, who lived down the street from me. Sitting at the Café de Paris on Via Veneto sipping a double espresso, Hank complained to me, "The Street"—Hank called Via Veneto the Street—"has gone to the dogs. You can't even call it 'son of *la dolce vita*' anymore."

He was right. I got to know photographer Ivan Kroshenko, a Russian-born cameraman who was known as "the king of the paparazzi." Ivan had been around forever. Over a campari at Doney's, across the street from the Café de Paris, Ivan recalled, "You could see the best of Europe here. Every night it was like a big elegant party on the street. There were the directors such as Federico Fellini and Michelangelo Antonioni, all the big stars, the literary and society people, and some wonderful oddballs. Those were the days, Burton and Taylor, Gina and Sophia, Bardot and Ekberg, princes and contessas. The whole works.

"But a photographer had to be fast, like a good commando. Surprise was the key. You had to know whether to use a telephoto lens, or disguise a camera in a cigarette pack. You learned the back door to places. You had to go in like a panther, not like an elephant."

At the time, now thought by social historians to be the height of the *dolce vita* period, Richard Burton and Liz Taylor were filming *Cleopatra* outside Rome. "I followed them one night," said paparazzo Kroshenko, "and they ran off the road in their car on the way back to their villa. I took pictures of them dazed by the crash. The pictures were big stuff and I got twenty thousand dollars for them for twenty minutes' work. A thousand dollars a minute!

"It was never difficult to find the celebrities. The word would be spread by airline or hotel publicity people. I didn't feel I was invading their privacy because it was the celebrities themselves who were going out in public with somebody else's wife."

It was Kroshenko, a Russian soldier who defected after World War II, who got the shot at the Hostaria dell'Orso—by outflanking security men and entering through the kitchen—of Liz Taylor dining with Aristotle Onassis, when he was supposed to have eyes only for his wife, Jacqueline Kennedy Onassis.

"Actually there was always a *dolce vita* in Rome," Ivan concluded. "But we photographers showed the world that it existed and, then, there seemed to be an insatiable demand for pictures. It was a great journalistic invention. But it's all changed now. All you get along the Street are tourists, and hookers, hookers, hookers."

Though some actors and actresses are neurotic, self-centered, and ill-informed, others are thoughtful and introspective, like Marcello Mastroianni, the star of the film *La Dolce Vita*. I had lunch with Mastroianni one day at his favorite restaurant, Nino's, around the corner from my office on the Piazza di Spagna. The actor, dressed in a cashmere turtleneck sweater and a sports jacket, had just turned fifty and was reflecting on this heavy milestone, a possible millstone for an actor.

"It is as if I am starting all over again at fifty," he said after the Tuscan bean soup. "An actor entering his fifties must find new roles. I want not just to be a good actor but to play parts that reflect my age and my time. My favorite role was the movie director in Fellini's *8½*, because he was representative of his time—sensitive, intelligent, impotent. And now, fifteen years later, I want to find an equivalent role, a man representative of his time."

In facing up to the rigors of age, Marcello seemed to have no illusions about himself, telling me that he was uncomfortable about his image on the screen as the quintessential Latin lover. "It's not easy to be thought of as a great lover in real life," he said. "I feel ashamed of the publicity buildup. Women who meet you believe you must be different, something special. After all, I am only an ordinary man. Probably, the little clerk in a government office is a better lover. I can rely on my image, but he has to work hard to be a successful lover—and no doubt is. One time I did a musical about Rudolph Valentino. Poor Valentino. Once he was portrayed as a great lover on the screen, he ceased making love in real life.

"It is difficult to measure up to images. That's why it is easier for an actor to have a relationship with an actress than a nonactress. Actresses understand the problem. You don't have to perform for an audience. An actress knows that beneath the image, actors are not different from others. With an actress, you don't have to play a role. Remember, Bill, that actresses are usually beautiful. And beauty is a miracle. It is exciting to discover that an actress is not really like her publicity, to find the real person there—gentle, intelligent, fragile. This can be an exciting discovery. And nobody knows, just you. Her real personality is a big secret, except to you."

Mastroianni had widely publicized affairs with actresses Faye Dunaway and Catherine Deneuve, and his separations were equally widely reported in the European press. "The worst thing is to break up with an actress you love," he said, slowly drinking a glass of Chianti

Classico. "Everyone knows. The actor says, 'I still want love.' But this appears grotesque, because an actor in anguish still looks like he is acting. Friends do not accept his pain, or the fact that he can be serious. They say, 'Oh, come on, you can have any woman you want.' But the thing is, I don't want any woman, I only want one woman, the woman I love."

Mastroianni said he wished he'd had more children but no longer expected to. "In principle," he told me, "I believe in having one great love in your life, and being faithful. I would have liked it that way—but it didn't happen. It is very hard, almost impossible, for two people to live together permanently. To do this, you must be so honest, intelligent, and generous, and sacrifice so much ego. You need too many good qualities to make it work permanently. I deeply admire a couple that can go through life together. But it is so difficult today. Men are confused. And women, too, have discovered more freedom, and they want to be available for other experiences. Then, too, actors are always trying to find themselves. They are like children. I don't mean stupid, but childlike, never maturing. We have the same fantasies that children do—and perhaps that is why we are so good with children.

"Actors tend to like children and young people. At fifty, one is tired. But young people are fresh in body and mind. That is perhaps why men at fifty take up with girls in their twenties. It's a way of renewal."

I asked Mastroianni about his own future—is there life after fifty? "We older people are so afraid of everything, including solitude," he answered in his soft, deep voice. "We are too worried about the future. We need young people around. They want to change the world. They have their targets, and older people, perhaps, have lost their targets. The young give us strength. I enjoy playing roles in international films which are usually more challenging than movies solely for the Italian audience. But the Italian films do well, and sometimes an actor makes a film just to pay for a villa or swimming pool.

"So I am optimistic about life and about Italy, too, though one must have a melancholy side. I want to do roles that will reflect my age and experience—that's why I say I am starting all over again. For people of my generation, this is a difficult time, a rudderless period, when we don't have the confidence we once did. At fifty, you don't have the strength and enthusiasm to throw yourself into new adventures as you did at thirty-five."

Mastroianni paused, stared into his espresso, and said of the future, "I am in the position of a man waiting for a train, a train that might not stop at his station."

I liked chatting with Mastroianni. He had a reflective turn of mind and didn't seem as full of himself as some actors. When I was a younger reporter, I welcomed the chance to do a piece on a well-known model or actress. It then seemed glamorous. But the years in war zones had left me much less impressed with the stars of the celluloid world. So I decided I'd only do pieces on people that seemed to offer something special in the way of insights rather than because they happened to be hot properties at the time.

I found Claudia Cardinale in a thoughtful mood, too, when I drove out to her villa on Via Cassia north of Rome to have lunch with her—a light, delicious lasagna and crisp, tangy salad, prepared by her own hand. Claudia was tall, willowy, elegant, with a ready smile and a wit, a product of her heritage—born in Tunis of an Italian father and French mother. She had gone through a traumatic period: She had become a pronounced feminist, obtained a divorce from her husband, producer Franco Cristaldi, and severed her long-term contract with his film company, and therefore, faced an uncertain professional future.

But she was upbeat about the experience. "For the first time I really felt free," she said, mixing the salad on the patio of a garden. "For fifteen years, I was considered and treated like an object or a project to be manufactured and merchandised. For much of my adult life, I was someone else's creation—they decided what movies I should play in, what clothes to wear, how to have my hair done, and even what friends to have. My personal life was all mixed up with my professional life, arranged by others. It was difficult to sort it out. It was as if I were something operated by remote control."

I knew her friends were surprised that a person of her intelligence and taste should have become something of a cinematic chattel, locked into a long-term contract reminiscent of the days of the major Hollywood studio pacts, a generation before. "I hadn't wanted to become an actress," she explained. "But then I found myself at the Venice Film Festival, in *Big Deal on Madonna Street,* and it was a whole new world, like being on the moon. I had the fortune or misfortune to be successful right away, and before I knew it, I was trapped in this artificial way of life. I was just a young girl from Africa, and, while I didn't want to be a star, I was not a recluse, and I was pleased to be recognized. I like to have people like me."

Over the years, she said, her marriage became one of convenience, and her professional life was dictated by her husband's company. Frustrations mounted. "I started refusing roles, not because I
was temperamental but because I wanted more intelligent parts. In
Italy, women actresses are usually cast only as sex objects. It is really
absurd to treat women this way—women, after all, are capable of more
in life than making love—but it is very difficult to find intelligent parts
for women in films."

She told me about meeting the Neapolitan director, Pasquale
Squitieri. "Pasquale didn't give a damn about the usual things," a
mutual friend told me at an aside during lunch. "He was simple and
straightforward and their relationship blossomed into a love affair."

"I decided that it was time to break with my husband," Cardinale
said. "I wanted to simplify my life, get out of my film contract and
become a real person again. In a way, I think my husband understood,
though I spent months fighting with lawyers over the contract. It is
difficult for a woman to be independent and I think women everywhere
have the same problems trying to assert their independence. That
doesn't mean I am against men—quite the contrary—but I am for
greater independence for women. But being independent can be difficult for an actress. It means you do not take the first part that comes
along. It means reading scripts and talking to writers about creating
intelligent parts for women. It means not working regularly. I like to
work and I love working hard with a good company and a good
director. But for years my life seemed to be a succession of ending one
film and beginning another. I felt like a slave. So for the moment, I am
content just taking time out to live."

Another actress who freely spoke her mind, I found, was Ava
Gardner, whom I went out to see on the Rome set of a potboiler called
The Cassandra Crossing, a film I have seen several times in lonely
hotel rooms in Riyadh and Damascus on closed-circuit television. It
had been a long, arduous day for Ava, and now, she kicked off her
shoes, slumped in a canvas chair, lit a cigarette, and poured a couple
of plastic cupfuls of white wine.

"I've got a touch of the flu, baby," she said in her throaty voice.
Still a woman of remarkable beauty, with flashing, slanted green eyes,
lustrous hair, and a handsome figure. "I don't feel well. I found out last
night there have been problems getting my salary on this picture. My
business manager advised me to stop working this morning but the di-

rector, George Cosmatos, is a dear man, and I didn't want to let him down. This money problem has something to do with the agents. Christ, they get ten percent for making my life miserable. They're all rotten sods who think actors are stupid. Dumb I may be, but stupid I'm not.

"George asked me to play this role: a middle-aged lady with a rich husband and a young lover, both bastards. But the real reason I'm in this picture is money, baby, pure and simple. You know, I'm not an actress, really. I may have a certain something. But what is it? It sure as hell ain't acting. I've never been an actress."

Actress or not, she was popular with the other members of the cast, which included such luminaries as Sophia Loren, Burt Lancaster, Martin Sheen, Richard Harris, Ingrid Thulin, Lee Strasberg, O. J. Simpson, and that Hollywood veteran Lionel Stander. As Stander told me between takes: "Ava and Sophia are truly fine actresses. There are some remarkable younger actresses around today, but few have that bigger-than-life quality you find in Ava and Sophia. It is a kind of magic that is increasingly rare."

I found Ava, after a quarter century in films, to be well preserved at fifty-four. She'd led a tempestuous, hard-drinking life with failed marriages to Mickey Rooney, Artie Shaw, and Frank Sinatra. She'd had a tumultuous life in Madrid, but had now settled down to a quieter existence in London.

She pulled on her cup of wine and told me, "I've really only loved three men. My husbands. I'm closer to Frank now than the others. Frank is an exceptional man, and one of the kindest persons I have ever met.

"You know, I truly fell in love only three times in my life—with the men I married. I had affairs with other men, but I wasn't in love with them, and I didn't marry them. If I'm not in love, I find it very difficult for a physical relationship."

Martin Sheen's wife approached. "Could I trouble you for a signature on this photograph?" she asked politely. " 'Tain't no trouble at all, honey," said Ava, her drawl deepening. "Happy to do it." She wrote, "For my dear baby, Martin, much love. Ava."

"I'm not comfortable acting," said Gardner, returning to the subject. "I rarely read the whole script for a film, and sometimes not even all of my part. They say that good dubbers make bad actors and vice versa. Well, Clark Gable and I were known as the quickest at dubbing roles at MGM, so I guess that tells you something about my acting ability.

"I've never been happy in the movie world. I know it's ungrateful to complain—you accept the money and you accept what goes with it. The loss of privacy. The constant spotlight. You go out for an evening and everyone watches to see whether you take one drink or three drinks before dinner. What I like about London is you can take your dog for a walk in the park and nobody notices you. To me, sanity is more important than stardom. The important thing is to survive as a person. Survival is the thing."

I asked her about being in the public limelight and she poured me more wine before replying. "Over the years, I've come to hate the press, the way words get twisted. It hurts to see these twisted things in print, it really hurts. It makes you mistrust newspapers. I'd like very much sometime to write a book and take what's been written about me, all the lies and misquotes, and then print the truth. But I probably won't. It would take too much time, and I'm too lazy. I've chosen to live in London because it is a pleasant place, very civilized. But I don't consider myself a European, or an expatriate. I consider myself an American. You bet your ass I do, baby."

Miss Gardner emptied the last of the wine from the plastic cup, smiled wanly at me, and said, "Today hasn't been my best day. So I'm going to bed early tonight. That's my main cure for everything: early to bed, early to rise, makes an old lady wealthy and wise."

It was 6:00 P.M. and director Cosmatos called, "Ava, Sophia, one last take, please." The actresses went through the final scene without a hitch and the director said, "Cut. That's very good. That's it for today." Ava Gardner put her arm around Sophia Loren and gave her an affectionate hug, breaking into a broad smile. "You're doing great, baby, great," she said.

Later, I chatted with Sophia Loren, whom I had first met in Naples when she was filming Pirandello's *The Voyage* with Richard Burton and Vittorio de Sica directing. "Ava's a delight to work with," said Sophia. "And a fine actress. She's also a beautiful woman and a wonderful companion. This has not been an easy movie to do—we're shooting out of sequence and most of the scenes take place on a constricted set—inside a train."

Sophia Loren, in turn, has been admired by most of her colleagues, unusual for an actress who could easily have turned into a cordially detested prima donna, like some others in the Italian cinema. She is outgoing and generous and usually has her mother somewhere around the set. "Mama's not getting any younger," she once told me, "and I want her to feel included." La Loren was a self-made product, rising out of the Neapolitan slums to the level of international stardom, which few other Italian actresses have achieved. She was originally spotted in a crowd of extras by Italy's foremost casting director Guidarino Guidi, who told me, "She had that certain something—beyond her beauty. Call it bearing, carriage, or character. But when she opened her mouth, we were horrified. It was the worst sort of vulgar Neapolitan speech. But Sophia did what most Italian actors don't do—she worked hard on her diction. And now her Italian is impeccable and her English is good enough to shoot sound-on-film for international productions."

Guidi elaborated, "Much of Italian acting is based on comedy. And so much of comedy in Italy is the humor of regionalism. A heavy Neapolitan dialect, for instance, can be used only for comedy—never taken seriously for tragedy. How can you get actors to speak English for an international audience when they can't even speak Italian? It is curious that in a country that idolizes cinema stars, we have less than a handful of world-class actors. You mention Marcello Mastroianni and Sophia Loren and you fall off quickly. Let's face it, Italian actors and actresses are like mozzarella cheese—they don't travel very well or very far."

I always found Richard Burton warm, pleasant, and outgoing on the set of a movie, a true professional when he wasn't drinking. When he was on the bottle, he was a different man. Nigel Dempster, London's leading gossip columnist, told me about the time when, based in New York for the *Daily Mail*, he went out to Long Island to ask Burton about his latest breakup with Elizabeth Taylor. He sent in his British passport to the guarded, private mansion as a way of proving his identity. It was about nine o'clock in the morning and Burton was already hitting the vodka bottle. Dempster was offered a drink and the columnist sent word to the guardhouse that Burton wanted no more journalist callers. Three hours and a vodka bottle later, both gentlemen were well on their way—Burton to bed and Dempster to phone in his exclusive—with a passel of reporters still clamoring empty-handed outside the gate.

I liked actors with a rogue male quality about them—people like Burton. So I was enthusiastic when the office accepted my suggestion that I fly to Marrakesh in Morocco to do a piece on the filming of Rudyard Kipling's story "The Man Who Would Be King," in the High Atlas Mountains. The movie was being directed by John Huston

and starred Michael Caine and Sean Connery. The setting was meant
to duplicate the North-West Frontier country in Pakistan—another part
of the world that fascinated me. I drove up a winding road to a dusty
village called Tagadirt-El-Bour and found the location company in full
swing.

Huston said hello and told me about the story: "It's a great
adventure tale, with excitement, color, spectacle, and humor. It's also
a splendid story of two tough and likeable rogues who are loyal to each
other and to their ideals, such as they are. They are not little men." It
sounded like my kind of movie.

The script appeared tailored for the British stars, with their
working-class backgrounds and service in the armed forces. I thought
Caine and Connery naturals in the roles of the two profane musketeers.

"I've been friends with Michael for twenty years," Connery told
me, "but this is the first chance I've had to work with him. He's great
fun, a grand bloke." He rolled up his undershirt sleeve, exposing a
tattoo on his right forearm—not a fake Marlboro-man paste-on but the
real thing: a dagger through a heart with the inscription SCOTLAND
FOREVER, a souvenir from the Royal Navy, which he joined from
Edinburgh at sixteen. Caine served with the Royal Fusiliers, recruited
from cockney London, in West Berlin and Korea, and said of Huston,
"John knows what he wants and takes pains to get it. But there is
always room for improvisation. In my regiment, we had a real London
cockney sergeant who used to scream at recruits, 'Fall in by threes.
That's one behind the other—twice.' So we worked that line into a
scene.

"John doesn't muck about much," added Caine. "He might just
say one word like, 'Faster,' or 'Slower.' Sounds simple. But you
change the speed of your phrasing and it changes the rhythm and the
whole tone of the scene."

I watched Connery and Caine working together, amused by their
wisecracks, setting an infectious tone that prevaded the company. At
one point, they were waiting to get aboard horses, wearing uniforms of
sergeants in the British Army.

"Michael, old boy," asked Connery, "didn't you wear one of
those kits in *Zulu*?"

"Bloody right, luv," quipped Caine. "In me first film I was a
lieutenant. Twelve years later and I'm demoted back to sergeant. No
bloody justice."

Connery noticed that one of the extras in the line of march was swinging his sword perilously close to the soldier behind him. "Look here, man," said Connery. "Carry your sword like this. You're about to castrate your mate behind you. He wouldn't like that, now, would he?"

Later, I sat outside a tent with Caine and Connery and we got to talking about the movie business from an actor's point of view. Caine nudged Connery and said with a smile, "Good actors don't try to upstage each other. Hell, you need the other actor's lines to make any sense of your own lines. Nowadays, there's no room in this business for stupid temperament. When you see a chronic display of temper, you can almost be sure the actor is covering up insecurities or lack of confidence." He pointed a finger at Connery and added, "You can be sure that with Sean and myself there is no lack of confidence because we are extremely experienced actors."

"That doesn't mean we are any good," cracked Connery. "But we sure as bloody hell are experienced.

"Another important thing," he added "when you've got a piece of the gross—which we have—you're interested in the good of the movie, and there's no room for jealousies."

"I don't know what Sean's making from this picture," said Caine, loosening his shirt, "but I don't care. The way I see it, if you get what you ask for, then whatever anybody else makes is irrelevant."

Both men looked their parts, brawny and tanned, certainly no juvenile matinee idols. "Ten years ago, I couldn't have played this part," said the forty-one-year-old Caine. "I would simply have been too young-looking. But this is a heavyweight role with lots of comedy. So age has its advantages."

At forty-four, Connery's hair was receding and graying, but he was little concerned about maintaining the looks of the younger James Bond. "Frankly," he said, "I don't like to wear a bloody wig. If the role requires one, I'll put the damn thing on, but I would prefer to be natural. Fortunately, I don't need a wig in this part. The other day, John Huston told me to take the straw out of my moustache. I told him, that's no bloody straw, that's gray hair."

Michael Caine said a few words in French to the Moroccan extra, and Connery observed, "I envy Michael's ability to speak French. When I was in school, I had the choice of learning French or metal-working. My father asked me, 'Who do you know in France?' So I took metalworking."

I had done a piece on the increasing political activism among actors in Britain during the preceding election; I had interviewed Vanessa Redgrave, a candidate for a Parliament seat who insisted on reading me the manifesto of her Workers Revolutionary party—despite the fact that I had read it and everything else in the tiny West Ham office while awaiting her very belated arrival. I asked Connery about the subject.

"The Scottish nationalists asked me to stand as a candidate, but I wouldn't want to devote anything less than full time to a job like that, and my work is acting. I'm not one of those armchair socialists, the actors and actresses campaigning on revolutionary party platforms. I don't like rich actors telling me about the problems of the working class, people who got their information only by reading about it. That sticks in my throat. I'm from the bloody working class and I know what the pluses and minuses are. As long as unions are more concerned with the downfall of capitalism than wages, it defeats the purpose of the exercise. The British have to learn that profit is not a dirty word. I don't see much hope for England unless management and labor can talk the same language."

I found it pleasant to be with two old pros—much as I had with Ava Gardner and Sophia Loren—who liked and respected each other, and who in turn were highly regarded by their fellow actors and technicians in the company, up there in the mountains.

"I spent a lot of time learning this profession," Caine said by way of explanation, "and I know how much a decent word is appreciated. So I always try to speak to everyone in the company and to come up with a joke. Sean is great to work with—I'd like to make another picture with him."

Back in Rome, an actress friend introduced me to director Bernardo Bertolucci, whose movie *Last Tango in Paris*, which he wrote and directed, had become a controversial international block-buster, with Marlon Brando and Maria Schneider in the leading roles. I invited him to lunch, and over a steak Florentine, I asked him about the subject matter: a couple who meet apartment hunting and embark on a frenetic three-day love affair—with graphic language and sexual scenes, including sodomy and masturbation.

"Pornography is a word that never came to my mind when I was making the film," Bertolucci said. "I didn't even know whether I would actually shoot the erotic scenes. But it seemed to me that it was more authentic to film the scenes rather than leaving them to the morbid imagination. Otherwise, I thought it would be like making a western without any gunplay.''

Tall, dark, shy, soft-spoken, Bertolucci added, ''The language, after all, is the language most of us use. And the erotic scenes? Well, the scenes may upset some people. But the film is full of things that upset me, too.''

He paused, thought, and then said, ''Actually, *Last Tango* is a rather sentimental picture. Whether it is art is a matter of opinion. But it is about a man whose marriage is a failure and who seeks some kind of authenticity in modern life. He finds this authenticity through Eros. I'm trying to get rid of the obsessive American image of sex as Doris Day in pajamas. You might call this film *An American in Paris— Twenty Years Later.''*

The Bertolucci film-making style is one of improvising. ''I'm always ready to change any script,'' he said. ''The script is something to read and forget about. It is boring to shoot every line and scene from the printed page. There are no surprises that way. In *Tango* I told Marlon that it was important to forget about the script and to create something fresh during the shooting, a cinéma vérité. Marlon did so and changed a lot of his dialogue on the set.''

Though a Marxist, Bertolucci's politics rarely intrude in his films. However, he told me, he drew heavily on psychoanalytic theory, particularly that of Wilhelm Reich. He said he had been undergoing psychoanalysis since he was twenty-eight (he was then thirty-one) and said it deeply influenced him. But it hadn't stopped him from having a string of girl friends.

Bernardo readily admitted to me that he actively sought success. ''Subconsciously, I have been looking for success in that I would like the widest possible audience for my work. I believe in communion with people. And I don't believe much in luck. I believe that we have to create luck for ourselves, even if, at the time, we may not realize we are doing this. Success is only important when you don't have it. When you have it, it doesn't mean anything.

''My good friend Alberto Moravia called me the other day to tell me that all you have to do is eat success—that is, live with the experience. If you have a good stomach, you can digest success. You chew it, swallow it, forget about it, and go on about your work.''

If Bertolucci is an example of director as improviser, Billy Wilder is the man who likes to get his cinematic ducks all in a row well before shooting. I called on him at the Rome studio where he was filming a comedy called *Avanti* with Jack Lemmon, Walter Matthau, and Juliet Mills. He told me the previous year he had landed in Rome during a hotel service workers' strike and there was no hot water available. So the Hollywood jack-of-all-arts strolled up to Via Veneto and accepted the solicitation of a local sporting lady. "Imagine her surprise," he recalled, "when I disappeared into her bathroom, took my bath, dressed, deposited the fee on the dresser—while she awaited me in bed—and bid her *arrivederci*."

Of the Italian catch-as-catch-can style of putting a film together, Wilder countered, "I like an orderly production. I find that if there is a lot of confusion during the making of a film, you usually get confusion on the screen. For a comedy, a good script is essential. You can't go out on the set with a company that is costing you twenty thousand or thirty thousand dollars a day and wait for the muse to kiss your brow. You don't hope that you or your actors will come up with great jokes or dialogue on the spur of the moment. They won't. Sure, you want to stay flexible and incorporate suggestions made on the set as you go along. But you don't depend on it. It is my experience that you get only three percent or at the most five percent with those improvised bursts of inspiration. Good film comedy is not created by winging it but by preparation. And it doesn't hurt to have pros in the cast. You don't find a Cary Grant, a Carole Lombard, or a Jack Lemmon on the street. Lemmon is marvelous in comedy, both visually and verbally. You can't analyze it. He was born with it."

Despite his eminence in the field, Wilder preferred not to reminisce about his past successes: *Sunset Boulevard, The Apartment, Some Like It Hot, One-Two-Three, Seven-Year Itch, Stalag 17, The Lost Weekend, Double Indemnity,* and *Ninotchka.*

"I don't look back," he said, shades shielding his eyes from the bright Roman sun. "Maybe I'll remember a good ten-minute stretch of film. But what counts is what you are working on now. Of course you hate to remember the failures. The trouble with Hollywood is that it doesn't bury its dead. A bad picture hangs around for years to haunt you on the late, late show. The great agony in film-making is that you don't have any tryouts in Boston or New Haven. Once it's filmed, it's too late. Nor do I believe the stories about redoing a picture in the cutting room. It's got to be there. It's got to play.

"Sometimes as you go along, the picture seems to taste good and you get the feeling that it's all going to jell. But the worst feeling for a director is to be two thirds through a movie and then feel it beginning to curdle. You're not like a painter, able to toss out the canvas and start over. You're painting on a canvas that has cost from one million to eight million dollars and you can't throw it away. Pictures cost so much today and the number of box-office successes is so few that it is an enormous gamble to make a movie. Not only money is involved: You've invested a year of your life and energies. It can be heartbreaking.

"Filming a comedy is a terribly tricky business. Each day you keep fashioning segments of a jigsaw puzzle and hope that all the little pieces will make a coherent whole. You also have to improve the smallest details, for if you polish up each detail in a comedy, the sum total will show through. So you can never be sloppy with detail, timing, and nuance. Comedy is such a fragile product made for such a fickle audience. You live with the constant fear of winding up with egg on your face. You hope that what seemed fresh when you wrote and filmed it will be fresh when seen by the audience. If the audience is unresponsive when you are waiting for laughs, the silence is shattering. And there is always that mysterious element in comedy: Have we got it? Have we conjured up the two hours of magic to make them forget their popcorn and talk about the film for twenty minutes in the drugstore afterward?

"You think you have caught something in a film. But you never really know until the sneak preview in Pomona whether you have conjured up the magic—whether you will hear that priceless sound of laughter in the theater."

Having talked to directors representing various approaches to cinema, I asked casting director Guidarino Guidi for a drink at the Café de Paris on Via Veneto for his views on Italian directors. He was a highly regarded authority on Italian film-making, though his name is unknown outside Italy, and he was not afraid to speak out forthrightly with his peppery views.

He told me that Italy lagged far behind other countries in the theater because actors and actresses, with a few exceptions, lacked a national theatrical consciousness. "That's why our actors are limited," he observed. "Take a Sicilian actor: He feels uneasy in Rome, lost in Florence, and if he gets as far north as Venice, he thinks he is in a foreign country.

"But Italian directors have not succumbed to regionalism, though in some cases, like Fellini's, their sense of place has been a source of great strength. That's why they have achieved an international identity."

I asked him to discuss the various Italian directors and he gave me these thumbnail critiques. I wrote furiously in my notebook, ignoring my drink. I think Guidi's assessments have stood up well.

Roberto Rossellini: "He changed the way movies were made and the way reality was perceived. But realism in film-making caught up with him and he never recovered. Now he has faded badly, and he has even rejected his best period, not even sure that it was right."

Vittorio de Sica: "He was a stage star for years before directing and that is why he could get such intimacy into a film. Half Neapolitan, he understood the human heart, and could produce emotion on the screen. At his best, he was a great director."

Franco Zeffirelli: "He is overly concerned with spectacle. Simplicity is not his forte. But he has tremendous taste, and with his background as a set designer, knows the visual arts well. But for all his ability in composition, something is lacking at the core. He sees the trees but not the forest. Yet his trees are marvelous."

Luchino Visconti: "He never lost sight of the forest, though many of his pictures are flawed. Actually, his best work was probably in opera, where he made all the theatrical elements come together best. At his peak, he could control both the details and the whole to perfection."

Michaelangelo Antonioni: "Next to Visconti, the least provincial of all Italian directors. But in becoming an intellectual, he tried to intellectualize his films. And in so doing he lost his touch. He seems to be going through some kind of identity crisis to find out who he really is. It shows, and his films have become a bore."

Pier Paolo Pasolini: "He was a friend but I didn't like his films. They were very cultured but he was trying to say things on the screen that were better suited for print. He was an intelligent, acute observer, but he thought cinematic form was not important. So his films were primitive and haphazard. Only his early films were good."

Bernardo Bertolucci: "By contrast, Bernardo pays too much attention to form. Each frame is composed, too much so. He has become an interior decorator. I thought *Last Tango* was overpraised. Though Bertolucci and Pasolini address themselves to the same issues, Bertolucci has much less to say. The fact that his last film, *Novacento* [1900] ran six hours after the final cutting tells you something very unfortunate about his work."

Lina Wertmuller: "She's tremendously popular with the New York critics, but in Europe we think she is superficial and vulgar. In *Swept Away,* after five minutes, you've seen it all. And in her films, she despises women, turning them into whores and rascals. Perhaps that's why American critics find her interesting. She has turned the American matriarchy—wives and mothers—into the villains.''

Liliana Caviani: ''Vulgar, vulgar. Seeking only commercial success. Let's forget her.''

Federico Fellini: ''He is the best. He does things nobody else can do. Sometimes he misses, but he always conveys the magic. His mistakes are always intelligent ones. He has a special vision of the world and manages to get it on film. He is a director at once simple and baroque, and he has the courage to be his own man and make films his own way. You are not indifferent to a Fellini film: You either love it or hate it. You are not bored. At his best, he creates that special magic only cinema can impart.''

Guidi, who comes from an aristocratic Tuscan family, landed his first job at twenty-two as a casting assistant on *Quo Vadis?*, then worked for Fellini and Dino de Laurentiis. At forty-five, he decided to become an agent specializing in up-and-coming actors and actresses.

''I despised agents,'' he told me, laughing as he did so. ''And I still do, except for myself. When you examine what we do, though, you find that casting directors help create films—but agents can create careers. And, in the end, that is more fun, more satisfying and lasting.''

On the eve of the 1973 Mideast war, I drove to Caprarola, north of Rome, to a sixteenth-century villa where *The Abdication* was being shot with Liv Ullmann and Peter Finch. The Norwegian actress had thrown herself into the role of Queen Christina, the Swedish monarch who abdicated in 1654 to become a Roman Catholic.

''I don't think I've ever been as much influenced by a role as this one,'' she told me; she was wearing riding clothes and resting against a balustrade. ''There are so many historical versions of Queen Christina—that she was a terrible whore, or that she was a lesbian, or even that she was a hermaphrodite—you can choose your own version. Christina was the women's liberationist of her time. She was a troubled woman looking for fulfillment. She dared to make her own life, to break from conventions. She couldn't cope with marriage or children. She didn't behave as a woman was supposed to; she went to extremes and a lot of people hated her for that. The challenge is to show Christina's unloved nature and her vulnerability—after her abdication and arrival in Rome.''

Ullmann told me she was angry at *Time* magazine, which had just done a cover story on her. She said the original reporter assigned to spend a couple of weeks with her was intelligent and serious—but his long file did not contain enough material about her sex life. So New York assigned another reporter, who kept probing into the details of her relationship with the Swedish director, Ingmar Bergman, by whom she had a child. She told the reporter to get lost. She told me she couldn't understand why a national newsmagazine was interested in her sex life. This I thought sounded a bit naïve, coming from a very intelligent and worldly lady.

Liv Ullmann liked to tell self-deprecatory stories about herself, such as the time at a Hollywood party when she was told that Mae West wanted to meet her. The ancient Miss West was escorted across a room by two young men. She gazed intently at the blue-eyed Norwegian actress through heavy crooked eyelashes and held her hand. As Mae West turned away, Liv heard her say, "Who the hell was that?"

Peter Finch complained to me that they wanted to put a lot of makeup on his face—as Cardinal Azzolino, the Vatican politician who was assigned to determine the validity of Queen Christina's conversion.

"I've spent fifty-three years earning these wrinkles," he grumbled, "and I don't want them wiped out overnight."

Finch fished a cigarette out of his trouser pocket under the scarlet robes of a prince of the Church and remarked, "Actually, I don't mind this getup, except for the high-heeled shoes—they're killing me. I don't know how the ladies stand them. I find that a cardinal's costume is somehow very manly. And do you know something? Women on the set tell me they find me—as a cardinal—rather interesting. Maybe it has something to do with the supposed unattainability. But they say they find the number intriguing and sexy."

The Abdication did not do very well at the box office; neither did many of the films I watched being made. One reason, I thought, was that the scripts—or at least the outlines I read—were weak and lacked strong narratives. I mean, what do you do with Pirandello on screen, even when you've got Richard Burton and Sophia Loren in the picture? That's why *The Voyage* flopped. I certainly can't pick a box-office winner. But many of the films in the making I covered looked like sure losers. When once I asked Richard Burton how he got tangled up in a nonstarter, he replied simply, "An actor's got to work."

On the other hand, Michael Caine took the position: "You don't go into a film thinking, 'This is a load of crap but I need the money,' although when you saw the film you might think that. I do things that I like and then make sure that I get the maximum amount of money out of it. I figure if I'm going to work, someone's going to make massive amounts of money. One of the people is going to be me."

CHAPTER EIGHT

Revolution in China

FROM ROME, I acted as a roving fireman, wandering afar, not only to the Middle East, but from Timbuktu to Katmandu, from Peoria (to find out whether the McGovern presidential ticket would play) to Peking.

Arnaud de Borchgrave, based in Geneva, and I had been included on the 1973 inaugural flight of Ethiopian Airlines to China and I flew from Rome to Addis Ababa. I was dining in the hotel restaurant with my nose in a book about China when I noticed a handsome couple dancing. They were extremely graceful. They sat down at the booth next to me, and only then did I realize they were Candice Bergen and William Holden. He had business interests in East Africa and was passing through. Candy had just completed a photo-reporting trip to Kenya with the Masai tribe and she had gotten an interview with aging Emperor Haile Selassie at the royal palace in Addis. Arnaud and I took her to dinner the following evening and she told us of her problems with the Masai chief. "He assumed because he was the chief and I was a woman that he could exercise his rights in bed," laughed Candy. "It wasn't easy letting him know that I didn't come with the territory." Candy is bright and straightforward and admitted she got a greater thrill seeing her name over a story than on the screen.

We took off for China the next day, flying all night over the Indian Ocean and the subcontinent. My first glimpse of China the next morning was from thirty-three thousand feet with the dawn firing the tips of the serrated Wu-Liang Mountains, through the valleys of which coursed the headwaters of the Salween, Mekong, and Red rivers. Then we picked up the great arc of the Yangtze River and followed it eastward toward the rising sun. However, we were diverted by ground fog at Shanghai to Canton, several hundred miles to the south. This worried me because I assumed the Ethiopian crew members were not familiar with this airport, which had to be approached by a tricky flight up the Pearl River estuary. The big 707 eased down through the soup, with me nervously nipping at a brandy flask, and broke into the clear just over the junks and sampans. In the Canton waiting room, a pigtailed waitress offered us coffee. I practiced my Chinese by saying, *"Shee-shee,"* which means, "Thanks." "Don't mention it," she replied in English.

Later in Shanghai, the world's most populous city with twelve million souls, we were put up at the Peace Hotel, formerly the Cathay, where Noël Coward wrote *Private Lives*. The signs were in Chinese, English, and Russian, the room threadbare but clean, with plenty of floor boys and quick service. De Borchgrave and I doubled up and our room boy told us we need not lock the door. "Nothing is stolen in revolutionary China," said our interpreter.

Arnaud was furious. Although he had been working on this trip for weeks, writing letters and sending telexes trying to set up appointments with Premier Chou En-lai and Chairman Mao Tse-tung, *Newsweek*'s foreign editor, Ed Klein, at the last minute had grabbed a seat on a similar inaugural flight by Pakistan Airlines, which was extending its route from Shanghai to Peking, and he hadn't bothered to notify De Borchgrave. The Chinese, who go by the bureaucratic rule book, were totally confused: Klein claimed he was Arnaud's boss and therefore the recipient of any major interviews; Arnaud said that he was the chief foreign correspondent and Klein was only in effect a clerk. The confusion resulted in neither journalist getting an interview with either of the two leaders.

Arnaud, Roy Rowan of *Time* magazine, Charles Devine of the *Reader's Digest,* and I took a walk along the famous old Bund on the Wang-Poo riverfront, once the haunt of good-time girls and remittance men. We foreigners attracted quite a crowd of onlookers. Of the excursion Devine wrote, "Tuohy is marked by a heavy shock of silver-white hair. I had the feeling the Chinese thought that Tuohy was some kind of Caucasian potentate and that De Borchgrave, Rowan, and I were part of his palace guard."

At dinner that night, we were served up a typical meal: sauteéd duck cubes with chili sauce, sauteéd pork slices with bamboo shoots, sauteéd shrimps with tomato sauce, cabbage sauteéd in chicken fat, crisp duck, mushroom soup, rice, green tea, and beer. We also quaffed during toasts a lethal, kirschlike potion called mao-tai. The toasts were quite amusing: "To the Imperial Government of Ethiopia and its anti-imperialists struggle." Damn clever, those Chinese.

At dinner, I asked San Kuo-chang, editor of *Wan Wei*, the local literary gazette, how China had received the news of the death of Defense Minister Lin Piao, who was reportedly killed in a plane crash in Mongolia while trying to flee the country after an abortive coup against Mao. "We did not print the story," he said. "Everybody knows what happened. So there's no need to repeat it. Anyway, it's all over now."

I was up at six o'clock the next morning, peering out the window at the bustling waterfront: foghorns, sirens, whirring cranes, and the park filled with people. Outside, I watched the Chinese going through their morning exercises undaunted by the chill wind. A group of older people performed the slow-motion boxinglike movements known as tai chi. Younger men and women followed their instructor's balletlike movements. He wore a red sweater, which was the only sign of color I saw in men's clothing in China, except on the stage.

We flew to Peking in a Soviet-made Il-62, which my interpreter told me privately the Chinese were not happy with. They were expecting to get Boeing 707s. We crossed the North China Plain, all browns, buffs, and yellows, wheat country like South Dakota. We drove into the Chinese capital with its stately boulevards, the people moving at a much slower pace than in Shanghai, and it was hard to believe seven million lived there. The hotel corridor was studded with spittoons, for the Chinese leadership, despite a national campaign, had still not eradicated the custom of hawking and spitting.

At lunch, I asked a teacher about the condition of women in revolutionary China. "Women have become the equals of men," she said. "All jobs are open to all and the salaries of men and women are the same in my job. But in many areas, we still have to raise the position of women because, in the feudal times before liberation, they were treated as inferiors."

And a woman executive on the revolutionary committee, Mrs. Chen Shan-lian, told me, "To realize the magnitude of this revolution you must know that within the lifetime of older women in China, their feet were bound and hobbled because men thought this beautiful. Baby girls were sometimes put to death or sold into bondage because their families could not afford to feed them. Girls were subject to arranged marriages. Sometimes they were sold off as child brides. In the old days, women could not obtain divorces nor could widows remarry. Only well-to-do girls could obtain higher education and the only work women could do outside the home was the backbreaking stoop labor in the fields. But now, we have women party members, doctors, nurses, interpreters, taxi drivers, pilots, soldiers, and peasants.''

That evening, I had a woman cabdriver: they seemed to pilot at least half of Peking's three hundred taxis. There were few restaurants open late, though, and Peking seemed deader than Peoria. I dined with Jim Pringle, the Reuters bureau chief I'd known in Saigon. Pringle, a Scotsman, was quite a ladies' man and I asked him what the situation was like in Peking for a bachelor like himself. He just returned from a reporting trip to the capital of Outer Mongolia and answered, ''Bill, I had to go all the way to Ulan Bator to get laid.''

En route back to the hotel, a friend pointed out a light burning in an upstairs room in the Great Hall of the People. ''That's Chou's office,'' he said. ''We think he's got an apartment there, too.''

On Sunday, we visited both a Protestant chapel and a Catholic church but there were only a handful of worshipers at the services. I was told there was a mosque in Peking but no synagogue. Since proselytizing is not allowed, I got the impression that the Chinese were letting Western religion die out as the older parishioners died off. ''Religions were a foreign import,'' a Chinese journalist told me. ''We don't need religion. We have the thoughts of Mao to guide us.''

Unexpectedly, our group—that is, the official party from Ethiopia—received a hasty summons: Prime Minister Chou En-lai would receive us in the Great Hall of the People on Tien An Men Square. We gathered in a room that could easily hold a couple of jumbo jets and the magnetic leader walked briskly in. His brushed-back black hair was streaked with gray. But at seventy-four, his eyebrows were full and dark. Though only five feet, five inches tall, he projected an aura of great presence and assurance, a curious amalgam of tension and serenity. I shook hands with him and noticed that his right arm was injured—during the Long March of 1936, an aide told me—and he held it with his left hand afterward. Chou wore a well-tailored gray tunic suit, a shade different in color from those of the other high officials with him. He moved easily from table to table, shifting from small talk through interpreters to serious questions, clinking his glass of mao-tai in a personal toast to each of us at the various tables. At one point, he summoned an official we had been trying to see—with merely a word to a subordinate. When asked why some Chinese officials were so difficult to contact, he replied urbanely, "They are still too worried about being seen with foreigners."

I asked him what was the greatest remaining obstacle to U.S.-Chinese relations, and he replied in a slightly ironic tone, "You know the answer. You must realize that Taiwan is a province of China. That will solve everything and we will then shake hands."

Chou then gave us the first tip-off that there would be an exchange of news correspondents based in the United States and China. And he accurately predicted that the United States and North Vietnam would reach agreement in Geneva.

After an hour of moving from table to table answering questions—a bravura performance—he waved a graceful good-bye and left the Great Hall of the People, alone.

During our ten-day visit, we saw steel mills, farming communities, textile factories, housing projects, silk-spinning plants, schools, day-care centers, and hospitals. At one school, Mrs. Shi Jing Shan, who was in charge, told me, "We teach our children according to the policy of Chairman Mao. Through his teaching, the student can develop morally, intellectually, and physically, to become a socialist worker." I asked a six-year-old boy what he wanted to be when he grew up. "A worker, or soldier, or peasant," he said. A six-year-old girl replied, "Peasant."

I found that in revolutionary China, sex did not rear its ugly head, at least not so that you could notice. The country, in fact, seemed to have turned into a vast puritanical society, like a great Red monastery, and not at all like my youthful days in Tsingtao.

The nation that had invented the enticing slit-skirt cheongsam had become the least permissive society in Asia. No romance in movies or literature. No displays of public affection. No sex-oriented ads anywhere. Officials told me they were trying to keep the birth rate down to two children per family through increased use of contraceptives, reduced sexual activity, and later marriages.

Roy Rowan, who had been based in China between the end of World War II and the communist takeover in 1949, tried to get our interpreter, Mr. Yu, to refresh his memory about some curse words he once used. "Please," said Mr. Yu, "we do not swear in revolutionary China."

One morning at breakfast in Hangchow, a lovely resort city with ingratiating gardens and lakes, we sat next to the Cuban table tennis team. Our interpreter, Mr. Yu, said Chinese sports are not competitive, though the national team strives for proficiency. "Friendship first, competition second," he said. Two nights before, we learned, the provincial Chinese team beat the Cuban national team. But to help the Cubans save face, the Chinese let the Cubans win over a university team. "Friendship first, competition second."

We headed south for the emerald-green fields of South China, and the surrounding palm trees seemed to make the people themselves softer, gayer, and more talkative than those in the harsh northern plains. Canton's semiannual trade fair draws thousands of foreigners and thus the city is more comfortable with strangers. "That's the hotel we reserve for the Japanese," said my escort-interpreter. "We want to separate them from the human beings." I gathered there was still no love lost in Sino-Japanese relations.

In Canton's hospital, we watched two operations involving acupuncture anesthesia going on simultaneously in adjoining theaters. A fifty-six-year-old woman had her right breast removed because of a cancerous tumor while, next door, a thirty-six-year-old woman was having a benign thyroid tumor taken out. The surgeons proceeded quickly and skillfully with the patients fully conscious, showing no sign of pain. The thyroid patient looked up at us, smiled, and waved.

Toward the end of the trip, Mr. Yu asked me why I was working so hard, taking so many notes. I couldn't resist. "Chairman Nixon," I said, "says we must all work hard for the state and we must be right in thinking and purge ourselves of error." Mr. Yu laughed. Impulsively, I gave him a present, though it was against the rules; I slipped him my gold Cross pen. He asked how much it cost. I said, "Fifteen dollars," or whatever, and he said that it was too expensive and he couldn't accept it. I thought fast and said, "Hong Kong dollars," which were five to the U.S. dollar, and made the pen acceptable.

At Canton, I boarded the clean, comfortable diesel-powered express called the East is Red for Hong Kong, moving past paddy fields with bullocks pulling plows in terraced hillsides. Ahead lay westernized Asia: autos and advertising, Coca-Cola and hamburgers, mascaraed Chinese girls in hip-hugging jeans, the captivating fruits of a rowdy, capitalistic society. Behind lay China, Chunghua, the center of the world, with a billion people—austere, monumental, mystifying, incredibly beautiful.

*   *   *

A foreign correspondent gets more than a passing acquaintance with the Four Horsemen of the Apocalypse: death, war, pestilence, and famine. In the summer of 1973, I flew to the Sahelian Zone of Africa during the first of the major famines to strike that unlucky continent. In Arabic, *sahel* means "edge of the desert," and this region comprises the southern rim of the Sahara, that great expanse of sand which stretches from the Atlantic to the Red Sea. The desert has been steadily encroaching on savanna lands to the south, forcing nomads to trek south, wiping out their herds of camels, sheep and goats, and threatening them with extinction.

The chief victims were the Tuaregs, the Saharan warrior-nomads of Caucasian stock—a tall, graceful race of striking bearing and beauty; their piercing blue eyes covered by white turbans, and their bodies sheathed in long indigo robes, which gives them the name "blue people." They preferred to drive their cattle back and forth across the desert and savanna lands, according to the season, rather than settling down to farm. As British anthropologist F. R. Rodd wrote: "The men are born to walk and move as kings. They stride along swiftly and easily like princes of the earth, fearing no man, cringing before none and consciously superior to other people." But the long drought in the Sahel has whittled away the population, possibly now not much more than one hundred thousand but no one knows.

The Tuaregs, a branch of the North African Berbers, were for centuries the lords of the Sahara, who taxed the gold and salt caravans, served as a link between the Mediterranean and central African cultures, and raided southern tribes for food, tribute, and slaves. Even in the extremity of famine, their society remains stratified, with a servant class that does the menial chores—since the warriors believe that manual labor is undignified. But the drought has played havoc with their civilization.

From Bamako, the capital of landlocked Mali where United Nations' officials were trying to organize famine relief, I hopped a ride on a U.S. Air Force C-130 transport lugging a cargo of emergency food supplies to Timbuktu. To me, as a schoolboy, Timbuktu was always synonymous with the outpost at the end of the line, the remotest place on earth. As the plane circled over the great bend of the Niger River, I at first had difficulty making out the town, so deeply did its mud huts blend in with the surrounding baked earth.

Once known as "the pearl of the desert," a major transit point for caravans coming down from the Sahara to the north, linking up with traders from the south, Timbuktu transshipped gold from Ghana and salt from Chad. It was an oasis from the harsh, vast desert. Now the town was rundown, the streets full of drifting sand, the sky gray from particles in the air. On landing, we unloaded sorghum, wheat, powdered milk, and corn. For, as the backwater administrative headquarters of Mali's northern region, Timbuktu had become the focal point for the thousands of nomads whose animals had died in the drought and who themselves were driven by hunger to seek refuge. The food was unloaded by tribesmen garbed in long robes, who placed the 125-pound bags of sorghum on their heads to carry them off.

Around Timbuktu, in goatskin tents the Tuaregs were suffering the most, yet with their classic view of townspeople, one tall tribesman ordered a government official in Timbuktu, "Give me food, slave."

Some Tuaregs, I was told, went insane or allowed themselves to waste away rather than adjusting to life in a refugee camp, and their graves stretched from Timbuktu in Mali to Agadez and Niamey in Niger. The bleached bones of their cattle stretched more than a thousand miles from the Sahara to Nigeria.

"But other Tuaregs now seem to realize their plight and have shown a willingness to change," a local official said. "But who knows whether in good years they will feel the ancient wanderlust, leave the farming communities to trek through the desert again—only to face starvation in the next long drought cycle?"

I watched a doctor at the clinic bury an infant in a makeshift new graveyard in a field of stunted millet plants. "Many of the old and very young are beyond help by the time they get here," a Red Cross worker told me. "They are sick with malnutrition, debilitated to the degree where we can do nothing for them. They are at the last point in life."

A trickle of rain began to fall while I was there, but one of the officials said that rain may have come too late. "The rains leave them cold and wet, easy victims for pneumonia in their weakened state," said the Red Cross worker.

"Unless they change from their nomadic ways, the Tuareg way of life is in grave jeopardy. Modern civilization, even by African standards, has passed them by. It is as if we are watching a race dying before our very eyes."

In Ouagadougou, the capital of Upper Volta whose name has been changed to Burkina, I found a superb restaurant run by a group of lay nuns who had a branch in Da Lat, Vietnam; and in Rome, both of which I had visited. The meal was delicious though I'll be the first to admit that there is something wrong with a world that provides a fine French restaurant in a town surrounded by famished Africans.

Sitting there over the coffee, I wondered if there was something wrong with me, being able to enjoy a meal while across Africa millions were starving. Yet, I thought, there was little I could do personally, and the restaurant, after all, was there. Perhaps my stories about the plight of the famine victims would help their lot. Nature had been cruel. But so had they contributed to the famine by overgrazing the land, interfering with nature's processes, intensifying the drought. And what could you say or do about the governments, those leaders in Mali, Burkina, Niger, Chad, the Sudan, Ethiopia, Somalia, who had been so blind to the problems of the drought and who so often used foreign food aid and funds to line their own pockets? Yet if I concentrated on how government officials skimmed off incoming supplies, would I not contribute to the general ennui of the First World when faced with Third World problems? I had no answers. I was watching a way of life die, as well as thousands of people, and I felt helpless. I drank my coffee and ordered a second cognac.

I encountered a similar problem in another part of the world, this time in Bangladesh, where mismanagement and corruption had led to widespread poverty, malnutrition, and ultimately revolution. I was in Washington on home leave in 1975 when Sheik Mujib Rahman, hailed as the father of Bangladesh, was assassinated. The foreign editor asked me if I could get to Dacca as soon as possible. I flew to Rome, changed clothes, and continued on to Bangkok just in time to catch the first plane allowed into Dacca in the wake of the coup d'etat. Dacca was a mess. Young officers had staged the coup one night in August 1975, rolled out of their cantonments and headed for Mujib's quarters. When the shooting ended, the president had been slaughtered along with fourteen members of his family including, sons, wives, and children.

The young Turks complained to us of their discontent because of Sheik Mujib's dictatorial yet dilatory ways of running his nation of eighty million people. Plain citizens and soldiers who fought the war of independence against Pakistan in 1972 were deeply unhappy with Mujib's tolerance of corruption and with the vicious behavior of his personal militiamen, who terrorized the countryside.

"It appeared that the officers wanted to wipe out the dynasty, root and branch," a Western diplomat told me on my arrival. They did so, but set the country up for a series of military leaders imposing martial law.

Wandering around Dacca, in the short time I had, I wondered whether any regime could run the country properly. In the streets of the moldering capital, children were hollow-eyed and gaunt, their sad faces reflecting the hunger pains that gnawed at swollen bellies. Many seemed reduced by poverty to a near-animal existence, with precious little hope for a future.

"It's a question of which of the Four Horsemen of the Apocalypse will reach here first," observed a United Nations official. For Bangladesh, the world's eighth most populous nation, has the highest population growth rate in Asia and the lowest per capita income. It had the dubious distinction of being first among what has come to be known as the Fourth World, countries set apart by grinding poverty from the developing nations of the Third World. I asked myself, Can Bangladesh be saved? Or should foreign aid funds be directed to countries with more of a future?

"Bangladesh need not be viewed as hopeless," a leading agronomist responded. "But saving the country will take an act of massive political will. The figures tell the story in a nutshell. Food production is growing by one percent while the population is increasing by three percent. There is no technical reason why Bangladesh cannot grow enough food to support one hundred fifty million people; it is a matter of political leadership and will."

Sheik Mujib, in the eyes of the army, did not have that will.

Hardly had we journalists pieced together a coherent account of what had happened or was going to happen, when the new government decided it had been a mistake to let us in—and we were all ordered out on the next flight, back to Bangkok. Some of my colleagues noted with irony that it was the foreign media coverage of East Bengal's plight that led to the Indian intervention, which assured Bangladeshi independence and freed Mujib from Pakistani captivity.

But Bangladesh was not the only country, of course, to expel foreign correspondents. The range of nations that allows the foreign press in and out is rapidly diminishing. The media—particularly reporters from Western democracies—are viewed as subversive and treacherous by an increasing number of Third World strongmen. Entry visas are difficult to get, sources are shut down, and censorship imposed. This view of foreign correspondents has almost been institutionalized by the current leadership of the United Nations Educational,

Scientific, and Cultural Organization (UNESCO), which believes the Western press is negatively slanted in its Third World coverage, and has advocated licensing journalists. Indeed, the scope for operating freely as a foreign correspondent has significantly narrowed in my time.

In Bangkok, I thought I'd do a couple of stories that I never had time for in the Far East, since my work was so exclusively devoted to Vietnam. One was a visit to Katmandu, which while I lived in Saigon, was depicted as a kind of peaceful Shangri-la, where hippies could puff away on dope in the shadow of the highest mountains on earth.

Hugh Mulligan had caught that mood with a lead from Katmandu: "There is no high like the high you get in the high Himalaya Mountains."

However, I was more interested in seeking out the Gurkhas, those tough little Nepalese mercenaries who had fought with the British Army for nearly two hundred years, who were truly "war followers." I had seen the doughty troopers, wearing their kukri knives, on duty in Oman, Hong Kong, Cyprus, and even Buckingham Palace.

En route, we flew at thirty-five thousand feet over an amazing sight: the Ganges River in massive flood, its mud-brown waters covering hundreds of thousands of miles of fields and towns—shimmering on a clear day. It was an awesome vision, particularly when I thought of the anguish it must be causing, as it stretched from horizon to horizon.

I was somewhat disappointed with Katmandu: The main square seemed to be used as an outdoor privy and stank. I was, however, taken with the huge, watchful Buddha on the gilded walls of the great Swayambhu Temple, designed to protect this Himalayan Shangri-la from harmdoers. It is perhaps no coincidence that Nepal's existence depends on its ability to ward off encroachment by either of its giant neighbors: China and India. The old town was a jumble of gongs, bells, and drums beaten by the purple-robed monks who administer the many temples, some trimmed with erotic carvings. The carvings are meant to fend off the goddess of storms, who is said to be rather prudish and thus would not descend on a place with such an outrageous display of sexual fun and games. Nepal survives through coexistence: between China and India; and Hinduism and Buddhism. The Nepalese, in fact, have come to accept Buddha as the incarnation of the Hindu god Vishnu. Sacred cows dozed in the center of busy streets, forcing traffic to detour. Small boys spun prayer wheels outside temples. Others flew their colorful, darting minikites from rooftops or the city parks. Outside the royal palace, immaculate Gurkha soldiers stood guard. The scents of curry and exotic spices were in the air. But the great flood of hippies in search of a high Himalayan high seemed to have dwindled to a trickle. Though you could still easily purchase ganja, the local base for hashish, on Darma Path, known to thousands of counterculturalists as Freak Street, the few young Westerners I saw tended to be more deeply motivated, some having taken up transcendental meditation.

I wanted to take a flight to get a good look at Mount Everest, at 29,028 feet the highest peak on earth, known locally as Chomolongma, or Mother Goddess of the World. But the monsoon season was closing in and heavy clouds covered eastern Nepal. So instead, I hired a driver to take me out through the glorious Katmandu Valley to visit the sturdy, two-story, lemon-colored barracks with green shutters with the sign reading BRITISH GURKHA TRANSIT CAMP.

I was met by the commander, a short, compact major with a ready smile named Gambahadur Gurung. He was an officer with the 6th Queen Elizabeth's Own Gurkha Rifles. Major Gurung showed me around the place; the walls were lined with the regimental badges: the 2nd King Edward VII's Own Gurkha Rifles, the 6th Gurkhas, the 7th Duke of Edinburgh's Own Gurkhas, and the 10th Princess Mary's Own Gurkhas.

The major wore the attire of a Gurkha officer: a green drill uniform with silver badges and a trim, wide-brimmed hat worn at a rakish angle. As we strolled, we chatted about the history of the Gurkhas. Over the centuries, the tribesmen coming from around the town of Gurkha, west of Katmandu, hired themselves out to the princelings of India to fight the border wars against Tibetans, Chinese, Baluchi, and Pathans. Early in the nineteenth century, the British began recruiting Gurkhas for duty, first in India, and then with Her Majesty's forces elsewhere in the world.

The British entered World War II with ten Gurkha regiments of two battalions each of about twenty thousand men. They won an inordinate number of Victoria Crosses, Britain's highest decoration for valor. And their deeds were the stuff of legend: Fighting near Monte Cassino in Italy, a Gurkha patrol found four sleeping Germans. They beheaded two of them, but left the other two alone, so as to transmit their panic to other troops—the Gurkha brand of psychological warfare.

Late in the war, the call went out to a Gurkha regiment for one hundred volunteers for airborne training. The British officers explained that the jump would be from a safe height of one thousand feet or more, but were surprised to find only forty men volunteering. A corporal in explaining his mates' reluctance to press forward muttered that five hundred feet was quite high enough to jump from. The officer explained that the parachutes almost never failed to open. "Oh, parachutes," said the surprised corporal when the device was explained. "That's different." And every man in the regiment stepped forward.

There was also the rifleman who escaped from a Japanese prison camp in Burma and walked for five months before reaching British lines in India, using a map he had somehow acquired. Intelligence officers examined the trooper and found all the trails and river fordings he crossed duly marked. But it turned out to be useless for their purposes: the Gurkha had been using a street map of London.

The late author John Masters, a decorated Gurkha field officer in Burma in World War II, said of them: "The distinguishing marks of the Gurkha are usually a Mongolian appearance, short stature, a merry disposition, and an indefinable quality that is hard to pin down with one word. Straightness, honesty, naturalness, loyalty, courage—all these are in it, but none is quite right, for the quality embraces all these."

By the end of World War II, the Gurkhas, totaled fifty-five battalions and had fought on every front, from Burma to France.

Major Gurung told me he had been in the Gurkhas for twenty-seven of his forty-three years—a very senior officer indeed. "I hope we are not witnessing the beginning of the end of the Gurkha battalions serving in the British Army," he said. "I would like to see the Gurkhas continue to play a strong role in the British forces. But here in the camp I see more old Gurkhas passing back through on their way to retirement than young Gurkhas being recruited for service.

"We used to recruit more than one thousand soldiers a year," mused the major. "Young shepherd boys from the hills. They make the best soldiers. Some are under age and insist they are sixteen. I myself enlisted when I was sixteen. But nowadays, we recruit only about three hundred boys a year."

With the dwindling responsibilities of empire, Britain has cut back on its ground forces, including Gurkhas. And with that reduction, a traditional way of life in Himalayan valleys is disappearing: the Gurkha soldier returning to his mountain village after a long, profitable military career and living happily ever after. For with the rising cost of living, a Gurkha's retirement pay no longer is sufficient to make ends meet.

Major Gurung introduced me to Padam Kumar Subba, a lean, moustached rifleman who had served in Malaysia, Borneo, Singapore, and Hong Kong. He wore civilian clothes with the Brigade of Gurkhas tie—crossed kukri knives on a green field. He was twenty-nine. Subba said he would have stayed in the Gurkhas for another enlistment: "But we were phasing back in strength and I was discharged. I don't want to go back to the hills so I am planning to stay here in Katmandu. I am hoping to become a tourist guide."

That seemed an anticlimax for a mountain tribesman. Yet I suppose it's a reflection of the changing nature of the modern world. Some retired soldiers want to go back home; others do not or cannot.

I asked Major Gurung about his plans.

"I have had a fine career," he said, not mentioning the ribbons for valor he wore on his chest. "I think the high point was leading Gurkha troops on guard duty at Buckingham Palace. I've had a good life as a Gurkha and I'm only sorry that there may not be room for young men, like myself once, to make the army their career.

"My career is about over now and, like the others, I will retire, too. It's time for me to settle down and do a little farming out in western Nepal."

He could have been a foreign correspondent speaking! How many times have I heard war reporters say they are looking forward to the day when they've got a nest egg for a ranch in Montana (Nick Proffitt) or a farm in Oregon (Jack Foisie) or a cabin in Vermont (Ward Just). I'm afraid it wouldn't work for me. As a city boy, I get uncomfortable after extended periods in the country. And I wouldn't really know what to do in retirement. I don't fish. I don't hunt. I don't garden. I'm not particularly reflective. I like drinking and talking to people. Call it an impoverishment of spirit, but I've always planned on working until the end.

My next plan was to get to the North-West Frontier Province in Pakistan and the Khyber Pass, an area that had long fascinated me. To do so I had to transit India. So I flew to Calcutta, about which my friend Jack Langguth once remarked, "Calcutta is a black hole."

Actually, I found the place rather appealing. I suppose I'm one of the few people who went to Calcutta as a tourist but was surprised that it was seething with life; and the architecture of the British Raj was still impressive. The Bengalis were lively and energetic, and I thought Calcutta a hell of a lot less depressing than Dacca.

I wanted to reach Lahore in Pakistan to see an American diplomat who I was told knew everything about the Pathan tribe of the North-West Frontier. I took an Indian Airlines flight to Amritsar, the sacred city of the Sikhs, at the Indian border of the great Punjab Plain. A taxi took me to the Golden Temple—the Sikh shrine—which was set on an island in a small lake in the middle of town. Once again, I found the rough rasp of religion, this time Sikhs versus Hindus, who were on the verge of their bloody clashes. At the border I was crossing, it was Hindus versus Muslims. In Katmandu, it was Hindus versus Buddhists. In Vietnam, it was Buddhists versus Catholics. In Ireland, it was Catholics versus Protestants. In Lebanon, Christians versus Muslims. And in Palestine, Muslims versus Jews. I had seen more blood shed over religion than politics or money. Would it ever end? Not as long as deep religious differences exist, I'm afraid.

At the border, which I reached by taxi, the Indians gave me a hard time, confiscating most of my notes and clippings, presumably because Prime Minister Indira Gandhi was conducting a vendetta against the press. After being held up for a couple of hours—I was the only person crossing the border—I was permitted to pass through. I was reminded of the crack made by Joe Fried of the New York *Daily News* who had spent some very frustrating months in New Delhi, "When it comes to the Indians, I'm on the side of the cowboys."

Lahore boasted a spectacular Mogul mosque; those emperors, really, were the greatest architects in the subcontinent. The city was garnished with structures of red sandstone and just out of town were the Gardens of Shalimar. I had an informative session with the American consul, who like some British diplomats, was captivated by the North-West Frontier Province and the Hindu Kush beyond. I flew on to Rawalpindi, the former capital which has been superseded by the new—and very dull—city of Islamabad. I quickly rented a car and driver and headed west across the Punjab, over the Indus River, and up into Peshawar, the colorful, flavorsome, dusty, market town, and capital of the North-West Frontier.

I drove into the gray-brown, rocky thirty-three-mile defile of the Khyber Pass, which falls mainly inside the Pakistan border with Afghanistan—a thin artery of government presence surrounded by a tribal no-man's-land. The pass was lined with the regimental plaques of the units that fought there over the decades, and it bristled with forts, artillery positions, and concrete tank-traps. High in the mountains, I stopped at the old Kiplingesque fort with crenellated parapets that garrisoned the troops of the fabled Khyber Rifles. But the regiment was not just a colorful anachronism. Even in the late twentieth century, the Khyber Rifles sallied forth to keep the peace in this troubled part of the world, the North-West Frontier Province of Pakistan.

The Frontier is the heart of the land of the Pathans, the fierce, independent, warlike tribal people whose fifteen million ethnic members inhabit one hundred thousand square miles of rugged high country on both sides of the Afghan-Pakistani border.

"There has always been a certain amount of trouble in the North-West Frontier," an official told me. "The Pathans today are restless. Even those in the settled areas feel neglected, that they are not getting a fair share of government development funds."

The Pathans form the largest tribal society in Asia, if not the world—they are extremely individualistic, and many give no allegiance to any central government authority. For hundreds of years, the Pathans have defended their strategic homeland, which lies athwart the main invasion route between the dry, barren plains of central Asia and the lush lowlands of the Indian subcontinent. Through the Khyber have marched the invaders: Persians, Greeks, Scythians, Parthians, Tartars, Moguls, and Afghans. The pass played a central role in the British defense of India, though the colonial troops never entirely succeeded in subduing the Pathans and suffered historic defeats at their hands. The lean, dynamic Pathans proved to be superlative warriors, masters of small-unit tactics and the use of mountainous terrain. It was to subdue the Pathan fighters that a soft, lead bullet was devised in a district of Calcutta called Dum Dum.

A Pathan, a Peshawar official told me, is the best of friends and the worst of enemies. They fight no-holds-barred: Torture and excruciating death for prisoners are part of the drill. Under Pakistani rule, the North-West Frontier is divided into a settled area, the lowlands toward the Indus River to the east, and a tribal area in the mountains to the west. The three million or so Pathans in the Pakistani tribal areas are a law unto themselves. Each family—the Mohammedzai, the Afridi, the Yusefzai, the Wazirs, the Sinwards, the Mahsud, the Khattak, and a dozen lesser ones—follow their own rules and recognize no central authority. The government's writ extends only along the major highways. There are no police or tax collectors.

The Pathan law is known as *Paktunwali,* or "the way of the

Pathans.'' It includes *melmastiya,* or hospitality; *manawati,* the right of sanctuary or asylum; and *badel,* or revenge. The harsh code, and disputes over land, women, or fancied slights, lead to long-standing blood feuds in the North-West Frontier. And the Pathan militiamen, like the Khyber Rifles and the Waziristan Scouts, keep the peace when serious incidents occur, operating out of ancient forts in the mountains.

North of the North-West Frontier, the Gilgit Scouts and the Northern Scouts—the former with an ibex, the latter with a snow leopard, for regimental badges—keep the peace in the ceiling of the world where the Himalayas, the Hindu Kush, and the Pamir mountain ranges come together.

Even before the Soviets invaded Afghanistan, there was a certain amount of trouble with the tribes of the North-West Frontier—and now the Pathans on the Afghan side of the border remain independent of the government and harass Soviet forces.

A Pathan specialist, Sultan Bahadar Yusefzai, over tea in the mountains, told me that a Pathan likes two things: a guest in his house and a gun on his shoulder. ''That makes him feel secure and comfortable,'' said Yusefzai. ''We call ourselves Pushtuns or Pukutuns, that is, those who speak Pushtu, our language. The word Pathan is a corruption by the British but it has stuck.''

Pathans dress in turbans, baggy pants, and robes, and most of those I saw carried rifles. They have a Semitic look and are often tall and handsome, with blue eyes. Many Pathans believe they are descended from a lost tribe of Israel, though some ethnologists dispute this.

''Many believe we came from Israel and that God has chosen us to rule,'' Yusefzai insisted.

The Pathans make natural leaders: the former president of Afghanistan Daud Mohammed Khan, whose overthrow triggered the series of events leading to the Soviet invasion, was a Pathan, as were former Pakistani leaders President Ayub Khan and General Yahya Khan.

Curiously, Pathans in the settled areas—several million—have quickly adapted to modern life, I learned, and have become proficient in the army, politics, and business. There are even farmers in California today whose fathers were born on the rocky flanks of the Khyber Pass.

But many Pathans prefer the traditional life, in which smuggling merchandise coming up from Karachi or homegrown local opium provide a thriving living in the mountains. So despite the Pakistani government's attempt to integrate the men of the North-West Frontier into modern life through improved economic benefits, it still seemed to me to be a long time before all Pathans trade in their swords for plowshares, their rifles for calculators.

In a way, I thought this was proper and poetic. With the Tuaregs facing extinction or citification and Gurkhas turning into tourist guides, the Pathans retained a kind of noble spirit I couldn't help admiring.

My paper was interested in doing a major story on the Indian Ocean as a developing cockpit between the U.S. and Soviet fleets, similar to a previous analysis I had done on the superpowers competing in the Mediterranean. For generations, the Indian Ocean was considered a backwater mainly because, while full of commerce, it was a well-policed British lake. But as the sun set on the British Empire, and London reduced its military commitments "east of Suez" (a catch phrase for the decision), a power vacuum developed and the superpowers gradually moved in.

I flew to Bombay to talk to Indian naval officers and then headed for Djibouti on the Horn of Africa at the entrance to the Red Sea. I took an Air India flight because it stopped at Aden in South Yemen, off limits to American journalists, but I hoped to talk my way into getting a transit visa at the airport. The South Yemeni officials didn't buy my pitch and wouldn't let me out of Aden airport. So I caught the local puddle-jumper to Djibouti. Meanwhile, my baggage was mistakenly forwarded to Nairobi, strangely the only time I've lost any gear while flying. It caught up with me in Addis Ababa.

With the Suez Canal reopened, the Djibouti port was doing a thriving business: Long, low tankers nosed into the crowded harbor; chunky freighters cast off lines and put to sea; sleek warships rode at anchor, alert and ready for action.

For across the northwest quadrant of the Indian Ocean moved 75 percent of Western Europe's crude oil and 85 percent of Japan's in addition to one quarter of the petroleum products imported by the United States. Further, the Indian Ocean carried more commerce than the North Atlantic: At any given time, fully half the world's seaborne oil sailed across those waters.

Djibouti was one of the few specks remaining in the once-vast French empire in Africa. It was the capital of what used to be called French Somaliland; was then called the French Territory of the Afars and the Issas, after the two leading tribes; and later became the Republic of Djibouti. But the French ran the military show and I looked up an intelligence officer I knew, who used to be with the Foreign Legion.

"The stakes in the Indian Ocean are high," he told me in his office in an old, colonial structure. "That's why the superpowers are moving into the area and that's why we keep a sizable force here, too. The name of the game is oil and that means the industrial economy of the Western world and Japan. That's why the Légion Éstrangère is still here."

Indeed, Djibouti was one of the last foreign outposts of the Foreign Legion, one of the world's famed military elites. I saw legionnaires strolling in their white kepis in the streets of the town, which once exported frankincense and myrrh and now dealt in dates, camels, and shipping. The Foreign Legion had always been based abroad, first at its headquarters at Sidi-bel-Abbès in Algeria and later from Aubagne in southern France.

Since its founding in 1831, the Legion had managed to conjure up an image of sacrifice, heroism, and mystery, and had been the subject of many novels and movies. Life in the Legion could be brutal, harsh, and demanding, subject to arbitrary, draconian discipline. Of the hundreds of thousands who joined—for a minimum five-year hitch—from more than one hundred countries, thirty-five thousand died in the service of the Legion.

But the Foreign Legion also gave its members a new identity, even a new nationality if they wanted one. More important, it provided them with a home, often their only home, a family, a way of life. Not for nothing was its motto: *Legio patria nostra,* "The Legion is our fatherland."

During world wars, the Legion enlisted such unlikely members as Arthur Koestler, Cole Porter, Ali Khan, and Prince Aage of Denmark. A young well-born Englishman named Simon Murray who served for five years in Algeria during that colonial war later reflected, "It was a magnificent experience, we had a camaraderie that was unparalleled."

I sat drinking pastis at a sidewalk café patronized by legionnaires. Most were members of the 13th DBLE, the veteran 13th Demi-Brigade, which had fought at El Alamein during World War II and Dien Bien Phu in 1954, among other places. It was now based in Djibouti and sent out regular patrols along the borders with Ethiopia and Somalia. I also noticed legionnaires wearing the green berets with the flash—a winged hand clenching a dagger—of the 2nd REP, the Legion's parachute regiment. The 2nd REP jumped at Kolwezi in Zaire in May 1978 to rescue the Europeans trapped in a civil war and it continues to serve as France's quick-reaction force. I would meet them again in Beirut.

I chatted with a couple of closely barbered, sun-brown legionnaires, who appeared to be as lean and fit as any troops I had seen. One, who spoke with a German accent, complained that there weren't enough Germans still entering the Legion. A Frenchman laughed, and agreed. Another legionnaire suggested that life for the troops was getting easier now that the old Beau Geste forts in the Sahara were long gone.

He dragged on a Gauloise and said, "We need to be hard and tough to remain the best, the elite."

Well, I thought, the Foreign Legion certainly was an elite, right up there among Western forces with the British Royal Marine Commandos, the German alpine troops and the paras of most countries— the modern equivalent of the Persian Immortals and the Spartan Three Hundred. Perhaps the only superior forces were super-elites like the U.S. Special Forces and the British SAS.

Yet I couldn't help thinking, too, that elite forces had to be cleverly used to make any military sense. World War II and Vietnam were replete with examples of their misuse in combat situations. Elite forces are designed for high-risk roles, which means that the most-qualified soldiers suffer the highest casualties. If the operation is of extreme value, the risk may be worth the price. But if the mission is marginal, then the lives of the best soldiers are frittered away. It's another catch-22: You select the finest soldiers and then destroy them.

Further, creating elite forces means stripping other units of the volunteers, the best-motivated, best-qualified men. These soldiers could well have used their expertise to train and lead companies and battalions throughout the army—rather than be bunched up in elite units that were often butchered because of their risky assignments. In the crunch, nervous senior commanders often use elite forces as ordinary infantry units because of the pressing battlefield demands. For instance the U.S. Army following World War II built up a mystique about the "airborne," yet in Vietnam, you could count the number of serious U.S. parachute operations on the fingers of one hand.

Still, as a journalist I am interested in expertise of any sort. And among military troops, I am inevitably drawn to observe the actions of the elite, the best. And while it may not be fashionable in U.S. graduate business school circles these days, there's something about the idea of ''all for one and one for all''—the spirit behind many military elite forces—that is deeply appealing to me.

Over the years, I had been in and out of Cyprus many times. It served as a kind of R and R center from the Middle East, a dramatic island with fine beaches and the legendary birthplace of Aphrodite, goddess of love and beauty. The beauty was in abundance; we correspondents favored the lovely fishing port of Kyrenia on the north coast and the town of Bellepais above it. But there was precious little love around.

In the struggle for independence against the British, the Furies had wracked the island. In the aftermath, two differing communities laid claim to the same soil: Greek Christians and Turkish Muslims. The capital of Nicosia was divided by a ''green line,'' so called because it was drawn on a map by a British officer with a green grease-pencil. The Greeks with a population of 500,000 tended to dominate the 125,000 Turks, who lived mostly in enclaves.

I was in Rome in 1974 when I heard the report that the Greek colonels in charge in Athens had allowed a third-rate Cypriot politician named Nikos Sampson to stage a coup against President Makarios in order to achieve *enosis,* or ''union'' with Greece. What on earth did they think the Turks were going to do? I wondered. Sit back idly and take it?

The answer wasn't long in coming. The Turks invaded by a paratroop drop and by sea. Suddenly, the whole southeastern flank of NATO was jeopardized by a possible war between its members, Greece and Turkey. The office called to ask if I could get to Cyprus on the Turkish side, since our man in Beirut was heading for Nicosia. I took the first plane to Ankara, musing en route that the Greeks were in a no-win situation. The Turkish Army outnumbered the Greeks by three to one. Cyprus, at the eastern end of the Mediterranean, was also at the extreme range of Greek fighters, while within easy protection of warplanes in southern Turkey. Further, the Greek Dodecanese Islands all lay under the shadow of Turkish guns along the eastern Aegean Sea, easy pickings for an amphibious assault.

Therefore, I was quite happy to be on the Turkish side. In a conflict, I prefer both professionally and personally to be on the side with the best chance of winning. Ideology is second to survival.

Ankara is one of the more depressing capitals around, but I walked into the hotel lobby and spotted Rauf Dentash, head of the Turkish Cypriot community who gave me a rundown on the situation and a good story to boot. I also ran into Eddie Adams, my photographer pal from Vietnam and Israel. We arranged for a car and driver and spent the next fourteen hours heading for the port of Mersin. The goddamn driver almost killed us passing a truck on a mountain curve with a car coming from the other direction. He actually clipped the truck with his rear fender darting back in but we didn't bother to stop. That ended any sleep I might get. I stayed wide awake, front-seat-driving the idiot behind the wheel.

In Mersin we managed to board a Turkish PT boat, and took off for Kyrenia on the north coast of Cyprus. I lay down on the pitching deck for the voyage across the Mediterranean. It was cold and wet. As the sun set, the waves began breaking over the bow, drenching me. Christ, I was wet. I tried ducking into the stuffy cabin but the smoke from the crew's evil-smelling cigarettes and the engine oil put me off. I stayed on deck and suffered, my typewriter as a pillow.

We arrived after midnight, slipping into the darkened port and a blacked-out town whose only sound was the slap of rifle bolts clicking and the challenge from a Turkish sentry. They put us up at the Atlantis Hotel which was full of broken glass. It covered my bed so I slept in my clothes. The corridor reeked from the telltale odor of a dead body somewhere in the stairwell.

Kyrenia had been one of the loveliest resort towns in the Mediterranean, a charming Greek fishing village set on a small gem of a harbor. Morning showed the streets of Kyrenia—which Turkey now called Girne—to be deserted except for Turkish soldiers. There was no light, power, or running water. Even the cemetery was gripped by the standstill. Burials of casualties were held up by the lack of Greek gravediggers, and Turkish Muslims refused to enter Christian burial grounds.

We hitched a ride to Bellepais, above Kyrenia, where many American and British expatriates lived and which was the setting in Lawrence Durrell's prophetic story of Cypriot violence, *Bitter Lemons*. The Turkish flag was hoisted above the old Christian abbey ruins, with a Turkish soldier standing guard beneath. At the Tree of Idleness Café, owner Savvas Kourtellas lunched with his family. Four Britons sipped gin and tonics on a patio under a mulberry tree. The side of the hills had been blackened from air strikes and artillery.

The Brits told me that about two hundred Greek residents fled, but others arrived, believing Bellepais to be a possible sanctuary because of its large foreign colony.

In Kyrenia, both Greeks and Turks pondered the island's future. I walked over to the big, whitewashed Dome Hotel, once a splendid resort, where now about five hundred Greek Cypriots were being detained, partly for their protection and partly, Turkish officials candidly admitted, as hostages pending the fate of thousands of Turkish Cypriots being held on the south side of the island.

I saw a political aide to Turkish premier Bulent Ecevit and he told me that he was prepared to release the hostages, but only when assured the Turkish Cypriot civilians would not be harmed. "The Greek villages on our side are mostly empty," he said. "But we would welcome the Greeks if they wanted to come to our side."

At the harbor, I found Arif Hussein, a boatman who had worked with various American film crews who used Kyrenia as a backdrop for thrillers. Arif, once deferential, now spoke in tones of authority. "We will allow the Greeks to come back," he said. "But now it will be the Turks who will be in charge. We will run the government, the administration, the police force. For years, we were the second-class citizens when it came to business. That will all have to change."

I looked up the retired British rector of St. Andrew's Anglican Church, the Reverend Evelyn Chavasse, whom I used to see in the old days. He shook his head at the idiocy of the Greek Cypriots' attempting to overthrow their own president and said sadly, "This island is full of hatred. It will take a very long time to heal this hatred." It was *Bitter Lemons* all over again.

As I was leaving, a Turkish official took me aside and said, "Look. Don't listen to propaganda from the other side. I don't think the Greeks and Turks can live together. Side by side, maybe, but not together. Most of us think there should be a boundary between us."

I boarded a troopship with some of the paratroopers who had taken the island; looking tough as tungsten, they were returning to Turkey for the victory parade; as far as they were concerned, it was all wrapped up. As we backed away from the quay, I looked over the postcard view and again marveled at the stupidity of the Greek Cypriots in Nicosia and the Greek politicians in Athens who thought they could topple Makarios and present the Turks with a *fait accompli*. After thousands of years living next to them, they still didn't know the Turks.

In Ankara, I ran into an old friend, Leo Hochstetter, the short, genial Middle East representative of the Motion Picture Export Association of America, who had served in Istanbul in American intelligence during World War II and had plenty of contacts. Leo had just come from a successful mission to Egypt—for Hollywood, not the CIA.

"I've just rehabilitated Tarzan in Egypt," he said over a stiff scotch.

"Go on," I said, pulling out my notebook.

"The Egyptian censor said that Tarzan was in disrepute. He was an imperialist. I'm not kidding. Maybe they were, influenced by some of their sub-Sahara friends, but they said old Tarz treated the Africans worse than the apes. So he must have been a CIA agent. They banned all the Tarzan pictures. The flicks had been good money-makers for Hollywood in Egypt. So I got the censors and the Culture Ministry officials around a table in Cairo and made my pitch: I reminded them that Tarzan had been a classic adventure story before politics came into the picture. The minister luckily remembered how much he had enjoyed Tarzan in his youth. So we hammered out an agreement that Tarz could be admitted to Egypt as long as we moved a few objectionable passages. Tarzan has cleaned up his act."

Leo had a witty way of dealing with touchy subjects. Of Jewish descent, he was once asked by an Arab immigration officer at an airport whether Hochstetter was a Jewish name. "Not necessarily," replied Leo and got the visa.

As a young reporter, I was intrigued by the stories of travelers who explored the remote land of Kurdistan and of the Kurdish leader, General Mullah Mustafa Barzani, the grizzled old warrior who had fought a long, vain struggle for Kurdish independence from his mountain redoubt.

On a trip to Baghdad, I contacted officials of the Kurdish Democratic party. They indicated that if I could get to an area high in the mountains near the Iranian border, a contact would try to set up a meeting with General Barzani in his lair. I hired a car and driver and set out on the long, grinding drive north from Baghdad along the east bank of Tigris River across the great Mesopotamian plain, through the oil fields around Kirkuk, and into Erbil, the administrative capital of Iraqi Kurdistan. From Erbil, we swung northeast into the mountains, up through long, winding ravines with snow-covered peaks. As the road roughened and narrowed, I could see how the Kurds could become so deeply attached to their wild and forbidding country. I could also see how men with ancient weapons could hold off a modern army in this forbidding terrain.

Barzani had been fighting all his life for independence, first taking up arms in 1930 to establish a state for the twelve million ethnic Kurds who live in an ill-defined area called Kurdistan comprising parts of Iraq, Iran, Syria, Turkey, and the Soviet Union. At one point, the Kurds got the short-lived Kurdish Mehadad Republic in northern Iran—supported by the Russians—until that collapsed and Barzani was forced to retreat into the Soviet Union. The hard fact of realpolitik was that the countries in the area were prepared to support the Kurds—as long as they were fighting for autonomy in a neighboring, antagonistic state. None of the countries was prepared even to consider setting up a Kurdish nation within its own boundaries.

We came to a small, rough camp called Nawperdan, at the confluence of two mountain streams near the Iranian border. I found a tiny office in a hut, run by a physician in his early thirties named Mahmoud Uthman, who told me that by day he served on the seven-man Kurdish Democratic party central committee, and at night ran his clinic. Dr. Uthman had been fighting with Barzani for seven years and he said with passion, "General Barzani is the one, undisputed leader of the Kurdish people. It is not an easy life up here. But it is better to live a hard life among free people than to live the easy life down there with the others."

He used an old crank-operated field telephone to get through to the chieftain's hideout. Then, he invited me into a beat-up Land-Rover for a jarring drive by night over a long, hand-hewn trail to a tiny village called Dilmin, a dozen mud-brick shacks occupied by Barzani's staff and their families.

I walked through a curtain that served as a door to the simple hut into a room lined with oilcloth. There was a wood-burning stove glowing on a hard-packed earth floor covered with bright oriental carpets. Barzani was there; he stuck out his hand in greeting. He offered me a cigarette from a pack of Dunhills. When I declined, he took a cheap Iraqi cigarette and stuck it into a foot-long homemade holder and lit up.

The old guerrilla looked ferocious: arching eyebrows like eagle wings, a big, bristling black moustache, and a stocky, muscular frame despite his sixty-seven years and infirmities. He was a very commanding presence.

The general wore a tan uniform cut in the Kurdish national style, a sort of baggy jump suit, and a faded red-and-white turban with a Sam Browne belt holding an automatic pistol. He had a huge curved dagger stuck inside a blue waist sash. He spoke in a surprisingly soft voice in Kurdish, translated by Dr. Uthman. Barzani was obsessed by the idea that the United States should support Kurdish national aspirations.

"We are a poor people, always oppressed by the powerful," he said. "So we need strong friends like the United States. Look on a map and you will see how strategically placed we are.

"We have fought the Iraqis for ten years for our rights." And he added that he was buoyed by the fact that, a few months before, the Kurds in Baghdad had signed an agreement that granted limited autonomy in local rule to the Kurds. At the time, the Kurds were getting support from the CIA through Iran, since the Shah thought it useful to have the regime in Iraq pinned down trying to repress the Kurds.

"We have been terribly damaged by ten years of war," Barzani declared. "We need development projects, roads, schools, modern agriculture, factories. We need hospitals and doctors. Dr. Uthman will tell you that Kurdistan is a veritable museum of diseases. We must compensate for the destruction. We must fulfill the needs of our people."

I asked him about his own enduring success as a military leader. He smiled and replied, "Just common sense and practical experience. After years and years of fighting, you get so you learn something about it all."

Then he asked me, "Can't you tell your government to give us direct support?"

I told him I didn't see the United States alienating either the Turks or the Iranians, with whom Washington was on friendly terms, or even the Russians, by pushing for an independent Kurdistan. Nor did I see the United States going out of its way to offend the Iraqis, even though diplomatic relations had been broken since the 1967 Arab-Israeli war.

Barzani seemed depressed at my remarks. I suggested he send Dr. Uthman to the United States to speak to American audiences on the subject of an independent Kurdistan to see if he could drum up any political support.

I asked him about his long career and he said, "I have never thought of myself as an exceptional leader. Roosevelt, Churchill, Stalin, Eisenhower, de Gaulle, Kennedy, Nasser—they have all come and gone. A leader should be judged by what he has done for his people. I am satisfied—to a degree—with what I have done with my life. We have gained some fruits but not everything we wanted. Even now, only God knows what the future will bring to us.

"Looking back, I suppose most men have some regrets on what they might have done or what they should not have done or what they left unaccomplished. I am one of those men."

Barzani gave me a ceremonial black-and-gold Kurdish dagger as a present. I thanked him and wished him luck. But the future did not bring much luck to General Barzani.

In 1975, I happened to be in Tehran when the Shah of Iran signed a deal with Iraqi leader Saddam Hussein. The Iraqis agreed to concede the eastern half of the Shatt-al-Arab waterway to Iran in exchange for the Shah's promise to stop supporting the Iraqi Kurds. Without a fresh supply of ammunition, the guerrilla fighting was doomed and the Baghdad regime warned the Kurds that they had a ceasefire until April 30—after which armed Kurds would be shot on sight and their villages bombed and shelled.

I headed for Kurdistan, bumming a ride in a Land-Rover with a British doctor, who was with the Save the Children Fund. We drove all day and well into the night, bedding down with Kurdish friends in a small town near the border. The following morning we departed early and talked our way past the frontier guards to enter Iraq. There we found a pitiable sight: Whole families with their meager belongings sat by the side of the road in bitterly cold weather waiting to be picked up by Iranian Army trucks and taken to refugee camps on the Iranian side of the border. The road, calf-deep in mud, was jammed with army trucks, civilian pickup trucks, jeeps, and every other available vehicle. Along the roadside, Kurdish herders drove cattle, sheep, goats, even ducks and turkeys. Above the road in the snow-clad hills, guerrillas moved east along the trails dressed in tribal turbans and baggy pants, carrying weapons.

Barzani, faced with the option of submitting to the Iraqi government or continuing a hopeless battle without ammunition, had decided to call off the fight for the time being. "The Kurdish revolution is finished," one of his lieutenants told me in the town of Derbend. "Fourteen years we have fought and now they have killed the revolution."

"Until a few days ago, the old man still thought that somehow the Americans or Russians would come to his aid. Barzani doesn't know the realpolitik of oil and detente. We have been sold for a barrel of oil.'' And a sergeant added, ''Right now we are done for and so is the revolution. Perhaps things will change later but now we are leaving Iraq.''

It was a sad sight: Barzani depressed and shattered; the tough, proud, usually cheerful Kurds, retreating across the border. Barzani died in the United States a few years later, a heartbroken and bitter man. The Kurds remained without a national state.

Poor Barzani. He was a victim of international power politics. He was supported in his lifelong struggle for an independent Kurdistan by the Shah and CIA only as long as it suited their interests. When it no longer did, he was unceremoniously dumped. The CIA stopped delivering arms; the Shah closed the border. Barzani accused Washington and Tehran of betrayal. But why would he ever have thought national leaders in the United States or Iran would behave otherwise? Certainly not on behalf of Kurdistan. Still, what else could he do? Poor Barzani.

I rode the long, grueling drive back to Tehran roughing out a dramatic account of the Kurdish evacuation of Iraq, only to find the English language paper in the capital carrying an even more dramatic—and significant—exodus. The retreat of the South Vietnamese troops from the Central Highlands, the beginning of the collapse of the South Vietnamese government. The plight of the Kurds, as usual, was overshadowed by other events. A few days later, I was on a plane heading for Saigon.

CHAPTER NINE

Fall of Saigon

THE AIR VIETNAM CARAVELLE from Singapore swooped steeply into Tan Son Nhut airport, a departure from the gradual approach that could expose the plane to hostile fire. It was a sharp warning that things were hairy around Saigon at the beginning of April 1975. I hadn't been back to Saigon since the end of 1968, and though the jumbled scene at the airport looked familiar, much else had changed.

U.S. armed forces had pulled out in 1973 after a shaky ceasefire arranged by Henry Kissinger and Hanoi's Le Duc Tho. "Vietnamization" had taken place, meaning the South Vietnamese were left to hack it on their own. But the regime of President Nguyen Van Thieu remained as corrupt as ever. Worse, Thieu continued to fill senior military posts with incompetent cronies: Personal loyalty was more important for advancement than military expertise. Army morale had dropped accordingly, particularly with the U.S. forces no longer on call in a crunch. And so when the North Vietnamese launched their early 1975 offensive in the Central Highlands, the South Vietnamese wilted in front of them. Now the situation was desperate.

That desperation was evident at the airport, which was in its usual state of chaos, heightened by the tension generated by frightened crowds straining and struggling to buy tickets for flights out of the country. I found a taxi for the ride into town, and soon was surrounded by traffic and the stench wafting up from the canals along the northern slum districts.

The cab pulled up to the arcade of the Continental Palace, my old hotel, and I spotted *Newsweek*'s Loren Jenkins, now Hong Kong bureau chief, in the lobby. He arranged a hard-to-get room for me and gave me a fill in. The situation was much worse than it was being depicted by the U.S. ambassador in Saigon, Graham Martin, and Secretary of State Kissinger in Washington. The precipitous and ill-planned evacuation of the Central Highlands—after the capture by the North Vietnamese of the provincial capital of Ban Me Thuot—on the orders of President Nguyen Van Thieu had led to the rapid unraveling of South Vietnamese military forces stationed in the northern part of the country. Pleiku and Kontum had been abandoned on March 15, to the amazement of the North Vietnamese generals, who reacted quickly by assaulting Hue, which fell on March 25, followed by the capital of I Corps, Da Nang, on March 30. By the time I arrived, familiar strongholds like Qui Nhon, Nha Trang, and Cam Ranh Bay had also gone down the drain.

The fall of these cities had been accompanied by panic-stricken evacuation scenes, flashed by television around the world, which had sapped South Vietnamese morale and left the army in a shambles. The U.S. Congress seemed indifferent to Saigon's plight and refused to appropriate the emergency millions in military aid funds requested by President Ford. Despite the obvious deterioration, Ambassador Graham stoutly insisted that a defense line could be established north of Saigon, a much-reduced but nevertheless viable state established in what was left of the South, and therefore the United States should not further erode a grim situation by the premature evacuation of Americans or Vietnamese nationals.

Martin was living in a dreamworld, as the CIA and field officers in the embassy fully knew. But he was backed up by Kissinger, who seemed to believe that Washington could pull some kind of diplomatic solution out of the hat, a conjuring trick that would see Hanoi agreeing to stop the military drive somewhere north of the capital and accept a ceasefire that would allow the Saigon government to pull itself together politically and militarily.

I strolled around town that first day, looking up old acquaintances and contacts, and the mood was unrelievedly ominous. Absolutely no one shared Graham Martin's bizarre optimism.

"We are fearful," an old Vietnamese acquaintance told me, when

I dropped by his empty office. "We can't understand what has happened in the North. It seems as if things are disintegrating all around us."

I bumped into a Vietnamese journalist friend, who added, "People just can't get used to the idea that the Americans are not going to bail them out. So for the first time many of the middle-class people who took U.S. assistance for granted are now having to make crucial decisions about their future."

At the hotel, a waiter who used to serve French soldiers a generation before, said plaintively, "All is lost, I think. I will stay, however. What can I do? Where else can I go? I hope they will bear nothing personal against me."

Those Vietnamese with money, however, were queueing at the banks to withdraw funds and purchase airline tickets out. Others who had neither the money nor the exit visas to flee were buying rice and other foodstuffs as a hedge against the uncertain future.

The next day, I managed to get a briefing from the military affairs specialist at the U.S. embassy. He took an extremely dim view of the ability of the South Vietnamese forces to resist total defeat now that they were on the run, holding only one third of their country. I was surprised to find such a frank and pessimistic report from someone in the same building whence issued the ambassador's continuing hopeful appraisals. The analyst described the military reverses of the past month as "catastrophic" and predicted the situation could only grow worse. He, and others, were bitterly critical of President Thieu's decision to abandon the highlands without an overall plan for the orderly withdrawal of soldiers and civilians, which led to a massive rout, with few shooting contacts with the enemy. There were now about four hundred thousand front-line North Vietnamese troops in the South and almost all of them were in a position to be deployed shortly against Saigon itself, or vectored at regrouped South Vietnamese forces in the Mekong Delta area.

Further, there were only six regular divisions of the South Vietnamese Army left intact, together with remnants of crack marine and airborne units. But three of the divisions were based in the Delta for use against Vietcong, leaving only the other three divisions to guard the northern, western, and northeastern approaches to the capital. Once the North Vietnamese moved into position around Saigon, the dispirited, enervated South Vietnamese Army would be outnumbered by three to one.

"It's only a question of time," said the analyst. "If the North chooses to apply the pressure now, I don't see much hope."

I walked over to the home of George McArthur, now the *Los Angeles Times* bureau chief in Saigon, who lived in a bungalow a half block from President Thieu's Independence Palace. George was a veteran Far East hand, having covered the Korean War for the Associated Press, and been in and out of Vietnam for a couple of decades. He had joined the *Times* in Saigon in 1970 and was as knowledgeable as any journalist in Southeast Asia. But I was appalled when I saw him: He had had an emergency operation after a ruptured appendix, which was followed by a bout with peritonitis. He looked awful and could hardly walk. Why on earth he had not been medevaced, I don't know. Possibly, he didn't inform the foreign desk how bad he felt. But it was too late now to get him to fly out: George was determined to see the story through to its bitter outcome. He had an old Thompson submachine gun propped up in his bedroom and intended to use it in self-defense if he had to.

He offered me a stiff scotch and I told him I planned to write a gloomy piece that evening about the prospects of the Saigon regime, pegged to the military situation.

"George," I said, "as far as I'm concerned, I'm here to help you. It's your bureau and I'll do anything you want me to do, going out in the field or running copy for you."

McArthur's villa was just across the broad Thong Nhut Boulevard from our office, which was in the house of Reuters news agency. Because of the time difference with Los Angeles, George could put together a first edition story late at night and then place a 9:00 A.M. call to his friend Tom Polgar, the CIA station chief at the embassy, for an overnight updating for our final edition. McArthur's cook would usually take his copy across the street for telexing to the United States. We decided that I'd drive to Vung Tau, the fishing port southeast of Saigon, to do a story about the refugees who were arriving by boat and barge from the captured cities along the coast.

The next morning, Loren Jenkins and I drove in the *Newsweek* minimoke, a kind of low-slung jeep, over the now-dangerous road through the rubber plantations down to the resort town on the South China Sea the French called Cap St. Jacques. En route, Loren told me he had been on a trekking trip in the Himalayas, climbing nineteen-thousand-foot peaks, when a messenger got through to him after several days' journey on foot in eastern Nepal. *Newsweek*'s cable ordered him to break off his vacation and get to Saigon pronto. Loren said he had been sorely tempted to scribble down an answer to New York for the runner: "Your message garbled. Please repeat."

In Vung Tau, we threaded our way through mobs of refugees to the port area to inspect a newly arrived barge. What we found was a horrifying sight—made more gruesome by the incongruous setting near brilliant blossoms of the flamboyant trees and crimson bougainvillea flowers.

An ungainly flat-bottom barge, with a vast deck the size of a football field, had come in the night before, towed all the way down the South China Sea from Da Nang in the north. Aboard had been hundreds of soldiers, women, and children, incredibly packed together, who had been exposed to the harsh sun and the fierce salt spray of the sea. As the survivors had struggled off the barge, they left behind at least a score of dead, impacted human bodies and possessions ground down into a foot-deep strata that lay like a nightmarish carpet across the deck of the barge. Bodies, pots, pans, clothing, suitcases, motorbikes, military helmets, duffel bags, rifles, and human waste were intermingled in a ghastly devil's layer cake. Soldiers wearing the 3rd Army Division patch, who had been entrusted with the defense of Da Nang, sorted through the debris and removed corpses. One woman lay with her body in a protective position around her baby. They were both dead. From starvation? Thirst? Suffocation? Trampled? No one could say. Probably no one knew.

"I don't like taking pictures of dead bodies," said a Japanese photographer who joined us on the barge. "But these don't resemble bodies. More like human garbage."

At the makeshift refugee camp set up near the port, we ran into an English teacher, a short, wiry man named Nguyen Ha Thanh, who had boarded a ship in Da Nang to escape. He said quietly, "A million or more people would have liked to leave the Da Nang and Hue areas. But only a few of us were lucky to get out by ship. My father and mother weren't able to get permission to get on the boat. But they are old and perhaps the communists will not harm them. I lived for twenty years in Da Nang and because I was a schoolteacher, I was afraid for my family."

Thanh, who appeared to be neither rich nor influential, took his savings worth two hundred dollars, a few handbags with possessions, his wife, and five children—ranging from two to eleven—and managed to find a place on a Vietnamese ship moored off Da Nang.

"We left the twenty-sixth of March," he recalled. "There were at least five thousand people on board and some children died. We got to Cam Ranh Bay and waited three days. There, soldiers, or people wearing military tunics, searched me and took my money. Now I have nothing, just what you see." He pointed to a couple of airline bags. The voyage aboard a second ship from Cam Ranh Bay to Vung Tau took three more days, on only one of which did the passengers have anything to eat or drink.

"We were hungry and thirsty," he said. "It was just terrible and we are lucky to be alive. We cannot understand why the government behaves this way. They had lots of troops in Hue and Da Nang. There were no VC there. Why run away? And when the government told the troops and the people to leave, they didn't have any ships to take us away. And now, nobody seems to know what to do, not the government or anyone else. I just arrived today. Perhaps I can find some friends from Da Nang who will know what to do. I feel like most of the people. We don't believe in the government because the government and the soldiers did not try to protect the people."

It was a depressing day and we drove back to Saigon in silence.

The next morning, I found myself running copy for McArthur. An angry Vietnamese Air Force pilot bombed the Presidential Palace across from George's bungalow. He had a grandstand seat for the attack. I carried his copy to our office down the street, a page at a time. Finally, when police cordoned off the area, George phoned the end of the story to me at the office and I put it on the telex to Los Angeles.

Later in the day, Loren and I drove out to see Air Marshal Nguyen Cao Ky, whom I had accompanied on several trips when based in Saigon. Successively head of the air force, national premier, and then vice-president, Ky had broken with Thieu and was without a job. The flamboyant pilot welcomed us with a beer at his heavily guarded villa at Tan Son Nhut and I noted that he had his personal helicopter standing by. For all his braggadocio, I found Ky a straighter shooter than most of the Vietnamese brass, and he was refreshingly forthright about the military prospects. His view differed considerably from the upbeat line being pushed by Saigon and Washington.

He told us that any military victory by the South Vietnamese armed forces was now simply "impossible," adding, "We are only trying to stop the debacle of collapse. We couldn't think of a military victory now. We must face up to reality. Thieu has shown he is not capable of leading the country in war. And he is incapable of achieving peace. He is responsible for the debacle because he made all the decisions about the withdrawal personally. He gave orders directly to the corps commanders, bypassing the military high command. He has become isolated from the senior military leadership. His chief adviser is General Dang Van Quang, a corrupt man with a bad reputation, hated even more than Thieu.''

Wearing his midnight-black flying suit, Ky lowered his voice and said that the only political hope for the South Vietnamese would be Thieu's resignation and the formation of a government of a "national salvation front" composed of military and civilian leaders. "For the first time in my whole life, I feel really pessimistic," he said as he stared out on the lawn where his helicopter was parked. "The situation is desperate.''

Indeed it was. The North Vietnamese were tightening the ring around Saigon, with the South Vietnamese holding the key crossroads town of Xuan Loc, thirty-eight miles northeast of Saigon and the headquarters of the 18th Army Division, which had the responsibility for defending the northeastern approaches to the capital. By the time I drove up Highway 1 to Xuan Loc, it was cut off: South Vietnamese defended it, but supplies and reinforcements could only arrive by helicopter. I watched a company of the airborne unload from trucks and wait for helicopters to fly them inside the Xuan Loc perimeter.

"The battle for Saigon was begun right here," a stocky captain wearing paratrooper camouflage, said as he buckled up to board the Chinook. "What happens here will determine what happens everywhere else.''

The airborne formed the army's strategic reserve: It was the best unit in the armed forces; and committing it to Xuan Loc meant that the critical battle was shaping up here. The Vietnamese, however, were not allowing reporters to accompany their troops, and since there was also a rigorous sunset curfew in Saigon, it was necessary to return to the city to file stories to Los Angeles before dark.

After writing our stories, we would generally gather around the Continental Palace Hotel for dinner and drinks. Many drinks. Old friends were on hand. David Greenway, who was with me in Hue, was now with the *Washington Post;* Don Oberdorfer of the same paper; Colin Smith of *The Observer* of London; Phil Caputo, who had served in Vietnam as a Marine lieutenant, was with the *Chicago Tribune;* Bill McWhirter of *Time* magazine; Keyes Beech, the veteran Far East hand of the *Chicago Daily News;* Bob Shaplen of the *New Yorker;* Bud

Merrick, of *U.S. News and World Report;* David Lamb, formerly with
the United Press in Saigon, who had arrived the same day I did for my
own paper; Sandy Gall of British independent television; Mike
Nicholson also of ITN; Martin Woollacott of the *Guardian;* Stewart
Dalby of the *Financial Times;* John Pilger of London's *Daily Mirror;*
Malcolm Browne, who won a Pulitzer wih the Associated Press in
Saigon, now returning for the *New York Times;* Nik Wheeler, the fine
photographer shooting for *Newsweek;* and Loren, who directed
Newsweek's sharp team of Nick Proffitt, Tony Clifton, and Vietnamese-
speaking Ron Moreau.

And then there were others, notably Hunter S. Thompson, who
was sent to Vietnam for *Rolling Stone.* Thompson and Jenkins had
spent a lot of time in Aspen together, and Loren more or less took the
famous "gonzo" journalist under his wing. Hunter was a strange
customer: He loped around Saigon wearing a Hawaiian-style sport
shirt, tennis shorts, and sneakers, along with green sunglasses, and a
long cigarette holder. A tall, gangly man who also sported a bulldozer
driver's cap, he cut a unique sartorial figure in Saigon.

As the days went on, the tension built up among the press corps.
The tension was caused by the certainty that Saigon was going to fall
but an uncertainty about how that fall would come about. Would there
be heavy shelling and later door-to-door fighting? Would there be a
bloodbath with the communists getting even with anyone identified
with the United States or the South Vietnamese regime? Would the
South Vietnamese themselves, in rage and frustration, turn on the
Americans who were deserting them and lash out at any "round-eye"
they encountered? There were plenty of scenarios making the rounds,
none of them pleasant to contemplate. As George McArthur put it over
a drink one night: "Anyone who isn't scared here is a fool. There are
some fools around—but not many."

I noticed my own consumption of whiskey was rising, a drink
before lunch to steady the nerves. Some reporters decided to arm
themselves in case their rooms were invaded by panic-crazed South
Vietnamese seeking vengeance. Others took the view that the only
course of action, if things came to that, was to say, "Sorry about
that," avoid a firefight, and hope for the best. Not being handy with
weapons, I wasn't sure what to do. In any case, most of us drifted by
the military black market to buy steel helmets and flak jackets to stash
in our rooms. Increasingly, young men with guns were menacing
reporters returning to the hotel after dark after filing stories. As of now

they were only demanding cigarettes and piaster notes. But anarchy was obviously setting in.

Hunter Thompson had flown to Hong Kong to write a long piece for *Rolling Stone*. But, unexpectedly, he returned, telling us he was unable to write properly and wanted to come back for a final look. Then he planned to go on to Laos, of all places. Thompson was an electronics freak and had brought back a suitcase loaded with various new paraphernalia, including a batch of walkie-talkies that he claimed could save our lives—by permitting us to communicate with each other. That night, he began screaming that we had to try out the radios and he ran up to his room and started calling, "Whiskey Echo Bravo, this is Sierra Yankee Tango," or whatever call signs he dreamed up for us. None of us sitting in the hotel garden paid any attention, so he returned, thoroughly miffed. He headed for the john but fell over, crashing through a trellis like a dawn redwood going down. We decided to leave him to sleep it off.

The next day, Hunter told us he had heard a rumor that the Vietnamese around the hotel thought he was an agent for the CIA and thus was a possible target for any hard feelings against American personnel. Thompson wondered how the Vietnamese could ever mistake a character like himself, with his outlandish gear, for a CIA spook.

"You don't know the Vietnamese mentality," I teased. "They think a CIA agent would dress exactly like you to confuse them."

"Goddammit," Thompson shouted. "Don't these goddamned Vietnamese know that I'm a fucking dope fiend, that I'm on the FBI's most-wanted list?"

Hunter departed shortly after, spending time in Hong Kong and Bali and running up a large expense account, but he never did write anything in that period about the fall of Saigon, one of the more dramatic stories of the decade, except for a short telex message that editor Jan Wenner published—presumably for want of a proper story. I suspect the reason for his writer's block was that for the first time in his career he had come up against genuine fear and loathing, and he couldn't handle it artistically. After all, if in his book *Fear and Loathing on the Campaign Trail* he chose to describe dear old Hubert Humphrey as a "treacherous, gutless old wardheeler who should be put in a goddamn bottle and sent out on the Japanese current," what sort of language had he left for real villains?

*　　*　　*

For a change of pace, I wandered over to the Cercle Sportif, the once-posh, French-designed country club in a residential quarter not far from Independence Palace. There, the Vietnamese tried to keep a stiff upper lip.

White-jacketed waiters served members tall lemonades and gin-and-tonics. A messenger passed by, tinkling a tiny bell indicating a phone call for the member whose name was scrawled on a blackboard he carried. Players banged tennis balls back and forth under the tall tamarind trees. Other members played the French bowling game, *boules,* and nannies escorted small children around the playground, as they had my son several years before. But below the surface appearance of normality, those at the Cercle were more apprehensive than most in Saigon, and with good reason, since they belonged to the ruling class.

"All the Vietnamese here are scared to death," remarked a Vietnamese-speaking American businessman, whom I suspected of being a spook, at poolside. "They don't know what to do. For the first time, the knowledge is sinking in that this is really it, that the South Vietnamese defense is on the verge of collapse, and that they, being relatively well-off, will fare badly under a communist regime. You'll notice that the young Vietnamese girls are a bit more friendly toward Western men than they have been in the past. Their first question is, Are you married?"

The Vietnamese young women, particularly those who thought they or their well-to-do families would be singled out for recrimination, believed that marriage to a Westerner meant a one-way ticket to safety. And they were not above arranging marriages of convenience to get them out of the stricken country.

On my way out of the club, I noticed a newly posted letter on the bulletin board that showed that even the privileged were catching on. It read, "Because of the current situation, the board of directors has decided to stop the admission of new members and their families for an indefinite period."

Well-off girls weren't the only ones looking for husbands who could get them out. The B-girls along Tu-Do and Nguyen Hue streets also pleaded with American customers to marry or adopt them so they could get exit papers and a plane ride from Tan Son Nhut. In this regard, I was lucky. I had been taking out an exotic half-Vietnamese, half-Cambodian lady, who I thought might ask me to get her out. But she had no intention of leaving. She told me one night she had decided to leave Saigon for her family home in the Delta. I gave her a packet of green dollars and was relieved that I would not have to feel responsible for her safety. I did sign documents for old acquaintances who would come up to the table at the Continental and push forms at us. Whether or not my signature did any good, I never found out. Panic was in the air; there was a mood not unlike the atmosphere in the movie *The Deer Hunter*. However, the idea set forth in the film that Chinese gamblers in the final days would be sitting around a den betting on drug-crazed American GIs playing Russian roulette was simply ludicrous. At this period, all the Chinese and everyone else with any sense were hunkered down in their homes with their money buried under the floorboards.

On most mornings, I would try to drive to an outpost outside of Saigon to get some firsthand feel of the military situation. Everywhere it was the same story. The situation was deteriorating quickly. What South Vietnamese troops were available were simply no match for the oncoming North Vietnamese divisions.

We concentrated on Xuan Loc, the key to the northern defense of Saigon where the South Vietnamese were still holding out, but now they were surrounded and the closest we could get was Hung Nghai, a village seven miles to the west. Artillery rounds were falling between Xuan Loc and the major city of Bien Hoa, the last bastion before Saigon. With incoming shells interdicting the highway, clearly we were well past the beginning of the end.

One morning on the way back from Bien Hoa, I stopped off at the Vietnamese military cemetery at Vinh Phu, which was the nation's equivalent of Arlington National Cemetery. In a way, it was an oasis of tranquillity in the hurly-burly of the war swirling around. But it was an oasis of sorrow. I found the widow of First Lieutenant Tran Van Dai, who had been killed fighting with the 18th Division in the defense of Xuan Loc a few days before. Her eyes were full of tears as she approached her husband's coffin, draped with the yellow-and-red national flag. She lit a stick of incense at the Buddhist shrine and bowed.

"I knew he was going to die," she told me as she wiped her eyes and put the handkerchief into her loose black slacks. She wore a simple flowered blouse and her jet hair was pulled back close to her head. "I went to a fortune-teller and she told me my husband would be killed in April 1975. He was thirty years old and we were married three years ago when I was eighteen. He was a happy, joyful man. I was living with him in the garrison at Xuan Loc but three weeks ago when the fighting began, he insisted I come to Saigon. He used to write letters telling me how well his unit had been fighting and always ended by promising to tell me more about the war. In his letters, he did not say anything about the danger. The only time he mentioned death to me, he said he wanted children very much. He said that if he had a child he would be happy to die. But we never had any children.''

On Tuesday, April 17, we learned that Phnom Penh, the Cambodian capital, had been evacuated by the Americans and fallen to the Khmer Rouge. The news spurred some forward movement in the evacuation of Saigon, where there had been grave problems. Ambassador Martin continued to insist that any large-scale evacuation would panic the Vietnamese and destroy whatever will they had left to defend the capital and the Delta. Martin was backed up by Tom Polgar, the CIA station chief, who had been deluded by the Polish and the Hungarian members of the International Control Commission into thinking a ceasefire could be arranged. This would presumably allow the United States to initiate an orderly evacuation of all the Americans and Vietnamese they were responsible for. In Washington, Secretary of State Kissinger went along with this line of thinking convinced that the Russians, too, would aid in making a deal with Hanoi. At the same time, the brighter, energetic field officers in the embassy and CIA were pleading with their superiors to get the so-called high-risk Vietnamese—those who had worked in sensitive positions for the United States or the Saigon regime—out of the country before it was too late.

Some lower-level American officials had set up a ''black'' operation to remove these Vietnamese, most of whom insisted that their large families be evacuated, too. This meant that many American officials were simply flounting the Kissinger-Graham orders and making sure their own employees got out. The media, too, organized its own black flights leaving Tan Son Nhut in the middle of the night. Aboard were longtime Vietnamese employees who believed themselves to be on the communist blacklist because of their association with U.S. news agencies. One afternoon, Loren Jenkins asked me to accompany him to the airport that night: He was taking out Eliane, the bureau secretary, who wanted to get out of the country.

Driving a Volkswagen, we picked her up at her house, placed her luggage in the trunk, and got her to lie down in the backseat under a spread. We drove through darkened streets, and at Tan Son Nhut, we talked our way past the guards and located the out-of-the-way hangar being used as a terminal for the clandestine traffic to Bangkok. She thanked us profusely. We said good-bye quickly and drove off. The dispatchers didn't want parked cars or extended farewells calling attention to the operation. George McArthur did the same for the *L.A. Times* interpreter, Pham Khi Long, who stuck with us, working every day, almost to the end. Our office secretary, Mai Lan, got out on her own. She told George she wanted a five-day vacation to get married. It turned out she married a visa, and an American got her out on an official-dependents flight.

Meanwhile, the embassy and media head offices were all urging the Saigon bureaus to cut back to bare minimums. Sam Jameson, the *Los Angeles Times* regular Tokyo man; Dave Lamb, who arrived on the same day I did; and I volunteered to hang on until the end. But George and Los Angeles insisted we reduce staff. Sam, having been there the longest, was the first to go, on a commerical flight, and took all our excess baggage with him to Hong Kong. Lamb was next, on the last commerical flight out, and George and I were left to cover the end game in Saigon.

It was never clear to me how the final official U.S. evacuation would be handled. The embassy was in a state of chaos and no authoritative word came from that source, only that Americans would be warned in time. Some of the non-American reporters still in Saigon wondered aloud whether they would get advance word of an American evacuation. We held an impromptu meeting in the rooftop bar of the Caravelle, and Loren Jenkins and I volunteered to notify our British, French, Australian, and Italian comrades as soon as we got anything definite. We appointed a foreign journalist on each floor of the Caravelle and Continental across the street, whom Loren or I would notify, and they, in turn, would alert everyone on their floors. There were rumors that the Saigon armed forces radio would play "I'm Dreaming of a White Christmas" as the signal to get ready to move out. The idea, in theory, was that reporters and other Americans still behind would assemble at various points in the downtown area and be picked up by helicopters or buses.

It all sounded rather hit-or-miss to me, and I suggested to Jenkins that we personally reconnoiter the U.S. embassy. I didn't see the point of standing around a street corner or hotel roof when the balloon went up, waiting for transport that might never arrive. And, I thought, the embassy would be where the action was; that would be the focus of the story of the American departure from Saigon. I had already done a story about the swarms of Vietnamese at the embassy gates and at the consulate next door seeking U.S. visas, and the mobs were still there when we drove by. We decided that the mass of people would make it difficult to enter the front of the embassy once the panic set in. We drove around the backside of the compound, where few people had recourse to visit, and found a gate guarded by Marines. We agreed this would be our goal when it all hit the fan. It remains a mystery to me why, when the day finally came, some of our colleagues lined up docilely at the various checkpoints waiting for buses that never came, or did but couldn't make it to the airport or port for the last boats and choppers leaving the stricken city.

Some of those final evenings were a blur. I was in Jenkins's room one night when he somehow got through a conference call to New York. Editor Edward Kosner had the idea that their team, now down to Loren and Nick Proffitt and photographers, should clear out. They were furious, arguing that they were in a better position to determine when to leave than editors in New York. Kosner, too, was angry, finally shouting something like "Okay, you can stay, but it's your ass, not our responsibility what happens to you anymore." Jenkins and Proffitt broke out into wild laughter: They knew that if they had bugged out and *Time* magazine's correspondent remained behind, they'd be the ones to look foolish, not the New York editors. Then the *Newsweek* cover editor got on the phone and asked why they didn't have pictures of North Vietnamese tanks, which he seemed to think were being posed by their drivers on Highway 1 for souvenir snapshots. I remembered that the very same editor had made the same silly requests of me ten years before when I was *Newsweek*'s bureau chief in Saigon. He expected a photographer to be assigned to the field for a couple of days and return with a Pulitzer Prize combat shot. And this particular editor never recognized the difference between an armored personnel carrier and a real tank. Things hadn't changed much in the upper echelons in New York, and we did some drinking after that evening call.

At the U.S. embassy and in Washington, the senior U.S. diplomats still thought that some last-hour deal could be made with Hanoi through various Eastern European intermediaries. But now it also seemed that any agreement was contingent on the resignation of President Thieu. Ideally, suggested the French ambassador, who was also in the act, Thieu would be replaced by General Duong Van "Big" Minh, thought to be more acceptable to both Hanoi and the Vietcong leaders of their Provisional Revolutionary Government. My own trips to the Vietcong mission at the International Peace Supervisory Force, set up under the 1973 accords, convinced me that the mission leader, a tough, little colonel named Vo Dong Giang, was in no mood to accept anything other than an unconditional surrender on the part of the Saigon regime, no matter who headed it. Behind his fenced-in compound at the airport, Giang brushed off suggestions that a new government in Saigon would prompt the communists to allow the United States a "decent interval" in which to evacuate Americans and Vietnamese who wished to depart their land. "The Ford administration should let the South Vietnamese settle their own affairs," he said bluntly, clearly a rejection of the idea of a peaceful mass evacuation organized by the Americans.

On April 21, the city of Xuan Loc fell to the North Vietnamese. That evening, President Thieu announced his resignation on national radio. In a long, rambling harangue, Thieu typically blamed everything on the Americans and Congress's failure to appropriate the emergency funds for additional military hardware—rather than on his own disastrous decision to pull out of the Central Highlands and to let this complicated operation remain in the hands of his incompetent military cronies. "You have let our combatants die," he told the Americans. "This is an inhumane act by an inhumane ally."

But the South Vietnamese politicians, in their own intractable and predictable way, refused to go along with the U.S.-French scenario. The elderly Vice-President Tran Van Huong insisted on his constitutional role, which meant succeeding the president. As Huong, Big Minh, and the politicans dithered, Kissinger finally ordered Martin in Saigon to get on with the evacuation of Americans still in the country—though little attention was paid to the loyal Vietnamese, who were expecting to be looked after and who were most at risk in the wake of a communist victory.

One problem was that many hard-core Americans, besides the media, preferred to hang on until the last minute. These were what the embassy officials referred to as the "woodwork types," meaning that very late in the day, unexpected U.S. citizens would come out of the woodwork to be evacuated, thereby complicating any last-ditch arrangements. Some were construction workers on various projects, others ex-GIs, or deserters, who had married or were living with Vietnamese women in a kind of underground existence. For instance, I discovered an American Legion post, of all things, in Saigon—a stucco villa set behind whitewashed walls. The place looked like a setting out of an old Warner Brothers movie, with a barmaid serving

Vietnamese beer, a billiard table, a dartboard on the plastered wall above black Leatherette chairs, and a stereo playing "What Now, My Love?" One man at the bar was eating french fries with catsup and sipping a bourbon.

A deep woodwork type, a tall American black, dressed in a tank top and jeans, told me, "Don't use my name, but I've been here since 1967 when I arrived with the air cavalry. I got a Vietnamese wife and I really like it here. So I don't want to be stampeded into leaving. Besides, I think there's going to be some American helicopters flying around this town looking for dudes who never got the word—and I'll just wave 'em down, show 'em my American passport, and get 'em to take me out."

Another customer at the bar, a husky white man who said he was a contract employee for the U.S. Defense Attaché's Office, sipped his "33" locally made beer, and explained, "I'm waiting for my wife to make her good-byes and it sure as hell is taking her a long time. You know the Vietnamese, they are very family-minded and they got to see everybody and go through a hell of a lot of walla-walla. She's down in the Delta today but she'll be back and maybe we can bug out this weekend."

With the inexorable sweep of the North Vietnamese forces toward Saigon, it was difficult to travel very far out of the capital area, though we continued to drive across the Newport Bridge and up the road past Bien Hoa and the span over the Dong Nai River. You couldn't get much farther than the rubber plantations north of Bien Hoa. The North Vietnamese were shelling the road, and with little tactical intelligence available it was difficult to know just how far advanced the enemy troops were. One morning, before taking off for Bien Hoa, I chatted briefly with the French photographer Michel Laurent at breakfast in the hotel garden. He was a handsome, boyish, quiet-mannered guy who had won the Pulitzer Prize for the Associated Press in the Bangladesh war. We wished each other luck. But his ran out that day. He was filming north of Bien Hoa and kept taking pictures even after he'd got shots of North Vietnamese soldiers through his long lens. Fearless, foolhardy, perhaps, he continued taking pictures from far too close a range. The approaching soldiers opened up with automatic fire, killing him instantly.

The next day, Nick Proffitt and I drove to the airport to watch the American and Vietnamese evacuees loading up on military flights to Clark Air Force Base in the Philippines. Americans married to or connected with Vietnamese women were frantically trying to round up all their "dependents" and get them manifested on flights. The list bore names that were a curious mixture of East and West: Schwartz, Vo Thi Bach; Carpenter, Nguyen Kim Long; and the Smith family, Robert, Mai, Hung, and Troc. One American wearing a cap with a Budweiser label told me he had adopted his wife's sister as his "daughter," since daughters and sons had a higher priority in the evacuation, which by now was proceeding at flank speed despite Ambassador Martin's strictures. Another American civilian, in a smartly tailored safari outfit, complained, "I told my girl I'd marry her and take out our two kids. But now she wants to bring out her father and mother, brother and sisters, and even the aunt. I don't know how I'm going to get them all out or how I'll support them in the States."

Another American civilian signing on the flight manifest summed up the mood with the current expression, "*Fini,* bye-bye, Vietnam."

Proffitt and I heard the United States was shutting down all its operations in the vast Defense Attaché's Office at Tan Son Nhut, so we decided to stop off at the post exchange on the way back to town. We found the Vietnamese salesgirls in the process of closing the place up for good. This, I remarked to Proffitt, surely spelled the end of the American involvement. One of the valid criticisms made of the American military style over the years was its overreliance on creature comforts from the States—refrigerators, air conditioners, and the rest. Still, Nick and I bought a couple of bottles of champagne, which appeared to me to be the very last sale. We drank it that evening in the hotel garden along with some delicious crayfish that Bill McWhirter brought back from a dangerous reporting run to Vung Tau.

Saigon was unraveling quickly in what Murray Sayle called "a war movie without a plot." The curfew was tightened, meaning you had to spend the evenings in the hotel or risk getting shot by edgy police and the local militia forces, mostly trigger-prone young boys with huge rifles. Embassies pulled out their people via their own military air transport, some like the Canadians without so much as a good-bye to loyal Vietnamese employees who had served them for years and expected to be evacuated, too. When the British left, the consul general gave the keys to the Embassy Club to Sandy Gall, the tall, engaging Scottish TV correspondent whose nose was broken almost as badly as mine. He looked after his mates. Two of the last lunches I had in Saigon were on the greensward of the club, with picnic meals provided by the Caravelle, and white wine from the Vietnamese steward. This, as the world was crumbling around us.

Several of the British correspondents and old hands like the AP's Peter Arnett, a plucky New Zealander who won the Pulitzer Prize in Vietnam, had decided to stay on after the expected fall of Saigon and skip whatever evacuation was devised. I stopped by the office of the Associated Press and chatted with George Esper, who had remained in Vietnam since my previous tour and who had married a Vietnamese woman. George asked me what I intended to do and what I thought about his remaining behind.

"Frankly, George," I said, "I'm planning to bug out with the final evacuation. It's not really my story. I got in late and I don't have that proprietary feeling about it. I don't think the North Vietnamese would try to harm us but they might keep us under house arrest in our rooms, for days, or weeks. I have a young son and I've never won the father-of-the-year award. I want to see him soon. But you're intimately identified with the story. Physically, your office is pretty safe, with some floors over you to protect from artillery, and you're off the street so mobs ought not invade the place. So it's up to you." George stayed.

In late April, Thieu flew from Saigon to Taiwan with his family and a heavy load of gold bullion. But the squabbling Vietnamese politicians were still unable to come up with a new government that— according to the scenario concocted by Kissinger, Martin, Polgar, and company—would be able to negotiate a compromise ceasefire with the North Vietnamese. By now, the "black" evacuation operation was in full flight, with U.S. officials moving many Vietnamese to the airport for unofficial evacuation. But there was no careful attention paid to priorities. Low-risk families were getting on planes; high-risk Vietnamese were kept in the dark. And because Martin had stalled for so long, the road to Vung Tau was now cut off, and there was no longer hope of a major seaborne operation from there, as had originally been discussed. Many lower-level U.S. officials believed they had a debt of honor to the Vietnamese who worked for them in sensitive positions, and that debt, in large measure, went unhonored—as Frank Snepp, who was in the CIA station, has so chillingly detailed in his book on the fall, *Decent Interval*.

Early on the morning of April 27, the North Vietnamese launched a rocket attack on Saigon. In the false dawn, five powerful missiles slammed into the city, killing a half-dozen civilians and wounding many more. When I heard the first explosions, I scuttled for the hotel bathroom, as in Amman, to get as many walls as possible between me and incoming fire. When the attack ceased, I saw a peasant women in the street outside the hotel, her body crumpled on the sidewalk where a rocket had hit close by. I walked down Tu-Do to the Majestic Hotel on the river. There a rocket had slammed into the top floor, wiping it out and killing the night watchman who was sitting near the blast. Still another missile landed in a slum, setting fire to dozens of hovels.

At the Continental, I picked up Loren Jenkins and we boarded the minimoke for the ride north. There were even more refugees jamming the four-lane highway, streaming southward—in cars of every description, hanging onto buses, with thousands of peasants on foot. There were also among them hundreds, perhaps thousands, of soldiers—undisciplined and split off from their units. The civilians carried pots, rice, vegetables, bread, chickens, ducks. In the massive tide sweeping south, a few units, the marines and airborne, were heading north to bolster the defenses on the north side of the Dong Nai River. the refugees said they were from Long Thanh, the district town that had just been overrun, and from outlying areas of Bien Hoa, which had been badly shelled. We were seeing the collapse of the outer defenses of Saigon. The huge Bien Hoa Bridge itself was a scene of massive confusion, with paratroopers allowing only refugees on foot to cross to the south, holding back hundreds of trucks, cars, motorcycles, and bicycles. Loren was trying to coordinate coverage with a couple of *Newsweek* photographers and I was getting jumpy waiting around for him to make contact. I realized we weren't going to get much farther forward, and I worried about being prevented by the army or the mass of refugees from reaching Saigon. This was a dramatic, significant story and I wanted to get back to the telex before nightfall to file it.

I saw a Roman Catholic nun, wearing a white habit with a black hood, trudging past and asked her why she was fleeing. She told me she had been born in North Vietnam, came south as a young girl, and was running away again. "The VC come so we go," she said simply, as if that explained everything—and for hundreds of thousands of refugees, it did.

As we retreated back across the bridge, incoming mortar shells began landing near an army post on the south bank of the river. The soldiers fired their mortars back. This meant the enemy could not be far away. I heard the sound of small arms fire erupting, which was even more ominous. There was no way, with all these refugees, that the government troops could hold the river line. On the way back to

Saigon, we saw the police shunting the refugee flow off to hamlets near the highway. Among them were barefoot montagnards, who carried their rude axes on their shoulders, and, even by refugee standards, looked forlorn.

In Saigon, we stopped by George McArthur's villa to check in and he told us the northwest road to Tay Ninh was cut at Cu Chi, leaving the 25th Division immobilized, and Highway 4, the main road to the Delta, was also severed. The capital was isolated. "It won't be long now," I said, stating the obvious.

"Not for you," George said. "I've arranged to get you on a military flight out tomorrow—if they're still flying."

I protested that we agreed I should stay with him until the end. But he insisted that there was no point in having two of us getting in each other's way. And he wanted me to get out while I could. He said I would have to argue with our editors in Los Angeles to overrule his decision. McArthur had been in Vietnam continuously for ten years and if he wanted to be the last man out for the paper, so be it. It was his bureau. I had a farewell meal at the hotel that night and Loren ragged me about bugging out—which didn't improve my mood. But I reminded him to head for the embassy when the time came and not hang around some street corner. I went to bed that night expecting another rocket attack and slept in my clothes.

The next morning, I awakened to the sound of automatic weapons fire coming from a Vietcong commando squad that had sprayed the highway just over the Newport Bridge. This tactic shut down the Saigon–Bien Hoa highway. I heard the communists were shelling Bien Hoa and the big air base there. From the U.S. embassy's point of view, the only hope now was that the delayed swearing-in of Big Minh as president would encourage Hanoi to allow the Americans to make an orderly evacuation. But Martin and Polgar were still living in a diplomatic dreamworld. I paid my bill at the Continental and walked to George's house, carrying only my handbag with a portable typewriter inside. I had a farewell drink—mine was a triple—with him and rode with his cook-driver out to Tan Son Nhut. I noted with some irony the memorial at the airport entrance to the non-Vietnamese soldiers who served in Vietnam, which was inscribed THE NOBLE SACRIFICE OF THE ALLIED SOLDIERS WILL NEVER BE FORGOTTEN.

Hundreds of Vietnamese civilians were lined up in the Defense Attaché compound waiting to get on U.S. military flights that were finally arriving from Clark Field, mainly C-130 Hercules. U.S. State and Defense officials worked quickly and efficiently under great stress. Hundreds of the Vietnamese were evacuated that day and I boarded one of the last flights out.

As I approached the Air Force guard who was going over passengers with a hand-held sensor looking for weapons, the woman in front of me prompted a squeak in the machine when it passed over her waist.

"You got gold in a belt?" asked the security man with a smile.

"Yes," she replied, looking nervous.

"Okay," he said. "Go on through."

I boarded a camouflaged C-130 with about 175 passengers, almost all Vietnamese except for a half-dozen Americans. For the Vietnamese, it was a flight to freedom. We were "combat-loaded," that is, we sat on the metal decking with our legs under huge canvas straps rigged horizontally across the plane's belly. The C-130 quickly revved its four engines, screamed down the runway, and climbed in a steep, spiraling bank with the crew members at the open rear doors looking for missiles coming our way. If they saw any, they would fire flare guns, hoping the intense heat of the burning flares would divert the heat-seeking missiles from our engine exhaust. We climbed in tight circles to twenty-thousand feet and then headed due east for the Philippines.

I was wedged in next to a young Vietnamese woman who, above the racket of the engines and hiss of the hydraulic system, told me she was Lan Thi Rush, married to an America AID official named Bruce Rush. She was taking her family to his hometown of Louisville, Kentucky. Meanwhile, she was acting as a counselor to the other Vietnamese, all of whom were nervous and apprehensive about flying, and the uncertain future. They were sorrowful about leaving their homeland, probably forever, but relieved to be out after the weeks of sweating out departure formalities.

"I wanted to take my relatives to my husband's family," Mrs. Rush told me. "I took a vote in my family. My father and mother chose to remain behind as did others. But a brother and sister and two cousins wanted to go, so I am escorting them out."

I struggled out from under the strapping and climbed the ladder to the flight deck. The pilot, Air Force captain Hank MacQueen, turned his head to the rear and said, "I sure hate to see them so uncomfortable back here. It's a four-hour flight to Clark in this aircraft, and it's sure as hell not first class on Pan American."

MacQueen was a trim, rusty-haired pilot who used to fly B-52s. "I flew bombers over Vietnam for three years," he said, "but that was a very impersonal thing. This crew is damn glad to have a hand in saving lives and we're eager to do something for these people. Considering the circumstances and the conditions, they have been extremely cooperative and well-behaved."

As the sun lowered over the South China Sea, Captain MacQueen plugged me into the radio circuit: Word came through that five North Vietnamese pilots, flying captured A-37 attack planes, had dropped a half-dozen bombs on the Saigon runway, temporarily closing the airport. That sounded like very bad news to us: The evacuation flights would be interrupted until the field was opened again—if then.

We landed at Clark and the dazed passengers were greeted by a welcoming committee of U.S. Air Force personnel who poured water and soft drinks, and served bologna sandwiches, eagerly munched by the children. Our passengers were told, however, that the Philippine refugee camps were all filled and they would have to continue eastward to Guam Island. I decided to accompany the group for the story I was doing. After a two-hour layover, we were loaded aboard a C-141 Starlifter full-jet cargo transport. We still sat under the strapping but the loadmaster had found some carpeting material and laid it over the steel decking for our comfort.

Just as we were taking off, the pilot announced, "We've just been informed that Guam is also filled up so we'll be heading for Wake Island."

I'm sure the passengers had never heard of Wake. To me it was the island captured by the Japanese in 1941 after a valiant defense by the U.S. Marines. But it meant a six-hour flight through the dark instead of the expected three and a half hours to Guam. We landed before dawn. Mrs. Rush smoothed her hair, straightened her dress, and led her relatives down the flight ramp. An Air Force colonel greeted the new arrivals: "Welcome to Wake Island. The living conditions are austere but more comfortable than Clark or Guam and the food is good. Our big problem is producing enough fresh water so please conserve it."

I said good-bye to the Rush family and looked for a phone to call my office in Los Angeles. Somehow I had the idea that Wake Island was still a mid-Pacific Pan Am base, with a hotel and flight service to the West Coast. I was soon disabused of that notion. Pan Am had ceased stopping at Wake with the advent of the jet. There were no private hotels, no commerical air service anywhere, and there was only one telephone line to the United States, which was booked up by GIs for days. There was obviously no way I was going to get my story from Wake to L.A.

The pilot of the Starlifter told me his squadron was based at Clark and he was flying back as soon as he refueled. I bummed a ride and had the cavernous interior all to myself. I lay down, took a nap, then wrote a story on my portable. I climbed to the flight deck and shot the breeze with the crew, who were eager to show me their state-of-the-art controls. It was a strange feeling—flying halfway across the Pacific and back, as if on a lark.

I watched the sky lighten and tinge the magnificent cumulus clouds with morning pastels, pink, rose, azure, gold. My rhapsodic mood ended when we received an emergency radio message relayed from Saigon: The fixed-wing airlift was halted because of the shelling of Tan Son Nhut; the large-scale military evacuation by helicopter was ordered to begin. The last two American servicemen to die in Vietnam were killed in the airport shelling: Marine Corporal Charles McMahon and Marine Land Corporal Darwin Judge. They joined fifty-eight thousand other American dead during the long, excruciating involvement in Vietnam.

We landed at Clark in the afternoon. My story was overtaken by events: the final exodus of Americans from Vietnam. U.S. helicopter crews and Marine security forces did a superb job in evacuating those in the embassy compound and the airport. But hundreds of vulnerable Vietnamese allies had been left behind to an unknown fate because of the failure of Kissinger and Martin to provide for them. It seemed to me then one of the sorriest episodes in contemporary American history. It still does.

CHAPTER TEN

Darkest Italy

WHILE BASED IN Rome, I returned there from one of my trips to find that an epidemic of cholera had broken out in Torre del Greco, a small town just south of Naples on the bay. At least eleven people had died and hundreds more were hospitalized. I was late on the story, in 1973, and phoned an Italian girl who knew the dialect and would, I thought, be a fine interpreter. I suggested we jump into my Alfa and run down to Positano on this nice sunny weekend for some good fish and white wine. Lovely, she said. Only one thing, I said. Would she mind if we stopped off in Torre to do a little reporting on the cholera situation?

"Cholera," she said. "You've got a lot of nerve, you bastard." And hung up.

I managed to contact a pluckier lady and we sped down to Torre del Greco, where a great crush of people were trying desperately to get inoculated against the disease: Ten people had already died. The crowd surrounded the local movie theater, which had been converted into a makeshift clinic. Women raised their children high, pleading and screaming to be admitted. Each time a score of policemen would admit more people, the rest of the crowd would surge forward, almost out of control. A man emerged, rubbed his newly vaccinated arm, and yelled, "This is a disgrace. Keep order! Keep order!" A policeman surveying the chaotic scene turned up his eyes and palms in Neapolitan fashion. I found the locals, like myself, were somewhat mystified by the nature of cholera and how it was contracted. The best guess was that it came from contaminated water supplies. The acute bacteria infection in the intestine produced a dangerous diarrhea and dehydration. Symptoms included both severe vomiting and diarrhea.

"The people laugh with one eye," a local journalist told me, "and cry with the other. We have been warned not to drink the water or eat fruit. Lemons are said to be an antidote so the price in the market has doubled."

A young girl piped up, "Maybe we shouldn't be standing around talking to one another, we might catch something. But we can't spend all day in the house listening to the radio. We have to talk to somebody."

The cities along the Bay of Naples smelled of disinfectant sprayed on the streets. Ambulances, sirens blaring, sped through the narrow streets. The bars were empty. No one was buying produce at the local markets. It was not hard to see how cholera had gotten a grip on this city of eighty thousand, with its lovely view of Sorrento across the bay. Torre del Greco was grubby and sanitation rudimentary. The streets reeked of urine and accumulated garbage being burned. The walls of the town and neighboring Ercolano (the site of the Roman town Herculaneum, which was destroyed with Pompeii in the Vesuvius eruption of A.D. 79) were papered with official warnings, telling people to avoid shellfish, open markets, and swimming. They also urged proper sanitary measures. Loudspeakers backed up the warnings. U.S. medics from the Sixth Fleet, many of whose ships were home-ported at Naples, pitched in giving cholera shots. Finally, the local authorities decided the disease came from infected mussels and banned the sale.

"The garbage strike here did not help things," one official told us. "Maybe that's why the cholera started here." Another citizen ventured, "We heard that it was a sailor from Ercolano who spread the cholera from Tunisia—but nobody knows for sure."

"Most of us have been vaccinated now," a teenage boy told me. "But we are told that it takes six days to become effective so we will just have to wait to see what happens." A local health official said that they expected to have inoculated two million people by that Saturday evening.

Foreign tourists were keeping well clear of the Bay of Naples, as well as Sorrento and the Amalfi Coast, and all the big hotels were virutally empty, though this was the height of the season. We had no trouble finding a table at a popular restaurant at Santa Lucia in Naples; however we avoided the fish and stuck to the wine. Luckily for Torre del Greco, in the next day or so, the preventive medicine precautions took hold and the epidemic waned.

In northern Italy a few years later, I ran into another form of pestilence. In 1976, a poisonous vapor had spread in a cloud from a chemical plant over the town of Seveso near Milan. The chemical called TCDD (tetrachlorodibenzodioxin), used in making a bactericide widely employed in the cosmetics industry and also in a herbicide, had leaked out of an overheated reactor, spread around the countryside, and lodged in the soil.

Loren Jenkins had just been transferred by *Newsweek* from Hong Kong to Rome as bureau chief and we flew to Milan, rented a car, and drove to Seveso. It was set in a pleasant region between Milan and Lake Como called the Brianza, known for its orchards and vegetable gardens. By the time we arrived, thirty-five people had been hospitalized and many hundreds moved out of their homes. Doctors were making blood tests of about fifteen thousand people. But the scene was one of confusion.

A large area of the community was sealed off, with men in white protective suits, like something out of a science fiction movie, taking readings on instruments to record the degree of contamination. They carried the carcasses of pets in garbage bags for autopsies. Residents told us they thought these men in white had gone into the quarantined area to feed the animals left behind. But the orders were changed and now all pets and domestic animals were to be destroyed.

We found a man named Mario Asnaghi, who lived in a house near the plant and who pointed to the now-vacant factory. "The cloud was grayish-white and looked like steam," he recalled. "It was acrid-smelling and was strong enough to make you want to vomit. We closed our doors and windows but the stuff settled into the ground. The young kids became sick, and some of them broke out in rashes."

Company officials at the Icmesa factory, a subsidiary of Hoffman-La Roche of Switzerland, were slow to inform anyone of the danger involved. Local officials, too, did not spread word of the contaminants. Some residents said that during the week, they were told by local authorities not to eat or drink local products. Most residents, however, said they had no official notification of any trouble.

Rumors abounded: The factory was supposedly making toxic gases for the NATO Alliance; the Americans had an antidote for the poison but would not part with it. "I can't find anyone around here who knows what is going on," complained a mother with two children. "Nobody knows whether we can go back to our homes in a week, a month, a year—or ever."

We ran across another sticky issue. Dr. Gianni Remotti, the local health officer, mentioned to us, "If we find pregnant women adversely affected, we will offer them the option of a therapeutic abortion."

A cleaning woman at the school, which was doubling as a medical center and civic meeting place, overheard the doctor's remarks, and objected, "Abortions are a crime and a sin."

"Nonsense," said a young mother who had just finished a series of blood tests. "Is it not sinful to bear a misformed baby which will have to spend its life in an institution? How much more humane to have an abortion!"

We found the few remaining residents in that part of town from which all inhabitants had not yet been evacuated incensed at the Swiss-based chemical company, whose officials were patently slow in warning townspeople about the inherent dangers in the leak—not unlike Bhopal in India and Chernobyl in the Ukraine a few years later.

Further, city councilman Giuseppe Asigna bitterly told us, "This disaster has affected thousands. We are destroying their crops and animals. They can't go home. And the Swiss who turned the plant into one for using dangerous chemicals are now embargoing food products from our area. How crazy!"

We spent several hours that day inverviewing residents and officials. I was impressed by what one victim told me. "If there had been an earthquake here," he said, "you would see the damage all around. In this thing, you see no signs of a disaster. But for us who live here, this has been an awful, mysterious disaster just the same."

We decided to drive to Lake Como for a meal. It was one of those incongruities a foreign correspondent runs into: From the middle of a stricken, poisonous environment, we were suddenly transported to the lavish Villa d'Este for a sumptuous meal. Needless to say, we made no mention to the headwaiter whence we had just come. I'm sure we would not have been permitted in.

It was from Milan, too, that Jenkins and I set off on our ride to Istanbul aboard the fabled *Orient Express*. I had learned from Robin

Stafford, the Rome correspondent of the London *Daily Express,* that a group of railroad buffs were organizing a re-creation of the *Orient Express* as it was in its glory days, using some of the same *fin-de-siècle* dining cars. The trip was being kept quiet because the organizers feared that advance publicity might inspire a robbery or kidnapping attempt on the gold-plated passenger list.

I looked forward to the ride: Graham Greene, Eric Ambler, Agatha Christie, and Ian Fleming had made the *Orient Express* the setting for thrillers. And we'd be traveling in the same cars that carried its celebrated baggage of royalty, adventurers, femmes fatales, spies, courtesans, tycoons, and con men: "the train of kings," as it was called, "and the king of trains." The first *Orient Express* left Paris in 1883 via Vienna, Budapest, and Bucharest to the Black Sea, where passengers took a boat for the final leg to Constantinople. After the Simplon Tunnel was bored through the Swiss Alps, the train, renamed the *Simplon-Orient,* took the shorter route via Lausanne, Milan, Trieste, Zagreb, Belgrade, and Sofia to renamed Istanbul. During the 1920s and 1930s, several intelligence agents including at least one American actually disappeared from the train. Shut down by World War II, the *Orient Express* was revived, but like American luxury trains, lost out to air travel. In 1962, the *Orient Express* ceased its deluxe service, and was reconstituted as a second-class contraption called the Direct Orient with no restaurant car and a clientele consisting mainly of Turkish workers, young people traveling on the cheap, and the occasional railway aficionado.

Our trip also marked the one hundredth anniversary of the International Wagon-Lits Company, which put together four vintage sleeping cars, plus another for the staff, a baggage car, a belle epoque restaurant car, a lounge car, and a shower car—all to be pulled, we were told, by a classic steam engine. Our route would take us through Italy, Yugoslavia, Bulgaria, to Turkey. Three days and two nights during which anything could happen—mystery, adventure, even romance. After all, our guest list included Prince and Princess Arimberto Ludovisi Boncompagni, whose family provided Italy with a couple of popes; Contessa Fanny Branca di Romanico of the Fernet-Branca liquor family; several other assorted members of minor European nobility; some business magnates; and a few odds and sods like us. I insisted to Jenkins that we bring along dinner jackets and a few bottles of Château Latour for a proper evening.

The first jarring note came at Milan's Central Station when—with

Italian television cameras rolling—an engineer in a colorful bandana, cap and coveralls, boarded the engine, cranked up the steam, and pulled the train, with its long royal-blue coaches trimmed in gold, slowly forward. This was a half hour before we were scheduled to depart, and the locomotive, a small 2-8-0 made in 1915, looked suspiciously underpowered. Could this teakettle get us to Trieste? I wondered. Sure enough, as soon as the TV cameras packed up, the train stopped. The steam engine was uncoupled and chugged off—alone. A few minutes later a huge, modern electric engine backed onto Track 11 and hooked up to the *Orient Express* with the same engineer behind the controls. Only now he was wearing the standard gray uniform of the Italian State Railways.

What the hell was going on? I asked. The engineer looked sheepish. "The steam engine was for show," he explained. "It only makes sixty kilometers an hour. It might not have pulled the train out of the station, let alone to Trieste."

Jenkins was furious. He declared loudly that he had been duped, that the voyage we had paid our money for was a fraud. But I thought the missing steam engine had a nice, Italian touch to it, adding a little spice to the story.

As we rolled across the flat, rich plains of Lombardy, I struck up a conversation with two beautifully turned out women in the lounge car. If they were fellow passengers, the trip was looking considerably up. My hopes for finding a femme fatale though were short-lived.

The first woman introduced herself in French. *"Enchanté,"* I said, hopefully.

"Wagon-Lits publicity," she said, all business.

The second woman was slender and statuesque; she might have been a descendant of the Borgias. She extended her hand. "Pleased," I said, bowing.

"Italian Railways promotion," she said, equally matter-of-factly.

"Perhaps you would join us for lunch," I said, noting that the cuisine was said to be worth a *Michelin* star or two.

"Afraid not," said the Borgia lady. "We're getting off at Verona, the first stop." So much for the femmes fatales.

At Trieste, we were taken on a tour of the handsome city, the old Hapsburg empire gateway to the sea. Back at the train, a tall woman in jeans came up, and asked, "Do you speak English?"

"More or less."

"Is it true that Frank Sinatra is aboard the *Orient Express*? My daughter heard the rumor at school and would like an autograph.''

"There is no Sinatra aboard," I said, "and no steam engine, either."

At dinner, we were seated next to two Yugoslavian women, dressed in native costumes that made them seem appealingly like spies.

"Welcome to the People's Soviet Republic of Yugoslavia," one said, and they introduced themselves as state tourism officials. So much for female espionage agents.

We rattled across Slovenia and Croatia at night and the next morning stopped off in Belgrade for another quick tour. By cocktail time, we had entered Bulgaria, where King Boris would board the train to drive the locomotive personally at breakneck speed, heedless of the peasants or their flocks. In Sofia, we viewed the city and returned to the train for a black-tie dinner, which began with iced champagne served while we were still in Sofia station. Bulgarian folk dancers performed for us on the station platform. The irony of us capitalists sitting down to a fancy dinner while communist dancers entertained us was not lost on the ravishing Contessa Branca. Wearing golden earrings and a ruby-and-diamond ring, she remarked, "I supposed we should get used to this and how it is done. The way things are going in Italy these days, I wouldn't be surprised to see a trainload of Bulgarians pulling into Milan station and we Italians doing a dance for them!"

Someone asked the contessa about the Bulgarian royal family. "My dear," she said, "it was a dreadful dynasty. The only European royal house worse than the Bulgarians were the Belgians."

Jenkins and I had a private laugh at this remark and included it in our stories, mainly for the sake of Arnaud de Borchgrave, who was born a Belgian count. He still believes we invented the line to needle him.

We were told over cognac that Turkish border authorities would awaken us at 5:00 A.M. to check our passports. An Italian princess muttered, "If there are going to be any murders on the *Orient Express,* it will be the Turk who wakes me up at that hour."

I tried using the shower car that night. It had eight separate cabins, each with a confusing array of handles and valves to adjust the spray and temperature. I managed, but only barely. I could see why the women aboard the train decided to give it a pass. As one told me: "Imagine banging around a curve with your eyes full of soap and fiddling with the wrong lever. You could scald yourself to death. I prefer a sponge bath in my compartment."

Sometime during the night in Bulgaria, a genuine steam engine was hooked on to the train and we passed through several tunnels. The next morning a thin layer of soot and coal dust covered the compartment. So much for the Golden Age of Steam.

As we neared Istanbul, the Turks coupled on a tiny steam engine for the photographers to mark our arrival. But it pulled us so slowly up a grade near the station that I noticed cyclists on an adjacent road going faster than the famed *Orient Express*. Over a last cup of espresso, I asked the irrepressible Fanny Branca whether she could envisage much romance aboard the storied *Orient Express*.

"My dear," she said, "we talk about jet lag and forget what train lag was like. The trouble with a long train ride like this is that it leaves you too fatigued to be very romantic."

Fifty-four hours and 1,305 miles out of Milan, we chugged into Istanbul, the women anxious to debark for a roomy hotel room and a hot bath. I asked the porter, Pietro, how he rated the *Orient Express* in terms of romantic liaisons. "I wouldn't know, *signore*," he said. "This is my first trip. Better luck in Istanbul."

When Jenkins arrived in Rome to open a *Newsweek* bureau, I offered him room in the spacious quarters of the *Los Angeles Times* on the Piazza di Spagna with a view of the church of the Trinita dei Monte at the top of the Spanish Steps. It was really an unrivaled place to work. One lunchtime in May 1976, we were sitting in Nino's, that fine Tuscan restaurant around the corner from the office, when we got word a severe earthquake had struck the Friuli region in the northeastern corner of Italy. A couple of hours later, we were at the Venice airport, renting a powerful Alfetta and driving north toward the stricken area. We moved up the Tagliamento River valley, one of the loveliest parts of Italy, to the pleasant town of Gemona del Friuli. This was the area that Ernest Hemingway depicted so graphically in *A Farewell to Arms*, describing the Italian retreat in World War I.

The place lay in ruins. Centuries-old structures, including churches with priceless frescoes. Bulldozers worked to lift the floors of apartment buildings that had collapsed in heaps. We spent six hours visiting the most severely hit communities. Everywhere the story was the same: Rubble filled the streets; trench-digging machines clawed at structures to locate the missing. Houses caved in on top of residents, and rescue workers struggled to free the bodies. The injured were taken to hospitals or aid stations; the dead to temporary morgues.

In Maiano, a five-story apartment house had collapsed like a concertina on the main street. Bodies were being moved to the gymnasium that served as a makeshift morgue. They were placed in shiny wooden coffins lined with plastic bags and stretched out in long rows, while grief-stricken relatives came to identify the bodies. A man named Guido Riva who lived next to the Maiano church told me, "When the earthquake struck, the church towers fell on my house. It began to collapse but I managed to get my family out to safety. My mother was trapped and I pulled her and three children out. Thank God we are still alive."

The electric power was shut off, so after dark rescue workers used generator-driven searchlights to continue rescue operations. I saw some soldiers digging with their hands into the rubble: Observers said they believed they had heard a child's cry from under the wreckage. Sometime after midnight, we drove back to Udine, the capital of Friuli. Luckily, its splendid combination of architectural styles—Venetian, Renaissance, and Austro-Hungarian—were undamaged by the quake.

I managed to get through to Los Angeles by telephone with the story. By now, the hotel kitchen was long since closed. We went to bed hungry. At dawn the next day, we headed back to the quake zone and spent several hours reporting, visiting hospitals, churches, and Red Cross units. In Gemona, I met Mario Zamaro, who was still searching for his wife and two young children. At one point, rescuers found a handbag in the wreckage. "That is hers," said the distraught Zamaro, wringing his hands. A while later, the soldiers found some knitting. But there were no cries and it seemed almost impossible that there could be any survivors. Zamaro put his head down in a state of shock and was silent. Later in the day, the worst was confirmed: His wife and children were found buried in the wreckage, dead.

Near the center of the city, the thirteenth-century Cathedral of Mary of the Assumption was in shambles. The historic old campanile was shattered, the bells fallen into the stone rubble at the base of the tower. The whole side of the Gothic church simply disappeared, along with the frescoes and paintings that lined the walls. Down the street behind arcade shops, the city's second church, which had a famous Madonna, was wiped out. The top half of the bell tower was missing. "We had just reroofed the campanile a week ago," said a townsman. "We were so proud of it that we had held a feast day. Now it is gone— part of this terrible disaster."

I remember one priest, looking at his collapsed church, and saying, "Five hundred years of history, all just lying here."

By nightfall, we had been to every afflicted village, and our notebooks were brimming. We decided to drive back to Venice to file. We checked into the Gritti Palace Hotel and headed for Harry's Bar for a late dinner. I was aware how odd it was that having just covered an earthquake we were eating a meal in one of the best restaurants in Europe. Some might think it crass to be enjoying ourselves in such a way, after what we had seen. But I don't think so. I've missed enough meals on stories or made do with C rations that I take my gastronomic windfalls when I can. I eat up and thank my good fortune.

In fact, the food in Italy is so good, a reporter can't help but write about it. I learned our managing editor was fascinated by white truffles and I volunteered to do a story about them. Above and beyond the call of duty, you might say. I drove to Tuscany to see an old pal, Arnaldo La Cagnina, who had been an NBC correspondent in the Middle East and was now a country squire producing his own estate-bottled Chianti Classico near Greve. We had been copy boys together on the *San Francisco Chronicle,* and since then he had developed a knack for marrying heiresses. His first two wives were beautiful Americans; his third, the lovely Claude de France, the former Duchess of Aosta. Once I was sitting in Hanno's Corner, a saloon across from the *Chronicle,* when Arnaldo breezed in, dressed in white tie and tails, bound for some very social charity ball. He borrowed five bucks from me, and I always hoped that the loan may have gotten him started in the upper reaches of the social stratosphere.

Arnaldo with the help of his second wife had purchased a sensational eleventh-century castle between Siena and Florence, redone the place, and filled it with tasteful antiques while revitalizing the surrounding vineyards. It was harvest time, so I gathered story material on the *vendemmia,* the grape gathering, and the efforts of the Chianti producers to upgrade their wine, which had an unfounded reputation as "dago red" in some parts of the world. Then, we drove across the Apennines into the Po Valley and stopped for lunch at Cantarelli's, which I found out was the best mom-and-pop restaurant in Europe. It was located at a small crossroads near Parma in Emilia, very much off the beaten track. But outside of what looked like a musty country store were parked large and fancy cars, many bearing Milan plates, including a Rolls-Royce.

Behind the racks of sausages, cheeses, and fresh pasta in the grocery side were two small back rooms with scarcely a dozen tables. It was a hard palce to find but the keen-nosed inspectors from the *Guide Michelin* had sought out Cantarelli's and awarded it two stars.

At the time, *Michelin* had never awarded an Italian restaurant the top three stars, which was rightly resented by Italian food buffs and chalked up to French chauvinism. Recommended was the guinea hen with cream, the duck with cognac, or the beef tongue soufflé, and the local sparkling wine, Lambrusco. At the tables, film people rubbed elbows with the local farmers. The cooking was superlative, as the best Italian cuisine can be: simple, straightforward, fresh, tasty. Later, over a glass of old armagnac, Giuseppi Cantarelli talked about the philosophy of running their restaurant.

"We decided to keep the place small," he said. "We never serve more than fifty people at any meal. If we expanded, we could make more money but we would have to hire more help and lose the family atmosphere. I just wouldn't be able to look after the customers as well. As you can see, there is not much fuss here. We try to keep things simple. This is not one of those places with beautiful tables but little substance."

Emerging from the kitchen, which was bigger than the dining space, Mirella Cantarelli, a warm, broad, handsome woman swathed in a rough apron, sat down. I asked her how she pursued excellence. "By getting mad and screaming," she said. "While our menu is not large, everything on it is a speciality of the house, whether antipasto, pasta, risotto, meat, or dessert. Some of our dishes are based on old recipes and others I adapted on my own. I don't like to copy other restaurants' dishes."

I wondered about the future of such a small family-run place. Mrs. Cantarelli thought a moment, and answered, "It is more and more difficult to maintain quality. Some of the fine traditions of growing food in Italy are becoming lost in the modern age. The pace of life is increasing and there is less demand for the kind of meat that you cannot produce mechanically. It is difficult to maintain the flavor of good food."

The Cantarellis had one son, then seventeen. "Whether he will decide to take over the business is up to him," she said. "A few more years in the business will tell. This is the kind of work you have to do with passion—or not at all. We love to do things well here."

Sadly, in 1983, the Cantarellis decided to retire when their son opted to do something else in life. In keeping with their spirit, they did not sell their restaurant, but shut it down. With them into retirement went one of the truly fine country restaurants in Europe.

We continued across the province of Parma, where the great local ham and cheese is made. Parmesan cheese is sometimes called "the truffles of the poor" because the high-protein stuff is grated over many dishes—pasta, soup, rice, vegetables—and is nourishing and filling. But we were headed for the country of the truffles of the rich.

They come from Alba in southern Piedmont, situated in the limestone hills that produce many of Italy's finest red wines: barolos, barberas, barbarescos, dolcettos, nebbiolos. The autumn crop of truffles had been disappointing, we learned on arrival, and the cost had soared to more than four hundred dollars a pound, pricier than caviar. Alba is the marketing center for the legendary white truffle, a fragrant delicacy that gourmets rate higher on the taste scale than the black truffle, even those from the Périgord region of France. Truffles are difficult to find and describe: a strange form of underground fungus that grows often in symbiosis with the roots of trees like the oak, poplar, willow, and chestnut. The Alba region, or Langhe, has a near monopoly on the white truffle, which is actually a dirty brownish color on the outside and beige on the inside. Sliced very thin, the aromatic, musky truffle is sprinkled, like Parmesan cheese, on all sorts of dishes in Italy—pasta, meat, eggs, risotto. Scrambled eggs, for instance, with truffles sprinkled over them is a rare treat.

Truffles have long been reputed to have aphrodisiac qualities. The white truffle, wrote sixteenth-century Italian botanist Castor Durante, "excites the sexual appetite and increases the number of sperm." Napoleon Bonaparte, after capturing Alba in 1796, credited his truffle eating with producing a son. All in all, truffles seem to measure up to the great French gastronomist Anthelme Brillat-Savarin's description: "the white diamonds of the kitchen."

In France, truffles are often found by pigs, who have a nose for the scent of the underground tuber. But the swine tend to eat the truffles unless restrained. The Italians prefer to use dogs. A well-trained truffle-hound is dearly prized around Alba. Or as someone put it: "They're worth their weight in truffles."

Why are truffles so scarce? Raul Molina, vice-president of the annual truffle fair in Alba, put to us his theory that the lack of the delicacy in recent years was due to farmers increasingly turning their fields into vineyards because of the high prices for Piedmont wines. "In effect," he said, "the vines are the killers of truffles. The truffle grows with the large trees, but the trees are being cut down so the farmers can plant grapes for barolo and barbaresco wines, since we are in their official zone. So the truffles are disappearing."

I chatted with Mario Morra, whose family cans and exports a large percentage of Italian white truffles. His father, Giacomo, was known as "the king of the white truffles" and handled one of the biggest on record, which weighed 2,520 grams and which he called the Kohinoor of truffles. The Morra family devised a way to bottle and can truffles that preserves much of their flavor. Ordinarily, white truffles, unless packed in rice or some such protective agent, lose their aroma within a month of being unearthed, and eventually are worth less than a potato. Morra also packs truffles in a paste form, used in truffle sandwiches, which are sold in Italy's smarter cafés. In the restaurant of Morra's family hotel in Alba, he served us a six-course meal, each of which featured truffles. After about the third course, I thought I had enough of the white diamonds, and traveling solo, I wasn't able to test their aphrodisiac properties.

Truffles, wine, coffee, pasta, olives, in time, I did stories on most of these subjects. Sitting in Nino's, I happened to peruse the label on a bottle of Fiuggi mineral water on the table. It was a testimonial that read, in Italian, "I have been drinking this water, morning and night, from a spring forty miles outside of Rome. This has broken my kidney stones and I am now able to pass them." When I noted that the endorsement had been written in 1549 by the great Renaissance artist Michelangelo Buonarroti to his nephew, I knew it was an ad man's dream, something like Pope John XXIII plugging Budweiser beer. So I pursued my research into the Italian mania for mineral water. Some three hundred brands are sold, each claiming to supply its customers the equivalent of the fountain of youth. My favorite *acqua minerale,* San Pellegrino, says it is "unrivaled for curing uric diathesis, gout, gravel stones in the bladder and kidneys and liver, catarrh of the stomach, bowels and bladder, congestion and swelling of the liver from diseases of the stomach and intestines, infections, fever, malaria and alcoholism, and the gouty manifestations of the skin." Not bad for fifty cents a bottle.

In Rome, I lived on Via Margutta, a street of artists' studios and roof gardens under the brow of the Borghese Park. In the movie *Roman Holiday,* which I admired as a young reporter in San Francisco, Gregory Peck played a foreign correspondent who lived on the street, so for me it was a bit like a fantasy come true. In those days, I drank grappa, the fiery brandy, or more properly marc, with coffee after meals. I discovered that an army captain of Alpine troops in World War I had said of grappa, "It is like a mule. It has no ancestors and no hope for descendants. It zigzags down your throat just as the mountain mule walks. You can rest on it if you are tired, shield yourself with it if you're being shot at, sleep under it if the sun is too hot. You can talk to it and it will answer, you can weep and be comforted, and if you're really determined to die, it will smile at you.'' That paean prompted me to look further into the subject, and I found that grappa makers were trying to rid themselves of the image of a soldier's drink and appeal to a younger generation. I'm afraid it was a doomed effort. By the time I left Italy, I'd had my fill of grappa, but it did indeed provide me solace in times of need.

I found a darker side of the country in the Italian south. The island of Sicily is one of the most haunting places on earth, really a country to itself with indescribably beautiful settings. It is also the land of the Mafia. This was the period when the *Godfather* movies came out, and some critics thought the films painted too sympathetic a portrait of the secret society. I flew to Palermo, rented a car, and drove into the interior to Corleone, the scruffy hill town that gave its name to the leading family in *The Godfather*. Corleone was a historic Mafia center, and the crippling effects of the internecine warfare between the feuding factions left a grim stamp on the melancholy town of winding streets, unpainted stone houses, overhanging iron balconies, and silent citizens.

In Corleone and the surrounding farmland, more than two hundred murders were said to have occurred between 1944 and 1958. The population dwindled from twenty thousand to twelve thousand, and many of those left behind were women and children. I looked up Mayor Michele La Torre in his office in the town hall, adorned with a crucifix and the seal of the city, whose name means ''lion heart'': a lion holding a heart in its paw. The church bells rang from the cathedral next door. La Torre read *The Godfather,* called *Il Padrino* in Italian, but he hadn't yet seen the movie, which had opened in Palermo.

''The book was interesting and the author knew something of the criminal life in the United States,'' said the thirty-six-year-old mayor, who wore a neat dark blue suit. ''But I don't think the Sicilian scenes had much to do with Corleone. Most people who have seen the movie think that it glorifies the Mafia, making them into heroes, and this is bad. By the way, in Sicily, Vito Corleone would be known as Don Vito, not Don Corleone.''

The mayor denied there was any local activity by the Mafia,

which he referred to as "the organized delinquency." Yet in the next breath, he pointed to the root problem. "Our young men have left to go to America or northern Italy. Unemployment is our major problem. The agricultural base is decaying. People are leaving the fields barren to go to the cities. We badly need jobs here and when people are down-and-out there is more likelihood of criminal activity."

But criminal activity means the Mafia. Mayor La Torre indicated that the organization was much weaker in the hills here than in the bigger cities. In its way, I learned, Corleone typified the changes in the Mafia taking place on the sun-washed island, which has been ruled by Phoenicians, Greeks, Romans, Arabs, Normans, Swabians, French, Spaniards, and now even Italians. The Mafia had its origin in the centuries-old struggle of Sicilians to fend off the yoke of foreign rulers. Thus "the honored society" developed, operating under the code of *omerta*, or "silence," with its leaders dispensing justice and patronage, taking the law into their own hands, usually with the *lupara*, the Sicilian hunter's shotgun. The Mafia's influence was paramount in western Sicily, where education, public services, and economic development were weakest. Though Mafia capos, or chiefs, liked to depict themselves as justice-minded Robin Hoods, in time they invariably backed the rich, landowning baronial families in any showdown with the poor farmer.

In 1915, for instance, when Corleone's brilliant socialist agrarian reformer, Bernardino Verro, tried to organize the farmers to secure a decent share of their profits, he was assassinated by the Mafia. That was the end of educational and agricultural reform in Corleone. During the 1930s and 1940s, the old order of doing things was reflected in the dominating person of Dr. Michele Navarra, the area's leading physician, a rich civic leader, and a power in the Christian Democratic party. He was also a leader of the Mafia.

Navarra's protégé was a young shepherd, Luciano Liggio, who was intelligent, energetic, brave, ruthless, and cruel. He wanted to adopt "new" ways for the Mafia, branching out into broader criminal areas. Dr. Navarra resisted—urging caution, content with the old ways. In the 1950s, a new dam was proposed for the Corleone area. Navarra opposed it because it would interfere with his traditional control of the sparse water supplies. Liggio, however, argued for the dam because it would provide new opportunities to make more money. The disagreement resulted in a war between the factions, a bloody period for Corleone. It culminated in 1958 when Liggio's men riddled Navarra in his car with seventy-seven submachine gun bullets. Liggio was arrested for several murders but managed to slip away, and Corleone rested easier, with the action shifting to the bigger cities.

In the capital of Palermo, the new Mafia has moved into racketeering in a big way: gambling, building construction, business licensing, the port, fishing, meat, fruit and vegetable markets, and drugs. Mafia members also buy up valuable land at cut-rate prices because, in the words of one official, "they made the seller an offer he can't refuse."

I called on Roberto Ciuni, an editor of Palermo's *Giornale di Sicilia,* who was an expert on the Mafia and an outspoken critic of it, in his office in downtown Palermo. "The Mafia has changed from a feudal, rural base to an urban one," he told me. "We have seen a shift from the old Mafia to the new Mafia. Corleone is a symbol of the old order giving way to the new. The old Mafiosi wanted respect and dignity and power. There is a Sicilian saying: To command is better than to make love! The new Mafiosi are pragmatic. They care nothing about esteem and honor. They are common criminals who would sell their mothers to make money. Liggio was like that. Three hundred years ago, Italian politicians followed the rules laid down by Niccolò Machiavelli. Today they seem to be following the political principles of the Mafia: protection, privilege, secrecy, the mentality of the family, producing votes. The national government set out to Italianize Sicily but in many ways we have succeeded in Sicilianizing Italy."

Ciuni sighed at the size of the task of reducing the power of the Mafia. "We have a long struggle ahead to defeat these people on this island and in this country," he said. "And the struggle is not helped by depictions like *The Godfather.* The movie is too seductive. The Mafia likes this portrayal. Don Vito, his family, and the Mafia come out too clean. This is very wrong because it is like telling people to look up to Bonnie and Clyde."

The nearest region on the Italian mainland to Sicily is Calabria, a wild, rugged place of vast beauty and dark violence. I was introduced to Calabria by a native, Elisabetta, a raven-haired, intelligent Italian beauty, with moods as deep as the region. She took me through the forests of the Aspromonte, the toe of the Italian boot, stunningly clad in autumn's scarlets, hennas, and golds. It is splendid country of remote hilltop villages, Greek ruins, massive olive trees, magnificent coastlines, and vineyards planted on slopes slanting into the sea so sharply that the grapes must be harvested from boats.

Since the days of the Roman Empire, Calabria has been the birth-place of rugged folk, and once provided gladiators for the Colosseum, Like Sicily, Calabria was long ruled by a succession of foreigners, which encouraged native resistance that often took the form of banditry. Lawlessness is still a common way of life, and the government, more often than not, is viewed as the enemy. A local version of the Mafia grew up here, known as the N'dragheta—the name is thought to derive from a dialect word meaning "belt," giving the sense of a tight circle of relatives. Once a kind of family protective organization, the Calabrian Mafia increasingly turned to racketeering, kidnapping, and extortion. The accompanying bloodshed stems mainly from internal squabbles over the huge spoils.

"The Calabrian Mafia has changed its shepherd's boots for the well-polished shoes and the double-breasted suit," Luigi Malafarina, a writer on the subject, told me. The shift in Mafia activities was galvanized by the government's decision to bring industrialization to Italy's impoverished south, first by building a multibillion-dollar, four-lane autostrada from Rome to Reggio Calabria, then by erecting a huge steel mill at Gioia Tauro, which critics call "a cathedral in the desert." An estimated 20 percent of construction costs were ripped off by the Mafia over the years, officials said privately. Masked men sometimes appeared at construction sites, ordering workers off the job until the extortion payments were met.

When sought by police, fugitives sought refuge in the Aspromonte, called Italy's Wild West. There, the outlaws, known as *latitanti*, operated with a certain style, protecting themselves with a network of armed patrols, guard dogs, and radio-equipped cars. The local police are widely believed to have reached a modus vivendi with the *latitanti*. For fugitives, prices run high: $1.00 for the same day's newspaper, $12.00 for a pack of cigarettes, $1.25 for a single bullet. Many hiding out are Mafisosi, others ordinary criminals; some are involved in vendettas in the many blood feuds between Calabrian families. The outlaws raise money through extortion. A note to a prominent local doctor complimented him on his medical successes and suggested that it would be in his and his family's interest to drop off the equivalent of $100,000 in a nylon sack at the appointed place on a mountain road. The note was signed, "The Anonymous Outlaws." The funds were deposited.

Aspromonte outlaws were also blamed for the kidnapping of the grandson of oil billionaire J. Paul Getty, who was held in Calabria and finally released after an ear was cut off to encourage payment. One

Mafia leader, Saveria Mammoliti, who was charged with the kidnapping, broke out of prison, hid out in the Aspromonte, but came out to marry his fiancée in a church wedding in her hometown of Castellace. He took her to the Aspromonte for a two-week honeymoon before returning her to her parents' home. Similarly, Mammoliti summoned a local architect and a lawyer to his mountain hideaway to inquire whether they thought he should invest considerable funds in a new tourist complex in Calabria.

I called on Judge Domenico de Caridi at his home along the beachfront at Reggio, overlooking the Strait of Messina, with the hills of Sicily hovering in the distance. The graying, bespectacled judge was a pronounced foe of the Calabrian Mafia. A few months previously, the judge's car was blown up in front of his house. A month later, he was ambushed by four bandits while driving on a back road. One assailant, spotting from an olive tree, alerted three others who brandished machine guns and ordered him to stop. Instead, he accelerated and sped away, despite a tire shot out.

"I don't think they wanted to kill or kidnap me," the judge said evenly, sipping a glass of red wine. "I think they wanted to intimidate me—and not only me, but other judges as well. The situation with the outlaws is very serious, very deep, with vast repercussions. Every day, the acts of crime become more glaring, daring, and arrogant. Somehow we have to revitalize public institutions and generate popular opinion against these criminals."

In his book *Old Calabria,* Norman Douglas observed in 1915, "The Aspromonte, the roughest corner of Italy, is a place of misunderstandings; the knife decides promptly who is right or wrong." The knife, today, has been replaced by the shotgun, the submachine gun, and the explosive charge, but lawlessness is still a usual style of life, and family feuds are often settled by violent means. As we traveled through the Aspromonte, Elisabetta introduced me to Seminara, a community of thirty-two hundred souls, wracked by a vendetta between two families—the Pellegrinos and the Gioffres—which made the Hatfields and the McCoys seem tame.

Seminara looks like a western frontier town—before law arrived—roughhewn, dilapidated, without any special character, having been reconstructed in helter-skelter fashion after the 1908 earthquake that ravaged western Calabria. Its chief grace note is the enormous olive trees that grow just outside of town, the largest in the world, as big as oaks.

"We called our square the Piazza of the Thirty-three Crosses, for the number of people killed there,'' explained a local lawyer to whom Elisabetta introduced me. ''Violence is in the land. It is in the blood. In the last two years, twelve members of the two feuding clans were killed and about forty wounded. But there's not much the police can do about it. These people observe the code of *omerta*. No one reports any crimes. No one even admits that any trouble has occurred. So the law cannot be enforced.''

Just before my visit, a woman member of the Gioffre family was shot and badly wounded as she slept in bed. According to town gossip, she was warned of her fate by letter, but no one, of course, went to the police. The current vendetta began two years before in the town square. Though there had been bad blood between the two farming families, the incident that triggered the latest round of violence was set off when a half-crazy member of the Pellegrino clan brandished the deeply insulting *cornuto* (''"cuckold"'') sign at a Gioffre and sharp words were exchanged. Killing and counterkilling ensued. A shepherd who helped a wounded member of the Gioffres was himself killed for his Good Samaritan services. Once, one family was taking its victim to the cemetery, and a member of the other clan leaped in front of the cortege with a drawn submachine gun.

''Drop the coffin,'' he yelled. ''This man was a killer and doesn't deserve to be buried with respect.''

The mourners dropped the casket and fled, but the incident only fueled their desire for revenge.

Two ten-year-old members of each family attended the same school and, curiously, became friends, according to their schoolteacher. Because of the feud, the teacher planned to put the boys in different classsrooms—but they both objected. ''I know when we are older we may have to kill each other, '' one boy told his teacher. ''But right now let us be friends together.''

Not all the violence in Seminara is attributed to the Gioffres and Pellegrinos. Other people are touchy, too, as was illustrated by two incidents that occurred not long before I arrived. In the first, a towns-man who kept ringing the church bells to celebrate the election of a new mayor was shot out of the belfry by a supporter of the opposition candidate who considered the action a personal insult. In the second, an irate father shot a married man he found in bed with his daughter. One of the father's women relatives repeatedly said publicly of the dead man, ''He got what he deserved.'' She was murdered not long after because, it was said, she gratuitously added insult to injury.

Sociological researchers from Italian universities have dropped into Seminara to delve into the culture that creates the climate for vendettas. But they never get very far, for the families simply will not talk.

I was introduced to Francesco Colicchia, the local pharmacist who doubled informally as the town sociologist. He offered me a chair in his store, and observed, "To understand the violence, you have to understand the isolation of this part of Calabria. Like the American West, these people feel cut off from the normal channels of government and of justice. Each person believes that only the family can obtain justice and that he personally must right any wrong done to the family. In Calabria, honor is everything. People are touchy and easily offended. Once a family feels offended, it is up to the members to avenge that hurt, and that can lead to a vendetta."

After filling a prescription for a woman garbed in funereal black, the pharmacist mentioned that on occasion women of both feuding families have been in his pharmacy at the same time. "They stand at different sides of the room and do not look at one another or speak," he said.

In explaining the iron code of *omerta,* Colicchia continued, "If four of us were sitting right here and somebody came and shot one of us, the others would have seen nothing and would know nothing about it. The only way to solve this state of things is to give the society faith and hope that government can guarantee justice. But that government authority doesn't exist in Seminara and these people believe that they must resolve these matters themselves. So it will go on and on. I think this feud will only end when one family is wiped out. And that may take half a century. One of the families could move away and that might end it. But this would amount to surrender, so I don't think it would ever happen."

I once took a trip to Verona to examine the most famous Italian feud, that between the Montagues and Capulets, celebrated by Shakespeare in *Romeo and Juliet.* I visited that captivating city on the Veneto's Adige River to check into reports that young people were still writing to the star-crossed lovers there. Sure enough, letters from all over the world were delivered to the graceful, cloistered Capuchin Church of San Francesco, where Juliet's marble tomb lies next to the chapel in which the young couple was said to have been married shortly before their deaths. That, if it ever happened, was seven hundred years ago, yet the letters, written on fancy stationery or copybook sheets, arrived at the rate of a dozen a month in Verona.

The city was the scene of the Shakespeare tragedy, based on a tale by Luigi da Porto written in 1531, which in turn was founded on the early-fourteenth-century romance of Romeo Montecchi (Montague) and Giuletta Capuletti (Capulet). The warring families certainly existed, and the Capulet home, dating from the thirteenth century, has been restored, with a marble balcony jutting out over the courtyard.

I was shown a sampling of letters written to "Dear Juliet" by the custodian.

"I'm writing about a problem that is much like the problem that you and Romeo had," said one from Florida. "I am in love with a man who is of a different race and religion. Our plans were to be married as soon as possible, but after revealing them to our parents, we ran into trouble. Our parents strongly disagreed. Please send me your advice as soon as possible. Sincerely. Sharon."

Or this from Los Angeles: "Dear Juliet. I have this terrible problem. I have loved a boy named Gary. How can I get him to love me? A true believer in you. Best regards. Joy."

A girl in Washington wrote: "Dear Juliet. I hope will all my heart you can help me with a problem. I am shy. I like a boy named Ed who is sort of like Romeo—a love-them-and-leave-them type. I just can't seem to say anything intelligent to him. What should I do? Love, and bless you. Loretta. P.S. Thanks a lot."

Some letters came from Italian girls with a more florid style. "Dear Giuletta," wrote a girl from Trieste, "I put myself into your compassionate hands because I am alone in the world without assistance, protection, and advice. I place my hope in you, protectoress of all pure suffering hearts."

In the splendid city of charming squares, lovely architecture, and cypress-covered hillsides dotted with Palladian villas, I discovered that the warder at the Church of San Francesco, a man named Ettore Solimani, had taken the unofficial title "Secretary to Juliet" and answered every letter that arrived. An old-fashioned romantic, Solimani used to say, "Juliet died for love, so all of us must live for love." When asked whether the couple really existed, he would say, "What does history really matter? For us, Juliet lives. She lives in our hearts."

When Solimani retired, Professor Gino Beltramini took over the task of answering the letters and as he told me, "I used to respond to each letter separately, with suggestions and indications based on good sense—trying never to forget differences in religion, civilization, and ways of life. You cannot give the same sort of advice to an Italian or European girl as you do to an American. I also tried to take the utmost care in raising spirits, and never depress hopes too far.''

But the local papers and television teams discovered that the kindly professor was answering letters—and splashed the story. The flashy publicity convinced Beltramini to retire, too. As he explained to me, ''This whole correspondence belongs in the field of legends and dreams. And it's not really fitting for an old man, over sixty, to become the embodiment of a dream figure. A heart is young, that's true enough. But I think of a young lady in distress, and realize that it will be a tottering old man handling her letter and advising her on her troubles. I decided that it just wasn't seemly. So I retired as Secretary to Juliet and the incoming letters are kept on file at the Municipal Building—but are unanswered any longer.''

Over the years, I have written stories on deeply controversial subjects: Vietnam, North Ireland, Cyprus, the Middle East. But the most heated reader reaction I've ever received stemmed from an article on the Italian husband as lover. Italian men are usually seen as the compleat Latin lover: handsome, stylish, attentive, devastating. In putting together the story, I talked to dozens of women who had married Italians and found them—as husbands—egocentric, neurotic, and compulsively unfaithful. One stunning American woman who lived in Italy for several years and was married to an Italian typically told me, ''Italian men are interesting lovers for a while—a short while. But basically, they are infantile, self-centered, hopelessly spoiled, and incapable of an adult relationship with their wives.''

Another handsome European woman who was married to an Italian confided, ''Italian men can never accept women as equals. They really believe that a woman is not worth having a serious discussion with: She only exists to be charmed, courted, and bedded. Ask an intelligent Italian about politics or any other serious topic and he will invariably reply, 'Bellissima, your eyes are so lovely, your hair so striking, et cetera.' He absolutely refuses to take a woman seriously on the intellectual level. This attitude can really turn you off.''

I noted a survey on sexual preferences taken by the Sicilian-born writer Lieta Harrison, who found that Italian wives complained that their husbands weren't good lovers. A large majority of the more than one thousand women interviewed maintained that while their men may

have been fine lovers during courtship, as husbands they were indifferent and selfish at lovemaking. "Italian husbands are disappointing
as lovers," she concluded, "overbearing as well as negligent, unprotec-
tive, and adulterous."

My old friend Oriana Fallaci, in describing why divorce was less
popular in Italy than in many other countries, said, "An Italian man
plays with other women like a soccer player with a football. But talk
about divorce and he has to face up to the facts: He isn't playing around
anymore. Since he views his wife as a mother figure, a divorce would
in effect make an orphan of him."

That concept of a wife as a mother figure seemed a central theme
underlying male attitudes, according to those I spoke with. Many
people I questioned, men and women alike, attributed the alleged
deficiencies of Italian husbands as lovers to the phenomenon known as
mammismo, which roughly translates as "momism."

"*Mammismo* is caused by the overprotective Italian mother ob-
sessively babying her male children, making them *mammoni,* or 'mama's boys,' " an Italian woman psychiatrist told me. "The Italian
male expects not only to be mothered by mothers, but later by wives,
and eventually by society at large. An Italian man's mother is the most
important and continuing influence in his life. When he says, 'I swear
on my mother,' it is the ultimate truth, much more sacred than swear-
ing an oath based on the Bible or on God. His mother dominates his
life, even after he is married. And if he is a bachelor, he frequently
continues to live at home all his life."

And an Italian woman friend of mine amplified, "It is a vicious
circle. Italian men place on a pedestal—as psychic virgins—their
mothers, their wives, their sisters, their daughters. All other women
are considered, in effect, women of easy virtue and thus fair game. So
when an Italian—who may have been a great lover in the courtship—
marries, his wife soon becomes a mother figure. And since the incest
taboo is very strong, he begins to look elsewhere for real sexual grat-
ification. The wives then channel their own sexual frustrations toward
their sons, spoiling them in the process. These narcissistic children
grow up to be Italian men and the whole process is repeated.

"One of the most serious problems in the Italian culture," added
psychiatrist Renata Gaddini, "is that children become 'mother-fixated,'
and the mother cannot cut the psychological umbilical cord to her
child."

I was introduced to clothes designer Osvaldo Testa at a party and
sounded him out on the subject. "Italian men are narcissistic," he

replied, "which is a result of *mammismo*. They are exalted by their mothers. The middle-class Italian woman is repressed sexually. She is not allowed freely to love her husband sensually. All her repressed sexual love comes out in admiration of her sons."

I also looked up writer Costanzo Costantini, whose book *The National Male* addressed the same theme. We met at the Caffè Greco on Via Condotti in Rome and he explained, "Italian male narcissism is everywhere. He is always looking in a mirror. And in a five-minute conversation, he will use the word 'I' dozens of times. It doesn't make much difference what level of education he has, or whether he is a literary figure or a communist official. All Italian men have been conditioned this way, including myself. I am only different in that I am more conscious of this quality in us."

Constantini and Italian women writers seemed agreed on the fact that an unfair double standard existed in most Italian marriages.

Gabriella Parca, whose book *The Sultans* explored the Italian male role in society, summed up her findings: "Once married, they want absolute faithfulness from their wives while reserving the right to remain an adolescent forever, ready for all adventures but unable to stand serious commitment."

And a woman sociologist told me, "An Italian husband may have two or three mistresses. He may take them even if he doesn't really want them, but because of his *bella figura*, his image. It's the expected thing. But he would consider himself justified in killing his wife if he found her unfaithful. I know a husband who bought a flat in which to pursue his extramarital dalliances, but to salve his conscience, he put the deed in his wife's name."

Finally, Adele Cambria, an Italian mother of two boys and a prominent feminist, explained to me, "Italian girls are taught from infancy to be deferential to Italian boys. They grow up believing they are second-class citizens—and they are. Until Italian women break out of their own stereotypes, they will continue to be treated solely as mother figures or sexual objects by their men." Ironically, Adele, who was separated from her husband, babied her own sons as much as any traditional Italian wife.

It seemed to me that the view of many modern women in Italy was that their Italian husbands were disappointing lovers, however ardent they might have been as swains. I went out of the way to make the point that the women were not impugning the virility of Italian men, only the men as husband-lovers.

Well, when the story came out, readers didn't wait to write. Some phoned the paper in Los Angeles to complain. One caller said I must be some kind of Irish homosexual to write such drivel. Another said he would like a crack at my wife or sister to show what stuff Italian men were made of. Some of the readers, particularly those with Italian names, seemed to think the story was somehow anti-Italian, which was not the case. I think many Italo-Americans in Los Angeles have forgotten how strong the differences are between assimilated Americans of Italian stock, and husbands in Italy. For all I know, the Italo-American may be the perfect mix in a husband—blending sex appeal with stability and concern for family values. Whatever the case, I was startled, but also amused, by the heat of the reaction to the article.

Among the women I had interviewed was Elda Gugliemetti, the glamorous manager of the NBC News bureau in Rome. Elda had spent most of her life in Italy. She had been married to an Italian count, but earlier had gone to Radcliffe College after the war. I once mentioned that she, coming from the remote Abruzzi Mountains, must have found Radcliffe an exciting, challenging place.

"Not really," she said. Puzzled, I asked why not. In her immaculate, perfectly parsed diction, she told me how she spent the war years. Though raised in Boston, she had returned to Italy with her father, and was cut off in the Abruzzi by the outbreak of war. As a young teenager, she had acted as a courier between downed American and British fliers, who bailed out in the mountains behind German lines, and the Italian resistance. She would relay messages and arrange for the airmen to be hidden until they could be smuggled south to the Allied zone in southern Italy. At the same time, the young German officer in charge of the Sulmona area, her hometown, used her as his interpreter since he spoke English but no Italian. The officer, a handsome captain, fell for her. As a budding young woman, she found him attractive. But she kept her loyalty to the resistance and for many months played a delicate game moving between the German occupier and the Allied fliers in the mountains. When, a couple of years later, she found herself at Radcliffe, surrounded by the daughters of bankers and businessmen, Elda said dryly, she found the quality of experience and discourse something of a comedown.

As a war correspondent, I've tried when possible to visit the locales of famous battles. The experience is instructive, though often depressing. One morning, I drove from Rome down the Liri Valley to Monte Cassino, the site of the Benedictine abbey that was fought over during World War II and finally destroyed along with the town of Cassino by massive Allied air raids. The bombing was one of the most criticized Allied acts in the war. And though the monastery has been fully restored atop the mountain, the memories remain fresh at the abbey and in the city of Cassino below.

I sought out Cassino's mayor, Antonio Ferraro, who told me he was sixteen at the time of the bombing in 1944 and forced by the German defenders to dig ditches in the town at the foot of the mountain. "It is all a very ugly memory," said the mayor. "There was no good reason for it. The bombing didn't help the Allied advance at all. Today our schoolchildren write essays about it, and make tape-recorded interviews with the survivors."

In 1944 on Allied war maps, Monte Cassino was simply Hill 516, commanding a network of valleys between Naples and Rome, but defended by tough, expert German airborne and mountain troops. The Allied drive northward had been stalled for two months, bogged down in the wet, cold mud of the rugged hills and lowlands. In January 1944, American troops had suffered sharp losses when they were repelled trying to cross the Rapido River. In February, the Americans were relieved by British Commonwealth soldiers under the command of New Zealand's General Bernard Freyberg, whose status was rather special. The overall Allied ground commander in Italy was Britain's General Harold Alexander. Under "Alex" and commanding the American Fifth Army was General Mark Clark. General Freyberg's New Zealand Corps came under Clark. But since Freyberg was also the representative of the New Zealand government in the Mediterranean Theater, he was treated with some deference by military superiors.

Before launching an attack in mid-February against Cassino and Monte Cassino, Freyberg declared it was a "military necessity" to destroy the abbey, which he claimed was being used by German observers and defenders. Clark was very much against the destruction of the monastery—which was founded in A.D. 529 by Saint Benedict—for historical, religious, political, as well as military reasons. He believed the Germans were not entrenched in the structure and its collapse would only make it easier for them to fight in the ruins. The French commander, General Alphonse Juin, probably the shrewdest Allied senior commander in the Italian campaign, agreed with Clark. He would have preferred to see the Cassino strongpoint outflanked and bypassed. But Freyberg was adamant that his own ground commanders said a successful attack could not be launched without previous bombing. Alexander backed him up. Mark Clark acquiesced since the ground attack was an "all-British" show. On February 15, 225 Allied bombers dropped 576 tons of high explosives on the monastery in what was then the heaviest raid of the war in support of a tactical target. Not only did the Germans then occupy the ruins but they beat back the assault of the New Zealand Corps. On March 15, the Allied command decided to hit the town of Cassino and turned it into rubble with 1,400 tons of explosives. The bombing made the task of the Allied battalions no easier. Monte Cassino was not finally taken until May 18 by Polish troops. The road to Rome was finally opened.

"They bombed and bombed," recalled Mayor Ferraro, "and they even bombed their own troops. They destroyed the town but it did them no good. Their tanks couldn't move through Cassino. And the German paratroopers who were holding the town repulsed them."

After the war, the Italian government provided the funds to restore the abbey from drawings made by the monks and built a new town in the Rapido River Valley. "We were never able to ascertain the exact number of civilian casualties," Ferraro commented sourly. "There were twenty-four thousand people in the town before the war, but many of them fled to relatives elsewhere and never came back. We have five war cemeteries near here. Italian, German, French, Polish, and British Commonwealth. In all, there are fifty thousand graves."

I climbed the heights to the abbey and encountered a septuagenarian monk who had survived the bombings, a lean, bent man called Don Agostino Saccomanno. He sat me down at a long wooden table in the refectory, offered me a strong espresso, and told me, "The strange thing is that many visitors think the Americans were to blame for the bombings. They weren't. It was the British. The Allies dropped warning leaflets, but we did not have time to flee. They bombed us the next day. There were no German troops in the abbey, only a few monks, and many civilian refugees. It was a great tragedy: Many lives were lost, a magnificent building with many of its art treasures destroyed. I asked then, and I ask now, To what end?"

Don Agostino got up from the table and escorted me toward the door. "If there is any good to come of it," he said, "perhaps it will be that the abbey will serve as a monument to peace, because the bombing achieved nothing but destruction, indignation, sorrow, and regret."

Not far from Cassino, on the Tyrrhenian Sea at Nettuno, is an American military cemetery for those who were killed in Italy in World

War II. On the day of my visit, a light wind off the Mediterranean rustled the stands of cypress and umbrella pines, fluttered the pink and white oleander blossoms, and stirred the two American flags on their tall standards. Here lay buried 7,862 American servicemen who fought in Sicily and slogged up the peninsula: Salerno, Cassino, Anzio, Rome, and the Gothic Line in Tuscany. The white marble headstones were arranged in gentle arcs in the deep green grass, forming a geometric pattern of crosses and Stars of David. Among the thousands of names, ranks, and home states were 488 crosses bearing the words, "Here Rests in Honored Glory a Comrade in Arms Known but to God." In the cemetery chapel, the walls carried the names of 3,094 men who were missing in action in land, sea, and air operations, listed in alphabetical order rather than by rank, with "Keene, Elmer, Private First Class, Maine," preceding "Keerans, Charles T. Jr., Brigadier General, North Carolina." Twenty-one pairs of brothers who died in Italy lie side by side in the cemetery.

I looked up Ralph Mancini, the soft-spoken superintendent, who was in his early sixties and told me he was a medic with the Fifth Army in Italy during the war, before taking a civil service job with the U.S. Battle Monuments Commission. He said that after the war American families were given the choice of leaving their fallen in Europe or bringing their bodies home. About 40 percent chose to keep their sons and husbands overseas, subscribing to the advice of General George C. Marshall, who said at the time, "With all my heart, I believe that no one who left a son overseas should doubt the fittingness of his final resting place. That he should have, for time unending, a part of the ground he so dearly bought is supremely right and fitting."

As we walked through the superbly tended grounds, Mancini reflected, "I've watched the trees and bushes grow during my twenty years here and each spring the place gets more beautiful. I feel very emotional about this place. I like keeping it looking lovely for the men who are buried here. I only hope people still appreciate what these boys did for their country. Sometimes foreign visitors ask me where the heroes are buried—they assume there is some special plot. I tell them they are all heroes here."

CHAPTER ELEVEN

Upheaval in Iran

I HAD JUST arrived for a short vacation with friends—in England's Lake District in late December 1978 when, checking into the resort hotel, I found a message awaiting me: "Call the office." I did and was asked by the foreign editor if I minded getting to Iran as soon as possible to cover the worsening crisis there. It was an inopportune time: I wanted to get a few days' rest and visit a restaurant Johnny Apple had touted. I got a couple of days' grace by pointing out that the Iranian embassy was shut down over the holiday weekend. But I was soon on a plane for Tehran.

As usual, Tehran was a complete disaster: The capital hadn't cleaned up its act since 1975, when I had spent two weeks in Iran. Traffic was unspeakable; gridlock was a way of life. But the Intercontinental Hotel was accommodating and filled with colleagues. For the dynasty of Shah Mohammed Reza Pahlavi, King of Kings and Light of the Aryans, was in mortal trouble: Street rioting was a daily occurrence, the country's workers were on strike, and oil production was down to a relative trickle. There were long queues at gas stations. I went quickly to work.

The story was a gripping one, worthy of the rash of thrillers written around the Shah and his oil wells: an Oriental autocrat, with a beautiful empress, who was determined to make his backward country the fifth most powerful industrialized nation in the world by the end of the century. The Shah meant well, launching the White Revolution (as opposed to the Red), and I think he genuinely had the best interests of his countrymen at heart. But in the course of his long regime, the Shah set up a feared and hated secret police, Savak; he throttled political activity; and, increasingly autocratic, he surrounded himself with a tiny coterie of incompetent and sycophantic advisers, a true Persian court. The Shah relished pomp as the successor to Cyrus the Great on the Peacock Throne, but actually the Pahlavi dynasty was only two generations along, founded by his father, Shah Reza, a former colonel in a cossack regiment who came to power in a coup d'etat in 1921, and was forced into exile by the British in 1941 as a Nazi sympathizer. The Shah also built an enormous military machine, far beyond the country's real needs, which the United States, Great Britain, and other European countries happily armed. And like other Middle Eastern autocrats, he funneled billions of dollars from oil revenues and contract rakeoffs into private bank accounts abroad, and into the ubiquitous Pahlavi Foundation.

On my previous trip, I had traveled widely in the vast country of forty million people and noted even then the disruptions caused by the White Revolution: The capital had become an overcrowded slum except for the lavish homes of the rich in suburban north Tehran where the royal palace was located; peasants were lured away from the farms to the cities but weren't suited to work in the new industries so hundreds of thousands of foreign workers were brought in; with the exodus from the farms, agricultural production fell and food had to be imported. The Shah's rationale was explained to me by one of his ministers: "We have only thirty years until the oil runs dry—by that time we must be properly industrialized with alternate sources of energy in gas and nuclear power. After fifteen years, we should be ready to use oil not as a fuel but as a base for all petrochemical products manufactured here."

It seemed logical, but that's not the way it worked out in practice. Instead, the vast oil revenues—on the order of twenty billion dollars a year—became a corrupting influence that pervaded the whole society. A new economic class was created: Wheeler-dealers who acted as go-betweens for contractors selling everything from nuclear plants to rice drew fat commissions for getting contracts from ministries or the royal palace. This enraged the *bazaaris,* the middle-class merchants who traditionally formed the commercial class in Iran. Further, most peasants who were supposed to benefit from land reform were forced to sell their small holdings because they were unprofitable. They moved to urban areas and brooded. Probably the Shah's biggest mistake was to alienate the fundamentalist mullahs, the Shia Muslim clergy who strongly influenced middle- and lower-class believers. Again, the Shah had good intentions: He wanted to secularize the country for economic progress, as Kemal Ataturk had attempted to do in Turkey. But in showing his contempt for the mullahs in many ways, the Shah only made it easier for the Ayatollah Ruhollah Khomeini to rally support from his position in exile, first in Iraq and then in France.

"There was a period in which the Shah could have done great things and regained his position with the people," a Western ambassador told me. "He had the oil money to satisfy most of the dissatisfied elements of the populace. But the money was misspent. Too much went into massive projects. And too much into waste and corruption. So the various elements in the society that should have been his natural supporters turned against him. The Shah never developed a genuine constituency among his people. Toward the end, he had only the rich and the army officer class behind him."

Not much of this seemed to register with the U.S. embassy in Tehran, as I found on my arrival. They played down the anti-Shah demonstrations that I covered almost daily. Under Ambassador William Sullivan, the embassy, like Graham Martin's in Saigon, had developed a bunker mentality. They appeared figuratively, to be smoking the same kind of opium. The political and CIA officers did not appear to sense the power of the opposition forces; they were chary of talking to the press; they seemed determined to paint the brightest possible picture of a regime that was rapidly approaching the brink. Possibly this may have been prompted by President Carter's personal friendship with the Shah; partly it was the Defense Department's and CIA's insistence that the Shah was our irreplaceable ally in Southwest Asia, home of our listening gear into the Soviet Union, protector of the oil fields, and bulwark against communist expansion in the Gulf. They believed the Shah could weather the crisis if the U.S.A. stood staunchly behind him. But they ignored the feeling of millions of Iranians who were turning against the Shah and his regime.

Early in 1978, Khomeini from his villa outside Paris stepped up his criticism of the Shah, and the tape cassettes of his anti-Pahlavi sermons were widely circulated in Iran's thousands of Shia mosques. Khomeini was deeply bitter about his exile and was also said to believe that Savak had murdered his brother. He blamed the Shah for this. Things came to a head when the Ayatollah's religious supporters staged a big rally in the holy city of Qom, about one hundred miles south of the capital. Army troops savagely repressed the demonstration, leaving scores dead and wounded. Forty days later—the length of the traditional mourning period—more demonstrations were held in various cities for the "martyrs" of Qom. Police and troops inflicted many casualties among the demonstrators. So began a second forty-day period, then another, and another, repeating with increasing intensity demonstrations, deaths, mourning, repression, and so on. In September, a mass demonstration in one of Tehran's main squares was torn apart by soldiers firing into the crowd. Scores were killed and what became known as "the massacre" marked the beginning of almost continuous insurrection against the regime of the Shah. The economy faltered, and ground down. Most workers went on strike. Martial law was imposed. In November, after a student was killed at Tehran University, students and faculty joined the active opposition and shut down the institution. Other centers of learning closed in sympathy. The Shah wavered between appointing soft-line civilian ministers and hard-line generals to his cabinet. But nothing seemed to work. The opposition mounted. Where once the dissidents might have been satisfied with more freedom, and later a genuine constitutional monarchy, they now demanded the ouster of the Shah as a minimum condition for the return to any sort of stability.

In early January, the Shah in a move designed to reverse his eroding position, approved the appointment of an opposition lawyer named Shapur Bakhtiar as prime minister to form still another government. But other opposition elements accused Bakhtiar of being a traitor for collaborating with what they called the "illegal monarchical regime." In the next few days, Bakhtiar insisted that the Shah should leave the country for a "temporary" period to allow his new government to dig in and win the confidence of the people. It was now clear to almost everyone, with the possible exception of the U.S. embassy, that the Shah would have to go—and once gone, would not soon, if ever, return.

During this period, it was difficult for us reporters to keep abreast of the breaking developments. We tried to get to the scene of demonstrations and riots to assess the size, intensity, and spontaneity of the crowds. We attempted to sort out claims and counterclaims: Did the military shoot first, or were they severely provoked? We tried to avoid being used by propagandists on both sides. We hired cars to traverse the city, calling on the various political factions to determine their latest positions. We made the diplomatic rounds: The Americans were hunkered down and useless, but the British ambassador, Sir Anthony Parsons, held a kind of late afternoon open house for journalists. Our group—Jon Randal of the *Washington Post,* Johnny Apple of the *New York Times,* Ray Moseley of the *Chicago Tribune,* Loren Jenkins of *Newsweek,* Martin Woollacott of the *Guardian*—would swap information with Parsons, who was no slouch at gathering facts. We'd sometimes meet for lunch at Leon's, whose borscht, caviar, and vodka, were a must. One day, I noticed the resident British spook lunching with a Russian. He was, we learned, a Soviet embassy KGB officer. After our lunch, which was loud and animated as we discussed the morning's events and discoveries, the two secret agents came over, introduced themselves, and asked, "What do you hear today?"

While we were among the most competitive reporters around, there was no way a single individual could gather and construct a coherent mosaic of any one day's swift-moving developments in Tehran, let alone the rest of the country. We were hampered by a moveable curfew in the evening, which interfered with dinner appointments with opposition or diplomatic sources. We had to be back at the hotel, usually by 9:30 P.M., to make sure the drivers could get home by the curfew. So we often pooled our data.

One night, Loren Jenkins and Barry Came of *Newsweek* ventured outside the hotel to check into the source of some shooting nearby. They were grabbed by soldiers, roughed up, tossed into the back of an armored car, and held for four hours before being released. Communications were difficult because the overseas telephone and telex operators were on strike. We couldn't make outgoing calls but instead waited for incoming calls from our office that could reach the hotel operators directly. There was no guarantee that a call from the office would get through to the hotel and as the night wore on, we'd "piggyback" at the end of a colleague's call, and his desk in Washington, New York, or Chicago, would relay it, in my case, to Los Angeles. As the drama built up, foreign editor Bob Gibson wanted to have two correspondents on duty in Iran at any one time. Our visas were only good for thirty days at a time, so Joe Alex Morris in Athens and Don Schanche in Cairo and I worked out a rotation system whereby two of us would be on deck.

The pressure on the Shah to leave finally became irresistible. On

January 16, the potentate, now fifty-nine and in failing health, departed from Tehran airport in a tearful ceremony. He canceled a press conference at the last minute, so no outsiders witnessed his leave-taking. His departure was kept secret but Joe Morris was at the airport and gathered up vivid details of the parting and phoned them to me at the hotel. I got Los Angeles on a second phone and quickly dictated the new lead to the previous day's story in time to make the final edition of the paper. The royal party included the Empress Farah, a few bodyguards, one of whom carried a box of Iranian soil. As soon as news of the departure was confirmed, the capital exploded in tumultuous excitement: Demonstrators filled the streets chanting, "The Shah is gone forever," and passed out flowers, as others tore down the city's monuments to the ruler and his father. The army sat quietly, watchfully, on the sidelines.

That afternoon, we dropped by to see Tony Parsons in the British compound and he pithily summed up the Shah's rule: "He totally failed to see why the people did not appreciate all that he was trying to do for them. He was convinced that he had rendered his country a great service. He kept telling me about the roads and the schools he was building. And he failed to see the resentment boiling up and that is overflowing tonight in Tehran."

The Shah left behind a fragile cabinet under the sixty-three-year-old Premier Bakhtiar, who was groping to establish his authority. But in Paris, Khomeini soon made clear his vehement objections to the new administration. There was going to be nothing but trouble ahead.

During the last few days before the Shah's flight into exile, some of us had made contact with a curious figure at the palace. He was an aide named Hossen Amir Sadeghi, who surfaced from nowhere, acting as a spokesman for the Shah. The morning after the departure, he called to invite us to take a tour of the Niavaran palace, northeast of the capital, as a way presumably of showing the world that the Shah and his empress had left behind almost all their personal possessions. The idea, I gathered, was to prove that the Iranian monarch was merely going on a short vacation, as he said. We entered the snow-covered grounds and found the buff marble palace looking impeccable. Inside, the mood of the Imperial Guard and private retainers was somber. But everything seemed to be in place: There were personal photographs everywhere, precious collections of Sumerian art objects, gifts from foreign dignitaries, and artworks by modern masters.

"Their majesties took only suitcases with clothes, nothing else," explained Sadeghi. "I'd say eighty-five percent of the palace furnishings are the personal effects of the monarch. But he himself lived in rather Spartan style. This is a sort of run-of-the-mill palace, not like Buckingham Palace. Actually, the Shah was a man of simple tastes. The art collection represents the taste of the empress. Don't worry about the crown jewels. They are here safe in Tehran. The royal couple did not take them."

I wandered around jotting notes about things I saw: sculptures by Giacometti and Brancusi, paintings by Utrillo and Modigliani, a personally signed painting by Marc Chagall, the empress's portrait by Andy Warhol dated 1976. Antique vases and glasses were everywhere. The furniture in the private apartments was period French.

As I scribbled in my notebook, Colin Smith, the feisty, fearless war correspondent of London's *Observer,* asked me what I was writing. I told him it was a kind of rough inventory of the works of art.

"What the hell, Tuohy," he said, "have you gone poofter on me?"

"Colin," I said, condescendingly, "you've got to realize there's more to being a foreign correspondent than knowing the range of an artillery piece or the caliber of a machine gun. You've got to know something about *art.*"

Smith seemed hesitant, then nodded reluctant agreement. "I take your point, Bill," he said.

In the first edition of the following Sunday's *Observer,* its sophisticated readers were introduced to two new Irish-American sculptors on the international art scene whose works were to be seen in the Niavaran palace: Jack O'Metti and Brian Cusi!

In showing me the Shah's spacious library, his aide, Hossen Sadeghi grumbled, "President Carter spent New Year's Eve here in 1977. He sat right in here. Ever since he put his foot in this country, we have been having a bad show. But it may have been our fault, too. These imperial courtiers surrounding the Shah were a parade of creeps. I have never seen two intelligent people like the monarchs surround themselves with a more shifty and incompetent group. His cronies were all political illiterates. For the past seven years, the Shah was ringed by an impenetrable circle of idiots."

Though Premier Bakhtiar still hoped to remain head of government, Khomeini's statements from Paris raked him daily, and the Ayatollah called for an Islamic fundamentalist government. The army was undecided whether to let events run their course—or trigger a coup that would put the military in control. The Americans sent a NATO general out to warn the military against taking power. The pro-Khomeini demonstrations continued. Iran was slipping into a violent interregnum.

I drove down to Qom, the dusty, dreary holy city where Khomeini had begun his organized dissent that eventually crumpled the regime. There were no television antennaes, bars, or cinemas in Qom; the women wore black, veiled cloaks, the chador. There were about five hundred mosques in the town of three hundred thousand in addition to holy shrines. I visited Ayatollah Kazem Shariatmadari, who was seventy-six and sat on the Persian carpet in his sparsely furnished room. He was a gentle-looking soul with a long gray beard and lively eyes behind horned-rimmed spectacles. Shariatmadari was the most important Shia leader inside Iran, with a personal following second only to that of Khomeini, and he had taken a tack on the side of moderation and coolness.

"I want a government based on laws," he told me. "And that is the kind of government we should think about creating. We have heard that the Ayatollah is calling for the formation of an Islamic revolutionary council. We haven't heard about the composition. If we do have a revolutionary council, we should then think of a way to form a government that will be a legal one—accepted not only by the people but by the army and also by other countries."

Friends of Shariatmadari said there was no rivalry between him and Khomeini. To me, Shariatmadari disclaimed any political ambitions. "You might as well ask me if I'm going to open a shop in the bazaar," he said. "Being a merchant is a job. Being a politician is a job. But it's not my job."

But about the future, the ayatollah was not hopeful. "I'm afraid something could happen to sink the country into more trouble and violence. I would try to stop it. I will do everything I can to stop violence." I asked the Islamic moderate whether his methods were different from Khomeini's, and he answered, "We might have different tactics, the use of violence for instance, but the end is the same—an Islamic republic."

Returning to Tehran, I thought that the moderate Shias would be no match for the grim determination of Khomeini when he chose to return to Iran. And it seemed his return would depend on whether the military would leave the Tehran airport open if he took off from Paris. In late January, the military authorities, who still functioned as the governors of cities and provinces, rashly announced that Khomeini was barred from returning to the country and they banned further political demonstrations. Khomeini supporters naturally announced a big demonstration for the following day. I expected a fresh outbreak of violence and it came.

I was up the next morning to watch the events unfold at the main traffic circle near the university, a frequent flashpoint between antigovernment demonstrators and the army. Paul Martin of *Newsweek* and I were talking to a group of students when the troops marched up the street toward us. The students had moved city buses across access streets as barricades. As the soldiers marched closer, some demonstrators tossed rocks and Molotov cocktails. The troops opened fire.

Martin and I dived for cover and scrambled into a doorway. It occurred to me that we were on the wrong side of the fence, so to speak, because being with the students we were targets for the soldiers. We tried to work our way along the main street to a side alley to get out of the main fields of fire. Soldiers positioned on rooftops shot down at the crowd, hitting several. One phalanx of troops bore down on the demonstrators, who had set fire to the buses by now. When the students dispersed, the soldiers opened fire with automatic rifles. I huddled in a doorway as the troops swept past toward the square, which they took over, and then began shooting at the students on the avenues leading away like spokes on a wheel. I saw a soldier kneeling down in a sharpshooter's position, taking careful aim before firing. He hit a demonstrator. After previous violence, Premier Bakhtiar had ordered the soldiers to fire only in the air. But I saw troops shooting their weapons in a flat trajectory. Many demonstrators seemed determined to draw fire. They surged forward until the bullets flew. Then they would scatter into doorways or alleys or behind parked cars. Whenever the troops ceased firing, the militants moved forward again to harass the soldiers with taunts and tossed rocks. Some students shouted, "*Jihad, jihad.*" Holy war. One young man tore off his jacket and beat his chest screaming, "Shoot me, shoot me." I saw a soldier in an alley, some distance from his unit. He was crying, and people helped him out of his uniform, apparently so that he could desert on the spot. From a distance, I could see the scene—amplified later by American television cameramen who filmed it with a long lens—where a soldier was beating a demonstrator with the butt of his rifle. Another trooper walked up and shot his fellow soldier in the head. He then ran off into the crowd, while a civilian grabbed the downed soldier's rifle and dashed off with it. The sirens of ambulances, screeching to pick up the dead and wounded, added to the clamor.

"The army is shooting at our people," one near-hysterical student told me. "They are supposed to be our brothers, but brothers don't shoot you down. Last week, we gave them flowers and they gave us back bullets today. So now we are going to give them back bullets. But we need guns to shoot back."

Unlike Beirut, few civilians had access to weapons under the Shah's regime. The firing died down as the demonstrators dispersed for the evening. I walked to nearby Daroosh Hospital to check on the casualties. There, a doctor in a bloodstained surgical gown in the emergency room, explained, "Most of the wounds we have been treating were in the stomach and chest. That means the soldiers were shooting to kill—not over heads or at people's feet."

I returned to the hotel to find that my colleague, Don Schanche, a man of great talent and panache, had broken his foot during his coverage of the day's violence along another street. In an outbreak of gunfire, someone had pushed him into a *jube,* one of the open trenches that serve as storm sewers in Tehran, running from the northern hills to the southern flats. Don had twisted his foot badly and his mood was not improved when he took cover in an armored personnel carrier and someone slammed the steel door on his hand. At the hospital, the doctor at first said the injury was only a sprain, but Schanche insisted on X rays, and sure enough, they showed a hairline fracture of the foot. The doctor slapped a plaster cast on his foot. Don seemed in good spirits at the hotel that night and said he intended to cover the demonstrations the following day, with the help of his cast, and a driver. The next day was a minor-key reprise, with more violence. That evening, I could see Schanche's pain had increased sharply, though he was loath to admit it. I learned that Pan Am had scheduled a special flight early the next day to Frankfurt and ordered Don to get on it— whatever the office might say about our then being down to a single correspondent in Tehran. He put up an argument, but, as with Jack Foisie and his kidney in Saigon, I had the last word. And a lucky thing it was. When Schanche landed in Frankfurt, he was met by his brother, a senior officer in the U.S. Army, who had him examined by the medics. They reported Don was within twenty-four hours of contracting gangrene: The Tehran doc had set the cast too tight and the foot, in swelling, pinched off the blood vessels, cutting off the circulation.

Strangely, while many of the demonstrators chanted anti-American slogans along with their plaints against the government, I did not get the feeling of any personal animosity against me as I made the journalistic rounds. Once at the university, a youth shouted at me, "Yankee, go home."

"Who, me?" I asked.

"No, not you." He smiled.

One morning, I wandered with an interpreter around the Grand Bazaar, a wonderful old place with a labyrinth of covered alleys and passageways. Where once thousands of Iranian merchants crammed the corridors to buy and sell—making deals for gold, carpets, and even steel—the bazaar was now largely deserted because of the general strike. I stopped at a fruit juice stand displaying glasses of orange, carrot, and pomegranate juice, and a pinkish mixture of carrot and yogurt. The rich purple pomegranate was particularly tasty as it washed down a steaming-hot plate of lima beans and turnips, nicely warming on a cold winter's day. This was the morning the U.S. embassy ordered government dependents out of the country, but the merchants and vendors I met were more than happy to chat amiably. One man offered me some pistachio nuts and commented, "The only answer to this is the return of the Ayatollah. If he comes back and tells the country to go to work, then we all will. He is a man of God, a man of the Book—the Koran."

In north Tehran, home of diplomats and politicians, the talk was of the need for constitutional legitimacy for the government. But in south Tehran, home of the working class around the Grand Bazaar, the issue of constitutionality seemed irrelevant. The bazaar was almost deserted because the merchants and their workers refused to raise their shutters or bend their muscles until Khomeini gave the word to the local mullahs, the Islamic clergy.

A watchman came up to the stand and commented, "We are waiting for the Ayatollah Khomeini. He represents the will of God. Nobody will go back to work until he tells us. They kept him out for fifteen years, and it's time that he came back."

It seemed to me that this attitude, however simplistic, was much more reflective of the masses than the constitutional theories, however high-minded, propounded by the liberal politicians in north Tehran, who were rightly fearful that Khomeini would name an alternative government on his return. They tried to figure out a way to admit the strongman into the country, while keeping him in some kind of political isolation.

The next day, the masses of south Tehran and the countryside got their wish: Khomeini returned on a chartered Air France 707 to a hysterical welcome. Then seventy-eight, the religious leader, who had not set foot in his native country since 1963, rode around Tehran in a Mercedes limousine as welcomers screamed, *"Allah akhbar,"* God is great. Again, I had an open phone line to Los Angeles and watched the events on the reopened television channel. I dictated the story to the office in time for the home edition.

Khomeini wasted no time in expressing his opposition to the Bakhtiar regime, which, he decreed, was a creature of the Shah. He announced that he was forming an Iranian Republic based on the teachings of Islam, headed by an "Islamic Revolutionary Council." As some two million Tehranis turned out to greet his triumphal rides around the city, Khomeini strongly criticized the United States and he warned the army against shooting at demonstrators. It was clear that a showdown was not far off.

However, my visa was expiring so I had to leave in a couple of days' time. In search of an average backwoods mullah to interview, Colin Smith and I drove to the Alborz Mountains, where by chance we witnessed a scene straight out of an ancient Persian miniature painting—hunters on foot pursuing their quarry with sticks and stones. We were driving along a rocky hillside, which, until the Shah departed, served as a royal game reserve. It was still a reserve but there were no Imperial Guards to protect it any longer. We saw some cars parked and their occupants staring eagerly across the valley so we stopped, too, to see what was up. On the opposite ridge, a graceful ibex, that endangered species of wild mountain goat, was picking its way along a steep slope, its slender horns rising elegantly above its lean, long body. Behind and above the ibex, a half-dozen men pursued the animal, like staghounds after a deer. The Shah allowed no shotguns or hunting rifles, and until a few weeks ago, no one would ever have dared set foot on the reserve. But now these tough and hardy mountain men carried long sticks, and, from time to time, tossed rocks above the ibex to force the beast down from the heights toward a stream that burbled along the valley floor. The men scrambled over rocks after the ibex, which seemed confused as it stumbled lower and lower—and farther from safety. Egged on by the shouts of encouragement from the bystanders on the road, the pursuers pressed closer, unfazed even when they slipped and skidded on the treacherous incline.

At last, the harried ibex made the wrong move. Instead of darting directly away from the pursuers on a horizontal or upward line, it moved even lower, and then slipped on the unsure footing and skidded into the far side of the stream. Yelling in triumph, the men bolted down the mountain side. The first two pursuers jumped into the icy, racing waters fed by the winter snowpack and, grabbing the ibex by the horns, dragged it out of the water and wrestled it to the ground.

As other hunters gathered around, joined by latecomers to the chase, a fight over the prize ensued, with the men beating each other with their sticks. Finally, two hunters pulled out long knives and severed the fine ibex's head and horns from the body and rushed off with the trophy while the others battled over the carcass.

I watched the scene in a kind of horror-stricken fascination. I wasn't sure whether to grieve for a rare ibex, or to admire the grit of the hunters. Was this a return to primitive barbarism? Or to the simplicities of natural life? Everything was rapidly changing in Iran. Was this some metaphor of things to come?

Thirty days after I arrived, I took off from Tehran leaving Joe Morris and Ken Freed, who had come out from Los Angeles, holding the fort. I was on a direct flight to Geneva so I managed to have dinner and some time with my son, who lived with his mother there. From there I flew to Paris for a couple of days off.

At nine o'clock on the morning of Saturday, February 10, Don Cook, our Paris bureau chief, called me at my hotel with the shattering news: "Joe Morris was killed this morning in Tehran. It's just come over the wire in the office."

I was stunned. But I dressed hastily and walked around the corner to our office on the Champs-Élysées. The details of Joe's death were still sketchy, but we pieced together what happened: Joe, Bill Branigin of the *Washington Post,* Ray Moseley of the *Chicago Tribune,* and Art Higbee of United Press International heard shooting coming from the air base that morning. They all jumped into a taxi and headed for the place, where dissident air force personnel were revolting against their superior officers—in what turned out to be the real revolution, the uprising of Khomeini sympathizers among troops against officers loyal to the Shah, the government, and the military high command. Firing between the air force cadets and the Imperial Guard drove the reporters to take refuge inside a store, and they went up to the first floor for a better look. A spray of bullets bracketed the building and everyone hit the deck. Joe was first up. He went to the window to see what was happening. A single bullet smashed through the blinds and hit him in the chest, killing him almost instantly. The three reporters carried him downstairs and with the help of some Iranian military volunteers got him to the hospital on the air base, where a doctor pronounced him dead.

I had succeeded Joe in Beirut and was very fond of him and his vivacious, German-born wife, Ulla. They had three young daughters. Don Cook and I decided to put together an appreciation, for Joe, at fifty-one, was the most respected U.S. correspondent in the Middle East. We found he had written a letter a few days previously to Jack Nelson, our Washington bureau chief, with some lines that could almost be his epitaph: "Life goes on here, most of it in Tehran, where I am due back Sunday after ten days off—and after four straight weeks on the job. It's a strain, family-wise and otherwise, but one rare chance to participate in a classic revolutionary situation. In other words, I look forward to going back."

That afternoon, I consulted with Bob Gibson, our foreign editor, and we decided that I would try to fly to Tehran and bring back Joe's body. Gibson meanwhile was flying to Athens to be with Ulla, as was Don Schanche from Germany where he was still recuperating. I took a taxi to the airport but the Air France people stalled for hours before announcing that the evening flight to Tehran was canceled because the airport was still closed in the wake of the revolution, which by now had seen the overthrow of the Bakhtiar government and the military high command.

The same thing happened the second day in Paris, so I flew to Athens with the rest of our group. Our Washington bureau cleared me to board any U.S. military transports going to Tehran to evacuate Americans. But Tehran airport remained closed under the new revolutionary regime, and no civilian or military aircraft were getting in. Don Schanche, joined by Dial Torgerson, our correspondent in Jerusalem, the *Washington Post*'s irreplaceable Jon Randal, who was a close friend of the Morris family, and I manned phones from Ulla's house seemingly around the clock to get through to someone in Tehran who could give us permission to fly in and recover Joe's body. After three fruitless days, Randal and I shifted to Amman, Jordan. Though Tehran airport was still closed, the American TV networks used a small charter airline called Arab Wings to fly out their film, and we thought they would be best plugged in to fly to Iran—if we could get permission.

After another night on the phone in Amman, Randal got through to a friend in the Foreign Ministry who seemed to understand our request for a one-time permission to land on humanitarian grounds.

Early the next morning, we boarded a tiny executive jet at Amman airfield, and took off, flying over Syria and Iraq. On entering Iranian air space, we were held up for a half hour, circling while our pilot communicated with Tehran tower, which had to clear things through the Foreign Ministry. Just when I thought the situation looked hopeless, the pilot received clearance to enter Iran and gave us the thumbs-up signal. For once in the muddled Middle East, things seemed to be going our way. Less than an hour later, we skimmed in for a landing at Tehran airport.

We found the airport in confusion. Revolutionary Guards quickly surrounded the plane. They had not been apprised of our arrival and thought we were foreign intelligence agents. They searched our baggage for weapons and held us at gunpoint until we began to sort things out. The leaders of the airport guards had heard of Morris's death and seemed eager to help; the trouble was that in this new revolutionary situation, nobody knew who was in charge. But we managed to convince the guards to let us use a phone at the airport to call higher authorities. Randal telephoned the Foreign Ministry. That straightened out, he managed to contact Ken Freed to say that we had a plane. Freed, and Bill Branigin and Bill Claiborne of the *Washington Post,* spent several hours arranging for the release and transport of Joe's body. There was nothing for me to do. I spent most of the day sitting near the plane guarded by soldiers with submachine guns. By late afternoon, the pilots were getting restive: The tower told them to take off by 5:00 P.M. At five, they pleaded for a bit more time and got a fifteen-minute extension. A few minutes before the deadline, an ambulance rolled up to the flight line: There were Freed, Branigin, Claiborne, and other helpful reporters with Joe's body in an ornate, carved wooden coffin with a cross on top.

Then came two agonizing problems. The otherwise irrational irregular guards reverted to bureaucratic instinct and demanded to see the official entry stamp in Joe's bloodstained passport. After searching for long minutes through the accordion folds of his many visas, I found the entry, and they dutifully stamped it with an exit visa. Then, I realized that as we manhandled the bulky zinc-lined coffin, it wouldn't fit through the aircraft's side door. However, the pilots managed to remove the trimming around the hatchway, and with that extra space, by twisting and tipping the coffin, we got it aboard.

Randal stayed behind and I escorted Joe's body out of Tehran. We zipped down the runway, refueled at Baghdad, and landed at Amman for a change of pilots. The Jordanian authorities, who respected Morris as a friend and journalist, waived formalities. I was given a hot, airline-style dinner and a cold beer, and late that evening we took off for Athens. It was a clear night with a brilliant full moon and I could see the Jordan River Valley with Jerusalem beyond. We flew past the ghostly snow-covered shoulders of Mount Hermon, over the bright lights of Damascus, banking to the west, above the Lebanon Mountains and burnt-out Beirut and then the mirrorlike Mediterranean and the troubled island of Cyprus. All the places Joe had covered during his fruitful career. Then we were down in Athens where Bob Gibson met me at the airport. I gave him Joe's passport, which he'd had in his breast pocket the day he was shot, and a Polaroid picture taken of him at the morgue, by way of establishing positive identity. No need to open the coffin. The next day, Ulla and Bob Gibson with two daughters accompanied Joe on his last flight home to America for burial in Connecticut.

The Cairo newspaper *Al Ahram* in its obituary of Joe Morris used the headline WHO SEARCH FOR TROUBLE DIE STANDING.

The following month, in March, I was back in Iran. Trouble had broken out in Kurdistan between the new, revolutionary regime, headed by Khomeini, and the fractious Kurds, who were still seeking autonomy and saw the political vacuum as an opportunity to pursue their grievances. With Phil Davison of Reuters, I drove for eight hours to Sanandaj, the center of the disturbances hard by the Iraqi border and not far from where I had watched the Kurdish exodus four years earlier. It was the beginning of springtime in Kurdistan, the rugged countryside full of cherry blossoms and rushing streams. The Kurdish rebels had surrounded an Iranian army garrison in the town and sporadic fire was exchanged between the sides. Phil and I darted from doorway to doorway on the main street, watching the fierce-looking Kurds, dressed in tribal turbans and baggy pants, armed with crossed bandoliers of cartridges and ancient rifles, firing at random toward the army garrison up the street.

We gathered that the Kurds were upset because the government shifted the contents of their grain silos to Tehran, which the locals took to be another way of repressing them. Beyond that, there was the perennial demands of the Kurds for more autonomy, for respect for their language, culture, and mores. I found one English-speaking Kurd, a tough, craggy-faced old boot named Ahmad Mohammadi sitting behind a sandbag, brandishing an Iranian automatic rifle and a revolver taken from police headquarters. He told me heatedly, "The army soldiers are supposed to be our friends. But not when they shoot at us. If they do that again, they will be finished. We want democracy for the Kurds."

The shooting erupted again. Some Kurds paused to kneel and fire their rifles toward the army barracks without taking careful aim. Others shot from rooftops. In one house where Kurds were firing from the rooftop, a housewife calmly poured us tea and shooed her young son away from the open veranda to keep him from being hit by a ricocheting bullet. The boy happily turned to an old Hollywood movie on the family's TV set.

On the main street, bullets whined and cracked overhead. Phil and I sought refuge in a nearby doorway. By chance, the occupants understood German—they had been guest workers in the country. Davison, a Scot, understood the language, too. So we conversed in German. The young housewife introduced herself as Parvaneh Ghorischi and offered us a delicious meal of kebab, rice, and Kurdistan's tasty, paper-thin bread shaped like a giant pizza. Then she broke out a bottle of Johnnie Walker scotch and poured a glass.

She smiled and said, "*Salemi mati.*" To your health. She laughed, adding, "You know, we could get twenty-five lashes under the new regime for drinking alcohol. But we Kurds don't like to be told by a government or by mullahs what or what not to drink. We want to educate our people. We have been backward for too long. And previous governments tended to keep things that way. But we've heard the nice words for too long—without any action. And now the government must be prepared for action—concessions in Kurdistan—or the only alternative will be more fighting."

We stayed in Sanandaj for a couple of days while a government delegation from Tehran tried to patch things up. Finally, both sides agreed to a ceasefire. The Kurdish prisoners in the army garrison were released. And the Kurds themselves lifted their siege. The city groped back to normal with butchers cutting up sheep on the sidewalks, vendors hawking vegetables, and housewives airing out their bedding. Once again the sticky and perhaps unsolvable problem of Kurdish autonomy was swept under the Persian carpet.

Back in Tehran, I was asked to cover a meeting of the Arab foreign ministers in the Iraqi capital Baghdad. But since Iran and Iraq were on the political outs, there were no direct flights between the countries. So I flew to Abadan, the big oil refinery complex on the Gulf, took a taxi through Khorramshahr to the border and walked across the flat, dusty country, hot as anywhere on earth. I had a good look at the terrain that was to become the scene of the war between Iran and Iraq, which I would have to describe the following year. At the frontier, I walked across and found another taxi on the Iraqi side, drove up the highway to the ferry at Kibasi across the Shatt-al-Arab, and rafted into Basra, the tropical, date-exporting river town, where I had lunch. That evening in Baghdad, I learned that Palestinian leader Yasir Arafat had walked out of the conference because the ministers wouldn't agree to his demands for economic sanctions against Egypt for signing a peace agreement with Israel. Once again, Arab leaders appeared unable to form a joint policy.

As the meeting ended, I was faced with the problem of getting back to Tehran, where I had plans to rendezvous with Loren Jenkins for a trip to Afghanistan. With no direct flights, I decided that having a valid Iranian visa, I'd drive to the border northeast of Baghdad, hire a taxi to Kermanshah, and fly to Tehran. An ABC-TV producer named Arden Ostrander asked to join me, and a fast drive of two hours took us to the border near Qasr-a-Shrin. But there an immigration officer wouldn't let us in, despite the fact that we had valid visas. He said we could only enter by plane through Tehran. After spending four hours at the border, we managed to get through by phone to an official in the Foreign Ministry, who ordered the immigration man to accept us. We then found a stubborn Iranian taxi driver who drove like hell for Kermanshah, but the border delay caused us to miss our flight, which actually left on time. I tried to talk our driver into taking us to Tehran, four hundred miles away, but he'd had enough of us. We found another taxi, whose driver was willing to go all the way, and set off. Somewhere around ten o'clock that night, we stopped for dinner at a roadside kebab joint. The driver finished his meal and walked out to the car leaving us with our tea. Ten minutes later, we got in the taxi, and found the driver messing around with a lot of paraphernalia in the front seat.

"What the hell is he doing?" asked Ostrander.

"He's making an after-dinner smoke of opium," I said.

"Do we want to ride with an opium addict?"

"Well," I replied, "out here in the middle of the Iranian desert, we don't have a hell of a lot of choice."

During the journey, I did my share of backseat driving from the front seat, and our sleepy driver moved slower and slower, until on entering Tehran about 3:30 A.M., we were down to a crawl. But I had made my plane by a couple of hours.

On November 4, 1979, the Iranian militants invaded the U.S. embassy, holding the personnel as hostages and demanding the return of the Shah as the ransom price. From my base in London, I was assigned to cover the Gulf in case U.S. carriers in the Arabian Sea took retaliatory action. In Bahrain, I bumped into Paul Martin of *Newsweek* and we thought we'd try to get close to the Strait of Hormuz because the Iranians were threatening to close it, stemming the flow of much of Europe's and Japan's oil from the Gulf. We called a pilotage outfit in Ras al-Khaimah and lined up a trip out into the Gulf to meet an incoming tanker. We flew to Dubai, without visas, and were held up for several hours at the airport until they let us in, but only for the day. So we hired a taxi for the ride through the United Arab Emirates, past Sharjah, Umm al Quum, Ajman, to Ras, and the border with Oman on the Mandaman Peninsula. We had missed our boat, but we talked with shipping pilots who guided the huge tankers in and out of the strait and we learned a salient fact, that much of the reporting about the its vulnerability was ill-founded: Hormuz was twenty-four miles wide and several hundred feet deep, so the sinking of one or more tankers by belligerents would hardly bottle up the Gulf and its precious oil.

In Bahrain, I managed to obtain an Iranian visa and flew to Tehran. The hostage story was big, but rather static. The embassy personnel were held inside the U.S. compound, and TV teams and print journalists assembled outside the gates every day to try to talk to the militant guards, as angry demonstrators paraded up and down for the cameras. Journalistically, the story was a stalemate.

In the United States, commentators like George Will called for the bombing of Iranian dams to force Khomeini to release the hostages, rather foolishly in my view. I thought this approach shortsighted and simplistic, and showing a total misreading of the nature of the Shia revolution in Iran, however unpalatable it was. For America's hands were tied in this situation. President Carter made the momentous mistake of making the release of the hostages the number one priority of his administration—to the exclusion of most other business. But there was no easy way to success, just as there was no simple device to get back the hostages from the U.S.S. *Pueblo,* taken by the North Koreans in 1968. President Johnson then played it cool. Carter didn't, though watching the nightly TV news films of the mobs in Tehran, with their banners reading DEATH TO CARTER and LONG LIVE KHOMEINI, one could sympathize with him.

In seeking a key to the solution, I called on a senior Western ambassador, who told me, "The best thing for the United States to do now is nothing. I know how difficult it is for America to accept such advice. Yet, if you want the hostages back alive, and sooner rather than later, the best, really the only course, to follow in the coming weeks is to cool it all down. Maintain quiet contacts with the Iranians, but avoid public declarations, threats, talk of sanctions, or use of force."

And an Asian ambassador I knew put it this way: "These are extremely temperamental, emotional people, and the United States has not recognized the depth of feeling against the Shah in this country. Every U.S. reaction promotes an equal and opposite reaction here. So what you have to do is break the symmetry of the situation. Let the Iranians blow off steam. Let them get the poison out of their systems. Threats only get the Iranian blood boiling—at the expense of the hostages. Force won't accomplish anything because the streak of Shia Islamic martyrdom that exists in the country would welcome suffering inflicted by a superpower. Let this thing play itself out. Don't keep it bubbling since it is clear that there is no quick or easy resolution."

Finally, an Iranian friend and a moderate who privately deeply objected to the seizure of the hostages, told me, "The main thing is to lower the temperature. The hostages will be released when Khomeini realizes they are no longer of any political use in Iran—and when he deems the chemistry is right. The U.S. captives will simply not be released through outside pressure, however unsatisfactory this fact of life is to the American mentality."

I made another trip to Qom to get a feel for how the mullahs were trying to run the country. There, I interviewed the chief judge of the Islamic Revolutionary Court, a hard-eyed, bearded mullah named Sadegh Khalkhali, who told me he had personally sentenced to death about 200 of the 750 people so far executed. The Islamic revolutionaries called him "the wrath of God" but he reminded me more of an oldtime hanging judge riding the circuits of the American West. He was appointed to the job by Ayatollah Khomeini and ordered the death of major figures in the Shah's regime. He bragged to me that he had encouraged the assassination on a Paris street of the son of Princess Ashref, the Shah's twin sister. And he added that he had put a price on the head of the ex-Shah and his wife.

Sitting cross-legged on a Persian carpet, the fifty-three-year-old mullah adjusted his long brown robe and told me he spent two years in jail for opposing the Shah's regime and was then banished to a remote province. He said he regularly had to report to Savak, the secret police, and his visitors were sometimes jailed or tortured. He said he had put the entire royal family on a hit list.

"If we find them," he declared, "we will kill them."

Khalkhali said he had no compunction about ordering the execution of former prime minister Amir Abbas Hoveida, though the official had not been implicated in any major "crimes" during his period in office. Self-righteous and self-assured, Khalkhali insisted he had meted out justice fairly. Almost plaintively, he asked me, "How can they call me the wrath of God? I cried for oppressed people when I was in jail. For any of the executions I ordered, God will give me a place in heaven."

Not far from Khalkhali's apartment, I watched the pilgrims file around the house used by Ayatollah Khomeini, who came out on the balcony from time to time to wave to the constant stream of people. At seventy-nine, the Ayatollah was still a spellbinding orator with glowering eyes, a white beard, and a dark turban. He was never considered much of a theological thinker, but through his personal magnetism became an ayatollah, which means "mark of God," a title not formally bestowed but which gradually accrued to senior mullahs who developed a loyal personal following.

I was with a diplomat friend who spoke Farsi and we heard the Imam say to the crowds, "I enjoy hearing and seeing you, because your applause is the continuation of the cry with which the usurper [the Shah] was thrown out. It is good that you continue to be agitated, because the enemies have not disappeared. Until the country is settled down, the people must remain fired up, ready to march and attack again. During my long lifetime, I have always been right about what I've said."

Afterward, my friend pointed out, "In dealing with the Imam, you have to forget about conventional concepts of diplomacy. For he believes in only two things: Allah and the masses. And that's why relations with him are so difficult. As for Allah, Khomeini is convinced that he has a direct connection with God and whatever he does is right. As for the masses, he doesn't really want to lead them. He just wants them on his side. And, therefore, he turns to demagoguery rather than leadership."

In Tehran, a former Iranian official amplified this line of thought, telling me, "It is important to understand that Khomeini has two obessions. The first is to return this country to Islamic fundamentalism—at whatever immediate cost. The other is his hatred of the Shah and his determination to bring him to Islamic justice. The United States has been singled out by Khomeini for special hatred because to him, it represents anti-Islamic values and is the one nation that worked hand in glove with the Shah and encouraged his worst excesses."

I flew back to London in December 1979 and was scheduled to return to Tehran late in April 1980, for a month's duty in Iran. But two days before I planned to arrive, President Carter decided to use force to free the hostages. The operation ended on the night of April 24–25 in the Iranian desert in flames: Three helicopters of the eight in the mission failed; Colonel Charlie Beckwith believed the five remaining helos weren't enough for his Delta Force; during the withdrawal, a chopper and a C-130 crashed into each other at Desert One; and the mission ended not only aborted but with loss of life.

The administration and the country seemed to experience something of a national trauma over the failure of the mission. But I thought the outcome had its brighter side, except for the lamentable loss of life: eight Marines and Air Force personnel were killed. For by attempting the raid, Carter got the right-wing critics off his back. The President had decided to go ahead, despite the objections of Secretary of State Cyrus Vance. It was the military that failed. When I heard the first reports of the rescue plan, I didn't believe that it could be carried off properly. As far as I could see, no one in government had taken into consideration that there were at least one hundred Americans, mainly media personnel, staying at the Intercontinental Hotel, let alone other Americans around town. So, even if Delta had managed a perfect raid—all hostages rescued with no loss of Iranian life—the militants could have still moved in on the hotel. Instead of fifty-two State Department hostages, they'd have a hundred or so media captives. Now, it may well be that few Americans would have much sympathy for media types who stick their noses in situations where they may not belong; still, it is hard to see how the administration could ignore another bunch of freshly taken hostages. And if any of the Revolutionary Guards were killed by the tough U.S. commando force, which was prepared to "take down" any opposition, I could easily see the militants executing an equal number of Americans after kangaroo-court show trials. Then what would the President be forced to do, hounded by hard-liners and media anchormen, editorialists, and columnists?

By the time the dust settled, reporters were let in again, and I got to Tehran, the Iranians had set up something called an International Conference on U.S. Intervention in Iran with an American delegation headed by ex-U.S. attorney general Ramsey Clark. Naturally, much of the conference was devoted to excoriating American support of the Shah. While the conference was a put-up job, Clark and members of the U.S. delegation did try vainly to find a formula to seek the release of the American captives.

During the conference, I managed to view a display of documents and equipment taken from the helicopters left behind at Desert One. I was appalled at the amount of sensitive information the Iranians had collected. There were pilots' notations on note pads with the routes in and out of Tehran delineated, along with radio frequencies and call signs—from the President and the Chairman of the Joint Chiefs of Staff on down. There was a captured U.S. satellite photo of the Desert One refueling point taken on March 30, 1980, and high-definition pictures of the U.S. embassy compound where the hostages were held and of the adjacent soccer stadium where the helicopters were to land. There were copies of the overall plan: "Day 1, ship to laager [the overnight hideaway near Tehran]," and "Day 2, laager to evacuation point." There were locations of "safe" houses in Tehran and a getaway plan for rescuers who might be left stranded.

There had apparently been no provision for destroying the helicopters or their sensitive material at Desert One. I could reconstruct the rescue plan in all its complexity, and it still seems to me impossibly involved. The helicopter force had to reach Desert One without alerting Iranian authorities although the site chosen was adjacent to a main road crossing the area. The C-130s had to land and refuel the helicopters in the dark, at the same time transferring the assault force to the choppers. The helos then had to fly to the "laager" outside Tehran, landing before dawn without attracting attention. The commando team would debark, be led to another hiding place some distance away, and spend the day there undercover. Meanwhile, the choppers would fly another fifteen minutes to a "hide" where they would lay low during the day.

In the evening, the commandos would be driven by truck into Tehran to the embassy compound, where they would breach the wall and rescue the hostages. Another unit would drive to the Iranian Foreign Ministry, many blocks away, to rescue the three U.S. diplomats who were being held there. The helicopters would then leave their lair and pick up the commandos and the hostages from the compound or from the stadium across the street and from the Foreign Ministry. The hostages and commando force aboard, the choppers would bring the rescued hostages and commandos to an unused airfield at Manzariyeh southwest of Tehran, where two C-141 Starlifters would land and take everyone aboard. The helicopters would be destroyed and the C-141s airlifted out of the country, with Navy carrier fighters flying air cover.

It was an audacious plan, but one, I thought, that had to work more perfectly than any U.S. military operation I had ever witnessed. After all, things do go wrong. And in the Delta Force plan there was precious little room for error, particularly for flying in under cover of darkness. While I had respected Colonel Beckwith in Vietnam, I thought the plan, as I read it, had less than an even chance of success. Since Delta Force was prepared—almost eager—to shoot anyone interfering with the operation, I wondered what would happen to any hostages left behind if Iranians were killed, or to the other Americans still living and working in Tehran.

As it was, the abortive raid showed what happens when the various arms of the U.S. military all insist on getting into the act: Navy helicopters, Marine pilots, Army commandos, Air Force transports, with a confused chain of command, particularly at Desert One. A complex rescue force that never once trained together or rehearsed the overall mission was not my idea of how to mount a successful operation. It did not surprise me that it failed.

During my stay, I also learned that the U.S. embassy personnel had left undestroyed vital and sensitive information about CIA activities and contacts that put friendly Iranians at great risk after the documents were discovered by the militants. Papers also identified the CIA station chief among the hostages. The intruders found such secret material as an "eyes only" cable from Washington detailing the State Department's thoughts on admitting the Shah to the United States; it was the Shah's admission that had prompted the seizure of the embassy.

Other Western diplomats I talked to were dumbfounded that such sensitive material would be left sitting around the files in the first place—let alone not destroyed during the three hours it took the militants to break into the security wings of the embassy. The Americans had had a previous warning: The militants had once before occupied the main building, though not for long.

"I learned a long time ago in the Middle East to keep my files bare," one ambassador in the area told me. "You don't need all that sensitive paper sitting around. If you really must have a certain document, you can have it sent in from the outside."

I could excuse helicopter pilots under the stress of Desert One for leaving documents behind, but why hadn't trained diplomats in a vulnerable U.S. embassy gotten rid of such material? Hadn't they learned anything from the fall of Saigon?

In the wake of the Desert One fiasco, the Revolutionary Guards became increasingly surly toward Americans in Tehran. One day, I noticed a mobile Red Cross caravan calling for blood donors. I had an idea: I'd give blood to the Iranians but on condition they gave me a donor's card in Farsi. I thought that if the mobs ever went on an anti-American rampage, my proof that I donated blood in Iran might at least gain me a quick death rather than being mucked over and dragged around the city behind a car. The blood bank staff were surprised but accepted my Aryan blood, and duly wrote out a letter thanking me, which I still have, just in case.

Later that year, I flew into Tehran, and some officious customs guards noting the usual journalistic gear—tape recorder, radio, Walkman, binoculars—decided I was a spy. It was no good suggesting that a real espionage agent wouldn't so obviously bring in electronic equipment in his bag—that wouldn't appeal to Iranian logic. Instead, I was hustled off to secret police headquarters in downtown Tehran, where I tried to get myself properly identified: The Foreign Ministry, which issued visas, and the National Guidance Ministry, which issued press credentials, never coordinated. So it was difficult for me to prove that I was a legitimate journalist. Luckily, I was still woozy from an all-night party at Loren and Nancy Jenkins's in Rome before catching the flight, so I napped for most of the day while the police straightened out my status in ways unbeknownst to me. After twelve hours, they released me, but someone wanted to keep my radio, suggesting it was contraband.

"OK," I said. "Just give me an official receipt." The official gave me the radio instead.

On this trip, I walked over to the regular Friday service at central Tehran's Abraham High School, which doubled as the Jewish synagogue. Iran has one of the oldest continuing Jewish communities on earth, dating from before the destruction of the First Temple in Jerusalem twenty-five hundred years ago. Cyrus the Great, the first

Persian monarch, freed the Jews from their Babylonian captivity in 529
B.C. At the end of World War II, there were some two hundred thousand Jews in Iran but half of those left for Israel at the time of independence in 1949, and the community continued to dwindle to about
forty thousand in 1980.

During the last days of the Shah, I had talked to the Jewish
community leaders and they were apprehensive because, whatever
they thought about the Shah's political rule, he had guaranteed Jews
the right to worship without restriction. Now, a few anti-Jewish slogans were scrawled on the wall of the high school building, along with
the huge letters, CIA. Inside, Jews said they were worried about the
latent anti-Semitism among the Shia Muslims; the Jews thought they
had been discriminated against in government jobs, perhaps because
most of them supported the Shah, as did much of Iran's middle-class
until the last year or so. I found the mood of those assembled tense and
uneasy.

"We are indebted to Ayatollah Khomeini for preserving our minority religious rights," one leader told me. "But we fear what some
future imam's attitude toward us might be in a fundamentalist Islamic
state."

The uncertain mood was intensified because a few weeks before
some Jews were executed on charges of treason and drug smuggling.
And about 120 others were imprisoned, many on unspecified charges.

"At times like these, we worry that we might be singled out,"
one of the Jewish community members confided to me. "So far, I
don't think we've been aimed at to any great extent. Basically, we're
in the same boat with other middle-class Iranians against whom the
revolution might be directed. But when revolutionaries look around for
someone to accuse, Jews make tempting targets."

Just before the evening service began, an elderly worshiper took
me aside and said, "We Jews are a recognized religious minority by
Khomeini. But that's only on paper. They still think we have disloyal
connections with Israel and Zionism. They charge us with crimes for
having contributed to Jewish funds. So we don't want to do anything
to upset the regime. They have executed a few Jews and you never
know who might be charged with being 'corrupt on earth.' "

Being "corrupt on earth" was the blanket charge used for a
variety of offenses—some leading to the death penalty.

"We have our problems," another member of the Abraham synagogue summed up, "but everyone in Iran has problems these days."

By this time, the Iranians were making it almost impossible for U.S. reporters to gain admission into the country. The only other American journalist in Iran then was Stuart Auerbach of the *Washington Post*. We spent most of the time covering the hostage crisis in Tehran, but I thought it would be worth our while to take a trip for a couple of days along the Caspian Sea, up to the Soviet border. Unlike the northwest province of Azerbaijan, the two Caspian provinces of Gilan and Mazandaran were not officially off limits to foreign journalists. I double-checked this with the National Guidance Ministry and they said, sure, go ahead, you don't need any official permission. I had my doubts, but I was eager to get out of the capital for some fresh air and a change of scenery. We hired a car and sped off at dawn north through the Alborz Mountains, which separate the capital from the Caspian coast. Most of Iran is a high desertlike plateau, but the Caspian slope of the Alborz is a green land dotted with rice fields, tea plantations, and orchards. The people along the coast seemed almost Mediterranean, after the grim citizens of the capital. They were easygoing, pleasure-loving, and high-spirited. The chador veil, increasingly foisted on women in Tehran, wasn't popular along the Caspian.

One woman at a soft-drink stand along the way told me, "If you say you are not close to the mullahs' revolution, you are more welcome here."

It was as if the harsh ideological winds of the mullahs from the inhospitable desert had been expended against the craggy Alborz, leaving the warm Caspian coast almost untouched with Islamic zeal. However, fundamentalism had left its mark. At some resorts, we found, local authorities banned mixed bathing, and in one town even prohibited women from entering the salt sea. At another spa, we learned, the mullah persuaded the mayor to divide the beach between sexes and ordered Revolutionary Guards to arrest violators. That didn't go down very well with resort operators or beachgoers.

Along the road, there were stands selling freshly caught fish, and an array of fruits and vegetables—melons, tomatoes, cucumbers, plums, onions, sour cherries. There was also honeydew melon juice churned in a blender. Many of the towns along the Caspian had a kind of Russian colonial look, each with a civic square like a stage set for a Chekhov play. Plaster was peeling from the buildings but they retained a threadbare charm.

Stopping for lunch and chatting with an English-speaking restaurateur, we learned that sturgeon was one of the main cash crops in the area, but fishing, which had been tightly controlled by the state, was now open to all. Officials feared that the Caspian sturgeon would soon become depleted, casting some doubt over the future of Iranian caviar.

We drove on to Astara, the lively town at the Soviet border. For most of its length, the Iranian frontier with Iran is grim and forboding, but in Astara, it follows a lazy stream with overhanging willows and lush green foliage. Not far from the rickety, single-lane bridge that spanned the river border, an Iranian truck driver was waiting to take a cargo of steel rods transshipped from the Soviet Union. Over a soft drink, he said openly, "We don't understand what the Russians are doing in Afghanistan. They tell us it was to fight U.S.-supported counterrevolutionaries. But we really don't trust the Russians. We've been invaded by them before."

When Khomeini took over power, Moscow quickly supported him, a move that embarrassed and weakened the Iranian Tudeh (Communist) party, which had traditionally called for a Marxist secular state, not an Islamic fundamentalist one.

We sought out the mayor, a man named, Hassan Zahmatkesh, who offered us a cold Pepsi and explained, "We hope the government will build a wider bridge so we can have two-way truck traffic. We have good relations with the Russian truck drivers who come over here. Basically, we look on them as guests, and we treat them that way. We're not frightened of the Russians. We sleep peacefully at night here."

Most of the townspeople in Astara welcomed the Soviet truck drivers, who stayed overnight in the customs area and shopped in the local stores, possibly perplexed if they read Farsi by the conflicting slogans on the walls—DEATH TO THE FEDAYEEN (the Marxist radicals) and LONG LIVE THE TUDEH PARTY. Soviet drivers sold or bartered fur hats to the Iranians, in exchange for jeans or jackknives, and especially henna hair dye and cheap cosmetics, which they took home for their women.

As we chatted with one of the Iranian drivers, a policeman from a nearby station, who had been watching us, came over and said, "You are not permitted to ask questions about the Russians."

He asked us for our identification and took us to the station, where he told us that journalists were not allowed in the sensitive border area. So we were taken to district police headquarters and held for an hour before I insisted they call a senior police or army officer. We then saw the head man, a colonel, and went through the same catch-22 routine:

324   DANGEROUS COMPANY

"You could be spies. Why have you no written permission to be here?"

"The Ministry of National Guidance said we didn't need permission."

"That is wrong, you need permission, and are breaking the law."

Finally, after calls to Tehran, we got through to the governor of the province, who ordered us released. But the local colonel, in an unintended takeoff of a western sheriff, ordered us to be out of town by sundown.

"But we haven't had anything to eat," I protested. "What about the famous Iranian hospitality to strangers?"

He relented and allowed us a farewell meal at a hostel in Astara, where we had intended to spend the night. A blue-eyed Circassian manager showed us the official menu.

"Do you have any caviar?" Stuart asked. It wasn't on the menu. The proprietor looked complicitous and disappeared. He returned with a hefty jar of caviar.

"That will have to be extra," he said, apologetically.

"No problem," I said. "By the way, you wouldn't have any vodka, would you?"

Again, looking conspiratorial, he departed and returned with a brown bag. Inside was a fifth of illegal Russian vodka. It made our day.

I didn't realize it at the time, but that was to be my last trip to Iran during the hostage crisis, which dragged on, as my sources had predicted, until the Iranians released the hostages when they no longer served an internal purpose.

Possibly because of his fixation on the issue, President Carter lost the election. The hostage drama illustrated among other things the limitations of American economic and military power, particularly when inappropriately deployed against ill-defined or unassailable targets. The North Vietnamese were a case in point, as were the Iranian Shia militants.

From London, I followed the denouement of the hostage story, and when they were finally released in January 1981, I was on hand at the Rhein-Main air base in Germany. I remained up all night in the bitterly cold weather, and shortly before dawn was warmed and rewarded by the sight of the hostages stepping down the ramp of the U.S. Nightingale hospital plane. They were free from their long, harrowing ordeal at last.

CHAPTER TWELVE

Bloody Ulster

IN JULY 1977, I flew to Northern Ireland to cover Queen Elizabeth's jubilee year visit to the troubled province of Ulster. Irish republicans mounted a massive protest demonstration in Belfast and British security was determined that no harm should befall the monarch. Along with *Newsweek*'s Malcolm MacPherson and Johnny Apple of the *New York Times,* I found myself caught in the middle of the fracas, one which followed a pattern that could almost have been scripted—with irate, young Irish Catholics on one side, and Ulster police and the British Army on the other.

The kids from the working-class Catholic neighborhoods of West Belfast—the Falls, the Ardoyne, Turf Lodge, Andersontown, Twinbrooks—gathered on the Lower Falls Road and announced they would march into the center of Belfast. The authorities, in turn, informed the marchers that parades were banned in the city center. The march began with dozens of women leading it, followed by hundreds of youths who moved down the Lower Falls Road, past the Divis Flats, heading toward the walled-off central shopping malls. At Castle Road, the boundary of the downtown area, the Royal Ulster Constabulary backed up by a battalion of the British Army waited to block the marchers' advance—with riot shields and helmets at the ready and a senior officer wielding a loudspeaker.

I began the day behind the police lines and watched as the officers readied themselves for the affray, unlimbering batons and weapons that fired plastic bullets. Overhead, a helicopter called a "heli-teli" transmitted a running televised transmission of the action, while behind police lines, cherry picker cranes hoisted police cameramen who shot individual photos of the demonstrators.

As the marchers approached the police lines, the chief constable warned through the loudspeaker, "You have no permit to march. You are breaking the law. Do not come any farther. Disperse and go back to your homes."

That warning touched off the next sequence. The women moved to the rear of the file and the young kids, egged on by adults, began throwing rocks. The pellets landed among the police officers, who fended them off with their shields or sought refuge inside their old-fashioned armored vehicles known as "pigs." The kids advanced closer shouting obscenities and chanting, "Brits out!" I narrowly avoided several of the rocks, cobblestones, and bottles the demonstrators were heaving at police lines, and decided to get to the other side to see things from there. It looked safer.

I made my way around a side street to come up behind the marchers. Half the demonstrators appeared to be genuinely angry but some of the young boys seemed to treat the event as an outing, happily snatching up rocks, running forward to pitch them, and then scooting back toward the rear again. The adults, whom the army calls "godfathers," encouraged the kids to hurl objects, but they didn't throw any themselves. This went on for a half hour or so, and then the police opened fire with plastic bullets, which are about an inch in diameter and three inches long. They sting badly when they hit and from close range, aimed at the head, can cause serious injury, even death.

Next, as the constabulary held the line across Castle Road, units of the army, in this case members of the Light Infantry Regiment, outflanked the marchers, and suddenly appeared on a side street. Then the "snatch squads" went to work, darting from the army ranks and seizing those thought to be ringleaders of the screaming rioters. The soldiers were armed with clubs rather than rifles, in case they were captured. Fights broke out as a unit of four soldiers grabbed a "godfather" and pulled him, yelling and kicking, back to an army vehicle. After several such forays, the soldiers had snatched a half-dozen adults and beaten off would-be rescuers, and with that, the steam seemed to go out of the demonstration, and gradually the kids dispersed back up Lower Falls Road.

I talked to one of the army officers, who explaining the military strategy in this kind of confrontation, told me, "Our aim is to use the minimum force necessary to end an illegal demonstration. We don't want to arrest kids. We are looking for those who provoke the children. The name of the game in these situations is selectivity. We try not to spread our net too wide in order not to offend the innocent. It is the godfathers we want, and we have been getting them."

I first visited Ulster in 1974, five years after the current "troubles" began. On my first day in Belfast, a car bomb exploded in the city center, alongside the tall barricades that cordoned off the shopping district. On my second visit, another bomb, five hundred pounds of gelignite, went off just across from my hotel, the Europa. The blast shattered windows and sent a plume of thick smoke billowing up over the city. Sirens screamed as police and firemen raced to the site. The area was sealed off. In the hotel lobby, I found a half-dozen fashion models checking into the hotel for a charity show. They had turned ashen at the front desk.

"That's the kind of thing that hurts business," remarked the hotel manager, R. Harper Brown, with studied understatement. "Strange, we haven't had an explosion that close for some time."

The hotel itself was the target of a dozen bomb attacks over the years, and you had to enter and leave the premises through a wooden shed where security men searched you. Brown, a dapper little man, had received the Order of the British Empire from Queen Elizabeth, perhaps the only hotelier ever decorated for keeping his place running in the face of terrorist attacks.

During the 1970s, Belfast had become the Beirut of Europe. In the United Kingdom, where police traditionally have gone unarmed, Belfast was patrolled by camouflaged soldiers with automatic rifles, often in armored cars, peering out anxiously for snipers. Soldiers and police holed up in fortresslike outposts surrounded by metal screens and barbed wire, floodlit all night. Much of West Belfast looked like Berlin after the war: Homes and shops were blackened and gutted. There were gaps in building lines where shops had been bombed and not restored. Graffiti was everywhere. Adults and children on the street seemed sullen and angry.

Yet there was another side to Belfast. I was taken on a pub crawl through the Protestant sector by a journalist friend. Once you were admitted into the bar, and spoken for, there was plenty of conviviality, despite the meanness of the streets outside. Later I went on a similar tour of the Catholic area and found much good cheer inside the bars. Perhaps it was alcohol-induced. But it provided me with another perspective to the grim Ulster scene. One night, for instance, I found myself with a party of attractive men and women, dancing at the roof nightclub of the Europa. The mood was of prewar Beirut or Dublin, rather than shell-shocked Belfast, and I had a better time than in many cities in Europe.

Still, Belfast was not like other European cities. To the east of the River Lagan, the city was largely middle-class Protestant; to the west, mostly working-class Catholic with large pockets of Protestants in enclaves like Shankhill Road. Both sides feared and distrusted each other.

The troubles had their roots deep in Irish history. Pope Adrian IV in the twelfth century granted the English Catholic king Henry II the right to conquer Ireland. During the Protestant Reformation that swept England, Scotland, and Wales under Henry VIII, Ireland remained Catholic. In the seventeenth century, Oliver Cromwell brutally repressed an Irish rebellion and sent emigrants from England and Scotland to the northern province of Ulster, as Englishmen were settled in the American colonies. In 1690, at the crucial Battle of the Boyne, the Catholic king James was decisively defeated by William of Orange, a Dutchman who subsequently became king of England. Aided by the mother country, the Protestant settlers prospered and became firmly entrenched. More important, they remained dedicated to the concept that Ulster was an integral part of the United Kingdom. Thus, Ulster retained its union with Great Britain even after southern Ireland became the Irish Free State and then the Republic of Ireland.

In 1969, frustrated by what they considered second-class-citizen status in Ulster—and discriminated against in jobs and housing—many of the province's five hundred thousand Catholics began a civil rights protest against the rule of Ulster's one million unionist majority. The demonstrations quickly disintegrated into near civil war between the two religious communities and British troops were sent in to restore order. The soldiers were first welcomed as protectors by the Catholic side but as the months wore on, the Catholics came to dislike and then detest the British troops, who often behaved boorishly as their numbers increased from six thousand to twenty-four thousand. Emotions turned to hatred in Londonderry on "Bloody Sunday," in January 1972, when British paratroopers fired into crowds killing thirteen people, all Catholics.

The Catholic militant groups were led by the IRA, the illegal Irish Republican Army, and its legal political arm Sinn Fein, which in Irish translates roughly as Ourselves Alone. The hard men of the IRA were the cutting edge in bombing and ambush attacks against the army, the Royal Ulster Constabulary, and sometimes civilian targets in Ulster or England.

The British Army maintained that it found itself caught between the two groups, whose implaccable hatred was primarily religious. It was also economic, the Protestant unionists being the haves and the Catholic republicans, the have-nots. The difference was also cultural: the Northern Protestants perceived themselves as better educated and more advanced than the southern Catholics. But religion, as far as I could see, lay at the heart of it all. The fundamentalist Protestants of Northern Ireland hate the pope and anything that smacks of papism. And for those who tend to play down the influence of religion in Ulster—or in Cyprus, Lebanon, Iran, Kashmir, or Sri Lanka, for that matter—I can only cite Mohandas K. Gandhi's dictum: "Those who say there is no connection between religion and politics know little about either."

I relished the story of a reporter friend who entered a bar in the Lower Falls Road, in Catholic territory, to phone his office and stayed for a beer. A group of locals observed him closely from their end of the bar, and one man, acting as an emissary, came over to ask the journalist:

"You a Yank?"

"Yes."

"Tell me, Yank, are you a Catholic or Protestant?"

"I suppose I'm an agnostic."

The emissary absorbed this for a moment, and then said, "Tell me, Yank, are you a Catholic agnostic or a Protestant agnostic?"

Shortly after the queen's visit, I spent some time on patrol with several different battalions of the British Army in Belfast and in the countryside. On my rounds, I found the soldiers to be reasonably well-behaved and thoroughly professional, particularly the officers. With a four-man patrol in the depressed, derelict Markets District, a Catholic area, I moved cautiously along the ill-named Joy Street. The troopers had rifles swung outward, watching for snipers.

"The main thing is to keep moving every twenty or thirty seconds," one squaddie told me, "so a sniper can't draw a bead on you. The IRA has declared us the targets so we want to make sure we are difficult targets."

That day, the patrol was led by Major David Grove, a squadron commander with the Royal Engineers, who explained, "Ordinarily we are stationed in West Germany with the Second Armored Division. But in Ulster, we, like the Royal Artillery, are used as infantry. Patrolling on foot is our key function. Each patrol has a specific mission—checking cars, houses, people, letting everyone know that we are here. Our basic unit is the four-man 'brick,' because we can build with them, putting two or three bricks together as the situation requires. Our soldiers have become remarkably observant. It may be that one house has suddenly ordered a couple of extra bottles of milk. That could mean visitors. Who are they? Each patrol is debriefed by an intelligence officer. Our soldiers put in a four-month tour here, and we keep them working twelve to sixteen hours a day, seven days a week. They go out on at least three patrols, night and day. It is a bit of a mental strain. You've got to be switched on all the time."

During the patrol, we stopped at a Provo hangout, the Markets Social Club, where the soldiers watched the men drinking at the bar or playing snooker. The proprietor, a former boxing trainer known as "Skin" Callaghan, offered Major Grove a drink, and turning to me said, "Nobody really wants the British Army in Northern Ireland. But we don't have too many complaints about them in this area. People are getting fed up with the troubles."

Just to the northwest of downtown Belfast lie New Lodge and the Ardoyne, militant Catholic areas, and Tiger Bay, an equally extremist Protestant neighborhood. The volatile "interface" between them was patrolled by a battalion of the Royal Greenjackets, who got their name because they wisely switched uniforms from scarlet to forest green while on duty in North America during the Revolutionary period.

"The paramount thing in our operations is good intelligence work," explained Lieutenant David Day, in his command post, which was lined with closeup maps with the Catholic areas in green, the Protestant in orange, and mixed neighborhoods cross-hatched. On the wall were photos of known or suspected IRA leaders in Belfast.

"We know who they are," said Day, "and we are sure that they know we know who they are. But we don't have enough evidence to lift them. So we keep an eye on them until we get enough to make a charge against them stick."

To garner intelligence, the Greenjackets maintained several observation posts, one of which was perched atop a fourteen-story apartment building, manned by soldiers around the clock. There I found a twenty-two-year-old corporal, Glenn Ternent, who spent four hours at a stretch peering down on the streets below. His equipment included a rifle with a high-powered telescopic sight, a camera with a long lens, and a log book in which to note anything suspicious, particularly in the two pubs on the street, which were frequented by IRA suspects. His concrete shelter had been chipped by incoming sniper bullets.

"After a while," observed the corporal, "we get to know the rhythm of the neighborhood and look for things that break the pattern. This may lead us to some of the hard men we are looking for."

Down below again, I drove off in a Land-Rover with the platoon leader, Lieutenant Henry Robinson. The radio crackled. Corporal Ternent in the observation tower reported a suspected gunman had entered one of the pubs. Robinson stopped our vehicle in front of the tavern while a soldier in the patrol covered us. He asked the suspect to step outside and informed him, "In the name of Her Majesty's forces, I arrest you."

The suspect was taken back to the command posts and turned over to the Royal Ulster Constabulary. Then the radio informed us that bombs were reported in a nearby shopping district. We sped off in the Land-Rover and found the bomb disposal team already on the scene. They disarmed two incendiary devices set in ordinary tape cassettes and left inside shops. Later in the day, two women pushing a baby carriage deposited similiar devices in downtown Belfast, setting off a dozen fires.

Like other military units, the Greenjackets used a new computer system that records background information about license plates so that soldiers at road checkpoints can get a quick fix by radio on the cars they stop.

"We think intelligence is paying dividends," said Lieutenant Day. "The Provo resources are drying up. Many Catholics now look on them as bullying gunmen who are disrupting normal living. What we are interested in is getting the godfathers, the ringleaders who incite the kids to violence but themselves stay under cover. Meanwhile, we are enabling the constabulary to return to these former no-go areas and provide some kind of orderly government presence. That doesn't mean the Catholics or the Protestants on the other side of the road necessarily like the British Army. But I think they realize there is no future with the Provos."

I had heard criticism of the use of the Royal Marines in Ulster:

These tough, well-trained battalions were likened to the paratroopers as being too brutal and insensitive for the delicate responsibilities in Northern Ireland. I spent a night on patrol with the seasoned 45 Royal Marine Commando, which had been accused by Catholic leaders of using undue force after a young marine was killed by a sniper in Turf Lodge.

"Overreacting?" said the battalion's commanding officer, Lieutenant Colonel John Grey. "They shot down one soldier and wounded three others. They fired at least twenty-five shots. We fired only two. We went into the area looking for the gunmen and we found five weapons. I don't think you can call that overreacting."

Grey strapped a pistol around his waist, cocked his green beret with the Marines flash, and said, "Frankly, I happen to think we are damn well suited for service in Northern Ireland. That is because our men are highly disciplined. The provocation in some of these hard areas—stoning, bottling, sniping—is such that you need disciplined soldiers who will not allow themselves to be provoked."

The colonel admitted that one of the severest tests facing young British soldiers in Ulster were the rules of engagement: when you could shoot and when you couldn't. The army issued a set of instructions listed on a "yellow card." But one of the Marine officers told me scornfully, "My God, you would have to be a lawyer to figure it out. These young soldiers have to make split-second decisions when they are being shot at. You know, this is really a corporal's war. They are the ones on the firing line making the critical decisions—whether to shoot back or not. By the time a senior officer arrives at the scene of an incident to sort things out, it is too late. The decisions have already been taken by the junior noncoms—for better or worse. And if a wrong decision is made, it may take us months to undo the damage in the particular area."

In South Armagh County, Crossmaglen is a Spartan-looking farm market town in an area of strong republican loyalties, a region the British Army calls Indian Country, for its hostility. It is a dangerous place where the IRA Provos for years crossed the unmarked border between Ulster and Eire almost at will. But now the British Army, spearheaded by the elite Special Air Service (SAS), stepped up its patrols and covert watching posts to hamper IRA activities. I watched patrols being inserted by helicopter in fields near the border. The men would lie in ambush for up to four days. Later, I had dinner in a company headquarters in Crossmaglen, a ramshackle outpost that reminded me of similar ones in Vietnam. The British soldiers called the post the Alamo. Major Ray Pett, who previously commanded Gurkha troops in the Far East, was in charge and he gave me this view commonly held by the British Army of its role in Northern Ireland:

"I think the army can be proud of what we are trying to do. We are not here because we like it. And we don't expect the people to like us. We wouldn't want a bunch of soldiers in our midst, either. But without us, this would be a very bloody place. With us, it is considerably less bloody. No officer thinks that there is a military solution to the problem of Northern Ireland. But with the level of terrorism reduced, maybe the politicians can get around to working out a nonmilitary solution."

Some weeks later, I returned to Crossmaglen in a rented car rather than by army helicopter. As I drove out into the undulating countryside from Belfast, through attractive fields with hedgerows, I noted how serene and beautiful is the northern landscape, every bit as felicitous as the south. I saw that some of the small cottages were flying the orange, white, and green tricolor of the Republic rather than the Union Jack. And the residents I talked to saw their situation in a quite different perspective from that of the British Army.

"The British think that South Armagh is the Wild West and we're the Indians," complained publican Paddy Short in his bar, as he drew me a pint of Guinness. "They don't realize the natives are far more intelligent than they think. We are smart enough, for instance, to know that we'd all be better off if the British troops would only get out. They're not down here to keep two different sides apart—there's only one side here. We ignore the army as we have right along. They come through in their patrols and armored cars but we take no notice of them and the shopkeepers neither speak to them nor serve them."

The pubkeeper, a cheery man of sixty-two with his hair only beginning to gray, added, "My family has lived in this very parish since the seventeenth century, and in this house since 1885. Yet the British think they can come in and tell us how to behave. Naturally we resent it. The army patrols the streets and the people stay inside. Since there's little work here, the bright young ones leave and the town wastes away."

Paddy Short poured me another jar and reflected, "This was a lovely little village, you know. In the olden days, it was peaceful and quiet. No big trucks passed through. In the summer, people would congregate around the square and musicians would play. There was talk and there was laughter. Now, if more than three people gather, they arrest you for unlawful assembly. What a sweet place it was then! Now, it is bleak, bleak. People don't come out on the street. The gaiety is gone.''

Driving out of town, I saw graffiti on a stone wall reading GOD MADE THE CATHOLICS AND THE ARMALITE MADE THEM EQUAL.

Indeed, the Armalite, or M-16, automatic rifle had become the status symbol of the IRA, the Irish Republican Army. Over the years, the strength and influence of the IRA has waxed and waned. The organization had its origin in the struggle for Irish independence beginning in 1919. The IRA opposed the creation of the Irish Free State, which led to the civil war of 1922–23. In 1969, a break occurred between IRA traditionalists, who sought power through political means, and a breakaway faction calling themselves the Provisional IRA, who argued that violence was the only effective answer. The ''Provos'' became more powerful and the regular IRA withered away. The IRA has gone through shifts of policy, particularly in their targeting: sometimes aiming only at the police and army; other times singling out ''soft'' civilian targets.

I had covered several such attacks: at Harrod's department store in London, for instance; a pub in Ballykelly in Ulster; the assassination of Lord Mountbatten in Donegal Bay in the Republic. In the last instance, I heard the preliminary report over the radio in London, flew to Dublin, and rented a car to drive across the island to Sligo. There I found that the World War II hero and postwar statesman was dead, along with his fourteen-year-old grandson and a local crew member on the boat that was booby-trapped. Four members of Mountbatten's family were wounded. He was seventy-nine and had never been involved in Irish affairs, except to visit his summer home at Classiebawn Castle. The IRA said the bombing was carried out ''to bring to the attention of the world the British occupation of the six northeast counties of Ireland.''

It was difficult for me to see how such an act gained any sympathy for the IRA cause, just as I don't believe bombing airliners contributes much understanding to Palestinian aims. While in the area, I visited the grave of the Nobel laureate poet William Butler Yeats, who though Protestant was an advocate of Irish independence. His tombstone bears the epitaph, which could be appropriate for some of the hard men involved in the Irish troubles: CAST A COLD EYE ON LIFE, ON DEATH. HORSEMAN PASS BY.

To look more closely into the IRA, I tracked down in Dublin Ruari O'Bradaigh, the president of the provisional Sinn Fein, who was known as Rory O'Brady before he gaelicized his name. I found him in a cluttered, tract-filled office in Parnell Square, just north of the River Liffey.

I asked him how he justified the terrorist tactics of the IRA and he answered, "The only way to get the British out of Ireland is through armed struggle. We have been in a situation of continuing violence against the British for eight hundred years. We want to disenchant the British people with their government's involvement in Ireland, to unify forces in opposition to the British presence, and to secure a British withdrawal. Toward that end, the economic bombing campaign and the war of attrition against Britian's armed forces have been conducted. One thing is certain. If the Protestants attack the Catholic communities in Belfast or Derry, it could lead to civil war. And if that happens, I don't think the Catholics in the south would just sit back and watch those in the north being killed."

O'Bradaigh, a seemingly mild-mannered man who wore spectacles and a tweed jacket with patch pockets but who had been a gun-toting revolutionary for most of his life, told me he had little more liking for the Irish government in Dublin than for British rule in Ulster.

"The Catholics in the north are the blacks," he said. "But the Protestants are only poor whites. The rule in the south is neocolonial, with imperialist puppets running things. We want to disestablish both states—in north and south. But that doesn't mean we want civil war."

I said that it looked like a formula for civil war to me. For what many American supporters of organizations like Noraid, the Irish Northern Aid Committee, do not realize is that Sinn Fein Provos want to establish a socialist regime in all of the island, or as O'Bradaigh put it, "a democratic socialist republic called New Ireland."

"The ideal solution," he said, "is a phased English withdrawal from Ireland and the creation of a new federal socialist system which would give each of the four traditional provinces—Ulster, Connaught, Munster, and Leinster—its own parliament and each local community control of its own affairs. The unionist-minded people [Protestants] would still have a working majority in the historic nine-county province of Ulster.

"But the means of production, distribution, and financial exchange must be controlled, and industries, agriculture and fisheries brought under state control. An upper limit will be placed on the amount of land any one individual may own. Larger tracts will be taken over and leased to groups of families to be run on cooperative lines. Private enterprise will still have a role to play in the economy. But it will be much smaller than it is today. Multinational corporations will not be allowed to have a controlling interest in Irish industry.''

In foreign affairs, O'Bradaigh went on, Ireland would have to reduce its ties with the European Economic Community, remain out of NATO, and expand trade with the smaller, neutral nations of Europe and the Third World. The Irish language would be reestablished as the principal community tongue of the Irish people. English would not be abolished but it would become a "secondary" language.

At this point, I wondered how Sinn Fein's program as enunciated by its president would sit with an average Third Avenue Irishman in New York.

The next day, I called on the noted Irish editor, Tim Pat Coogan, to see what he thought about the IRA as a future political force. Rather poetically, he told me, "The IRA is not a centralized movement with a head office, pensionable staff, and institutional mechanisms that carry it forward from one generation to another like a regular army. It is rather a wind in the corridors of Irish history, a rustle in the undergrowth of Irish politics, a spark that, if the wind blows favorably, suddenly ignites with literally napalmesque consequences.''

While in Dublin, I sounded out an Irish government official on the aims of the IRA, and he said bluntly, "I tend to think they are not very democratic. If they came to power by the barrel of a gun, they would probably hang on to power by the same gun barrel. They claim that Britain is the enemy now, but I think they have got Irish democracy in their gunsights, too.''

If the IRA was adamant in its aims, so were the Protestants. They had their own paramilitary groups and could be equally ruthless in carrying out various forms of terrorism. During the summer "marching season," members of the Orange Order delighted in tramping through the streets of Ulster cities—and into Catholic enclaves, too—pounding drums, playing fifes, and chanting slogans like, "To hell with the pope and popery, brass money and wooden shoes, and may the papishes be rammed, stammed, crammed into the big gun of Athalone and be blown to hell.''

What has struck me is the assumption by many IRA sympathizers, including those in the United States, that if British soldiers were to depart, the Irish republicans would soon take over, and the world would see a united Ireland. This view overlooks the fact that the Protestant unionists are a very tough tribe, rough as Carborundum, with a long history of military discipline and service in the British Army overseas. There are a million of them in Ulster and they were terrorizing the Catholics when the British Army arrived in force in 1969. The unionists are quite capable of setting up their own enclave or state, based around Belfast. I don't see how the IRA even together with the Republic of Ireland Army, which has no recent martial tradition, could roll up the Protestants, if they decided to hang tough. If the British pulled out, there could be a prolonged, unresolved conflict, with the possibility of dragging in all kinds of international opportunists.

In late 1980, I was in Ulster to cover a major hunger strike by IRA prisoners at the bleak, bare Maze prison in Long Kesh, an area south of Belfast. Seven convicted republican terrorists had been taking only water and salt since late October and were near death. In mid-December I was told that prison medical authorities expected the prisoners to be dead by Christmas. The inmates were demanding they be given special "political" rather than criminal status, a special category that had existed for both republican and unionist prisoners in the early 1970s. When that status was revoked in 1976, hundreds of IRA inmates began the "blanket protest," wearing only prison-issue blankets and refusing to don clothing. This was escalated to the "dirty protest," whereby prisoners refused to wash and smeared their cells with excrement. However, Margaret Thatcher's Conservative government opposed renewing the political status of prisoners convicted of terrorist offenses.

In Ireland, the use of the hunger strike as a protest could be traced back to the seventh and eighth centuries, when wronged persons would fast on the doorsteps of the offender, hoping to embarrass him into paying recompense or otherwise resolve the dispute. During the long period of English rule in Ireland, the hunger strike was used by prisoners opposing London. Later, rebellious IRA members tried the tactic against the newly created Irish Free State.

One of the best-known hunger strikers was the lord mayor of Cork, Terence McSwiney, who in 1922, charged with terrorism, starved himself to death in a London jail. Shortly before he died, McSwiney declared, "It is not those who can inflict the most, but those who can suffer the most, who will conquer." His words became an implicit battle cry for some republican prisoners.

For a period in recent years, British authorities had the option of force-feeding those on hunger strikes, which they did, for instance, in the case of the convicted Price sisters, Marian and Dolours. But backed by the guidelines of medical associations that force-feeding was a form of torture, the government decided against the practice. Thus, it appeared that the Maze men might die.

A few days before Christmas, however, the seven strikers suddenly ended their fast, thus defusing a tense situation. The Sinn Fein people said the strike was called off because the government granted certain concessions demanded by the prisoners.

One of the organizers of the Maze strike, though not a participant himself, was a twenty-seven-year-old prisoner named Bobby Sands. Early in 1981, Sands decided that the government had reneged on its agreement with the hunger strikers, and he began fasting on his own. A few weeks later, he was joined by other republican inmates in the Maze. Sands vowed to fast to the end.

Sands seemed an unlikely martyr. He was born in the predominately Protestant district of Rathcoole on the northern outskirts of Belfast, the eldest of four children. Friends said he worked as an apprentice in a manufacturing plant but was intimidated by Protestant employees and forced to leave. After the troubles started, according to IRA sources, the slightly built Sands joined up while in his teens. He was arrested in 1973 for armed robbery, jailed for five years, and released in 1976. Six months later, he was arrested, convicted on a firearms charge, and sentenced to fourteen years in prison.

On entering the Maze, Sands joined the dirty protest. He was elected spokesman for his wing of the H Block (the branches were named for their shape). When he went on his solitary strike, he soon gained international attention when Sinn Fein ran him as a candidate for the British Parliament from Fermanagh–South Tyrone, and he won. He was now Bobby Sands, M.P.

Many political figures from Irish prime minister Charles Haughey down pleaded with Sands to end his fast, but he refused. His plight was becoming a page one story, and I scheduled a trip to Belfast toward the end of March. However, my son in Geneva was planning to spend the weekend with me in London, so I met him at the airport and we got tickets for Belfast. By a rare quirk of Ulster weather, Belfast airport was snowed in. We quickly switched our tickets for a flight to Dublin, there rented a car, and drove at night through a snowstorm to reach Belfast. No sooner had we checked into the Europa than I received a call from his mother (I don't know how she tracked us down) wondering whether I wasn't necessarily exposing him to danger.

"He's a lot safer with me than in Madrid last summer," I said. Cyril had spent a couple of weeks in Spain on an exchange visit. But the father of the family turned out to be a cabinet minister, a target for Basque terrorists, and their apartment was surrounded by security men. I grumbled that if you worried about every possible danger, you'd never get out of bed in the morning.

In Belfast, tension was running high as Sands continued his fast. He wouldn't allow his case to be taken up by the European Commission on Human Rights when some of its representatives came to see him. In a last-hour appeal, Pope John Paul II sent his secretary, an Irish priest named Father John Magee, to Belfast to persuade Sands to end his fast. Though Sands thanked Father Magee for the pope's concern, he refused to take food. Finally, Sands's mother announced her son had asked her to promise not to intercede with the authorities if he became unconscious.

"I love my son," she said as she left the prison. "I promised I would do nothing. He's prepared for the end. It's up to him."

On Sunday, May 3, Sands lapsed into a coma. He was deteriorating rapidly. The next evening, I ran into a friend from the Northern Ireland office who told me confidentially the prison doctors said Sands was not expected to survive the night. I wrote a story based on the information for the first edition and alerted Mike Kennedy, a bright, young reporter from the *Los Angeles Times* Metro staff sent to Belfast to help out. I planned to remain up all night waiting for official word. About 1:30 A.M., I was having a drink with Jim Allen of the *Daily Telegraph* when he got a flash: Sands had died at 1:17 A.M., on the sixty-sixth day of his fast. I called Mike, awakening him, to get him headed toward Lower Falls Road, the Catholic stronghold. Then I dictated a new lead to my story. That done, I drove my rented car to the headquarters of Sinn Fein, arriving to see kneeling women, rosaries in hand, pounding trash can lids on the pavement as a sign of mourning. Young boys, some not even in their teens, were building barricades and fashioning Molotov cocktails on the sidewalks. The police and army were alerted. The kids began rioting when the police arrived and they in turn fired plastic bullets.

I saw that I left my car parked in no-man's-land and I jumped in to get it out of harm's way, around a corner. Just in time. Kids, wearing face masks, tossed their gasoline bombs in high, flaming arcs toward the police and troops. The young people behind their barricades cheered with each landing of a flaming bottle, and ducked the plastic bullets as best they could.

"Maggie Thatcher," screamed a woman, "if you could only be out here, we'd blow you to hell. You dirty, yellow bastard."

We had been the first reporters on the scene and Kennedy returned to the hotel to dictate material on the rioting. I remained in the Falls until sometime around 5:00 A.M. By then it was clear to me that the worst of the disturbances were over, so I drove back to the hotel to call in a final update to the story, which ran for a couple of thousand words in the home-delivered editions.

There was one unsavory, journalistic sidelight to the Sands story. The New York *Daily News* had sent a young columnist named Michael Daly to do stories from Belfast during the Sands hunger strike. A day or so after Sands's death, the *News* ran a dramatic Daly story about a British Army patrol, which had wounded a demonstrator a few hours after Sands's death. The story indicated that Daly had been with the patrol before, during, and after the shooting. Further, it included dialogue between members of the unit at the time of the incident. And it concluded with Daly following the patrol, which by coincidence just happened to end up in the morning light near Sands's family home. The general impression left by the story was that of hardened and callous officers and men, treating Irish Catholic demonstrators as little more than animals.

After the story appeared in New York, and its contents were relayed to London, the *Daily Mail* assigned a reporter to check out the British Army patrol and personnel alluded to by Daly. The *Mail* determined that an army patrol did indeed wound one demonstrating youngster in West Belfast that morning, but no reporters had accompanied the unit. The *Mail* also established that the patrol did not come from the barracks Daly said it had, nor could it have possibly ended up at Sands's home, a couple of miles away.

The story, the *Mail* said editorially, was manufactured "to stir up American public opinion against Britain and the British government. Almost everything which the author wrote is a work of pure imagination. What is presented as the news turns out to be a pack of lies."

The paper suggested that Daly's reporting was in the same category as that of Janet Cooke, the *Washington Post* reporter whose Pulitzer Prize-winning account of an eight-year-old drug addict turned out to be a hoax. When the *Mail*'s account appeared, Daly insisted he would "stick by my story" and that it was substantially true, but he then resigned. Anyone familiar with the British Army's practices at that time knew it was no longer taking reporters on patrol, that officers did not make such foolish remarks in front of journalists, and that patrol areas were confined to small areas: army units did not go wandering all over West Belfast.

I suppose columnists like Jimmy Breslin, who was Daly's mentor, can create their own cast of characters and events. But I don't think the Damon Runyon school of journalism, with its liberal mixture of fact and fiction, should be let loose on serious stories.

After Bobby Sands, nine other IRA prisoners fasted to their deaths, one after another. Following each death, there were riots in Belfast, but the British government was unyielding over their demands. In October, the Irish republican leadership in the Maze finally called off the strikes. Several days later, I flew to Belfast to inquire, Was it worth it?

In his small office on Lower Falls Road, I found Richard McCauley, a former IRA prisoner and now an official in Sinn Fein who was as informed and frank as anyone in the movement.

"The hunger strike failed," he said without qualification. "But there were positive by-products. The British government is more ostracized now than it has been for many years. Recruitment for the IRA is up. For the first time since the 1950s, republicans have been elected to the Irish and British parliaments by the people in the north. And the intrusion of the priests trying to end the strike by putting pressure on the prisoners' families shows that the republican movement is not a Catholic movement."

In the Ballymurphy area of West Belfast, I called on Father Desmond Wilson, a Catholic priest who was sympathetic to the republican movement but against the hunger strike. He told me, "It is a tremendous relief to people that the strike is over. At the same time, the element of trust of the government has fallen very low. The government did not realize how powerful the hunger strike was. When Bobby Sands died, I said, This is the beginning of the end of the British rule in Ireland."

Another Catholic priest, Father Dennis Faul, added, "I never liked the idea of the hunger strike. And not because I consider it suicide, which I don't. The hunger strike is a very noble form of protest with a long, legitimate history in Ireland. But the hunger strike should have been brought to an end after Bobby Sands's death. There was simply no reason for ten men to die.''

I met Sands's nineteen-year-old brother, Sean, and he said quietly, "We all love him—my parents and my sister and his friends. But it was his decision that he should lay down his life for his friends, for the republican cause, and for human justice for the prisoners. He didn't want to die. But he was his own man. I don't think his death was in vain.''

So the hunger strike victims became another link in the long, sorry chain of Ulster history. The situation in Northern Ireland reminded me of the religious wars that plagued Europe for centuries, but in modern times had seemed a relic of the past. It was clear to me that religion was at the root of the Northern Ireland problem, just as I believe it is in the Middle East and the Indian subcontinent.

Is there any solution in Ulster? Many observers think that ''power sharing'' would be a way to give the Catholics a greater say in the government of Northern Ireland and hence reduce the tensions in the province. Yet a formula devised in 1973 failed and another attempt foundered in 1986. Why?

"It's simple," said Protestant leader Harold McCusker, when I asked him why he was so adamantly against power sharing with the Catholics. "Democracy means majority rule. In Ulster, we are the majority. The Catholic minority wants to do away with our state and become part of a foreign country, Ireland. That's why we are so totally against power sharing.''

I asked the same question of Oliver Napier, a Catholic who attempted to bring together both religions in his Alliance party in Northern Ireland.

"Once you mention unity," he said, "you drive the Protestants up the wall. They view any kind of power sharing with people who insist on Irish unity as a kind of Trojan horse to get inside the walls. The Protestants see themselves becoming a minority in a country in which they would belong to an entirely different culture and religion.''

In defending power sharing, the moderate Catholic John Hume, one of the most admirable politicians in Ulster, pointed out to me, "The Protestants have to come to terms with the fact that it is Ireland they are living in—not England or Great Britain.''

But do the Protestants have to come to terms? Their conception that the Republic of Ireland is ruled by Rome, however arguable, is firmly strengthened in their minds when the voters in the South outlaw, as they have in national referendums, abortion and even divorce. The Protestants argue that they are not outsiders refusing to become "Irish"—but rather inhabitants of four hundred years' standing who have as much right to Ulster as the descendants of English settlers have to the United States.

Many republicans believe that politicians in London are determined to hang on to Ulster; that they genuinely want the province to remain part of the United Kingdom. I don't share that view. It is my experience that most British politicians, and the British voters at large, would dearly love to divest themselves of Ulster—if there were some way to do it that would not lead to civil war. British support for the intractable policies of Ulster Protestants is wearing thin. And some thoughtful observers believe the best way toward a peaceful solution is to let the Protestant politicians know that London will not write them a blank check indefinitely. But Prime Minister Thatcher has painted herself into something of a corner. For if she was willing to send a British task force eight thousand miles to fight to defend the right of a thousand Falkland Islanders to self-determination, how can she not allow the million Protestants to have similar rights just across the Irish Sea?

For its part, the British Army is more than happy to continue turning over security duties to the Royal Ulster Constabulary and the home-raised Ulster Defense Regiment. On one of my last trips to Northern Ireland with my new foreign editiior, Alvin Shuster, I stopped by the army headquarters at Lisburn to see Brigadier Michael Rose, who was in command of 39 Brigade, which had responsibility for Belfast. A brilliant and resourceful soldier, who was decorated for leading the crack SAS regiment in the Falklands, Rose answered my question forthrightly:

"You ask me what my policy is. I'll tell you. It's Brits out! But that being said, how does a responsible nation like Great Britain pull out its forces if it would lead to bloody carnage? I'm afraid that's what would happen here. And I'm afraid that's our problem here."

CHAPTER THIRTEEN

Once More Around the World

I WAS IN LONDON when the Falkland Islands were invaded by Argentina on April 2, 1982. I put in my bid to accompany the assembling British naval task force to the South Atlantic. But the Ministry of Defense refused to take any foreign reporters along. In fact, they took relatively few of their own journalists, and from all accounts handled them badly. I began writing one or two stories a day from London for the next eighty days, probably the longest sustained coverage of a single story that I have done. I might leave London for the day for interviews with military or naval experts or visit bases like Portsmouth, returning to my office to write in the evening. The senior officials at the Defense Ministry were generally unhelpful to the press. So there was a lot of bad blood around the government offices along Whitehall during the campaign. The saving grace was the British Army's director of press relations, Brigadier David Ramsbottom, a combat veteran who knew what he was talking about and never gave you a bum steer. The British Army had learned the hard way in Ulster that you needed good public relations, and they assigned to the job some of their brightest up-and-coming senior officers like Ramsbottom and his successor, Brigadier Michael Hobbs. The Royal Navy, on the other hand, was hopeless in presenting its case.

At the beginning of the crisis, most reporters in London accepted the word of various British officials on controversial matters, and correspondingly downgraded material coming from Argentinian sources. At first, this seemed reasonable: The straightforward Anglo-Saxon accounts seemed more credible than the excited, inflated Latin version of events. But as the conflict intensified, and with the landings at San Carlos about to begin, senior British officials began leaking misinformation to selected reporters, including myself, to confuse the Argentinians about their plans. By the end of the war, many reporters in London were giving more credence to statements from Buenos Aires than to British officials. And the British government's reputation for candor suffered accordingly. A parliamentary inquiry was set up afterward to probe into how the government made such a mess in its press relations.

Shortly after the war ended with the British capture of Port Stanley, the Ministry of Defense offered to fly a few foreign reporters belatedly to the Falklands. I was one. I had hoped to attend Johnny Apple's wedding to the beauteous Betsy: A party was to be held on a boat sailing along the Thames. But duty called and I saddled up for the flight to the Falklands. In its way, it was fascinating. We took a Royal Air Force VC-10 for the eight-hour jaunt to Ascension Island in the middle of the South Atlantic. We stopped to refuel at Dakar in case we couldn't land at the speck of land, and had to return to the African mainland. At Ascension, we got a helicopter ride around the island with a crew exploring the possibility of harnessing energy from volcanic geysers. Then we took off aboard a RAF C-130 Hercules for the fourteen-hour flight to Stanley. The plane was specially configured with extra fuel tanks inside the cargo bay. In the event Stanley was socked in, we had to arrive with enough fuel to get us back toward Ascension. So we had to refuel twice en route. I clambered up to the flight deck to watch our first refueling operation. Because the aerial tanker was a full-jet Victor whose minimum speed was about equal to the maximum speed of the prop-jet C-130, once we linked up with the refueling hose, we had to make a shallow dive of about ten thousand feet in order to keep the connection from parting in air. It was an eerie feeling diving behind the tail of a jet tanker over the South Atlantic.

The only bad moment of the flight came when over Stanley, we made one unsuccessful pass at the short runway and the pilot announced over the intercom, ''It's a bit foggy down there as you can see. If we miss our second pass, I'm afraid we'll have to go back to Ascension.''

I thought, Oh, Christ, no. Not a twenty-eight-hour nonstop flight in a cold, noisy, uncomfortable, combat-loaded Hercules with nothing to show for it, only the prospect of doing it all over again. South American airports were off limits to us. On the second pass, I strained with the pilot as if my mental efforts could help. Luckily, we skimmed in through the white stuff, and landed.

I found the Falklands, lying off the tip of South America, a dispiriting place. It was the worst time of winter there, a location where it was said you could experience all four seasons in a single day. Port Stanley, with its faded frame houses, had the improvised look of a turn-of-the-century western mining settlement. The inhabitants were upset because their remote, isolated way of life was totally disrupted by the war, and they were now faced with the presence of a large, permanent garrison of British soldiers.

I also sensed deep-seated tensions stemming from the Argentinian invasion. These feelings, stated and unstated, involved questions about how best the Falklanders should have reacted to the invasion, what degree of resistance to have put up, and the responsibilities of the islanders to one another. Some residents resented the fact that many British contract schoolteachers and others took advantage of an Argentinian offer to leave the Falklands after the invasion.

"They should have stayed behind with us," one high school student told me. "We won't feel the same about them again."

The community was also divided as to whether the capital should have been abandoned to the invaders, which would have made it easier for the British to attack since there would be no fear of injuring civilians. Those who stayed in Stanley rather than striking out for the countryside, known as the "camp," shared the view of the energetic and likeable local radio broadcaster, Patrick Watts, who told me, "There were those who believed that we who stayed behind were irresponsible. But I believe just the opposite to be true. I thought some of us had to remain and do our jobs—as long as most of the residents stayed in Stanley. Somebody had to keep the town running. We couldn't trust the Argies to do it."

But others thought that the population should have made it as difficult as possible for the Argentinians, letting them shift for themselves in the capital. One of these was town councillor Terry Peck, who told me he got out of Stanley at the first opportunity, left for a remote sheep farm, and made contact with advance units of the British forces as soon as they landed to provide them with intelligence.

One head of a family suggested the feelings of the locals were intensified because of the very compactness of Stanley. "This is, after all," he said, "a very small town, with all the little envies and petty jealousies you'd find in any such place. Living under an occupation and through the fighting has increased the tension."

I also found an adverse reaction setting in between the army and the islanders. Some of the Falklanders seemed to disapprove of the troops whose efforts broke the Argentinian yoke. And the soldiers privately told me they thought many of the islanders were ungrateful and took for granted their liberation and the sacrifice of some 250 dead British servicemen. The soldiers, too, made jokes about the islanders' backwardness, which they attributed to the inbred nature of the families. For their part, the residents resented what they considered an attitude of superiority by the military.

"They treat us like bumpkins," was the way one Falklander put it.

In looking over the islands, it occurred to me that at relatively little cost, Britain could have resettled the nine hundred or so families in New Zealand, Australia, the Orkneys, the Shetlands, or mainland Great Britain, where they could have a comfortable existence raising sheep. Then London could cede the islands to Argentina, thereby ending the anachronism of the Falklands, and repairing relations with Latin American nations over the issue of the Malvinas.

However, when I sounded out Prime Minister Thatcher the next time she had a chat with the American press, she was adamant that, as she put it, "the wishes of the Falkland islanders are paramount." So the views of a handful of people have precluded any settlement of the vexing issue during Thatcher's administration.

After the Israeli invasion of Lebanon in 1982, I flew to Tel Aviv and found the country in an uncharacteristic downbeat mood. The Christian militia's killing of Palestinians in the Sabra and Chatilla refugee camps in Beirut, apparently with the tacit approval of some Israeli military officers, had left a sour taste. I found Israelis in and out of the armed forces questioning the relationship between the military and the civilian government in a way that had never before occurred in that nation.

For I had been in Israel during the 1978 invasion of southern Lebanon, when in response to a terrorist attack on a civilian bus that left thirty-three Israelis dead, the army rolled north as far as the Litani

River. Then, I moved in behind the Israeli troops, with my old friend Amos Sapir, now a reserve major, and Hearst newspapers' John Harris. Shellfire echoed up front and jets screamed overhead. Tank treads rattled on the stony ground. The M-60 Patton tanks were followed by mechanized artillery, the long barrels of the 175s pointed menacingly northward. Smoke rose ahead where their shells hit. Even then, I got the impression that the Davidian finesse that had marked the army's style had been replaced by a kind of Goliathian stomping. In the hamlets, we moved through—Tibeh, Rashaya El-Fourkar, Nakar, Ras El-Maroun, Al Buss, Ras Al-Bayada—great craters had rent the earth, many houses were flattened, and dead animals lay in backyards.

In Bint Jebail, where the Palestinians operated, the walls were pockmarked with bullet and shell holes, and the streets were full of rubble, cartridges, shattered glass, and dangling telephone lines. Civilian cars, some with occupants still inside, had been crushed by the onrushing tanks as if hit by some giant drop-forge. The smell of decaying bodies wafted through the orange and olive groves. The main military problem with this use of massive force was that the fast-moving guerrillas were long gone by the time Israeli armor arrived in a village, leaving only innocent farmers and their families behind to bear the brunt of destruction. The mailed-fist technique was used to teach the Palestinians a lesson, but it was a lesson they refused to learn.

After the 1978 ceasefire, I rode again through southern Lebanon to the Litani with the United Nations peacekeeping forces from a different direction, which only confirmed my impression of widespread destruction that seemed to have no military justification.

However in 1978, most Israelis supported the decision to clean out southern Lebanon, though some critics objected to the heavy-handed tactics involved.

In 1982, in contrast, I wondered what had caused the widespread disquiet in Israel. Most of the people I saw indicated that it was Prime Minister Menachem Begin's decision to go beyond the originally out-lined war aims—the expulsion of the Palestinians along a twenty-five-mile border zone—to attack Beirut itself and occupy one third of Lebanon. In particular, these critics condemned the attack on Beirut, and the secrecy surrounding the government's decisions.

I looked up Hirsch Goodman, an old friend and the respected military correspondent of the *Jerusalem Post*—as well as an ex-paratroop officer—who told me, "There is a crisis of confidence, of trust, among senior officers in the army about the government. And this is filtering down through the ranks. There were no real reasons to advance beyond the original twenty-five-mile limit. Entering Beirut meant involvement in the madness of Lebanese politics. And military intelligence and Mossad [the Israeli secret intelligence service] advised against it. There was no clear benefit to engage the Syrian Army. It was a tangential operation and it cost an additional two hundred lives of Israeli soldiers. Finally, we exposed to the Syrians and other Arab states our new military capabilities—aircraft tactics, attack helicopters, tanks, antimissile defense, and logistics, as well as our maneuvering tactics, during the advance.''

The target of much of the criticism was my friend from the Sinai campaign of 1973, General Ariel "Arik" Sharon, who was Begin's defense minister. Sharon was accused by some of shifting the blame for the Sabra massacre from himself and Begin to the army—and of lying about his role in the invasion and his dealing with Lebanese Christian militia leaders. In various parts of Israel, reserve officers and enlisted troops signed petitions protesting the invasion of Lebanon and called for Sharon's ouster.

Ironically, the sagging army morale followed what most military analysts considered a superb feat of arms: The speed and precision of the invasion, the expert handling of air, land, and sea forces, were described to me by specialists as almost textbook perfect. Still, the operation had cost the Israelis at that point—some 400 dead—with more to come, compared to only 190 killed in the 1956 Sinai campaign, and 777 in the 1967 war in which Israeli forces retook the Sinai as well as the West Bank of the Jordan, and the Golan Heights.

I had iced coffee in a Jerusalem outdoor café with Avraham Burg, the twenty-seven-year-old son of Interior Minister Yosef Burg, who had volunteered as a sergeant in his old paratroop outfit despite a back injury. He fought in the bitter battle to take Sidon. Later, he became a leader in a protest movement called Soldiers Against Silence. He said his group had collected more than two thousand signatures before deciding that was enough to make the point.

"We purposely restricted those signing in support of our goals to front-line soldiers rather than peace activists," Burg told me, as we sat in the sun. "We are concerned with the damage inflicted on the army by the government's military policies. We believe that we didn't really know what we were fighting for and the government's real aims were disguised from us. Sharon has used the army for his own political goals, like pawns. This is a people's army, and we used to have an expression about our 'purity of arms.' Under Sharon, the army was not used in such a way as to maintain that purity.''

Even such a prominent establishment figure as Chaim Herzog, the former chief of military intelligence, ambassador to the United Nations, and future president, said, ''One thing is clear—the erosion which is all too evident in the defense establishment, as reflected by the tensions between the defense minister and his generals, constitutes a mortal danger to our society and to our democracy. If the government does not act immediately on this issue, it will bear the gravest possible responsibility before the people of Israel.''

In time, Begin gave in to the pressures and removed Sharon as defense minister, though the general remained in the cabinet and continued to justify his actions in Lebanon.

While in Israel, I spent a couple of days driving around occupied southern Lebanon, including a visit to Damour, a coastal town a dozen miles south of Beirut. Damour was a victim of the vicious eye-for-an-eye spiral that had wracked Lebanon since the civil war began in 1975. With its view of the Mediterranean through palms, pines, and cypresses, Damour was once the home of ten thousand Lebanese Christians. In January 1976, Palestinian guerrillas, enraged by a Christian attack earlier in the war on their refugee camp at Tel Zataar, assaulted and overran Damour. They drove out the inhabitants.

There, I found a short, chunky man wearing a polo shirt, shorts, and combat boots, who identified himself as Elia Aoun. He was working in the rubble of a house he said he was forced to evacuate six and a half years before. He carefully placed unexploded mortar shells on a stone balustrade amid the wreckage and told me, ''The Palestinians killed nine members of two families right in that house next to the church. And look what they did to the church.''

He escorted me inside what was once a jewel of a Byzantine stone chapel, the Church of St. Elias. The walls were scrawled with Palestinian slogans and papered with posters of Palestinian heroes. Three bull's-eyes were painted on the alcove behind the altar. They were scarred with bullets, evidence that it had been used as a target gallery. Outside in the graveyard, all the tombs had been opened, the marble covers shattered. Human bones lay helter-skelter in the graves. The burnt-out hulk of a jeep sat near a wall bearing a large handwritten sign: REVENGE FOR TEL ZATAAR.

The Israeli invasion drove the Palestinians out, and Christians like Aoun returned. He told me that some Christian militiamen who massacred the Palestinians at Sabra and Chatilla came from Damour. So, sadly, the cycle of violence continued, with Damour perhaps undergoing only the latest turn.

In September 1982, I headed for Beirut to help out Mike Kennedy who had been assigned to the Middle East after his stint in Belfast. The Beirut airport was closed so I flew to Larnaca in Cyprus and took the overnight ferry to the Lebanese capital. The first news I heard that morning was not auspicious.

Warships of the U.S. Sixth Fleet had opened fire against Druze positions in the mountains above the city. It was the first time that the U.S. Navy had seen fit to fire against any of the forces struggling for power in Lebanon. And, I thought, it didn't make much strategic sense.

After the Sabra-Chatilla massacres, the coverage of which had won Pulitzers for Loren Jenkins, now with the *Washington Post,* and Tom Friedman, of the *New York Times,* the United States had sent sixteen hundred Marines to Lebanon as part of a multinational peacekeeping force, along with the Italians, French, and British. At first, the Marines, like the British Army in Northern Ireland, were welcomed as protectors. But it was never clear how the Marines were supposed to avoid getting involved in the factional fighting. For the Christians saw the Marines' role as supporting the Lebanese Army and President Amin Gemayel; the Palestinians and Shias thought the Marines should protect them against Christian vengeance; and the Druze believed the Marines should keep the Christians from usurping their tribal territory in the Chouf Mountains above Beirut. For its part, Israel saw the Marines' presence as a symbol of American diplomatic support for a peace agreement between Jerusalem and the Lebanese government.

When the leathernecks first went ashore, their commander recommended that his unit occupy the high ground in the hills to the east of the airport, the defense of which was their main responsibility. The commander, with a sense of terrain and tactics, pointed out that the airfield was virtually indefensible since it had hills on two sides and its back was to the sea. But his request was overruled by Washington on political grounds: They were ordered to base on the airport alone.

For Secretary of State George Shultz and National Security Adviser Robert McFarlane had cast their lot with the enfeebled Gemayel government. U.S. support enabled Gemayel, a Maronite Christian, to stall efforts to draft a new constitution giving non-Christians a fairer share of power in Lebanon. It also seemed to put the Marines on the side of the Christians, even though they were stationed in Muslim territory.

Early in September, the Israelis summarily abandoned their positions in the Chouf, which resulted in heavy fighting for control of that vital area between the Lebanese Army and Christian militias on one side, and the tough Druze mountain people supported by Palestinians and Syrians on the other. The Marines were caught in the middle.

On September 12, Washington made an idiotic decision, one that would ultimately be disastrous for the Marines. Believing that the Christian mountain stronghold of Souq El Gharb was endangered by attacking Druze fighters, the administration declared that the defense of Souq was essential to the "safety of the Marines." This was silly since Druze and Shia gunners could already zero in on the leathernecks. The Marine commander, Colonel Timothy J. Geraghty, protested the announcement, warning that if the Sixth Fleet guns angered the Druze, "we'll get slaughtered down here."

But President Gemayel pressed Washington for U.S. naval gunfire and air strikes to defend Lebanese Army positions. The morning I arrived, the ships opened fire against Druze units in the hills. In the lobby of the Commodore Hotel, I could hear the rounds hurtling overhead.

Secretary Shultz and the U.S. embassy in Beirut argued that the naval gunfire was "defensive," which reminded me of the description of the Marines' role in Vietnam when they first landed in March 1965. I checked with the French, British, and Italian forces and they all expressed serious qualms that the United States was intervening on one side of what might be likened to a civil war. Further, they thought it ridiculous that Souq El Gharb was considered "vital to the safety of U.S. personnel," as Washington claimed in defending its new strategy.

Later that day, I drove out to the Marines' encampment to spend a couple of days with the grunts. Four Marines had been killed by random incoming fire in the previous days. A tough-looking gunnery sergeant, when I asked him about the tactical situation, said sarcastically, "It's goddamn lucky we are here on a peacekeeping mission because we are in the most untenable position of any American unit since General George Custer and the Seventh Cavalry at the Little Big Horn."

He was right. A series of hills overlooking the airport were held by Shia and Druze gunners. The Marines occupied trenches and bunkers surrounding the airfield—all on dead flat ground, totally exposed and undefendable.

"The distances are very short here," said a young captain as we walked toward the perimeter. "It's as if we were in Burbank, getting shelled from the Santa Monica mountains. Let's face it. We have no tactical advantage sitting here on the low ground. If we were in any rational situation, we'd take the high ground. As it is, we're protecting the airport as a symbol for the government. Except that the airport's been closed for weeks by shelling."

I clambered down into a bunker on the perimeter, dug from the red clay reminiscent of Vietnam, and found a twenty-five-year-old lieutenant named Ron Baczkowski, who told me that incoming fire had become routine. As he spoke, an artillery shell exploded some distance away, apparently intended for the Lebanese Army forces.

"Here we go again," said the officer. "What we have to worry about is stray incoming rounds, mixed with sniper fire. If we see somebody shooting at us, we can fire back. But we've got to be careful. We don't want to shoot into an area where innocent civilians could be hit."

In trying to explain the Marines' orders, Major Robert Jordan of the 24th Marine Amphibious Unit, told me, "We're careful to maintain our neutrality but still show anyone shooting at us that we are not paper tigers. When we were first fired at, we responded with illumination rounds to show them what we could do as a warning. When they kept it up, we fired the real thing. What we are doing is letting them know we have their phone number, and can dial it."

One of the Marines' problems, I learned, was that the Lebanese Army on one side of the airport had moved their positions closer to the U.S. forces, so shooting directed at the Christians from the Druze in the hills sometimes wandered over to Marine positions.

"We never know whether the fire we take is aimed at us or at the Lebanese," said a huge American-Samoan staff sergeant named Manusamoa Fiame, at the checkpoint he manned near a built-up community. "But when they fire our way, we shoot back. This post takes a lot of heat at night. They usually shoot from just behind those olive groves."

Privately, the Marines were critical of the newly reconstituted Lebanese Army. A young grunt dug in on the perimeter pointed out to me, "They don't seem to be methodical about clearing out houses from which they're taking fire. They just keep moving up the road and getting shot at. Hell, there's one artillery battery that has been firing all week long and the Lebs have never managed to hit it. They seem to use their artillery as an area weapon, just pumping rounds in the general direction of the target. They are never precise."

Trained for offensive action, the Marines felt constrained in their vague, ill-defined role as peacekeepers.

"By our being neutral," observed an officer over a cold can of beer, "yet by supporting the Lebanese government, we are supposed to be buying time for that government. Lots of luck. Being a peace-keeping force has plenty of frustrations. But our problems now should have been considered before they committed us, not here in midstream."

A few days later, I took a helicopter out to the nuclear-powered cruiser U.S.S. *Virginia,* one of the gunfire support ships in the Sixth Fleet patrolling offshore. The view from the ship's bridge looked like a postcard: sun sparkling on the Mediterranean, high-rise apartments on the corniche, beaches, and hills beyond. But I noticed dark smoke rising from the mountains where the warship's five-inch guns had pumped seventy-pound shells at the position of antigovernment forces. The *Virginia*'s officers said naval gunfire was being used because a moving ship was a more difficult target to hit than the stationary Marine artillery emplacements ashore.

Yet the *Virginia*'s gunnery officers had nothing to do with target selection. That was the responsibility of the higher command on another ship, which simply passed along map coordinates to the cruiser's gunnery officers.

I found it odd when an officer asked me, "Can you tell us what we've been hitting?"

As in Vietnam, the Navy seemed to be psychologically as well as physically removed from the direct action on the ground. One officer said to me, unofficially, that he understood the ship's targets to be tanks and rocket launchers in the mountains that had fired on the U.S. ambassador's residence in suburban Yarze.

I asked whether the *Virginia*'s shells, aimed from a distance of up to twelve miles, might not miss pinpoint targets.

"We won the 'E' for excellence in the Atlantic Fleet competition," explained a gunnery officer.

But, I asked, what was considered a direct hit.

"At the Culebra range off Puerto Rico," came the answer, "we consider anything within fifty yards a bull's-eye."

That might have been fine for naval gunfire pounding an enemy-held island in World War II, I thought, but fifty yards in a mountain village in Lebanon could mean the difference between hitting the target, a tank in the middle of a crossroads—or a school or church a few yards away.

Further, the *Virginia*'s officers admitted there were no U.S. personnel spotting from planes or forward observation posts to correct the fire. So it was difficult—impossible, really—for the gunners to know whether they were hitting any specific targets.

I'm afraid I left the ship unimpressed with the effectiveness of a naval cruiser as an appropriate weapon in the confused Lebanese situation. The powerful battleship U.S.S. *New Jersey* was due to arrive soon off Lebanon, having recently been taken out of mothballs. I had been aboard the battlewagon on a firing mission off North Vietnam in 1968. But it was one thing to hurl those seventeen-hundred-pound shells into a free-fire zone, where everything and everyone was considered enemy, and quite another to shoot into the Lebanese mountains aiming at "surgical" targets.

The next day, I found myself on the receiving end of the Sixth Fleet's guns. I had driven by a circuitious route—a curving road through aromatic groves of parasol pines with roughhewn mountains, yawning canyons, and unrivaled vistas—to get up to Aley, once a hill station resort for vacationing desert sheiks, but now a base for the Druze soldiers pushing along the mountain ridge south toward Souq El Gharb. During intermittent noontime shelling, I made my way to a small hospital in the middle of town, where an incoming round seemed to explode every minute or two.

"That last one was pretty close," dryly observed Dr. Abdel Abu-Assi, an American-trained physician, whose chin was a pepper-and-salt stubble, his eyes glazed with fatigue. Blast waves from the incoming artillery rattled the surgical instruments in his operating room and he complained to me, "The Lebanese Army shells us day and night, and now the American Navy is doing the same thing. I like Americans and the way they live. But I wish they would understand what this fighting is all about."

He adjusted his surgical cap and added earnestly, "This is not just a fight between Druze and Christians. It is a fight against a totally unfair government that has treated us worse than dogs or cats. We're trying to get the government to grant equal rights to all the people—as is done in the United States. The government troops will never succeed in conquering us by force."

Dr. Abu-Assi, a forty-year-old Lebanese who studied at Eastern Virginia Medical School and worked at hospitals in Newark, New Jersey, and Lincoln, Illinois, had been up all night and most of the morning and had just finished a noontime catnap when the new round of shelling erupted. He wore mismatched operating-room blue pajamas and directed three nurses as he treated wounded patients and then dispatched them to the safety of Sofar, a mountain town east of the shelling zone. The upper floors of the hospital had been hit repeatedly, so the medics worked in the basement.

During the Israeli occupation of the Chouf, the physician said, right-wing Christian militiamen were allowed—encouraged, in fact— to enter Druze villages and establish control under the protection of the Israelis. This simply exacerbated long-standing rivalries over turf in the villages.

Dr. Abu-Assi introduced me to a young woman anesthetist, wearing an operating smock and sneakers. She said to me, accusingly, "We want to know, why are the Americans helping this terrible government? This war is not just the Druze against the Christians. It is for all the Lebanese people who want equality. The government has abused all the Muslim sects—the Sunnis, the Shias, and even some other Christians—and the Falangist militia came here trying to kill us. So we don't want your Robert McFarlane making unjust deals."

Among the hospital nurses, I found Arita Gutoski, a twenty-eight-year-old American who had received her degree at the University of Wisconsin in Milwaukee and volunteered for service through the U.S. affiliate of Oxfam, the charitable agency.

"The thing that gets me the most," she said, taking a quick breather, "is the loss. The loss of families, the loss of spirit. The people are hiding in shelters most of the day and night—they are unable to walk in the open air without the threat of death or injury. I really don't think the American Marines are doing much good down there, especially when they shoot at us."

Overhearing the nurse, Dr. Abu-Assi added, "It is unfair for the Americans to take sides in this. Worse, they are backing the wrong side. This government has not provided what civilized people expect in their lives. So the American government should get out of Lebanon and let us settle our own affairs. Instead, they are shooting at us. The American naval ships have hit many houses up here, no matter what they say, so that means they are not firing simply at military targets. I repeat, it is wrong for America and Americans to act in this way."

Just then, an old man was carried into the basement receiving room with injuries from shellfire. The doctor bent over the gray-faced man on the operating table, placed a stethescope to his chest, and ordered intravenous fluids. After a quick but intensive examination, Abu-Assi looked up and in a hollow voice told me, "He is hurt but he will make it."

Farther down the mountain, I visited the headquarters of the British military contingent, which was located in an abandoned cigarette factory on a ridge overlooking the airport. The British had the smallest force—about a hundred—and were hospitable to reporters who liked to stop by their base because of its grandstand view, particularly of the Marines below and the fleet offshore. Some days, you could stand on the roof of the British base and hear the shells cracking overhead as Druze and army gunners exchanged rounds. One afternoon, I noticed a U.S. Marine equipped with long-range binoculars manning the bunker on the roof. I asked him about Bravo Company with which I had spent some time.

"I think the guys down there in Bravo are okay because they've dug in and got a lot of cover overhead around the perimeter," he said. "We're up here to see what's going on. Down there, we've been caught in the middle, so it's useful to come up here to get a different perspective on who's shooting at who."

Someone had taped a notice to the wall of the British operations office that read:

> It is the job of all dedicated officers and noncommissioned officers of the multinational force to analyze thoroughly all situations, anticipate problems prior to their occurring, have answers to those problems, and act accordingly and decisively to solve the problems when called on to do so. However, when you're up to your ass in alligators, it's difficult to remind yourself that your initial objective was to drain the swamp.

While the mission of the multinational force was not to drain the swamp, to clear Lebanon of its warring factions, the area often seemed to be overrun by alligators. Alligators with guns. The British, French, and Italians were more successful at appearing to be neutral. Through no fault of their own, however, the U.S. Marines backed up by the fleet increasingly were perceived as being partial to the Christian militiamen and the Lebanese Army. This did not bode well for the Marines.

I departed Beirut early in October, making my way south through countless checkpoints and crossing the border into Israel. On Sunday morning, October 23, 1983, a Muslim terrorist driving a flatbed truck loaded with twelve thousand pounds of high explosives—wrapped around butane gas canisters—crashed through the thin barbed-wire defenses at Marine headquarters at the airport, plowed into the entrance of a building serving as sleeping quarters, and blew it up. Some 240 Marines were killed or mortally wounded in the blast; more than 100 were wounded.

Infuriated, the Reagan administration promised retaliation. The *New Jersey* fired its sixteen-inch shells, which hit nothing of consequence. Carrier-launched jet fighter strikes, resulting in two downed American planes. A captured Navy flier was released from Syrian hands, not by threat of force, but by the intervention of the Reverend Jesse Jackson. On January 26, President Reagan totally reversed himself: The Marines whose presence was needed to safeguard the interests of the West were ordered back on ship. On March 30, the President announced the United States was unilaterally withdrawing from the multinational force, leaving its allies holding the bag.

So much for the Marines' "vital" presence in Lebanon. So much for armchair strategists in Washington dictating a totally flawed military and political policy in an area they little understood. Marine commanders were dreadfully remiss, of course, for not taking the necessary defense precautions at the base, particularly since the same type of attack was used to blow up the U.S. embassy in Beirut just six months before.

But the Marines were placed in an untenable tactical position because the U.S. secretary of state decided, for a while, that he needed a visible troop commitment to the shaky peace treaty he had fashioned between President Gemayel and the Israelis, an effort that was always doomed to failure in the Middle East. To this day, Gemayel has resisted making any significant concessions to the non-Christians. So Lebanon remains a mess, fragmented and in danger of breaking apart permanently.

The Gulf war between Iran and Iraq had been dragging on since 1980, the balance shifting first to one side and then the other. Iraq had opened the hostilities, but seeing his offensive bogged down, Iraqi president Saddam Hussein wanted to make a deal for peace. But that fierce Iranian leader, Ayatollah Khomeini, would have no peace until his archenemy, Saddam, was ousted.

You could tell how the war was going by noting which country was issuing visas to journalists. In 1984, Iraq approved my visa and I flew to Baghdad. The first problem was getting my portable typewriter past customs.

"Sorry, mister," said the man. "Typewriters are not allowed in the country."

"How can I write stories about the Iraqi defense effort without a typewriter?"

"Sorry, mister." Et cetera.

The Iraqis did not like typewriters because antigovernment tracts could be written on them, I was told later. Finally, after some histrionics and calls to the Information Ministry, I was allowed to bring in the portable. Another American reporter had his taken away to be picked up on his departure. But when he left the country, the customs room was locked.

Shortly before my visit, the Iranians had mounted a major offensive across the marshlands north of Basra, where the Tigris and Euphrates rivers join. Iranian troops managed to cross the frontier and occupy part of Majnoon Island, a low-lying piece of real estate in the middle of the marshes. They paid a steep price. Thousands of soldiers including teenage boys were slaughtered by Iraqi artillery and machine guns as they advanced in human waves reminiscent of World War I.

One morning I was taken by car on a drive of several hours to Bita, an islet in the marsh country along the Tigris River—east of the main Baghdad–Basra road. I passed the tomb of the Old Testament prophet Ezra to reach a village on the Iraqi front line. It was the closest settlement to the Iranian border and the mud huts in which residents lived were turned into bunkers for army defenders.

My escort, an Iraqi Army colonel wearing the black beret of the armored corps, pointed out the defensive positions, and said, "We've got infantry, armor, and artillery deployed around here. Any additional attack will cost the Iranians dearly. They got to within four miles of the Baghdad–Basra road. Their mortars were able to hit the highway. That was not a desirable state of affairs. But we drove them back past here. I think they have learned their lesson in this area."

Indeed, the Iraqi attack left bodies stacked almost waist high on the tiny bits of dry land at Bita. There were still pieces of bodies floating around the waters. And it seemed incredible that they could have mounted such a serious attack across this strange mixture of earth and lake.

This was the country of the marsh Arabs, more water than land, with hundreds of thousands of acres of bulrushes, papyrus, and other reeds, and the occasional clump of land. On bits of ground, the inhabitants built distinctive reed houses. There were few roads. Travel was by the long, slender reed canoes. The horizon was endless, the sky vacant, except for a relentless sun scorching everything below in the intense heat. For years, the marsh Arabs were known only to each other—and to anthropologists and naturalists who came to study the culture and abundant bird and fish life. And a few journalists like my friends Gavin Young and Nik Wheeler who produced an elegant pictorial book on the marsh Arabs.

The pastoral scene now had a military look: cannon, tanks, antiaircraft batteries, troops. Engineers attempted to flood out Iranian military positions by diverting the confluence of the Tigris and Euphrates rivers into the marsh lagoons, raising the water level above some of the low-lying islands.

Despite the military buildup, the marsh Arabs continued to pursue a pattern of living that has changed little since pre-Sumerian times. "They have followed this way of life for thousands of years," said the colonel. "It will take more than a war to change that."

But in Basra, I found, a classic way of life had changed drastically. Basra is the main port on the Shatt-al-Arab and the legendary home of Sinbad the Sailor. During the war, its docks were empty and it was regularly shelled by long-range Iranian artillery. Nevertheless, the Sheraton chain opened a new hotel there. It was designed to attract citizens from nearby Kuwait—an observant Muslim country that bans alcohol, gambling, and prostitution. By Gulf standards, Iraq was a liberated country that allowed wine, women, and song. So Kuwaiti sheiks, flush with their oil royalties, drove across the border to Basra for long weekends of gambling in the hotel casino, drinking wine from France, whiskey from Scotland and Kentucky, while entertaining sporting ladies imported from the Far East.

Though Iraq is mainly Sunni Muslim, it has a large Shia minority, as well as the two holiest cities in the Shia religion, Karbala and An Najaf. One day, I drove to the holy places, a couple of hours south of Baghdad. Karbala is graced by the golden dome of the Imam Hussein Mosque and An Najaf has a similar monument to honor Ali, the prophet Muhammad's son-in-law. Shias believe that Ali, and Ali's son, Hussein, were wrongfully deposed and that only their descendants are eligible to be the Imam, or leader of the faith. When Khomeini first went into exile from Iran, he came to Najaf to reside at the theological center there and to preach against the Shah. But in 1975, when the Shah made a deal with Saddam Hussein to settle their border problems and repress the Kurdish uprising, Khomeini was forced to stop his anti-Shah propaganda. The Ayatollah moved to Paris. Khomeini never forgave the Shah or Saddam. So the holy cities are shrines not only for Shias; for Iranians they involve a special tribute to Khomeini.

Thousands of Iraqi Shias who died in the war are buried at Najaf's huge Vale of Peace cemetery. I saw orange-and-white taxis from all over southern Iraq—where the Shia population is concentrated—driving along the highway with coffins lashed to their roof racks, mourners behind in other vehicles. Near the golden dome and two minarets of the Iman Hussein mosque, the Iraqis had positioned a captured Iranian tank as a monument.

Devout Iranians would dearly like to visit the cities. For instance, I talked to some young Iranian prisoners of war in a detention camp outside Baghdad and they told me they were instructed by their mullahs that, if they would attack boldly across the border, they would soon arrive at the holy city of Karbala, with the promise of eternal reward. However, the distance was actually two hundred miles and the only way the young Iranian soldiers eventually got to the shrine was on a bus tour, courtesy of their Iraqi captors.

I returned from the holy cities and Shia mysteries to my flashy, modern hotel in Baghdad. It had a well-stocked bar, open even during the Muslim fasting month of Ramadan, and a gambling casino with pretty girls from England working as croupiers and shills. On one Friday, the Muslim holy day, I decided to write by the pool. I was astonished to see three or four lovely English girls in bikinis, lying on their deck chairs, totally topless. Saddam's Baghdad was a long, long way from Khomeini's Tehran.

That distance was the problem in settling the Gulf war. For the war was really thirteen hundred years old, dating from the original religious conflict that splits Islam. The battle was not only between Arabs and Persians but between Muslim sects (Iranian Shias versus Iraqi Sunnis), visions (Iranian fundamentalism versus Iraqi secularism), and, today, personalities (Khomeini versus Saddam). The prize was immense: hegemony in the Gulf with its fabulous oil wealth.

Saddam Hussein foolishly started a war that he could not quickly end; he took on a nation of forty million with Shia fanatics prepared to die for their country, arrayed against his own country of only fourteen million. When Saddam realized his mistake, he found that Khomeini was not a leader to let bygones be bygones and agree to peace. Khomeini will settle only for Saddam's head.

"The war will only end with a change of heart in Tehran," Sir John Graham, the British ambassador, told me one night at dinner. "And that will probably come only after Khomeini no longer holds power in Iran."

In April 1984, I had a stroke of good fortune. North Vietnam was allowing in a limited number of foreign reporters to cover the thirtieth anniversary of the fall of Dien Bien Phu. Our man in Bangkok, who would normally have been assigned to the story, was on home leave, and foreign editor Al Shuster asked me if I'd be interested. It was a rhetorical question. After several long-distance calls to the Vietnamese press attaché in Bangkok, I was promised a visa and was off to Bangkok. I hadn't been to Vietnam since the fall of Saigon and I had never gotten north of the 17th Parallel except at sea.

I flew from Bangkok to Hanoi. The scars of the war were finally healing around the capital. The bomb craters near Gia Lam airfield had been converted into fishponds and the creaky old Long Bien Bridge across the Red River, which U.S. planes never managed to put out of action, was still in use. It was sometimes called the world's longest bridge because of the time needed to cross it. The two traffic lanes were separated by a railroad line over which elderly steam engines pulled long strings of cars. Traffic on each lane was reduced to the speed of a bicycle. However, a new bridge, the Long Thanh, with double lanes each way was being finished just upriver.

Outside Hanoi, drivers were crazy, blowing their horns loudly as if assuming all pedestrians, cyclists, and animals would quickly move aside as they charged their vehicles down the road with a fatalism worthy of their counterparts in the Middle East. Inside the city, things were quieter, for there were few cars and trucks to be seen. Instead, I was swamped in a sea of bicycles jamming the wide, French-designed, tree-shaded avenues. Tranquil Hanoi seemed out of key with most Asian cities and their cacophony.

My first hotel, the Hoa Binh (meaning Peace), was a disappointment, to say the least. The pipes had deteriorated and were being repaired. There was no hot water or running water for the toilet. But never mind. I was in Hanoi. In many ways, Hanoi was even prettier than Saigon since it had a central lake called Hoan Kiem in the middle of town, a lovely amenity, with a couple of smaller lakes not far away.

Around the lake were ice-cream parlors and teahouses, where the young set gathered for drinks and conversation. Few women were dressed in the traditional flowing costume known as the ao dai. Nearly everyone wore plain pajama-style garb, save for the young and affluent who preferred U.S.-style jeans.

The sidewalks were rolled up early in Hanoi. Power was shut down in various parts of the city during certain hours. The only lights at night often were the tiny lamps of cigarette sellers along the boulevards. It seemed to me that Hanoi, after so many years of struggle, had developed a stoicism, almost apathy, much different from the dynamism of other major Asian cities. I could have been in a city in Tibet. My pedicab creaked along empty, darkened streets. All was silent except for the whoosh of a passing bicycle. I never felt any sense of danger though I was a citizen of the country that had subjected the city to fearful bombings.

Under the few streetlights that were kept on in the block that housed the central post and telegraph office, young women walked together along the middle of the street, back and forth. At first, I thought they might literally be streetwalkers, but when I checked they said they were students who found it easier and cheaper to study their textbooks under the municipal lights than use small oil lamps at home.

I found a wonderful little restaurant on a back street that served delicious crab farci and pigeon with mushrooms. You entered the place through a smelly back alley that would have caused most food writers to faint, and the two upstairs rooms were among the grottiest I've ever been in. But the food was immaculate, the atmosphere raffish, and the proprietor came up with fine bottles of Bordeaux unavailable anywhere else in town. After dinner, I'd stroll back to my hotel past the Catholic cathedral and the lake, feeling euphoric. I seemed to be the only one out on the street after midnight, and this induced in me a mood of great calm.

The Information Ministry organized a trip in a small van to the Chinese border for a briefing on inroads the Peking troops were supposedly making against the Vietnamese. We rattled over a potholed road to the provincial capital of Lang Son, about ninety miles northeast of Hanoi. The senior provincial official, a man named Phi Long, was hospitable but he said we couldn't approach the border itself because it was too dangerous.

I scoffed at this, pointing out the only reason we made the long journey was to see the frontier and the Chinese positions beyond. I

went so far as to suggest there was no point in having lunch with him
if he couldn't get us to the border, which was what we had come for.
Finally, after several phone calls, he announced firing had subsided
and we could indeed drive to the border town of Dong Dang at the
Munan Pass, which served as a main road and rail artery during the
war, when China was Vietnam's ally. Peking sent military supplies to
Hanoi over what was then known as Friendship Pass.

Now, however, the historic enmity between Vietnam and China
had surfaced. The provincial officials showed us the wreckage left
behind from 1979 when the Chinese, in retaliation for the Vietnamese
invasion of Cambodia, crossed the border and shot up the countryside,
which still bore the scars: abandoned, half-destroyed houses and
downed bridges. It appeared the damage was left intact as proof of
Chinese aggression.

From a hill at the entrance to Dong Dang, I could see across the
valley to China. It was a classic Chinese sylvan scene except for the
two radar scanners monitoring activity along the frontier. A Vietnamese guide told me that the reverse side of the hill held a command post
for a Chinese assault battalion and for the artillery that covered the area
around the pass. The guide said, too, that four people had been killed
and fifty wounded in the past few days as the flare-ups continued. I
gathered from the trip that the military activity along the border had
become something of a spring rite, a Chinese reprisal for the annual
dry-season offensive the Vietnamese invariably kicked off in Cambodia. Both sides tended to exaggerate the extent of the conflict: the
Vietnamese, because they wanted to depict the Chinese as bullies
before the world; the Chinese, because they wished to emphasize their
commitment to the Cambodians.

Driving back to Hanoi over the fourth-class road, it struck me just
how desperately poor Vietnam was. Many bridges and structures had
simply never been repaired after the American bombing, though the
campaign had ended more than a decade before. There was very little
modern physical plant to be seen along the route. Buildings, bridges,
roads, communication lines, all seemed to be falling apart. Animals
were the main form of transport and water buffalos in the rice fields the
main beast of burden.

For despite its natural resources in coal and rice as well as water,
Vietnam remains one of the poorest countries in the world, with an
annual per capita income of around $140, and it is rapidly falling
behind its Asian neighbors.

What astonished me in Hanoi was the latest population figures I obtained. While I was in Vietnam in the 1960s, we usually listed the population of South Vietnam at fifteen or sixteen million, with a roughly equal figure for North Vietnam, or a total of some thirty million or so. In spite of the brutal years of war and the hundreds of thousands of deaths, the population of the country had soared to an incredible sixty million. What human fecundity! But this meant that a nation that was once the rice granary of Southeast Asia had trouble feeding itself.

Matters weren't helped by Vietnam's having a standing army of 1 million men, the third largest in the world, 160,000 of whom were stationed in Cambodia and another 40,000 in Laos. So thousands of men who might be working on farms were kept in the army, which was eating up one third of the national income.

In talking to officials in Hanoi, I gathered that they blamed Chinese aggression for some of their economic problems, since so much effort and manpower were devoted to the armed forces. For though the Vietnamese had fought, defeated or repulsed the Japanese, the French, the Americans and the Chinese, the country after a decade of reunification was economically hanging by its fingernails.

"Unfortunately, after forty years of war, the guns have not been silenced," a Communist party official named Hoang Tung told me. "So our first priority must be to repel the aggressor. Security must come before economic well-being. We are facing the greatest difficulties right now. The people are living a hard life but they are getting by. We're just making ends meet."

Economy Minister Tran Phuong was equally frank. "I don't want to hide the backward nature of our country," he said. "We haven't been able to make full use of our workers for many reasons. And it may take ten years to solve this."

Why had not the industrious Vietnamese prospered like other East Asian nations after reunification? The question fascinated me.

The consensus of experienced diplomats in the capital seemed to be that Vietnam's brand of state socialism turned out to be an unmitigated disaster.

"Under President Ho Chi Minh," a Western ambassador told me, "the Vietnamese leaders set their goals single-mindedly on creating a Vietnamese state through revolutionary warfare. They achieved that goal but they have not seemed to be able to do much else. So far, none of the old leaders has been able to make the shift from running a revolution to running a country, let alone a complex economy."

And another Western ambassador looked at it this way: "The North Vietnamese have a superb talent for war but, so far, not much else. They just don't know how to run things. Everything is stop and go. No one wants to make the tough decisions about the economy. Everyone keeps passing the buck up to the secret level of the politburo."

For instance, Scandinavian nations built plants: the Swedes a large paper mill, the Danes a cement factory, and the Finns a ship repair yard. But Westerners who visited these installations told me the Vietnamese had simply not learned to run them properly.

"They just haven't adjusted to the realities of running a factory," a Scandinavian diplomat explained, in exasperation. "They will take visitors to meet the girl on the assembly line who is said to have personally helped shoot down a B-52. As if that makes the factory function properly."

In my wanderings around the city, I saw small markets in the side streets, bustling with a lively trade in chickens, ducks, rabbits, rice, corn, greens, carrots, onions, cucumbers, tomatoes, pineapples, and fish.

I asked a UN official who had been based in Hanoi several years what to make of these free markets and he shrugged. "It's not socialism but it works. And therefore it's embarrassing to the regime. The whole system is a contradiction. Is it a socialist economy or a free economy or a mixed one? They seem to keep changing the signals."

A few days before the thirtieth anniversary of the fall of Dien Bien Phu, we set out aboard an old, yellow school bus for a trip to that historic valley in the northwestern corner of Vietnam. It was a long, bone-crunching two-day journey, three hundred miles over an unimproved road, across dozens of mountain ridges and deep valleys, climbing higher and higher. We set out through the lush, emerald-green fields of the Red River valley, passing an old baroque cathedral, a reminder of the long period of French rule. The road climbed through a bamboo forest into the foothills, and then, in a series of switchbacks with precipitous drops, into mountains shrouded in mists. We spent the first night in a small guest hostel in Son La, a provincial capital where the French once imprisoned such Communist nationalist figures as party leaders Le Duan and Truong Chinh. I squeezed myself into one of the underground punishment cells for a few minutes and I quickly got some inkling of the hatred the imprisoned Vietminh revolutionaries developed for French colonial rule and rulers.

On the second day's drive, I noticed how scarred the mountainsides were. The uninitiated, flying high overhead in a jetliner, might blame this on wartime air strikes or defoliant spray. But no. The hideous gaps were caused by the montagnard practice of slash-and-burn farming, that is, cutting down trees and burning them to provide a clearing and phosphate from the ashes, and planting a season's crop of manioc. The next season, they moved on to the next mountain.

We passed several convoys of soldiers in ancient trucks struggling over the roads, which turned off on the main highway to Laos, where the Vietnamese were supporting the Pathet Lao regime. Finally, toward late afternoon, we crested the last of the ridgelines and in a remote corner of the country, descended into the high, hot, flat valley of Dien Bien Phu.

The French had positioned their garrison of paratroopers and legionnaires in Dien Bien Phu because of its strategic location guarding the route into Laos. They wanted to lure the Vietminh into attacking what the French generals thought was an impregnable position. But the French had created a trap for themselves. They occupied only the valley floor, airstrip, and several surrounding hillocks, which they turned into strongpoints the French commander, Brigadier General Christian de Castries, reportedly named after his mistresses: Gabrielle, Anne-Marie, Beatrice, Hugette, Dominique, Claudine, Eliane, and Isabelle.

But the French neglected to occupy the higher ground beyond, believing that it wouldn't be necessary because the Vietminh couldn't drag heavy weapons over the rugged mountains. How wrong they were. Under the brilliant direction of General Vo Nguyen Giap, the Vietnamese did just that: They hauled by brute force heavy artillery pieces up into the mountains that ringed Dien Bien Phu and opened up a fifty-five-day siege that made life a literal hell for the French defenders. The Vietnamese cut them off from the world and forced a surrender on May 7, 1954.

I had spoken of the war to General Giap in Hanoi, who told me that American policymakers were poor students of history and hadn't learned of the power inherent in a "people's struggle."

"The Americans," he said in his quiet voice, "were on the side of the colonialists and Dien Bien Phu was the bell that tolled the twilight of colonialism."

Giap was then seventy-three and vice-premier; he was slight but erect with steel-gray hair, dressed in a simple green uniform with four gold stars on his red collar tabs but no ribbons or decorations, though he had won more than his share. For him, the lesson of the battle was the superiority of morale and motivation over firepower and hardware.

"The French had modern equipment and air strikes," he told me. "But the most important thing in war is people. Unfortunately, the American imperialists did not learn from experience. They are not good pupils. Wars of national liberation are bound to win—but American generals are not very apt students of history. Dien Bien Phu paved the way for us to defeat the French, later the Americans, and now to defend our country against the Chinese."

In Dien Bien Phu, I met Lieutenant Colonel Luong Din Chin, then commander of the military district who had been a young platoon leader in the final assault at Strongpoint Eliane. Standing atop the hill, the wiry, little soldier recalled, "We had the strongpoint surrounded and we tunneled in about one hundred yards with a two-thousand-pound load of explosives. The blast gave the signal for the final attack. It blew up many French defenders. We charged. It was very close quarters with grenades and bayonets and we finally conquered the hill."

De Castries surrendered his eleven thousand remaining men that afternoon. Some five thousand French troops, among the finest in the army, were killed during the siege.

The Vietnamese were turning the battlefield into a sort of national monument and tourist attraction, with de Castries's bunker preserved as well as the dugout in which the French artillery commander killed himself in mortification. For those French defenders, there was one testament to their sacrifice: a white cross on a gravelike mound erected by the Vietnamese with a plaque bearing the words THIS IS TO MARK THE GRAVES OF THE FRENCH SOLDIERS WHO DIED HERE.

In the village of Dien Bien Phu, which had a population of about thirty-five hundred, the Vietnamese had built a guest house for visitors. There was a small souvenir shop, selling rattan fans, canvas shoulder bags, and a tatty-looking tiger skin priced at $350. At the bar, a chipper young waitress served me a cold can of Japanese Asahi beer. I paid for it with a dollar bill. The waitress gave me back two U.S. dimes in change. All the way to Dien Bien Phu to find twenty cents American in change! There were few bars in the world, outside the United States, where you'd be given American coins back.

Instead of taking the grueling two-day trip back by bus, we were able to catch the weekly Air Vietnam flight direct to Hanoi. As we

waited on the tarmac, some soldiers appeared with two wounded comrades to be put aboard the plane. They had been hit near the Chinese
border, we learned, and one young trooper on a stretcher was only half
conscious, his blackened toes protruding from a dirty cast. His face
was contorted in pain but he made no sound. The plane landed, a
Soviet-made turboprop. But the three-man crew drove off into town for
lunch as we all stood by. It was blisteringly hot and the soldiers waited
patiently under the wing of the plane. Finally, the crew returned and
we all got aboard. In Hanoi, there was no ambulance or anyone else to
meet the soldiers. The badly injured man on the stretcher was carried
by porters to an alcove in the terminal where he lay in obvious discomfort. When we collected our baggage thirty minutes later and took
off for town, I noticed that the soldier still lay there.

In Hanoi, I again sought out Hoang Tung, the member of the
Secretariat of the Central Committee of the Communist party, to ask
him about American servicemen who were still listed as missing in
action during the war. The issue was a sensitive one in the United
States: In addition to the twenty-five hundred MIAs listed by the Pentagon, reports surfaced from time to time that U.S. servicemen were
being held alive in prison camps in Indochina. Such reports, however,
have never been confirmed by the Defense Department.

Tung flatly denied that any Americans were being held alive by
the Vietnamese, and he added that "to the best of my knowledge" no
U.S. prisoners were in captivity in Laos or Cambodia, either. The
official, who also edited the Communist paper *Nhan Dan,* was quick to
admit that resolving the MIA issue "would be good for relations
between the United States and Vietnam."

But when it came to searching for the remains of MIAs, Tung said
the United States and Vietnam had different priorities: The Vietnamese
simply did not have the time or resources to explore the mountainous
jungle locations where most of the missing fliers and soldiers were
thought to have perished. But his positive attitude about the matter may
have reflected the leadership's later decision to permit limited searches
by American teams to seek out crash sites.

Less emphatically, Tung denied the existence of a warehouse in
Hanoi where, some sources said, the remains of U.S. servicemen had
been collected and, from time to time, released to the Americans.

I sounded out Western diplomatic sources in Hanoi on the subject
and they agreed there was little possibility that any Americans were
still kept in detention. The Vietnamese had no reason for such action,

they said. However, one diplomat pointed out that there was always the possibility that some individual GIs, a half-dozen deserters or so, might be living in the backwoods with their women. Or there could be Frenchmen left behind from the previous war. The possible existence of such Westerners might, he said, account for the sporadic reports of mysterious sightings of Caucasians in the hills of Indochina.

My visa was running out and I dearly wanted to get to Saigon to see what it was like, though it was not on the official schedule. The Hanoi authorities tried to discourage me, indicating that not much was going on in the south. But I went to Duong Minh, the head of the foreign press section, and told him that while I had put in my formal application to see the tourism minister in Saigon, I really wanted to return simply for old times' sake. I had lived there for four years, I said, and my infant son grew up there. Minh was sympathetic: I was allowed to purchase a round-trip ticket for myself and an escort on the daily Air Vietnam 707 flight to Ho Chi Minh City.

I was up at 4:30 on a Sunday morning. I asked my driver to take me by the Catholic cathedral in Hanoi. The bells pealed across the city calling the faithful to worship, by far the loudest sound in the capital in the early hours. Inside the church, I saw that about two hundred people had turned up for the first mass of the day, celebrated by a priest dressed in ornate white-and-gold vestments. It all seemed so peaceful and old-fashioned, as if set in amber from a time before the upheavals of Vatican II changed the liturgy in Western churches. Outside, I had a traditional Vietnamese breakfast of pho, a tangy soup with meat and vegetable greens cooked in a pot at a sidewalk stand.

In Ho Chi Minh City, on the way to my hotel, the old Majestic, I asked the driver to stop by the cathedral in time to observe the end of a late-morning mass. There was a good-sized crowd, with younger worshipers than I had seen in Hanoi. I had scored a double-header in masses that Sunday morning in two cathedrals hundreds of miles apart. Not bad for a fallen-away Catholic.

Later that morning, I suggested a Sunday drive to Vung Tau, the resort on the South China Sea, where we used to go for the surf and lobster, and where Jenkins and I interviewed refugees from central Vietnam in 1975. Vung Tau also served as an R and R center for American troops. The French called the place Cap St.-Jacques and built bougainvillea-covered villas amid the stands of pines and palms, turning it into a Southeast Asian mini-Riviera. The beach club was still there, reserved for foreigners, but now the spacious beaches were filled with white-skinned, overweight Eastern Europeans and Russians.

I noted a sign in the beach club with regulations posted in Vietnamese, Russian, and English, warning THE OVERDOSE OF ALCOHOL IS UNADVISABLE BEFORE DIVING INTO THE WATER.

Another notice cautioned bathers IN CASE OF DANGER, YOU HAVE TO PAY FOR THE COST OF RESCUE SERVICES.

Though most of the Russians could not have been mistaken for anything else, one fellow had picked up some American sartorial ideas. He wore a denim work cap, cut-off jeans, and running shoes. Another potbellied man wore a T-shirt adorned with the five-ringed 1980 Moscow Olympics symbol. I tried to chat with him but he said, "No speak English. Speak Russian."

Many of the Russians on the beach were involved in the petroleum industry since Vung Tau was the center for offshore drilling in Vietnam. My escort and the driver told me that the Russians were unpopular in Vietnam, despite their economic aid and support for the country.

"They are arrogant and are cheap with their money," said the driver. "We still like the Americans better, when they come."

How strange. The Vietnamese still preferred Americans after all we had inflicted on them, despite our cultural incompatibility, and our rough, vulgar ways, we round-eyed bulls in an Asian china shop. But this was the same reaction I discovered in Cairo when the Russians were riding high under Nasser. There is an enormous potential reservoir of goodwill for Americans in many unlikely places. It's a pity we don't make better use of it.

Vung Tau was famous for its seafood, and I hosted lunch for my escort and driver with excellent lobster, crayfish, and shrimp and washed down by an imported, iced, French white wine.

Apart from the attraction of sun, sea, and seafood, Vung Tau drew hundreds of weekend visitors from distant places to an important Buddhist shrine. We drove past it and saw dozens of buses with day-trippers from as far away as the Mekong Delta.

"Southerners are much more superstitious than us northerners," said my escort who came from Hanoi and was visiting the south for the first time. "We have very few temples in the north."

Vung Tau's fishing harbor was also the jumping-off place for hundreds of "boat people," who secretly set out hoping for a better life elsewhere. These poor souls, I was told, had to pay up to two thousand dollars in hard currency to get aboard a boat for the chancy voyage to freedom.

On the way back to Saigon, I asked the driver to detour past Long

Binh, once the site of one of the largest U.S. military installations anywhere, the headquarters for the U.S. Army in Vietnam. There wasn't much left of it. The Vietnamese had not put the dozens of buildings to any use and the military complex seemed to be fading back into the jungle, like some kind of strange, secular Angkor Wat.

Back in Saigon, I had a chat with the head of tourism for Ho Chi Minh City, a small man named Nguyen Vu, who sketched out the country's plans to attract foreign visitors. He said he hoped that one day Americans would outnumber the Russians on the sands of Vung Tau. After several cups of tea, he asked me what I thought of the chances of luring Americans, particularly those who had lived, worked, or fought in Vietnam. I always thought that Vietnam was one of the most scenic places in the world, with its dramatic mountains, triple-canopy jungle, lush rice fields, long expanses of sandy beaches, lively cities, and graceful people. I told Vu I could see the attraction: tours of Ho Chi Minh City and Hanoi; a visit to the old imperial capital at Hue; Da Nang, and the remains of the Cham civilization; the coastal resort of Nha Trang; the mountain retreat of Da Lat; the Mekong Delta; the beautiful Hai Long Bay, with its islands in the northern Gulf of Tonkin. He suggested visits to the Vietcong tunnels around Cu Chi, or even a one-day trip down the Ho Chi Minh Trail. A two-week, all-inclusive trip for foreigners.

"It's a great idea, Mr. Vu," I said. "But you've got to do something about those crummy hotels in Hanoi. They're really dreadful, particularly for a tourist spending hard currency, not some Eastern European official on a free trip. But you also want to keep Vietnam unspoiled and not mess it up like the Spanish coast."

I suggested that he contact a professional outfit like the Club Méditerranée that knew how to construct comfortable quarters without spoiling the natural beauty in tropical vacation places. With the traditional French link to Vietnam, I said, I could see tourism developing, if not flourishing, given the right accommodations. I added I thought there'd be a market, too, for U.S. Vietnam veterans, who'd like to return some day after they had saved some money and were looking for an offbeat vacation. He nodded agreement. We left it at that.

I liked the Majestic, a tall, buff-colored hotel at the end of Tu-Do street on the Saigon River. I found many proper names in the city changed by the Communist regime, including, of course, Saigon itself. But few people called it Ho Chi Minh City, except officially. The Majestic was now the Cuu Long, or Nine Dragons, which was not bad.

The place still catered to foreign guests, but the Caravelle up the street was reserved for Eastern European VIPs. I knew my escort wanted to look up a brother he hadn't seen for some time, so I suggested he take the evening off. Besides, I wasn't crazy about having a government shadow.

I decided to try for dinner in Cholon, the Chinese section of town, at the Arc-en-ciel (Rainbow), which had been popular with Americans and the French before them. In front of the hotel, I spotted a pedicab driver, who, though aged, seemed eager. We rattled off down the wide boulevard known as Tran Hung Dao, after an ancient patriot whose name was still acceptable to the Communist regime. I was startled at the amount of traffic in early evening. There were few large cars, none of the trucks and jeeps that once clogged the streets. But there were thousands of motorbikes and hundreds of jitney buses spewing clouds of noxious fumes and creating a continual din. In the past, I had taken taxis to Cholon, and I now found the leisurely pace of the pedicab pleasant indeed. The street was crammed with sights and memories. As we creaked past the apartment blocks that once served as American military and CIA billets, I remembered the various occasions when we'd had to race there after a terrorist bomb had gone off. Now the sand-filled oil drums, which served as protection for the billets, had been removed but the wire netting installed to ward off grenade and rocket attacks was in many cases still in place.

As we bicycled down the boulevard, it seemed as if every one of the city's three million inhabitants was out on the street, moving with us, against us, or cutting across stream. In Cholon, the Arc-en-ciel was open for business. I asked the driver in French if he would wait.

"Sure, Joe, I wait," he said in English. "No sweat."

No sweat! That expression out of the past seemed to wipe away fifteen years.

The Arc was deafening with hi-fi speakers blaring out rock tapes, well past the threshold of pain. So I got back in the pedicab and drove to the Eskimo, another old favorite. It still wore a coat of green paint but looked empty and depressing so I headed back downtown. The driver suggested a Chinese place not far from the hotel. It was small but first-rate with excellent crab and rice.

Later, I strolled up the short main drag, which the French had called Rue Catinat, the Diem regime renamed Tu-Do (Freedom), and which was now changed to Dong Khoi (Uprising) Street. Most of the bars were still in place but converted to coffeehouses with new names.

They offered warm beer and sedate waitresses, a far cry from the riotous scenes that once characterized the joints. The miniskirted, gum-chewing bar girls were gone, many sent to rehabilitation camps. They were long freed, but there were still an estimated ten thousand inmates of the camps who had been designated war criminals and were incarcerated indefinitely.

I checked out Nguyen Hue, the Street of Flowers, where the blossom stands were still open, and saw a line of American sedans, the only ones I had seen in Vietnam. They were Chevrolets and Plymouths, painted red-and-white and used as limousines for wedding receptions and special events. Even under Communist rule, the Saigonais liked to put on the dog.

It was just before the 10:00 P.M. curfew and as I approached the Caravelle Hotel, a pretty girl sitting in a cyclo asked if I'd like to have a coffee, "after-hours."

Curious, I said yes. She waved down a second pedicab, which I clambered into. We proceeded in tandem to an attractive villa in the heart of the old foreign residential section, a couple of blocks north of the cathedral. There, couples sat at tables on the front lawn under the flame trees, with subdued lighting, and sipped coffee. I asked for a beer and a few minutes later, a can of Japanese brew appeared. The girl introduced me to her friend, equally winsome. I bought a round. My companion indicated discreetly that I might take one or both home. At a price, naturally. I was tempted. But I gathered they lived with relatives in a crowded quarter near the airport. The thought of skulking around a Vietnamese household, avoiding mothers and grandmothers, at midnight didn't appeal to me as much as it once might have. I tipped handsomely: I was heartened to find that the chance for hanky-panky still existed in Ho Chi Minh City.

The next morning, I found one of the liveliest markets I had seen in Asia. It was not far from the city hall and anything but secret. Yet on display at fantastically high prices was an incredible variety of consumer goods: cognac, bicycles, motorbikes, refrigerators, calculators, television sets, tape decks, videos, stereo equipment. The speakers were pouring forth American pop music, which seemed to have become firmly entrenched in this Communist stronghold. Some of the stands sold clothing, with T-shirts and jeans in great demand. The single most popular item appeared to be a blue denim cap with a badge over the beak, the sort of covering you saw on American golfers and farmers.

Much of the stuff came through the port of Saigon. I was told that three directors of customs had been fired for corruption in the past two years. I could believe it. With all those electronic delights, I could see, the temptation for skimming off a percentage was immense.

The city, by whatever name, still operated in the freewheeling, southern style it had when I lived there. Its temperament was totally different from the austere northern Hanoi. I decided that the Vietnam of the future would be more southern than northern if it were to prosper, though the north had won the war. Like Greece co-opting Rome. The southern Vietnamese approach is much more flexible and sophisticated, based on generations of dealing in a free market economy where the iron laws of supply and demand prevail. The southerners knew the mechanism of marketing, how to buy and sell rice. They had a natural bent for trade. And they viewed their northern comrades, who were tough enough warriors, the way big-city boys look patronizingly upon country cousins.

In a pedicab, I rode by the former Independence Palace, the gates of which were knocked down by North Vietnamese tanks two days after I left in 1975, officially ending the war. It was now called the People's Committee Hall. A few blocks up Thong Nhut Boulevard, the walled compound of the U.S. embassy was the Ministry for Petroleum. Across the street, the British embassy had been turned into a sports center.

I stopped at my old house at 9A Tu-Xuong Street. It hadn't changed much: a white stucco, two-story villa with a red tile roof behind a beige wall with a green iron gate. I wondered who lived there now, but I didn't inquire. My wife had bought some exquisite Vietnamese porcelain pieces when we lived there. I had never been much of a collector during my travels, but I thought I should obtain something while in Vietnam. I called on Mme. Nguyen Phuoc Dai, who was South Vietnam's first woman lawyer. In 1967, she was elected to the Senate, and became an outspoken opponent of the Thieu government. Despite her criticism (or more likely because of it), Mme. Dai was given a hard time by the new regime, her home was confiscated, and she was forced to move into her law office.

She had a wonderful collection of old Vietnamese pieces, which was buttressed by those of friends who wanted to sell their things for hard currency. I picked out a few small pieces: a lovely early Annamese twelfth-century bowl and a couple of thirteenth-century celadon dishes. She wrapped them professionally, and put them into a flight bag. I departed with some superlative mementoes of Vietnam.

Back at the main square, I passed the old Rex Hotel at the corner of Nguyen Hue and Le Loi. This used to be the headquarters for the U.S. Information Agency and was the location for the afternoon military briefing, "the Five O'clock Follies." Above the offices were rooms for U.S. Army officers, and the roof had a restaurant that featured outdoor steak barbecues. Curiously, I found the Rex still in operation as a hotel, renamed the Ben Thanh (Perfect Place). Even more curiously, the barbecues continued under new Communist management accompanied by a Saturday night dance that was the most popular social event of the week for the swinging, young Saigon crowd and visiting Communist firemen.

Across the street, I noticed dozens of new motorbikes parked outside a couple of the former high-rise hotels on Nguyen Hue Boulevard. I saw more of these outside one hotel than in all of Hanoi. Checking inside, I discovered that the coffee shops in these ex-hotels had all been converted into minitheaters to show videos imported from Paris on the weekly Air France flight. Watching the videos on Saturday and Sunday afternoons was the main entertainment for teenagers in Ho Chi Minh City—just as moviegoing had been for me at the Granada Theater in Chicago.

I walked into the old Continental Palace Hotel, where I lived for a year and spent the month of April in 1975. The place was a shambles: They were turning it into a guest house for official visitors and the lovely interior garden was filled with debris and building materials. The "Continental Shelf," where you could once sip drinks and watch Southeast Asia go by, was empty and sad.

Across the square, I took the elevator to the top of the Caravelle, where I had spent my first night in Saigon nearly twenty years before. The Caravelle, too, had a new name, Doc Lap (Independence). But the decor hadn't changed—all plate glass and marble. It remained as a generation of reporters remembered it. I walked out on the roof terrace in the rose light of late afternoon. The setting sun brought out the rich siena of the cathedral's brick facade, and it caught the Vietnamese flag—red with a yellow star—that fluttered from the city hall.

An elderly waiter with a familiar face brought me a can of Heineken in a silver wine cooler filled with ice. I was his only customer and he said, "Times are bad here now. I can make enough money for myself, but how do I support the rest of my family? Yes, there are plenty of things available in Saigon, but one has to pay a very high price. I can't afford the price. I remember the days when this hotel was full of American journalists. Those were the good times."

Good times for some, bad times for others. For tens of thousands of Americans, the trip to Vietnam had been a one-way ticket. I was one of the lucky ones. I had come to the country voluntarily. I had, despite the horror, been able to enjoy the city and country. As a reporter, I was involved in the most important story of my time. I had been unscathed physically, and unlike some friends, undamaged emotionally. The latter perhaps was a measure of insensitivity. I don't know.

On the terrace, I stared off toward the airport and remembered that the French military cemetery was still there. A reminder of a war before the Americans, equally frustrating and unsuccessful. But there is no memorial in Vietnam to the fifty-eight thousand Americans who lost their lives in the conflict. Only that black marble wall back in Washington with all those names.

I remembered how we used to gather on this terrace to watch the action when battles were close to the city. We journalists were outsiders here—observers, voyeurs—able to watch death and destruction at some remove, with a drink in our hand. We could depart when it suited us.

Twenty years later, I was back, again with a drink in my hand. I had been made to feel comfortable here, even welcome, despite the carnage wreaked by my generation. It was puzzling.

In the old days up here, the firing around the city seemed to increase at dusk; perhaps that was when the sound traveled more readily. It was dusk now, but all was calm as the tropical sky darkened from soft rose to deep violet. Even the noise of the motorbikes below seemed subdued. The loudest sound I could hear came from the black-and-white swallows, wheeling and crying just overhead.

Epilogue

I WAS SITTING in my office in London when the bad news came over the BBC newscast. Dial Torgerson, the *Los Angeles Times* bureau chief in Mexico City, had been killed by an explosion, believed to be a land mine, while reporting in Honduras near the Nicaraguan border.

Only a few weeks before, Dial and I had been together in Nicaragua. I was on special assignment to examine the comparisons being made of the U.S. involvement in Central America with that in Vietnam. We had rented a car in Managua and driven from the capital north toward the Honduran frontier to check on the extent of a raid by anti-Sandinista forces.

In Matagalpa, we were detained by the army police who said we had no permission to be in a restricted area. After a couple of hours, we were released and told to return to Managua. But first we had lunch in a pleasant bistro in the mountains. Torgerson had been based in Nairobi and Jerusalem for the *Times,* and he was an engaging and knowledgeable companion. He was more than helpful to me with insights on Central America, a region I'd never visited.

I was thinking about that trip when the phone rang from Los Angeles. An opinion page editor wondered if I could do an immediate story explaining "the philosophy" of why foreign correspondents take the risks they do. At first the request struck me as ghoulish, linked so

378

closely to Dial's death. The editor hadn't served abroad. How do you explain a correspondent's motivation to outsiders?

I said I'd think about it and call him back. By chance, I was on my way to a publisher's drink for *Newsweek*'s Tony Clifton, whose book on the Israeli invasion of Lebanon, *God Cried,* had just come out in England. When I arrived, a half-dozen old comrades were already at the bar. I thought I'd ask them: Why? Why did reporters who detested war keep going back? Why, like Torgerson, did they risk being blown away on an unmarked road in a remote country whose capital most readers couldn't pronounce?

Stewart Dalby of the London's *Financial Times,* whose shambling bulk was familiar to me from the mean streets of Belfast to Saigon, shrugged and said, "Curiosity, Bill, curiosity. We're all gossips, if we're any good at all. We want to be in on things when they happen. We want to be in on the know. And the bigger the show, the more we want to be in on it."

Tony Clifton thought a bit and said, "What makes the risk worth taking, I think, is a matter of journalistic conscience. In the end, there's simply no substitute for observing what has happened in an important situation. You can interview people later who say, 'I was there and I saw this or that.' But sometimes they're wrong, particularly when the event is politically charged. I think a journalist has got to be able to say, if he can, 'This happened. I know because I was there.' That knowledge is worth the risk."

And Michael Herr, that gentle soul who seemed so out of place in Vietnam yet wrote the memorable book *Dispatches,* observed, "The more I see of war correspondents, the more I doubt you can accept any reason one gives you for what he does, year after year, and why he does it. I can see why a young correspondent would get involved in Vietnam—once. I can't see how he would do it twice."

In looking back, I realize that I became a war reporter because wars are news, in the most serious sense. The hard fact is that the eventual fate of nations is often determined on the battlefield, whether the plains of Europe, the deserts of the Middle East or the jungles of Southeast Asia and Central America. To make sense out of what is going on, there is simply no substitute for being on the scene. In some countries, senior journalists restrict themselves to commenting on events. The American tradition happily is for reporters to get out and try to determine what happened, to lay a basis for informed comment.

As a foreign correspondent, I have written about politics, diplomacy, sports, archaeology, social trends, entertainment, just about everything. But war remains the most gripping subject of all. Some journalists thrive on danger itself. I am not one of them. I am extremely cautious within the sound of gunfire. Yet covering wars is in the nature of things exciting. Human conflict is a subject infused with the drama of men under stress at the cutting edge of life. On a personal level, there is a heightening of one's sensibilities and a deep satisfaction in the camaraderie found in a war zone.

At worst, the job of a foreign correspondent can be exhausting, dispiriting, frustrating, even humiliating, with moments of blind terror. It is, I suspect, less fun that it once was. We are often viewed as the enemy by governments and treated accordingly. Reliable information is harder to come by. Visas are more difficult to obtain. Travel is increasingly grim. The job takes its toll in broken marriages, soured romances, alcoholic burn-out, and corroding cynicism.

Over the years, I've become exceedingly skeptical of much of the human political motivation I've seen. It is not easy to accept the amount of callousness, ignorance, and arrogance I have found in high places. It is equally depressing to see the amount of blood spilled in the name of religion. And it is infuriating to discover American policymakers repeating the same mistakes abroad, sometimes at the cost of lives.

At its best, however, scouting for trouble that is brewing on the horizon, for events that affect human lives and destiny, can be stimulating, instructive, amusing, and satisfying. In a democracy, citizens need the information reporters can provide.

At its very best, foreign reporting can do good, changing things for the better. Has any of my reporting done so? I don't know. I hope so. Has it been worth it kicking around the world? Yes.

Index